Crested Ic9

Jeffrey G. Carswell

Jeffrey G. Carswell

About the Author

Jeff Carswell

Hero of the Thule Survivors Association, a participant in the cleanup at the top of the world, and the unbridled, relentless driving force behind Black Ice Shroud.

About the Book

The Ice Burns Black chronicles the cascading intrigue of international events, altered lives, and premature deaths resulting from the horrific crash of a nuclear-armed B52 bomber in Greenland. This broken-arrow incident and the cleanup of "hot" plutonium and uranium at the top of the world by Carswell and the other good Samaritans represents the quietest bombing in history to ultimately kill at least 129 innocent people.

Table of Contents

About the Author i

About the Book ii

PROLOGUE: READY. AIM. FIRE! 1

Chapter 1: A Day On The Ice 5

Chapter 2: The Sleeping Whale 21

Chapter 3: Pen Pals 53

Chapter 4: Hobo 28 Takes A Dive 67

Chapter 5: A Day In The Life 90

Chapter 6: Crested Ice 123

Chapter 7: First We Take Washington 140

Chapter 8: Project Crested Ice 178

Chapter 9: Science Attains Maturity 214

Chapter 10: ...Then We Take Copenhagen 249

Chapter 11: Success Plus Failure Equals Experience 267

EPILOGUE 310

PROLOGUE: READY. AIM. FIRE!

> In one sense truth alone can be exaggerated;
>
> nothing else can stand the strain.
>
> *Charles Dickens* G. K. CHESTERTON

JENS KRONBORG WAS only thirty-nine when he was saved from a painful lingering death from throat cancer by getting himself drowned in the sluggish Herlev river that creeps greyly through the western outskirts of Copenhagen.

Jens Kronborg was a fireman. And not merely in the obvious sense: the red blaze of his hair and beard that seemed to leap from his face, the intense blue of his eyes that washed over you as if scanning your very soul, the navy-blue uniform adorned with luminescent yellow-green stripes, the black top-boots, the hard, bell-shaped hat like a London bobby's, all of this did not fully capture the essence of Jens as a fireman. Nor did it matter that when the alarm rang out he would throw down his full house, spin down the polished brass pole like a grotesquely oversized gibbon, Jens was not a small man, and leap onto the fire engine to which he then clung like a Danish Buster Keaton, a human fuse of urgency, as it flung itself through the streets of Korsoer. Nor was it simply a matter of him periodically training a hose on blazing warehouses or gutted office blocks. Nor even the routine collection of his fortnightly pay cheque from the Korsoer and District Fire Brigade Central Administration and Personnel Offices in Hans Christian Andersen Straede.

No, Jens Kronborg was a fireman by vocation in the way a youth is drawn to the liberal professions in adolescence, dreams solidifying over a grueling apprenticeship, a youth's ambition hardened and polished by decades of exacting labor, dues meticulously paid.

And pay his dues he did. By the time death called him, he had been a fireman for twenty-three years. In 1966, when he applied to serve at the American air base in Thule, in Denmark's most remote north-western county, Greenland, he had already completed four years of firefighting. When he left Thule six years later, he returned to Korsoer largely unchanged in appearance but profoundly altered in his interior compass.

Time changes a man, of course, especially a man like Jens, observant, reflective, internally resonant. Life's events, trivial, grand, mundane, or catastrophic, activated a kind of resonator within him. The world outside he absorbed, processed, and transformed, a ceaseless mill grinding the experience of the universe into the refined flour of reflection. Jens Kronborg was, in essence, a northern worker-day Aristotle: a man meticulously measuring all he encountered, weighing it against the inner ledger of his own reason.

So, when cancer arrived at the too-early age of thirty-seven, Jens measured it against the whole of his life, and, drawing conclusions from the flimsiest evidence, the anecdotal inevitability of the disease, found it wholly unwelcome, consummately unreasonable. He knew that even the robust can be felled in an instant, that vitality can vanish to leave only a stark, emaciated shadow of the former self, wilting, wandering, wondering.

Yet he asked: why this loss of appetite, aching joints, blurred vision, bodily functions betraying him with painful erraticism? Were these the usual attendants of cancer, or something else? Jens thought not. He turned, again and again, to examine the fabric of his life, the weave of time, and invariably returned to Thule, the threads of memory tugging him there.

There, his life had been framed: his features half-blackened by the unrelenting dark of sunless days, half-reddened by infernos so vast they made him feel like a lone witness to a witches' Sabbath of extraordinary scale. In that crucible, he believed, lay the key to his present suffering.

Determined to confront the mystery, Jens reached out to the Danish Health Department, which suggested he contact the American Embassy. The next morning, he caught an early train to Copenhagen to speak with a representative of the American Public Relations Bureau.

That same evening, his wife, Marta, received a phone call.

"Mrs. Kronborg? Yes, hello. My name is O'Toole, Brig O'Toole. I'm with the American Public Relations Bureau here in Copenhagen. You are probably aware that your husband was coming to speak with me today? Yes. Good. Well… he hasn't shown up. He left for Copenhagen this morning? Hmm. I'm afraid I haven't seen him, Mrs. Kronborg. He just hasn't turned up. Has he called you to say he got the address mixed up, or…? Hmm. Well, I'm sure he's fine. But if he doesn't contact you tonight, perhaps you should notify the police. Oh, and could he call me tomorrow to arrange a new time? Thank you. Good night."

The next morning, at seven o'clock, Marta called the Copenhagen Police. She did not report her husband missing in the usual sense. Instead, she was requested to come to the capital to identify a body fished from the river by the water police just hours earlier.

The coroner's verdict: homicide by person or persons unknown. Jens' body bore multiple contusions across the shoulders and head; his wallet, watch, and wedding ring were gone. So, too, was the photocopy of his doctors' reports, which he had brought as supporting evidence. No one mentioned their absence, no one even knew such a document existed, not even Marta.

The funeral saw the entire Fire Brigade assembled. Fire Supervisor Marius Schmidt, a man who had worked alongside Jens for nearly twenty years, including the Thule years, squeezed Marta's hand with quiet, solemn sympathy.

"A shocking incident, Marta," he said. "It must have happened so quickly for someone to overcome a man like Jens."

"Well, he wasn't as strong as he used to be," Marta replied, her voice dry and measured.

Marius' brow furrowed in genuine surprise. "No? He looked fine. Was he ill?"

Marta fixed him with a look so steady it made him shift uncomfortably. "He had cancer," she said simply. Then, with the support of her sister and son, she was assisted to the car, leaving behind the echoes of a man who had measured the world, and himself, with a precision no illness, no catastrophe, could fully undo.

* * * * * *

MARIUS WAS PACING up and down like a one-man Salvation Army band, the ceaseless jingle of his keys forming a thin, metallic melody that matched the agitated rhythm of his hands. Each gesture carved the air sharply, as though he was conducting an orchestra only he could hear. The pipe clamped between his teeth, chewed almost into the grain, declared the true magnitude of his unrest. It had been over a year since Jens Kronborg's unhappy widow had left him standing alone in the drizzle at the cemetery, staring after her retreating figure as the earth settled on a coffin he still couldn't believe was real.

Now, on the desk in his study, lay a letter from her, a modest, neat envelope holding the quiet devastation of memory. In it, she reminded him of Jens' cancer and expressed her interest in joining the "B-52 Crested Ice Disaster Thule Radiation Victims' Association" (the Thule Association, as it was grimly nicknamed). The letter rested among a growing mountain of similar requests; some thirty had arrived *that very day alone*, a sudden surge of voices long silent, now awakened by some shared dread.

And on the floor nearby, trampled during one of his restless circuits of the room, lay a crumpled typewritten note. The creases cut through the neatly aligned letters like scars:

Mr. Schmidt,

Firemen shouldn't light fires; they should only put them out. Put this one out, Schmidt, before it burns you bad,

Signed,
No Friend of Yours

The starkness of the warning clung to the room like smoke, acrid and insinuating.

* * * * * *

THE VOICE OVER the phone carried an unmistakable Sydney-side Australian accent, breezy, confident, almost musical in its upward lilt. And yet, despite its attempt at friendliness, it caused Jeff Carswell's face to tighten, the muscles along his jaw fluttering with contained fury.

"Give it up, Jeffie-boy. Mixing yourself up with cranks and weirdos like Schmidt and those other foreigners, you'll just end up regretting it. Take my word for it, Jeff, you *will* regret it. And so will Sophia… and Phillip… and James. Take care now, lots of care. OK?"

The voice lingered on the names as if savoring them, pronouncing each with unnatural, syllabic precision:

So-phi-ya.

Phii-llipp, exploding on the *p* like a mini-detonation.

Jaa-messa, stretching the ending into a long, buzzing hiss.

A casual threat wrapped in singsong warmth, a lullaby sharpened to a blade. The kind of call that stayed with a man long after the receiver was placed gently, carefully, back into its cradle.

Chapter 1: A Day On The Ice

Forthwith upright he rears from off the pool

His mighty Stature

Paradise Lost: Book I   MILTON

ON THE ICE, you can see into eternity. Well, almost. The air possesses a glass-like clarity that mocks the European eye, stripping it of all familiar judgment. Distances collapse and expand in bewildering ways, so that what appears within reach may in fact be a day's march away, and what seems impossibly remote sits quietly at your feet. Just as, at the uppermost point of a sphere, motion dissolves into stillness, so too, at the top of the earth, space and time unmake themselves. The compass needle, that faithful servant of rational men, spins into a charming, useless dance, an elegant display of inconstant oscillations, mocking the very notion of direction.

Time itself becomes uncooperative. Seconds, minutes, hours, days, Western man's beloved units, do not belong here. They lose their meaning, their grip on movement. Time is measured instead by weather and wind, by the moody drift of snow, by the sudden silence of animals or their hurried return. A brief journey you swear will take two hours may stretch into a long, disorienting pilgrimage if the sky decides to turn or the wind begins to speak in one of its colder voices. And always, there remains the quiet possibility, known but unspoken, that you may never arrive at all. A shift in this strange region's unseen mechanics can flip you sideways into some chaos of drifting snow warp or one of the icy black holes the old explorers whispered about.

Here is a cold that feels as though it never belonged to this earth, a cold borrowed from some other, darker world. In winter, the temperature regularly plunges to dizzying depths: forty, forty-five degrees below zero. In such conditions, even the act of breathing becomes a wager. Inhaling through the nose risks freezing the delicate hairs within, snapping them off like brittle twigs. Breathing through the mouth means inviting air so cold it bites into the lungs with metal teeth. There is no safe method, only degrees of harm. Life here feels perpetually unsecured, fragile in every direction.

Ultimo Thule, once imagined as the planet's distant rim, somewhere beyond the Shetland Islands, proves in reality to lie much farther away even than imagination dares. The true Thule rests in the far northern crown of Greenland, a region so remote that only a few explorers, their names rising like faint echoes across time, have tread upon its extremity. To approach these wastes is to feel the world's rotation tug at you in strange ways. With every step closer to this arctic still point, one senses the entire planet spinning centripetally away. And to pause, truly pause, at that authentic stillness is to step outside the mortal framework of time and watch the earth's evolving and revolving with something approaching the eye of God.

The Inuit (Eskimos), who inhabit this translucent kingdom of ice, shrouded half the year in impenetrable darkness, and for the other half dazzled by the fragile, prismatic colours of refracted snowlight, possess myths born from the very palette of their environment. They believe the leaping flames of the Northern Lights are the souls of the dead playing ball with a walrus skull. They call it *arsarnerit*: the ball game. Another tale says the Lights are the souls of stillborn children dancing with their umbilical cords. Myths, of course, are structures built around experience; scaffolds for the unexplainable. And both these stories speak of the dead and their condition, an idea we may yet find instructive to keep in mind.

Meanwhile, the Inuit might well have recognised another kind of death game around 3:49 p.m. on January 21, 1968, when a giant B-52 Stratofortress carved its flaming arc across the sea ice. It came roaring out of the dark, a blazing globe of steel tearing through the frozen air. Then, as the hundred-metre flames of the bomber and its deadly nuclear cargo rose above the mangled gash of wreckage, challenging even the towering icebergs for dominion of the sky, the Inuit might have seen in it the image of the entire human race engaged in a macabre ball game with its own skull…

* * * * * *

MEMBERS OF THE local Inuit *Qaanaaq* (tribe) were the first to reach the wreck.

The eleven Danish fire trucks, massive, steel-bodied creatures far too heavy for the treacherous ocean ice, sat four miles away like stranded mechanical seals, their engines idle, their usefulness nullified. The fire had fused the ice into a tar-black sheet, and among the firefighters there was, beneath the formal urgency, a quiet sensation of relief. They understood precisely how extreme the risks were. The *Broken Arrow* training films they had watched repeatedly, grim, monotonous reels designed to prepare them for the unthinkable, had instructed them to approach a burning nuclear aircraft only from an oblique angle; to locate and flip an external switch before touching anything, lest the pilot-ejection system take the fireman's head clean off; and above all, *never*, under any circumstances, to touch the nuclear wreckage itself.

On previous occasions, when forced landings at the base suggested a bomber might be carrying a nuclear payload, many firemen spent their standard fifteen-minute waiting period writing last notes to their families. Fifteen minutes, because that was the accepted time the Russians had allocated between notification of missile launch and the arrival of the missile. A quarter hour to think of wives, children, debts, sins, and the long shadow of the Cold War.

This time, they never even got those fifteen minutes. Just a single, brutal concussion, the shattering thud that rocked the raised Arctic barracks to their foundations. No one panicked. But training, preparation, and reflex all evaporated in the face of something that simply could not be reached. The ice at the point of impact was perhaps a metre thick, but no one knew if it could support the fire vehicles. So the Danes and Americans, marooned four miles away on the fjord's perimeter with all their sophisticated firefighting equipment, became a kind of Western irrelevance. They could do no more than watch the fire devour everything, perhaps even the surviving crew, whose fate was unknown and unguessable.

Perhaps some of them wondered, in that moment, if they should already be cinders, fuel for the brief furnace of a manmade sun.

The only way to approach the wreck was by dogsled. In winter, the Arctic Ocean freezes over completely, and the coastal ice, fragile as a poorly laid carpet, fractures in summer into translucent prisms of delicate colour. In winter, however, it becomes a hard, sullen expanse, unforgiving but navigable. Without this ice, the Inuit would never have migrated, hunted, or sustained their nomadic lives.

The sleds used on thin ice are curious things. After the spring thaw, the Inuit gather exposed mud and store it through the warm months. In winter, they cake that mud onto the sled runners in layers at least ten centimetres deep; once frozen, they pare it with knives until smooth enough to glide across the ice. The final step is brushing on a thin layer of ice itself, spread like butter over the pastry. When that ice layer weakens through use, the runners are "retreaded" with urine. These simple, ingenious vehicles were the only means of reaching the smouldering wreckage in the immediate aftermath of the crash.

Nature always wins in the Arctic. The best human solutions merely bow to that truth. While Western technology sat impotent, eight dogs dragged their load of Inuit and military personnel toward the blackened scar of twisted metal. They moved fast: Arctic dogs always do. Their coats blend the brown of earth with the white of snow, their eyes forever scanning distances where no human eye could find even the suggestion of a horizon. They are kept constantly hungry, driven to a frenzy that fuels their speed, and sometimes that hunger exacts a human price. Each year, one or two infants perish at the jaws of a starving animal. It is a brutal toll, yet without the dogs there would be no travel, no hunting, no survival. No children at all.

But on that day, another predator, an alien one, posed a threat to the Inuit. Europeans struggled for centuries to adapt to the Arctic's austere brutality, but they did learn the essential rule of the hunt: sometimes, you sacrifice others. Two hundred metres from the B-52 wreck, the US military personnel stopped their advance and stepped off the sleds. The Inuit were sent onward, beyond the "zero line", to search for signs of life or remains of the crew.

It is comforting to recall, as we read reassurances printed in a small Midwestern newspaper desperate to calm public nerves, that:

"Thule Bombs Not Dangerous, Washington. No danger to human, plant, or animal life."

A relief indeed to know that hydrogen bombs are completely harmless.

Until they detonate, of course. At that point, they become something else entirely, bombs in every meaningful sense.

According to these calming articles, there was no risk from the burning plutonium, tritium, uranium, or chemical compounds comprising the bomb casings.

No radioactivity. No toxic contaminants. Nothing for the Inuit to fear.

Nothing for the military personnel watching from afar.

No reason for the firefighters to have been trained never to touch nuclear wreckage, nor to wear protective gear in the event of an accident.

Subsequently, however, after communication lines between Washington and Little Rock had time to stretch, distort, and falter, it was discovered that this report was not, in fact, entirely accurate.

Unfortunately, the chemical explosives inside hydrogen bombs detonate when heated and subjected to a sufficient impact. The onboard fire provided the heat. The bomber slamming into ocean ice at more than 500 miles per hour provided the impact. The resulting explosion shattered the bombs, the aircraft, and its cargo into over a million fragments of metal, smoke, and death, scattered across the frozen span of the fjord.

Wolstenholme Fjord, scene of the crash, was covered by the vast plain of frozen ocean that forms each Arctic winter, turning thousands of square miles of open water into temporary land. In the long polar darkness, visibility was poor, but the icebergs remained, towering monoliths, some rising over a hundred metres high, pure-white shards of ancient glaciers. Beautiful. Serene. Older than civilisation.

The bomber had refuelled midair half an hour earlier and was returning to its predetermined "figure-eight" flight path to make sure the scale of the flight is clear. When the fire ignited, the pilot headed for Thule, the closest landable site within a thousand miles. But as the fire grew out of control and the plane's fate became clear, he set the autopilot for Canada and ordered the crew to bail out.

Why Canada? Because the United States had a fly-over agreement with them. If the plane went down in international waters or on Canadian soil, the diplomatic fallout could be contained.

Denmark, however, was a different matter. Its government had promised the people, explicitly, repeatedly, that no nuclear-armed bombers flew over Danish territory, nor were nuclear weapons stored there. This was not just political rhetoric; it was written into the Danish Constitution.

A bomber with a nuclear payload crashing on Danish territory would expose not just an accident but a betrayal. A diplomatic sleight-of-hand. And the United States was in no mood to give the Soviet Union such a public relations gift.

Still, the Americans are an honourable people, and of course… we all trust in God.

* * * * * *

DIRECTIONS ARE NEVER easy for Europeans in the Arctic abyss. The very idea of orientation becomes a kind of cosmic joke. No compass has ever worked there; the magnetic field simply shrugs off human expectation. And so, as the fire chewed its ruthless way into the electrical circuitry, the doomed beast began to veer, slow at first, then with deranged certainty, turning to fly precisely where it was never meant to go: toward the isolated military installation at Thule, where some 3,000 souls were enjoying what passed for a relaxing Sunday afternoon on the edge of the world.

The B-52 did not descend but *lurched*, as if the machine itself were frantic, a frightened sun trying to escape pursuit. Through the unbroken arctic darkness it careered, too heavy with fire, too wounded to survive, until its right wing kissed the ocean ice. That soft, almost delicate touch became the trigger. The aircraft exploded in a cascade of alchemical frenzy, a mechanical starburst flaring where no stars should be.

Following the bombing of Hiroshima, President Truman remarked that the force of the sun had been unleashed on the enemy. Here, in the bleakest corner of the world, that same force flickered again, a dying sun groaning its last breath in the eternal night. It was not a nuclear blast, not the apocalyptic bloom the world feared, but by the skin of our teeth it evaded becoming one, and the shadow of that possibility lingered like a ghostly aftertaste.

The explosion, fuelled by a full load of JP-4, tore a wide hole in the ice, an immediate wound opening into the ocean beneath. Through it sank a portion of the shattered fragments: part of the fuselage, the engines, and one of the bombs. The hole closed quickly, sealing itself over as if the ice wished to hide the evidence, but glaciologists would later be able to detect its ghost-print, the scar within the layers. Two hundred metres of ice were coated with sprayed fuel, creating an ocean of flame in the instant aftermath. And wherever the fire spread, the plutonium, uranium, and the silent ingredients of the nuclear cocktail rode on its breath.

The fire lasted only some twenty minutes, short, furious, terrifyingly efficient. Yet the heaving glow from the cinders clung to the horizon, an ember refusing to die. The extreme heat lingered for more than two hours before the deep arctic blackness reclaimed its dominion. The grave may offer darkness and stillness, only the cavalier worm breaking monotony, but the Arctic delivers a different silence, the kind carved not merely from cold but from the absence of life itself. It is a void. The absence of absence. A stillness so complete it mocks the idea of negation.

Into this void the Inuit went, sent to scour the area as soon as the fire had finally succumbed to the cold. They entered a limbo world where danger lay like an invisible predator. The cold, the ice, the darkness, these you can sense, wrestle with, and understand. But nuclear radiation offers no scent, no shape, no glimmering warning. It does not announce itself. You cannot see it, hear it, touch it, taste it, or smell it. And if no sense can detect it, then, by the logic handed down in a land where survival is instinctual, there can be no reason to fear it.

Fear, like beauty, is in the eye of the beholder. And the beholders that night, the Europeans, shared looks heavy with recognition, eyes meeting in that dreadful flash of understanding that something irretrievable had occurred. All their training, all their doctrine, insisted the question was not how to avoid damage, but how to keep it *acceptable*. And so the silent consensus formed with the speed of a reflex: do not spread panic.

The Inuit were told nothing of any dangers.

* * * * * *

CONSEQUENTLY, THE INUIT knew nothing of any dangers.

The 'zero line', a term that sounds almost clinical in its simplicity, marks the invisible frontier inside which radioactivity is judged to reach levels considered an unacceptable risk. It is the boundary of a world reshaped by invisible forces. Within the zero line lies the so-called *hot zone*, where anyone venturing inside is required, by every established protocol, to take all necessary precautions: hermetically sealed protective clothing, breathing apparatus, and a barrier between flesh and the unseen.

But protocols are luxuries of those for whom danger is an intellectual concept, not an unfolding reality.

Mamarut Kujaukitsoq, one of the Inuit, was sent inside that zero line to shovel contaminated snow onto a sled so it could be removed and tested at the base. For the first twenty-four hours after the crash, Mamarut collected fragments from the wreckage across the two-hundred-metre square area designated as lethally dangerous. He wore no special clothing. His only breathing apparatus was his own pair of lungs, the same lungs that had carried him across frozen plains and winter seas all his life, now pressed into service against something no human instinct was shaped to recognize.

At that early stage of the emergency, there were no other means of transport. None. Two two-lane highways had to be carved across the ice before the European vehicles could even attempt to reach the site. In the meantime, the work fell as it always had in this region, to the people most familiar with the land, its cold, and its hardship.

Mamamrut helped build igloos and a rough cabin to shield workers from the midwinter brutality. The site lay fully exposed to the harshest of arctic winds, the kind that strips courage from the unprepared. He also assisted in constructing a makeshift heliport, a fragile platform meant to tether modern machinery to ancient ice.

Aron Duneq would spend several days inside the zero line. Shortly after the crash, he even sat close to the wreckage itself. An Inuit hunter from Qaanaq, the township the Americans built after forcibly removing the entire village that once stood at the Thule Base site, Aron was asked to assist the U.S. military in assessing post-crash conditions. He took on work as a cleaner and night guard, antithetical roles that nonetheless folded into the same grim task. Like Mamamrut, he helped build igloos. He gathered pieces of the broken plane. And, being human, he paused now and then to take a tea break, simple tea brewed from melted snow near the crash site.

Tea is a potent beverage in the Arctic: warm, fortifying, a tiny defiance against the cold. And snow on the ocean ice is the purest source one could hope for. But no one warned Aron that his tea that week came with extra-special properties. No one told him that "pure" was no longer the operative word.

The widow of Arnaeuniaq Qissuk has recalled that her husband worked in a capacity similar to Aron's during the rescue operation. His story mirrors the others: labor, exposure, oblivious proximity to danger, up until the moment of his death years later. He drowned on September 24, 1973, hunting from a boat in the deep Arctic region, in the old Inuit style. He died as generations had lived, thankfully unaware of the shadow that had once brushed against his life during the Thule clean-up. He never learned that his traditions had been threatened by forces no hunter's instinct could detect.

Ululik Duneq, another Inuit from Qaanaq, also worked inside the zero line. He helped establish a telephone line from Pituffik, the Inuit word for the air base, to the crash site. He shared Aron's tea breaks, sipping in companionable fashion from cups filled with nuclear tea. He, too, helped erect the igloos.

Arruteq Kristiansen was a handyman in Uummanaq, the name the Inuit use for the nearby village Europeans call Dundas. Being the only person in Dundas with sled dogs, he was approached by the Greenland Trade representative, Jens Zinglersen, and asked to join the search for the missing crew members who might have landed on the ocean ice. They found no one. But in the deep, punishing darkness, they passed close to the crash site. Had there been any danger from radiation, and there was, they would have walked straight into it. In fact, without realizing it, Arruteq returned home with radioactive particles clinging to his clothes and boots.

Arruteq never took part in the clean-up itself. He simply went back to his ordinary duties as a handyman at the telegraph station in Dundas, employed by the Ministry for Greenland, unaware that ordinary life had already been dusted with something irrevocably foreign.

* * * * * *

AGPALINQUAQ ANGINE AND Ajako Miteq were lucky, in their own hard-bitten way, to be given the chance to collect wreckage, build igloos, shovel radioactive snow, and drink what would later prove to be an infusion laced with plutonium. Agpalinquaq explained why.

"It is Sunday, January 21, 1968, around nine in the morning. Ajako and I are driving our dog sledge over the ice pack toward Agpat. We come across a crack in the ice and follow it until it leads us to the breathing hole of some seals. I poke two fingers down into the water to determine the direction of the current. Ajako checks the rifle for dirt and loads it. We sit to wait. It's around minus thirty-five degrees. But we are patient. We built an igloo for protection.

"The kids are playing outside. At about twenty to five, they rush inside shouting for us to come out. I'm the last one out. And there it is, a huge fire some four miles out on the ice, intense enough to make the icebergs and the mountain sides glow. A round black cloud, pulsating, is climbing into the sky. And then the sound of the explosion reaches us, and we are blown over. The kids scream. Some of us retreat into the igloo, me included.

"But I must come out again to see what is happening. What was it? A comet? A volcano? An aircraft? But we hadn't heard one, just saw the flames.

"In another igloo, the children are crying uncontrollably. The dogs are also starting to scream. We retreat inside again. Then out again to see what's going on. Ululik arrives from somewhere, and I suggest, 'Maybe a big stone from the sky.' No. Nothing. He just gestures with his arms, indicating a movement from above downward, at an angle. We watch the enormous fire, but it is freezing, at least thirty-five below zero, and our fur clothing is frozen solid because of our sweat. I go back inside.

"A little later, the Danish Military Liaison Officer, via the transistor radio we have with us, states that a B-52 bomber has crashed and that six men have jumped out with parachutes. He asks the Thule Eskimos to go out and look for any survivors. Ajako and I drive to Dundas at seventeen-thirty. The pall of smoke is flattening out. A light wind blows.

"The fire is still very intense at the crash site. Now and then it seems to stop, but that is only because an iceberg comes between us and the flames, blocking our view as we move quickly toward Dundas. We pass the pier at the base, and while Ajako keeps the dogs under control with the whip, I stop to speak with two Danes who advise that three crew members have been found. We continue toward Dundas, seeing many falling stars as we drive, something I am very used to after so many nights on the ice. As usual, the ice formations near Dundas are bad, making it hard to get into the village. I almost broke a leg on a crack in the ice while trying to move in. A man comes out to meet us. He is from Savigsavig. Others are already out searching for survivors. All evening, from eighteen-hundred hours to midnight, helicopters fly around the port area, over Dundas village and South Mountain.

"Agpalinquaq drops his fur clothes as soon as we get inside. It is warm, comfortable, and we move in to enjoy tea and bread. The children are playing with a puppy dog, and we are listening again to the Liaison Officer making announcements in both Danish and Greenlandic. We have to go out again and help. It is hard to pull on the frozen clothes and mittens; they stick to me and partly rip my skin. The extreme cold is most unpleasant when one has just come from a cozy, warm house. But after five or ten minutes on the dog sledge, one no longer feels it.

"The visibility is around one hundred yards, and oil drums I see as we drive appear as dark shapes against the white ice. Suddenly, the dogs go mad. They have found a breathing hole, and they run fast, barking furiously. I see a light and start driving toward it for a long time. Maybe it is Akudak. The light begins moving away. After a couple of hours, I see flashes of light close to land toward the north. My eyes are watering; it is possible the light is not real because of it. My forehead is hurting badly from the cold now, and I am getting very tired.

"I stop to rest and light the small gas lantern. Then 'it' begins in the south. I point 'it' out to Ajako. Maybe it is clouds. But it is not. It is like green zeppelins or silk covers being drawn upward into the sky from the southern horizon. The carpets move like yo-yos across the sky, up and down, climbing higher and higher each time. Thin silk shoots horizontally across the darkness, and by now it is almost upon us. It turns northwest, then north again, constantly shifting, shimmering, ghostly.

"Only the lantern hisses in the intense quiet of the night. Eventually, it reaches the northern horizon and looks like two folded seams, the silk rising vertically on both sides. The stars are visible through it. For a short time, a quarter of our sky is covered by pulsating, shimmering green light, immensely beautiful, until it disappears an hour later in the direction from which it came.

"We return home exhausted. I must have driven a hundred miles today. My moustache is frozen with tears, breath, and a runny nose. As soon as I lie down, I am asleep.

"Ajako is driving some distance behind me when his dogs find the body of the crew member killed when he left the aircraft in mid-air. We have been very close to his body several times as we moved across the area. We feel very sad."

* * * * * *

A GREENLANDER, THAT is a person of mixed Inuit and European blood, usually Danish, by the name of Jokum Heinrich was also among the first 'volunteers' in the rescue and clean up operations.

* * * * * *

THE AMERICANS ARE an honorable people.

* * * * * *

As a belated precaution, if one can even call it a precaution when the damage has already crept beneath the skin, the military decided to put several Inuit through medical examinations at the base. The whole affair became a kind of grim comedy, though no one laughed with any joy. The amusement came from the sheer absurdity of it: men who had lived their entire lives in harmony with the ice were suddenly being handled, inspected, and scrubbed like curiosities by representatives of a culture that assumed its power conferred its righteousness.

The humiliation was unintentional, perhaps, but no less profound for that.

None of the Inuit men had ever taken a shower. It wasn't neglect. It wasn't ignorance. It was survival. Life in the Arctic makes such indulgences both unnecessary and dangerous. Picture it: washing your hair inside an igloo, then stepping back into temperatures that could shatter breath itself. Your locks would freeze solid and snap clean off, drifting to the ice floor like brittle twigs offered to the wind.

Still, the military insisted.

Water, hot, foreign, running down skin unaccustomed to its touch, filled the men with unease. No temperature, no amount of scrubbing, could wash off the death clinging to them from their simple walks across the poisoned ice. Their clothing, taken and burned, was replaced with stiff military arctic gear. And as though to make amends for the indignity, someone offered them warm meals and a seat before a television screen. *I Love Lucy* flickered before eyes that had never seen moving images before, as if the laughter of strangers could stand in for what had already been set loose in their blood.

It took the United States military a while to realize that more families, hunting households crossing the ocean ice at the wrong time, had witnessed the explosion and simply continued home afterward, unaware of what had settled onto their parkas, mittens, boots, and breath. So the Americans dispatched a team to check the homes for contamination.

What they found there chilled them in a way no winter could.

Moving through the quiet dwellings, Geiger counters erupted in a furious chorus. The very clothes worn by the residents made the meters rattle like a plague of cicadas. Every object, every surface, was saturated. They followed the owner's footsteps through his home, into the lounge, up the stairs, across the bedroom, each click marking where death had walked beside him.

Everything in those houses had to be removed and destroyed. Everything except the people themselves.

Time, and the plutonium already nestled inside their bodies, would take care of that.

Still, in a gesture as helpless as it was honorable, the Americans assured the families that there was little cause for fear. That they would be fine. Those new clothes and clean belongings would put things right again.

No use crying over spilled plutonium.

The words hovered in the cold like a prayer made of smoke, brief, comforting, and untrue.

* * * * * *

Mamarut's decline began almost immediately after the crash. The pain settled into him like an unwelcome tenant, constant and unmoving. Lesions marked his skin. Sensation drained from his fingertips. Doctors tended to him as best they could, but nothing eased what had already begun its course. After months of suffering, he died.

Aron Duneq wore his own clothing for the first three days following the crash, polar bear trousers, polar bear boots, garments cut from animals as rare and valuable as they are essential for life on the ice. He had spent those days deep inside the zero line, helping search for survivors, unaware of what he was carrying home on his back. His clothes were taken with the explanation that they would be shipped to the United States for cleaning and returned. They never were. Nor were they replaced. A half hide for a pair of trousers is no small thing; in Greenland, such garments are a lifeline, not a luxury.

Aron suspected, even then, that something was wrong. His pockets held things he feared would betray him. The sled he rode became radioactive within a day. Even his pocket knife, his daily companion, registered contamination, so that each meal risked bringing plutonium to his lips. Only years later did he truly understand what he had been exposed to.

New clothes cannot undo what has entered his blood.

His health began to erode. Not catastrophically at first, nothing dramatic enough to force immediate alarm. Just a slow betrayal of his energy. A creeping lethargy. A sense of being unwell in ways he couldn't name. A few hours near the wreck, and he had stepped into a lifetime of pain.

Ululik Duneq's clothing wasn't tested until three days after the crash. By then, the damage was done. His legs swell constantly now. There is severe tingling, and ulcers grow between his toes. The skin along his scalp is marked and fragile. Doctors have searched for causes, but none can explain what is happening to him.

His case echoes many others, Danes and Americans who worked the clean-up, who have been told, in effect, that their bodies bear mysteries for which medicine has no language yet. Perhaps someday they will give it a name. *Duneq's Syndrome*, they might call it.

But a name will not give a man back his life.

Ululik can no longer hunt. With that, his traditional life has vanished. Social welfare is all that remains for him. He fathered seven children before the crash. Since then, none.

And so the list continues, a somber tally of the first men who reached the burning ice.

Arruteq Kristiansen developed tumours on the surface of his skin, *"they tickle a lot,"* he says with a strange, quiet humor. Before the crash, he fathered ten children. Afterward, none. But this, he notes, may not amount to much, his wife went on the pill after the crash. His dogs, however, tell the story more starkly. They had been strong, healthy sled dogs, tireless creatures of muscle and instinct. Within weeks, all were dead. They had helped search for the missing crewman; the snow they ate sealed their fate.

Agpalinquaq Angine was never asked to surrender his clothes. He lives now with ongoing heart attacks and a condition he calls *"fatting."* Pain walks with him everywhere. His one child was born before the crash.

Ajako Miteq cannot hunt anymore. His body trembles. His head aches. His back and feet have weakened. His skin is damaged and marked. He lives now on welfare. Of his four children, the two born before the crash are healthy. The two born after suffer from severe hearing problems.

Most of his dogs, those tied near the crash site while he and the others built igloos, shoveled snow, drank their tea, died within weeks. They had eaten the snow. Before death, they refused water, refused food, their bodies unraveling in ways hauntingly similar to human cancers. By spring, they were gone.

And then there is Jokum Heinrich.

He is now so ill he cannot hold a pen. In 1994, his niece guided his hand, writing down his words as he dictated from a hospital bed. In that letter, he told me he believed he was the last of the Greenlanders and Inuit who had worked after the crash still alive. He wrote as a man who knew his time was short.

A life measured now not in years but in borrowed hours.

* * * * *

But of course, the Inuit understand death differently. Suicide, in their world, has long existed not as an act of despair but as a final gesture of responsibility. To become a burden to one's hunting companions is unthinkable. The Arctic does not negotiate with weakness; it offers no shelter for the infirm. No European could endure it without Inuit knowledge. The ice takes all, and returns nothing. Yet many Inuit choose to give themselves to that frozen world willingly, because when life grows heavier than death, the journey into the foreign country becomes less a departure and more a release.

Inuit existence is an art shaped entirely by necessity. In their hands, the savage becomes tender; the terrible, familiar. For those whose suffering is born primarily in the mind, these people show an unusual resistance to pain, what Europeans see as a place of relentless danger, an environment of killing cold, endless night, and omnipresent threat, the Inuit experience as a landscape of severity, yes, but also of beauty, clarity, and intensity.

Life is lived entirely in the present. The next hunt, the next igloo or snow shelter, the next patch of safe ice, these are the horizons they navigate. When that present begins to dissolve, when the body can no longer spear a seal, or bring down a bear, or outwit a fox; when a man must ask for skins he can no longer earn and food he can no longer provide, he knows the stillness is calling him. Death, for him, is simply a move from one steady point to another. A place where spirits dance with children and elders alike.

Death is a transition. It is not something to fear.

But fear, fear can be taught.

* * * * * *

THE INUIT AROUND Thule are the purest of race of all the remaining natives of the far northern regions, the people least encumbered with Western values and material influences. They yet retain significant portions of their mythology, carrying it through generations as both compass and caution. Within their cosmology, there exists a lower and an upper world in the sky. The lower world mirrors this one, yet its sun and moon are fainter, and it is formed around hidden caverns and winding passages that echo the rhythms of the land. The upper world, by contrast, is brilliant: it revolves around a mountain and is populated by Innues, beings once men who, through transformation, have become stars. But in the perpetual nuclear night, both these Inuit worlds will be obscured. Nature itself will fracture; the ice will refract evil. Death, they understand, is part of the natural ends and beginnings of time; yet when a force arises that neither lives nor dies, but ensures that nothing survives, it moves beyond the spheres of both time and eternity, into a place that is the absolute negation of all things, including negation itself. A preternatural darkness with no possibility of light, a silence that cannot know sound or even its absence, and a time that began before time had any knowledge of start or stop: here, even the Inuit's ancient resilience falters.

They confront their own horrors, though of a natural kind, through the intercession of the sorcerers, or `angagoks,' men whose souls have been taken by wolves or bears and whose bodies are possessed by spirits. The angagoks are seers, able to perceive the Innua, the hidden, pulsing forces of nature. Their role is sacred: to ward off evil spirits, misfortune, storms, starvation, disease, and to discern crimes before they manifest.

Young men aspiring to the rank of angagok attach themselves to a seasoned practitioner. They train rigorously, entering states of consciousness akin to shamanistic trances. A variety of methods are employed to induce these trances. One approach is the complete abstinence from food and water until visions arise, dancing and twisting in the mind's eye. Another is a form of self-hypnosis: the aspirant isolates themselves in a remote place and engages in repetitive tasks, rubbing stones together for hours, even days. Eventually, spirits appear: sometimes no larger than a thumb, sometimes shaped like a frail old woman hiding beneath the ice; sometimes a dog-shaped earth spirit; perhaps a sphere fallen from the heavens; or a raven gliding silently across the sky.

Once the angagok masters trance induction, the next challenge is summoning the spirits to his aid. No method is universal; each angagok crafts his own ritual. He divides the supernatural world into categories, calling forth one spirit from each, forging pacts through vision and presence. He seeks spirits of the sun and moon, the departed ancestors, powerful animals, and even monstrous forms. Equally crucial is the skill to repel spirits from the underworld, the tonrats,' demons of vengeance capable of wreaking terrible destruction. Among these are Aikpalookvik, who dwells in the sea and seeks to devour sailors, and Keelut, the hairless dog-like pibloktoq, who drives men to sing, slash themselves, or lose their reason.

In the long, merciless darkness of winter, surrounded by these vivid terrors, the angagok works ceaselessly: no protection is too elaborate in that blind, frozen hell. Yet there exists one shape the spirits cannot comprehend, one form that eludes the cosmology of the Inuit: the smooth, symmetrical metal cylinder, a creature born not of myth but of human invention, a form of extinction beyond nature or imagination. This sleek, alien presence is the antithesis of the Inuit creation myth, wherein a raven, starting blindly in human form, stumbles through chaos until purpose becomes clear. The B-52 bird, conversely, moves with calculated knowledge, its human semblance hidden within, ending only in a cataclysm of fire and destruction.

The Inuit, who move in rhythm with the cycles of nature, the ebb and flow of moonlit tides and sunlit ice, naturally comprehend nothing of what is termed 'modern realities.' These realities, however, were terrifyingly real: the Soviet nuclear threat was authentic, and the nation's survival depended upon vigilance and preparedness. In this context, the production of a certain measure of nuclear waste, mostly harmless after all, was judged a tolerable cost by the United States, and by extension the world behind its skirts. And yet these realities, modern and lethal as they were, rendered the intricate mythologies of the Inuit almost invisible. The luminous worlds of spirits, the Innues and the tonrats, persisted as legends but no longer commanded attention. In a world poised on the brink of intercontinental annihilation, where the presence of nuclear weapons was a daily truth, the illusions of evil spirits and afterlife worlds simply withered, their magic overwhelmed by the cold, hard logic of civilization's fear.

* * * * * *

THE FIRST ATOMIC bomb was christened 'Trinity' by J. Robert Oppenheimer, after one of John Donne's Holy Sonnets.' A sobriquet more unholy might have been more appropriate: perhaps, as James Goldsmith termed it, the Devil's energy.' What is only living can only die. But nuclear waste is death itself, living at its own terrible, unyielding speed, indifferent to time, humanity, or the moral universe.

The prominent Australian scientist, Sir Mark Oliphant, who as a young man had worked under Rutherford and later became the Governor of the State of South Australia, observed the matter with solemn gravity on the fiftieth anniversary of the Hiroshima bomb: "I remain sad fifty years later that the search for knowledge of the structure of matter became the source of a killing agent that will threaten all mankind until it is banned." The melancholy in his words lies not merely in lost lives, but in the bitter irony of discovery turned weapon, curiosity transmuted into annihilation.

The Soviet Premier, Uncle Joe Stalin, once observed that the bomb was, after all, only designed to frighten people. It was only another instrument, in that respect, of the Terror: a policy as efficacious as it was brutal and random. No joy there, then: to properly export the Terror, sooner or later it would have been necessary to select a victim; perhaps a vulnerable city like Jakarta, or Saigon, might have served the Terror's purpose, and obliterate it. It is therefore not altogether surprising that more strong-minded observers took some comfort from the fact that, in 1964, four years before the Thule incident, the United States had the capacity to inflict 110 million Soviet deaths, as against the Soviets' comparatively paltry figure of thirty million US deaths.

In 1977, Zbigniew Brzezinski, a former assistant to the US President, once remarked that if ten percent of the world's population were destroyed by a nuclear holocaust, it would be a disaster beyond comprehension; yet, paradoxically, it would not represent the total destruction of humanity. Such non sequiturs confront the thinking mind, forcing contemplation of the incomprehension we call 'modern realities', a reality in which civilization wields the power to extinguish itself with a keystroke, yet continues to function as if such destruction were merely theoretical.

By the time the nuclear threat had retreated some thirty years later, a fearful symmetry had been established between the two powers: each could obliterate the other several times over, an equilibrium of annihilation resting uneasily on human arrogance and technological mastery.

* * * * * *

SO, WHILE THE Inuit retain their superstitions, their angagoks, their lost and wandering spirits, the frightful howl of vengeance in the wind, the chattering society of animals preying on themselves, the tumultuous sea that freezes solid in a moment, the civilized person lives with nightmares that intrude upon his very daylight hours with an intensity almost unbearable. Nightmares in which the divide between fact and dream becomes irrelevant, where the fragile span of a human life amounts to a mere 0.006666% of the time it takes plutonium to lose half its radioactivity; in which entire cities are reduced to nothing more than cold, strategic 'bargaining chips'; in which the 'period of interest' is measured not in months or years, but in the precise duration that human beings might endure the poisoned sanctuary of fallout shelters; and in which the grim euphemism of 'servicing the target' translates into the exactitude of a bomb strike, precise enough to erase lives, landscapes, and memory with mathematical indifference.

* * * * * *

There was, for instance, the crash at Lakenheath Royal Air Force base, twenty miles north of Cambridge, when a B-47 ran out of control on a runway and ploughed into a storage igloo containing several nuclear weapons. Within the igloo were three Mark 6 nuclear bombs, each four yards long and one yard in diameter, each containing eight thousand pounds of TNT, forming part of the trigger mechanism of the bombs themselves. The nightmare remained a nightmare only in prospect on this occasion, as firefighters, standing on a stage of incomprehensible terror, managed to douse the burning jet fuel before it could ignite the TNT. They laboured under the shadow of unimaginable annihilation, frantically trying to restrain forces that could have spewed radioactive material across the countryside. In the words of a RAF general on the scene, "it was possible part of eastern England would have become a desert." Another official commentator concluded that the outcome was the result of "tremendous heroism, good fortune, and the will of God," a trifecta that spared humanity from catastrophe on that occasion.

It is not possible to wake from this nightmare.

Nor from this one. Over the fishing village of Palomares in southern Spain, the nightmare combined all the elements of earth, air, fire, and water. During a routine high-altitude refuelling operation, a B-52 collided with the KC-135 fuel-tanker craft. The B-52 carried four nuclear bombs. The planes and two of the bombs exploded on impact, scattering plutonium across a hundred square miles of land and water. One of the intact bombs fell into the sea, prompting what has been described as "the most expensive, intensive, harrowing, and feverish underwater search for a man-made object in world history." Every second mattered: the bomb needed to be located and recovered before its poison could seep into the Mediterranean, an invisible and lethal tide threatening life far beyond human vision.

Some incidents occurred as almost asynchronous horrors, over in the blink of a dreamer turning in sleep. The nuclear weapon that fell from a B-36 near Kirtland Air Force Base in New Mexico, exploding completely on impact in the garden of Mr. Walter Greeg of Mars Bluff. The nuclear weapon accidentally jettisoned from a B-47 into a "sparsely populated area in South Carolina." The B-47 caught fire on takeoff at Dyess Air Force Base in Texas, scattering nuclear materials across the site. The B-52 that lost its right wing and jettisoned a twenty-four-megaton bomb into bushland. Yet it was only a dream, after all: when the bombs were eventually recovered, it was discovered that five of the six safety devices had failed. And everyone knows that that sort of improbable luck only ever happens in dreams, where reality and improbability entwine.

Disasters of the magnitude of Chernobyl and Three Mile Island rend the veil between possibility and fact. When the earth itself is deadened by creeping poison, it ceases to matter whether the cause was natural or manufactured; whether decay is wrought by invisible microorganisms, or by the slow, implacable burn of radioactive contamination that will endure for thousands of years. Just as when a tree falls in a forest, and no one hears it, it is doubtful that it truly fell, so too does the devastation of nuclear waste vanish with the death of its last human witness. Cockroaches, as ever, do not count as observers.

The problem is that humans do not count as participants. They survive only 400 rads of radiation, have soft outer shells, require elaborate protection in the form of fallout shelters, and possess an unparalleled capacity for self-destruction. Protective clothing may be devised, masks fitted, armour constructed, but they cannot substitute for the fragile, living body. Cockroaches, by contrast, wear a trinity of impervious chitinous layers, survive ten thousand rads, and consume almost anything, irradiated or not. The irony is elemental, cruel, and absolute.

Perhaps, however, the ice will remember something of the human world that once was. Not that it will care; it will only stare sullenly into itself, seeing nothing, knowing nothing. Yet the bones of the past are sprinkled throughout the tomb of the Arctic: the occasional sprightly mastodon, an angagok locked in grim embrace with a spirit, a wolf frozen in terror, and cockroaches of all ages, indifferent witnesses of what was lost.

In 120,000 years' time, when the creeping nuclear waste has decayed to half its lethality, perhaps there will remain a human or two, caught in a strange communion with a machine that belongs neither to this world nor the next. Perhaps then the machine will appear less alien, a little more natural, a little less like the silent bringer of death from which there is no release.

Chapter 2: The Sleeping Whale

"Can you draw out Leviathan with a fishhook,

or press down his tongue with a cord?"

JOB 41:1

GREENLAND STANDS AS one of the last truly silent places on Earth, a continent-sized island that remains, even in our age of satellite surveillance and global connectivity, profoundly and stubbornly unexplored. Its mystery is born from a twin curse of geography and climate: a paralyzing remoteness, and an environment that ranks among the planet's most mercilessly inhospitable. It does, technically, lay claim to the title of the world's largest island—a geographical fact often trotted out in trivia. Yet that very claim feels like a grand, icy deception, a piece of cartographic legerdemain made possible only by the enormously thick, permanent shroud of ice that smothers over eighty percent of its bulk. This is not an island of rock and soil so much as an island of ice, with land merely as its reluctant, buried foundation.

Apart from some few, fringing, and pitifully tiny skirts of exposed land along the violent meeting place of rock and ocean, the whole of Greenland's staggering 840,000 square miles lays imprisoned under glacial ice. This is not a frosting, but a continent-crushing burden, averaging a mind-numbing five thousand feet in thickness. Modern science, through radar soundings that map the ghostly topography beneath, has revealed a more startling and humbling truth. It seems the greater part of Greenland's mass, pressed down by the colossal weight of its own frozen cloak, actually lies submerged below the level of the sea. The island we name on maps is, in essence, a magnificent illusion. Strip away the ice that forms its central mountain ranges, its plains, its deep-cut valleys—ice that the brief, perfunctory kiss of the summer sun is powerless to truly assail—and the truth would be laid bare. Greenland would not be a single entity at all, but an elongated and disjointed archipelago, a shattered spine of dark rock drowned in the Arctic Sea.

Of the meagre and grudging fifteen percent of land that emerges, skeletal and temporary, during the warmer months, little even deigns to support life beyond the most tenacious. Tundra grasses cling in desperate patches, and the landscape is one of profound botanical austerity. No forests grace the stark, abrupt mountainous terrain that rises, fortress-like, directly from the frigid seas on all sides. The only arboreal presence is a few stunted and poor birches, some toughened willows bent double by the wind, and a little alder scrub that hugs the ground as if fearing the sky.

With a total population of only some 55,000 souls—a number smaller than a modest provincial town elsewhere—Greenland is a study in emptiness. It possesses not what you might call major centres of civilization. Its main cities, such as they are, can hardly invite comparison with the sprawling chaos of a Los Angeles; or even, for that matter, with a modest regional hub like Brownsville. One inevitable result of this dual curse of remoteness and inhospitality is that Greenland makes nary a dent upon the common global psyche. It exists in the peripheral vision of the world. Its single, feeble purchase on popular memory is, ironically, for its name: the world's most glaringly and poetically inappropriate toponym. 'Iceland,' that green and fertile place, had already been snapped up by the cocky little island to the east, leaving only the dismal 'Whiteland' or the curiously optimistic 'Greenland'—the latter sounding, to say the least, like a cruel or desperately hopeful joke.

Folklore says the name was bestowed by Erik the Red, the Norse exile who, with a Viking's shrewd sense of marketing, sought to attract settlers to his new-found territory. Yet another tale speaks of a lone missionary priest, arriving by ship in the fleeting height of summer, harboring in a southern fjord. From his deck, gazing across the water at the distant hillsides momentarily brushed with a scant and temporary green carpet, he was deceived by the apparent pleasantness, the merciful illusion of the season, and so baptized the land with its enduring, unlikely name. In my own imagination, I prefer a different scene: perhaps it was that same Erik, frowning over the dead, unvegetated fissures of the fiords, the grinding ice, the stone-grey skies, and opting for the dark, Norse solution of irony.

Politically, Greenland enjoys the complex status of an autonomous constituent country within the Realm of Denmark. Granted complete home-rule in 1979, it is a vast, frozen ward of that tiny, orderly kingdom of my birth. This arrangement allows Denmark, in a borrowed and peculiar way, to semi-achieve the old, grand boast of the nineteenth-century British Empire: for during a part of the year, thanks to this distant, icy possession, the sun truly never sets on Danish territory.

Since the time of the events recorded in the earlier parts of this narrative, my own coordinates have shifted. I have become an Australian citizen, and in the parlance of my new home, I now think of myself as a Mainlander. This is a term used in gentle opposition to the 'Taswegians,' who occupy the island about the size of Maine to the south. This shifted perspective has wrought a subtle change in my inner geography. I now find it curiously difficult to consider the small, windy town where I was born—Esbjerg, on the flat western coast of Denmark's Jutland peninsula—as belonging to any meaningful 'mainland,' though this is undoubtedly a physical fact.

For Denmark proper is itself a modest, fragmented entity. It consists of a slim, probing finger of the European continent pointing out into the North Sea towards Norway and Sweden; two medium-sized, cultured islands, Funen and Zealand (the latter bearing the capital, Copenhagen); and a graceful scattering of smaller isles. It is a compact and human-scaled realm. The sparsely populated, windswept and frozen wilderness of Greenland, by stark and awe-inspiring contrast, could contain within its icy borders several nations the size of this entire little European kingdom.

* * * * *

THE DENMARK INTO which I made my first, crying appearance on the morning of May 24, 1943, was not one of the happiest countries on earth. A deep, humiliating shadow lay over the land. The Nazis had occupied the country in a swift, brutal invasion early in 1940, installing a puppet regime that danced to Berlin's tune. Their reasons were coldly pragmatic: partly strategic, to secure the northern flank and complicate Allied air operations from England; and partly predatory, to plunder the little neighbour of its agricultural and industrial resources to feed the insatiable German war machine.

I arrived as the fifth addition to a family that was, like the nation itself, struggling under the weight of circumstance, of mixed social and economic background. The town of my childhood and adolescence, Esbjerg, is a practical, salt-bleached place of about 90,000 souls. It is Denmark's—and probably Northern Europe's—largest fishing port, a fact it proclaims with over seven miles of sturdy, functional quays smelling of diesel, brine, and decaying marine life. It was also one of the country's most vital trade ports, the conduit through which much of Denmark's exports—its butter, its bacon, its fish—were shipped out to a world at war.

After the War, my father, who had been a long-haul truck driver, never again set foot in Germany. His routes before and during the conflict had taken him across the torn-up face of Europe: into the heart of Germany, through France and Spain, down the length of Italy, and even across the Adriatic into the fractious landscapes of Yugoslavia and Greece. His refusal was absolute, and it was silent. It was not until January 1973, when he agreed to drive my new wife and me on a quick honeymoon jaunt across the southern Danish border to the German town of Flensburg, that I even realized this self-imposed exile had existed for nearly thirty years. The revelation came only in the casual aftermath of that trip; the full understanding of his stubborn, principled refusal I would not grasp until after his death.

Now, I understand the immense and quiet generosity of his gesture that day. Had I known the depth of the wound, the strength of the feeling, I would never have asked him to cross that line. My misconception had been born from a superficial observation: because he could speak some German and understood more, he often preferred to watch West German television, which was, without a doubt, vastly superior to the dreary, limited Danish TV of the time. I mistook pragmatism for affinity.

His precise reasons for this quiet, yet intensely burning animosity were never communicated to the family. He was a man of few words about the past, and the war was a closed book. On the rare occasions he referenced it, he offered only fragments, never the full story. He once made a brief, haunting reference to entering Hamburg the day after a heavy Allied bombing raid near the war's end. The bombing had spawned a firestorm of such biblical intensity that people died not from flame or collapse, but because the inferno had consumed all the available oxygen in vast swathes of the city. But that was all. In general, the assiduous, palpable avoidance of the topic by him and so many of his generation supplied endless fodder for a child's imagination. I supposed then, and still suppose now, that he had seen things that were simply incommunicable. From 1943 onwards, with the Reich collapsing in on itself, the Allies reducing German cities to cinders, and the machinery of the 'Final Solution' operating at a horrifying peak, Germany was, even for a bystander, a landscape of profound trauma.

My mother came from a different world. She was the eldest daughter of a well-to-do, landowning farming family from Jutland, the north-western region of Denmark that forms its continental arm. My grandparents' property, where I spent the long, luminous summers of my childhood, was set high upon a commanding rise above a deep fiord, its soil famously rich and productive.

Although my grandmother was ill for much of my youth—she had been kicked by a horse years earlier, an injury that left her in constant pain—I remember my holidays on the farm as a time of boundless, sun-drenched freedom. I knew, even as a boy, that my grandmother possessed a heart of genuine gold beneath a manner that could be harsh and abrupt—a combination, I now believe, of the unrelenting hardness of farm life and the private suffering borne from her injury. My grandfather, by contrast, was his wife's visible opposite: a jovial, warm, and expansive man, whose cheeks were perpetually ruddy and whose eyes crinkled with ready laughter. His skills in domestic crisis management were considerable and gentle.

I recall one instance vividly. When it came time for us to return to the city and to school, my siblings and I were desperate to take with us the rabbits we had been allowed to rear as pets during the holidays. This was, of course, wholly impractical for a family in a fair-sized city apartment. My grandfather, foreseeing tears and drama, executed a flawless diversion. A couple of days before our departure, he invented a story: a huge, sinister, black tailless tomcat had been seen slinking around the farmyard the previous night. He enlisted us as junior detectives, sending us on a solemn mission from one neighbouring farm to another to inquire about this marauding beast. We were so engrossed in this investigation, so convinced of the cat's monstrous responsibility, that the coincidental and timely disappearance of our rabbits was accepted as a tragic but logical outcome of the feline invasion.

As an adult, my experiences of the farm were, predictably, filtered through a more complex lens. Following my marriage, my wife Sophia and I visited, and were joined by her brother, John, and his wife, Rosella, who had travelled from their home in Venice. They had missed our wedding in Athens due to the political crisis over Cyprus, when all able-bodied Greek males were barred from leaving. The visit is cemented in memory for a moment of unintended and painful gallantry. John, ever the gentleman in unfamiliar territory, stepped up to the thin wire fence erected to restrain the cattle. He straddled it, offering a hand to help his wife step over. The piercing yelp and subsequent stream of colourful, Mediterranean-accented expletives that erupted from him informed us all that John had discovered, via the most direct experimental method, that the wire carried a sharp, humiliating electric current.

From the farmhouse, uninterrupted, majestic views were enjoyed over the lower country. The land swept down in long, graceful curves of patchworked paddocks and meadows to the steel-blue line of the fiord itself, perhaps a good three miles distant. The clarity of the northern air there lent those vistas a preternatural crispness and immediacy. Passing ships could be recognized with ease, their details sharp despite the miles. I remember once, with great excitement, identifying the sleek Danish Royal Yacht on its passage. That crystalline quality of light and air was a sensory benchmark in my life, one that would only be surpassed, and then only just, decades later by the views from P Mountain down over the Thule airbase to the frozen, awe-inspiring expanse of the Wolstenholme Fiord in northern Greenland.

* * * * * *

MAJOR RAILBACK RECEIVED the encrypted scramble message deep in the air-conditioned, fluorescent-lit bowels of a NORAD command bunker in Colorado. He was fully dressed, his go-bag in hand, before the two key words of the transmission truly sank in: destination Greenland.

"Well, at least it's not Green Bay," he thought, a grim, humorless twist touching his lips. "God, what a shithole that was. But Jesus… could Greenland be any better? What's even up there? How many warm bodies can there be within five hundred miles of the damn Arctic Circle?"

His mind, trained for contingency, immediately began calculating the logistics of informational minimization. This 'Broken Arrow'—the military's chillingly bland term for a nuclear weapon accident— would hinge on one thing: locating a pliable, isolated workforce that could be mobilized instantly to scrub the site clean before any 'bogies' (civilian eyes) could retrace the events or comprehend the fallout. *Christ,* he thought, *where are the clean-up crews going to come from? There aren't any bases up there.* But then, a sliver of cold comfort: with Vietnam bleeding across the television screens and dominating the headlines, just maybe he could spin the crash story, control the narrative before the raw, ugly 'facts' could metastasize in the press. In a place so empty, with so few military personnel, any leaks could be kept, at the very least, unconfirmable—the stuff of Arctic whisper.

"I've got to get those flyboys on ice, and fast," he muttered to himself, a mantra of containment, as he was driven through one of the myriad of reinforced tunnels carved beneath the Rocky Mountains, heading for the surface exit and waiting aircraft.

Engrossed in strategizing the cleanup of an incident that was still just codes and coordinates—a mystery wrapped in a crisis—Railback did not feel the car brake and draw to a smooth stop. Only when he heard a familiar, gravelly voice cut through his reverie did he surface. "Now, don't you start making decisions on your own up there, Major."

Railback looked up into the weary, pressure-cooked face of General Burton. "Of course not, sir," he said, his body snapping into a crisp salute automatically. "So, who will be making them for me? In any case, I plan to keep you completely informed, General. It'll be strict SOP, sir."

"I'm working on your chain of command now. And just you make sure it *is* SOP, Railback," Burton said, returning the salute with a perfunctory wave that was also a dismissal.

As the car pulled away, Railback's driver, a sharp-eyed sergeant, mused aloud, "The General's skivvies seemed a bit tight this morning, sir."

Railback stared ahead, his mind already miles north. "Well, after Palomares, and with McNamara and his whiz kids maybe looking for a reason to stop the birds from flying… everybody's watching their own ass, Sergeant. Let's just get me to a bird."

They drove on in silence. *SOP?* The thought nagged at him. If Burton wanted it done strictly by the book, why send *him*? Railback was the man you called when the book had been thrown out the window and into a ditch. He was a fixer, not a protocol officer. The General's unusual tension, now that the sergeant had pointed it out, was a bad sign. The long, loud flight to Thule in the fighter's rear seat would give him time not to rest, but to war-game every ugly scenario.

Shortly after the screaming take-off, Railback radioed ahead to Thule. The response delivered a crucial, unexpected piece of luck: a large population of Danish civilian workers—construction teams, technicians—were present on and around the base, along with a smaller, scattered native Inuit population. His mind clicked into overdrive. He quickly ordered that the 'point'—ground zero—be secured immediately, by dogsled if necessary. No excuses. If the goddamn Snowcats couldn't operate in that bush, then have the natives locate and secure it. Promise them 'whatever it takes'—his standard, blank-cheque order for cooperation. Then, start work on mobilising every single Dane who was available and could be persuaded, incentivized, or strong-armed to commence the clean-up. He'd be on site to assess the damage before they could cause too much trouble or ask too many questions. Medical teams were coming from God-knew-where, but he wasn't going to let this operation stall waiting for some by-the-book Air Force medical types.

Five hours later, Railback's first aerial view of the wreck site shocked him into a rare, silent stillness, veteran though he was of disasters across the globe. His mind performed a terrifying, instant calculation, extrapolating the carnage had this happened over Chicago, or London, or Moscow. WHITE. The world here was supposed to be infinite, virgin WHITE. But it was BLACK. A vast, grotesque stain of oily, pulverized BLACK.

"Let's get this bird on the ground. Now. ASAP," he commanded the pilot, his voice low and hard. "Yessir, Major," the pilot replied, his own voice strained. "Jesus, sir... looks like somebody tried to pave a parking lot right in the middle of hell's icebox."

On the ground, Railback moved like a force of nature, barking orders at anyone who crossed his path, officer or enlisted. He ignored protocol.

"Don't you want to check in with the Base CO first, sir?" asked a young, nervous line officer as Railback stormed past.

"If the fucking Base CO ain't here on the tarmac to meet me," Railback snapped without breaking stride, "then I guess he doesn't need to hear what I have to say. Get me out to that black ice, Captain." "Captain Burnett, sir. There's a chopper already warming up, sir."

"You got somebody out on 'point'?" Railback screamed, his voice fighting the growing whump-whump-whump of the helicopter blades. This was no time for pleasantries or introductions. "We've located it, sir. Sent native hunters out on sleds. We think we have bearings on most of the crew." "Well, I don't want that crew talking to *anyone* until I've talked to them first, Burnett. You read me? NO-fucking-ONE. If I hear the rescue crews did any more than ask them where they're hurt, I'll personally bust the son-of-a-bitch. GOT IT?"

"YESSIR."

"And I want to review any and every written report—eyewitness, mechanical, environmental—before they're so much as filed. I *own* the paper on this one." He closed the subject.

"YESSIR," Burnett's voice trailed after him as he ducked into the chopper's belly.

"Dammit!" Railback cursed inwardly as the craft lifted off. "This could get uglier than a divorce in a trailer park unless we can contain both material and conversation in the next forty-eight hours." An idea formed: maybe a sudden, convenient 'communications storm' needed to shut down all non-essential traffic to and from Thule until the bulk of the dirty work was done. *Thank God for Vietnam*, he thought again, a cynical prayer. If that wasn't the hottest hellhole on the nightly news, this screw-up would be the biggest story on the planet. Not the kind of publicity a Major who has his eye on a Light-Bird colonelcy needs at this point in his career. The chopper began to churn its way toward the spreading stain on the horizon.

"Hey, Cap," he spoke into the crackling com line to the pilot.

"Sir?"

"Get me a scrambled frequency back to the Thule command desk. Now."

"Aye, sir. You're patched."

"This is Major Railback. Any word on marshalling those Danish workers?" he demanded of whoever answered.

"Burnett here, sir. Yes sir, we're rounding them up now. Should we wait for the proper medical teams to screen them?"

"No, goddamnit! Use the medics you have on base for random testing. For the rest, you use the standard radioactive procedures manual. It's in your safe. You do have one, Captain? Just read the goddamn directions and follow them. Speed is what we need here if we're to clean this up before it gets politically radioactive, too. Chopper Zero out."

Railback let the handset sink slowly to his knee as the chopper began to circle, hovering over the heart of the disaster. Below lay what looked like a square mile of recently-tilled, loamy earth, except it was pitch black and lay in the middle of a stark, white moonscape. The scale of the explosion, the sheer physical insult of the plutonium spray, became horrifyingly apparent.

"My Lord," he muttered to himself, the profanity leaving him for a moment.

"General's on the horn again, Major," the pilot interrupted.

"Scramble it."

"Railback." It was Burton. "No bad news, now. Can you clean it up?"

"Yes, sir," Railback responded instantly. What other answer was there? "There's a large contingent of Danish nationals we can… co-opt to help out. Natives are cooperating on securing the point. I'll be getting a full damage assessment from our men on the ground shortly."

"I don't want the details, Major. I just want it done. And I want it done *by the book*."

Burton added, almost as an afterthought, his tone shifting to something less brusque, more conspiratorial,

"I don't need to remind you, Railback, that the politicians are looking for any excuse to ground our flying alert force. This is just the kind of ammunition they'd love to use to get to McNamara."

"Yes, sir. I understand the implications perfectly, sir," Railback answered, his jaw tight.

"Well, I'm trusting you to do the job as it needs to be done."

Railback thought, *Do you want the fucking job done, or do you want it done by the book? Make up your mind.*

He said, "I will need your full support, General. And I will need a free hand to make on-the ground decisions."

"I'm working on it in the highest quarters, Railback. I'll get back to you ASAP. NORAD out." The line went dead with a final click.

"Alright, Cap. I've seen enough," Railback said, shaking his head at the General's contradictory pressures. "Let's head for the barn. I've got to get my own crew out in the field—and find me somebody who can interpret whatever the hell language these Danish people speak."

"Most of them speak pretty good English, sir," the pilot offered.

"Well, shit," Railback said, a dark chuckle escaping him. He wasn't sure if that was a blessing or a curse, given his secondary brief of keeping the information flow to an absolute, needle-thin minimum. Whatever else happened, he had already decided: these Danish citizens were going to work for Uncle Sam, they were going to clean this mess, and they were going to do it with a smile or without one. It made no difference to him. Results were the only currency that mattered.

* * * * * *

SUBLIMINAL PROCESSES WORK upon us from beneath the surface of conscious thought, their influence felt but rarely seen. Looking back, I believe it was such an influence from my father—for there was never any direct pressure from that quarter—that gently steered me toward a career in international trade. The journey from truck-driving to shipbroking is a step made across a single generation, a quiet inheritance of movement and commerce.

However it may have been, by the time I finished my junior high equivalent, I was already resolved on a future in management and trade. My initial plan was to join Scandinavian Airlines as a cadet in aircraft management. That path seemed clear until a chance visit to a careers advisory exhibition reshaped my destiny.

I was wandering the hall aisle, moving from stall to stall, pausing to collect pamphlets or examine the displays with a teenager's idle curiosity. I happened to linger longer before a stall run by a shipbroking agency named J. Lauritzen's Successors. My attention was captured by the six-foot-long model of an oil tanker that dominated their display, its miniature decks and hatches a perfect, intricate world.

One of the company representatives sidled up to me, noting my interest. "You seem quite taken with the display," he observed. "What are you thinking of as a career?"

"Well, I've sort of decided to go for aircraft management. Scandinavian Airlines are looking for people right now. In fact, they've already written me a letter saying they are interested in considering me."

"Have you ever thought of shipbroking?" he pressed.

"No, never."

"Look, if you're considering a career in management and trade, the way to get in the door is on a boat," he grinned.

"It would need to be a wide door," I grinned back.

"Well, there you have it," he continued. "Ships open their own doors. But I'll tell you something. If you go for Scandy Air now, sure, you'll have a good job and good money: but, the career prospects are just that bit restricted as compared with shipbroking. From ships you can go to planes: but, from planes to ships…" He shrugged his shoulders. "It's like forcing oil into an engine with the funnel upside down."

Whether it was that analogy, or anything else he said; or whether it was just the magnetic pull of that perfect tanker model; I cannot say for sure. The only certainty is that for the next four years, I was concurrently working as a cadet and studying international trade, specializing in shipping—all without leaving my hometown of Esbjerg.

The on-the-job training was ruthlessly practical. It was less an education and more a series of initiations, rather as if a paratrooper were to train for jumps by first being pushed out of second-storey windows: survive twelve feet, and twenty thousand is just a matter of managing the vertigo.

There were no classroom simulations. My simulator on one occasion, during a particular nadir in relations between Greece and Turkey—the Cyprus Crisis—was a boatful of Turks with knives and another boat full of Greeks with volatile attitudes. My company was agent to both ships, and I had been sent to investigate after a frantic, wailing call from each captain. Their crews were in a tense Mexican standoff on the quay.

So, I pedalled my way down to the waterfront and, before I could properly find the brakes on my bicycle, I found myself standing on the wharf late on a chaotic night, well past midnight. I was suddenly the only barrier—a scrawny, pale teenager—standing between two opposing crews intent on carving each other up with scimitars and cargo hooks, all in the name of nationalist fervour.

I felt I had stumbled onto a set for *Treasure Island*, cast in the role of Jim Hawkins or a terrified cabin boy: the youthful, wide-eyed centre of a storm composed of great, heaving, hairy men with tattooed arms, reeking of alcohol and rage, screaming imponderables at each other in no common tongue. I thought quickly and decided the 'innocent abroad' was not the best persona for this developing situation.

So, I got mad too. I dredged up a choice few Danish imponderables close to my own heart, seasoning them with fragments from my English, German, and French reserves.

I started quivering and slow.

"If you drunken bloody fools don't get your stupid asses off my wharf right now and take your damned international incident with you somewhere else than my port, where I won't have to clean up the mess after you, and just get back onto your own friggin' ships and stay there, ..." I was by now at the top of my voice and pointing at the two crews' several ships, "... I'll,.. I'll (I'll what? Take their names and make them stay after school?) ... I'll see to it that your captains keep you brigged up for the rest of your stay here ... and make no damned mistake about that!"

I ended my peroration with a finger thrust close to the noses of the two men I supposed to be the opposing ringleaders.

Much to my profound relief, I felt the eyes of mutual hatred part from each other and turn instead to stares of incredulity, focused on the unlikely sight before them: a thin, pale Scandinavian teenager transforming into a concrete, shouting obstacle before their eyes. Each blinked a couple of times, lowered his weapon, and turned muttering back into the dark gang behind him.

Soon, I was alone on the wharf, the silence ringing in my ears. It only remained to have a firm word with the two ships' captains to ensure their respective crews remained on board for the length of their stay.

This done, I mounted my bike, which unaccountably wobbled so uncontrollably that I decided I had better just walk it, and made for home. A couple of blocks away from the waterfront, my bike had regained sufficient balance for me to mount it.

"That was pretty, well, exciting," I thought to myself. "I've just averted a serious incident of international dimensions. I've helped to avoid bloodshed!" I felt a flush of pride and satisfaction.

So, suffused with this bravado, I was just riding off from the verge when I was accosted by a police patrol car.

"Sonny, you've got no lights. You can't ride that bike at this time of night."

"But, how will I get home?" I felt instantly humiliated.

"Walk it, smartarse. Or we'll give you a lift you won't like."

"Yeah," put in the other, mumbling through a hamburger. "Under the ear."

So, I walked the rest of the way home, thoroughly deflated. An unknown and unrecognised hero of the Cyprus Crisis.

My training furnished several other, less dramatic occasions to practice my fledgling diplomatic and language skills.

The occasion of a national wharfies' strike nearly became the occasion of my migrating to Argentina.

An Argentinian shipping company had, at the time of the strike, a number of ships in Esbjerg, loading cylinders of natural gas for transport back to Buenos Aires. The dispute dragged on through three refractory months, during which time I got to know the Argentinian crew well and conceived the idea of going to live and work in their country. I went so far as to organise a job for myself there and was deep in the process of securing a visa when the collapse of the Argentinian economy gave me pause. I came that close to becoming a Spanish speaker and perhaps getting caught up, years later, in the inglorious Falklands War.

* * * * * *

HOWEVER, THAT WAS not to be. Instead, shortly after completing my degree, I fulfilled my obligatory military service to the Danish nation in the Royal Danish Air Force.

There was no glamour, no danger, and precious little excitement in being a peacetime draftee in the mid-sixties. Very little of the 'Right Stuff' came my way, I must admit, never leaving the ground in control of even a trainer. Instead, I spent fourteen months manning a series of remote, early-warning radar installations, most of which had an effectiveness rating of zero—a rating I would apply to my entire military experience were it not for the stark beauty of the locations.

Boot camp was down south on the border with Germany, where the first attacks had come in the last war. I was then stationed for a short time at a secret Air Force facility in a northern Copenhagen suburb.

One highlight of that dismal period was the secret amusement I derived from imagining what a passing onlooker must have made of the extraordinary daily sight. All a council worker or taxi-driver would have seen was a vacant, derelict block of land occupied solely by a single, solitary construction-site toilet. At around seven each morning, our hypothetical observer would have watched, cigarette forgotten on his lip, as that toilet swallowed over a hundred men in quick succession. At five-thirty each afternoon, the process reversed, the hundred-plus men emerging from the humble single-seater portable dunny to disperse to their homes.

The only other memorable circumstance was the bizarre number of Eastern Bloc spies who patrolled the area, offering lifts to young recruits emerging from His Majesty's Ship 'John' to drill them for information about the top-secret facility and perhaps crack the code of the 'powder room.'

I was then assigned to a major base at Skrydstrup, in southeastern Jutland. From there, I was seconded briefly to a radar tracking installation on a small island as close to East Germany as Denmark could get.

The radar itself was constructed on the highest, most windswept point of the island. Every day of that week, we had to trek up to the monitoring screen and tie it down against the wind, which even at its lightest seemed to threaten the structure. Consequently, once the screen was secured for the day, we spent the rest of it sleeping.

Shortly after returning to Skrydstrup, the early-warning station burned down while I was on duty. The enormous underground installation was completely destroyed. After that, I was posted to the radar station at Skagen, at the very northernmost tip of Jutland, where I definitively gave up smoking.

At Skagen, apart from admiring the area's spectacular natural beauty—where two seas meet in a perpetual, dramatic clash—there was a mind-numbing absence of anything to do. Our duties were limited to occasional marches on a windblown parade ground and interminable hours lounging in our quarters.

We were being driven mad by inertia. I suspect it may have been a very subtle psychological test devised by the military for the government: to see how much boredom and inanity a Dane could be exposed to before irreversible damage was done.

It had an extreme effect on me: it inured me to lonely, vast places; it solidified my determination to emigrate to just about anywhere else in the world; and it made me industrious for my own well-being.

The immediate effect was that I took on several part-time jobs. This helped mitigate the execrable boredom and eke out my miserable salary. First, I worked a short-term position as a hand in a huge freezer for a fish-exporting business. Then, I joined a small travel agency, holding practically a full-time position there while still performing my military duties.

In these ways, I spent fourteen months defending and protecting the Free World from the Communist threat at the height of the Cold War.

Upon completing my service, I accepted an offer of partnership in the travel agency and immediately set about expanding it to include a shipping component, finally putting my qualifications as a shipbroker to direct use.

The expanded agency became quite a successful little earner. However, my partners—a married couple—got stars in their eyes and wanted to expand in a different direction. Had their plan been almost anything else, I might have stayed on with them to this day. But they wanted to dive into the southern European holiday market, flying people on package tours to the Algarve, Mallorca, and the Costa del Sol.

I felt the market had already peaked and would quickly become overserviced. So, I declined to participate in the expansion and left the partnership altogether. I went to work as a shipping clerk with the Danish Construction Corporation, stationed at Thule Air Base in northern Greenland.

Unfortunately, I was proven correct in my prediction. The travel agency soon afterwards folded, with significant losses due to the attempt to compete with established, centrally located agencies in a saturated market.

I, meanwhile, was being fitted out with my Arctic gear, looking forward to a three-month stint during the summer resupply season at what felt like the last place on earth.

Five years, two days, and eight hours after I arrived in Greenland, my stint came to a close. The intervening years had held much overt good and much hidden ill. The good came in years of job satisfaction, close friendships, and youthful excitement in an extraordinary venue. The ill came secretly and sub-atomically in the unsought consequences of mankind's grappling with nature's foundations, and in the hubris and posturing that attended the effort to harness forces from that invisible, impossibly tiny realm.

* * * * * *

THE MEMORY OF Thule slept soundly after my departure in 1971. For the next fourteen years, it was just a memory of pleasant associations: long friendships begun, good times, excitement, and the satisfaction of personal and professional accomplishments. Barely a glimmer of disquiet remained over some features of the cleanup operation, 'Crested Ice,' in which I was proud to have played a minor, though useful, part. Photos, letters, 8mm films, pressed wildflowers, and a few select knick-knacks were the artifacts of this living memory. They were touchstones by which I could readily wake it, though it more often lay dormant as a potential experience than as a positive act of reflection.

Memories were not the only things lying dormant within me, however. The leviathan within, when woken, proved to be an emissary from the building blocks of nature gone awry: and the building blocks were stacked against me.

The first stirring of this waking monster came to my attention in January 1985. During a routine medical examination for a position with the Electricity Commission of New South Wales, north of Sydney, the doctor commented on my elevated blood pressure.

"I should keep an eye on that, if I were you," he suggested.

I was a little taken aback. "I've never in my life had high blood pressure," I said. "In fact, I've never had any health problems. I don't even have a regular GP."

"Hmm! Well, all the more reason to have it checked from time to time. I'm not suggesting there's a problem. It's just best to be on the safe side so that you don't present yourself with a, how can I put it?, with a nasty Christmas surprise in five years' time."

I examined closely the buttons on my shirt as I put it back on. "Well, thanks. I guess I'm getting into that age bracket where I need to take some precautions."

Once I got the job, though, the doctor's wise suggestions fell into abeyance.

Until, just before Easter of that same year.

It was lunchtime on day three of a senior management course I was attending, run by the Australian Graduate School of Management. I was lining up in the canteen amidst a bustle of managers when, out of nowhere, my chest exploded into pain. I almost fainted, falling against two very rotund and loquacious middle managers from a small Australian firm called BHP, in the queue before me.

One of them turned and caught me before I hit the floor. "Jeez, are you OK, mate?" he asked in the typical Australian idiom, supporting me about the shoulders.

I could only answer by shaking my head in the negative.

"Blimey, I think we'd better get this bloke to a doctor, Bob," said his companion. "He's lookin' a bit green about the gills!"

As my two new friends walked me bodily out of the canteen in search of a sick bay, I overheard a comment from the queue: "Food that good here, hey mate?"

The surgery having been found and me laid down on the couch, the doctor in attendance quickly ascertained that I was not having a heart attack, but that, whatever it was, "this injection is sure to stabilize you," and jabbed me with a needle the size of a Saturn V rocket. I remember little of the remaining two days of the course.

The event is memorable nevertheless, as it marked the beginning of a two-year stint of gradually worsening health and an almost endless series of medical tests.

* * * * * *

JOERGEN RASMUSSEN WAS a country boy from the Jutland Peninsula; solid, friendly, jovial, with a keen business sense. His work as a fireman at Thule did not sufficiently fill his time, so he took to importing goods to the base on behalf of the more financially secure Americans and Danes. Following his coup in managing to provide a made-to-order suit for a colleague—having taken the measurements and sent them to a tailor in Copenhagen—he became so successful that eventually his room was a storehouse of clothes, bags, pipes, shoes, and jewellery. He even set up a car-rental agency for anyone heading back to Copenhagen for a holiday; upon arrival at the airport, a car would be waiting.

Joergen made lots of money. But money was not his only interest.

Joergen would preside over card games in the barracks that would go on till all hours of the morning. The games were really a pretext for Joergen to soap-box on a wide variety of topics. These ranged from the comparative anthropology of the Danes and the native Greenlanders to the special problems encountered by Danes in imposing their education system on a Greenlandic culture that had no concept of requiring children to do anything they did not want to do.

Joergen made lots of money and eventually became the owner of several large apartment blocks in Copenhagen.

Joergen made lots of money; but Joergen died of cancer at forty-nine.

R.I.P. Joergen.

* * * * * *

ONE EVENING, NOT long after the attack at the management course, I was sitting in our lounge with Sophia and our younger son, James. Our elder son, Phillip, was out playing the newly popular sport of indoor cricket. We were watching a replay of *M.A.S.H.*, another televised facsimile of battlefield triage and big-top surgery. Without warning, I was overcome again by a crushing constellation of symptoms. With my layman's knowledge—gleaned from desultory reading over decades and the surreptitious dipping into disreputable magazines such as *Reader's Digest*—I believed it to be a heart attack.

"Sophia," I managed, my voice strangled by the pain, "I'm sick of this show."

She laughed and turned to give me a pat on the shoulder. Instead, the colour drained from her features. In one fluid motion, she pulled me to my feet and had me in the car, speeding toward Belmont Hospital before I could utter, 'not again.'

The busy medico in the emergency ward checked me over and assured me it was not a heart attack. Though in no position to do so, he suggested I was 'perhaps under a lot of strain at work lately?'

As for tests: every conceivable examination was performed. They searched for tumours of the brain, the chest, the stomach, and so on, ad nauseam. When nothing tangible was found to explain my deteriorating condition, the doctors grew more consternated. I began to feel they considered me a bit of a troublemaker, and perversely, I started to wish they would find *something*—just so they would have a concrete enemy to fight. My constant, debilitating vomiting, however, convinced them I was no malingerer. I had to restrain my temper whenever any of them suggested, however delicately, that my suffering might be stress-related.

"Well, of course it's stress-related," I once retorted in frustration, "I always throw up when I have to go into a staff canteen!" I was in another doctor's surgery following yet another bout of pain in my limbs, stomach, and chest, accompanied by dizzy spells.

"Very droll, I'm sure, Mr. Carswell. However, we must not overlook the possibility. It is not unusual for people with management responsibilities to suffer from some form of hypertension; and the higher you climb up the tree, the greater the responsibilities and the consequent pressures and stresses."

"With respect," I said, barely keeping the growing impatience from my voice, "I've been in management all my working life and have always been subject to its typical stresses. I am under no greater pressure now than I was when I worked, for example, as an executive officer with the Danish Construction Corporation on the US military base at Thule in the sixties. And back then, I felt no undue stress at all. I'm cut out for this sort of work, and I'm very happy doing it."

"But you are considerably older now, Mr. Carswell. The pressures are there and must tell on your frame sooner or later."

"Do you put down to stress every condition that you can't pinpoint?" I had lost my cool by now. "If it is stress, what sort of specialist can you send me to? After all, the solution to every problem is to pass it on, isn't it?"

Obviously, I had said nothing the doctor hadn't heard a thousand times before. He sat immutably behind his desk. "Well, Mr. Carswell, all the tests known to the practitioners of medicine in one of the most advanced clinics in the country have drawn a blank." He crossed his arms. "My suggestion is the causes of your condition—tiredness, discomfort, and nausea—are somehow related to life stresses. How, I am not expert to judge…"

"Indeed!" I assented, the word sharp.

"…Indeed. For which reason, my recommendation is that you attend some sessions with a psychologist. I can refer you to one quite close by, if you wish."

"A psychologist?" I was appalled.

"A psychologist would be in the best position to assess whether your condition is indeed emotionally based and to then suggest the most convenient treatment."

"In all seriousness," I asked, leaning forward, "Do you mean to tell me that, rather than admit to failure, you want *me* to?"

"I can only suggest to you what it is within my expert capability as a medical practitioner to suggest."

"I had not thought it possible before now that being practiced in medicine could diminish the soul," I responded angrily. "But so it must, if that is the only thing you can suggest."

A taut silence followed. The pursed lips of the man opposite me, across the professional distance of his desk, told me I had gone just far enough to pierce the armour. I relented slightly. "Write me the referral, then. It seems I am running out of options from the mainstream of medicine."

"It is all for the best," the doctor answered coldly as he scribbled on his pad, tore off the sheet, and handed it to me. "They have quite a good success rate these days, I'm told."

I took the sheet of paper, folded it slowly, and without another word, turned on my heel and marched out.

I never got around to visiting the kindly recommended psychologist. Apart from having not the slightest intention of making such a visit, I was soon afterwards offered a job in Melbourne, Victoria. I accepted it, and shortly thereafter, I went to live in the City on the Bay, where I still reside.

* * * * * *

WILLIE WAS OLDER than most on the base, around forty in 1968. Bushy eyebrows half hid his large, expressive eyes, and his broad, thick lips seemed ever on the verge of a smile. His hands were a captivating adjunct to his words, whizzing through the air before his interlocutor like a one-man flying circus. Willie had enough personality to fill three distinct lifetimes.

Willie One was an incredibly talented handyman and mechanic. Enormous, ancient diesel engines that others had abandoned to the ice and wind were barely a challenge for him. To watch Willie tinkering over and revivifying one of those mechanical hulks was to witness a lesson in total absorption, a perfect unity of the workman and his work.

Willie Two drank, and when he did, he turned nasty and belligerent. He was a heavy man who hit hard. Someone always regretted getting to know Willie Two. Yet the morning after battering someone's door to chipboard, he would remember it all and cheerfully ask, 'Well, was I the only one who saw the horse that kicked that door in?'

Willie Three loved fun and was usually open and voluble. On one occasion, however, his close friend Marius Schmidt noticed him being unusually secretive and quiet about a package he had received from Denmark. A few nights later, Marius, returning late to the barracks they shared, saw Willie's light still on, his door ajar. Naturally, he went to pay his mate a visit. Marius poked his head around the door to say hello and withdrew it in shock. A second, more cautious peek revealed the cascading hair, shapely bosom, low-cut dress, and high boots of a lady with her back turned, presumably in conversation with Willie. Then, Willie's large, laughing face appeared in Marius's. 'Isn't she great, Schmidt? She looks just like the real thing in those clothes, don't she?' He gave the immobile figure a push, and it fell to the floor—a full-sized blow-up doll. Willie's package had contained her wardrobe.

When at home in Denmark, Willie lived with his elderly mother, the only 'real' woman in the world for him.

Marius remembered many stories about Willie. He recounted how, once, the unique fauna of Thule made a grave impression on the back of Willie's head.

The fire station personnel had received a fresh supply of movies after a film-drought and were showing them one after another in a large garage used for instruction. Joergen, Willie, I, and most of the guys attended this marathon. Several nodded off, but not Willie. He sat with his chair leaning against the partially open garage door, propping it ajar to ensure a supply of fresh air.

We were on Polar-Bear Alert. The Air Police had radioed that one of the huge monsters was moving around the airfield near the fire station. A protected species, it was hoped it would move on without interference. So, Willie declared he would keep the bear out and let in only the air.

About halfway through *Come Back, Little Sheba*, the fire alarm sounded. Marius had to drive down to the port in a small pickup to deal with a contaminant spill. On his way back, hoping to catch the end of the film—being a fan of Burt Lancaster—he ran into a Thule Inuit with his dog team.

The Eskimo, using sign language, conveyed that one of his puppies was limping and needed help. Marius, also signing, explained the dog needed expert attention and that it would be a pity to have such a cute critter destroyed. He promised to take it to the hospital. The Eskimo, at that, pointed to his expensive Seiko watch, made a sign of four full circles with his index finger, and pointed toward the sun twice. Marius stood perplexed, chewing on his pipe. Suddenly, it struck him: ah, yes. Two days. They should meet in two days to report on the puppy's progress.

They hurried together up to the fire station with the puppy. They halted outside the garage, near the half-open door from which issued the sound of Willie's snoring. One of Willie's arms hung relaxed by his side, the palm facing invitingly backward. The puppy rushed over and licked his hand in joyful greeting.

Willie let out a roar like an air-raid siren, lost his balance, hit the ground with the back of his head, bounced up as if made of rubber, and scuttled off to safety behind the garage.

It was nearly half an hour before he could be convinced that the polar bear had not been responsible for his startlement.

The puppy, unfortunately, had to have its damaged leg amputated at the hospital. It went on to become something of a mascot there, as its Inuit owner had no use for a three-legged dog.

The polar bear, meantime, disdained to cause any alarm in person and moved off harmlessly, never knowing the panic it had caused in poor Willie.

Willie died of cancer. At his funeral, Marius discovered he had a son. When he heard the lad speak, Marius said to himself, 'Here is Willie Four.'

R.I.P. Willies One, Two and Three.

* * * * * *

WANTIRNA IS A pleasant residential suburb in the outer eastern part of Melbourne. Typical of the growth corridors that have seen the city slowly submerge the orchards and dairy farms since World War

II, it comprises a large number of well-defined rectangular blocks, hiding within themselves mazes of courts, crescents, and cul-de-sacs. It is easy enough to get into, but devilishly difficult to get out of. Within, the general atmosphere is one of peace and family contentment, while only yards away hum the busy thoroughfares of commerce and commuting.

"Yes, a nice area, Wantirna," said Doctor Dennis Shepherd, my new Melbourne GP, as he sat at his desk noting down the particulars of my medical history. "What is it, just forty minutes to the city and twenty to the Dandenongs? I suppose you've been out and had a look around the hills?"

I said I had.

"So, Jeff," he got down to business, his tone kind but direct. "Why have you not given up on the medical world, despite your lack of success in getting a useful diagnosis?"

It was a candid question and deserved an answer of the same quality. "I do admit to feelings of animosity toward a profession that cannot say when it's wrong, or at least admit that it cannot provide every answer."

Dennis remained silent, giving a slight nod to indicate he was listening. I went on. "What are my options? If I give up on the medical profession, that leaves me with turning to quackery and snake oils, and the endless, fruitless expenditure that entails; or, above and beyond the symptoms of intense discomfort and almost continuous nausea, contending with the distressing possibility that I'll never find a diagnosis and hence, no cure or alleviation."

I sighed lightly. "That prospect doesn't cheer me too much."

"Hmmm." Dennis was thoughtful and careful in his reply. "There is a danger in this profession, especially for general practitioners and specialists—I mean those who are not engaged in research, which is a genuinely humbling experience—but who work with the sick and desperate from day to day. They labour under the pressure of a public perception that their GP is the local conduit of the fount of all cures. The danger for the practitioner is to make the same mistake and confuse himself with his exalted position. It's a common misconception that medicine itself can do no wrong. Combine that with the case of the doctor who represents it, who is baffled, yet clings to the same misconception. He's confronted with a person in pain who has placed utter trust in him and believes he can do no wrong. Believe me, Jeff, it is not always the easiest, nor the most prudent and helpful thing to do for a desperate person: to evanesce an illusion on which he has pinned all his hopes."

He paused while I absorbed the point. "Besides which," he continued, "There are alternatives to conventional medicine that don't necessarily entail submitting yourself to a suspension of belief."

Dennis became animated, rising from behind his desk and coming toward me, his hands punctuating his words. "Western medicine is coming to appreciate more and more the as yet largely inexplicable effectiveness of acupuncture. Did you know, for instance, that there are hospitals in the US where anaesthetists have been quite put out of commission? The judicious placement of a number of needles in the body here and here and here," he pointed to various parts, "does just the same job as midazolam and suxamethonium. It's being found that conditions as widely varied as stomach ulcers, skin rashes, and period pains can be treated at least as effectively as with drugs and diet. And that's just the beginning!"

"Yes, I can see that," I ventured to break in with a smile.

"Ah, Jeff, you note my enthusiasm," he returned the smile. "But note too what some of the most highly regarded medical journals in the world have reported." He swept his hand toward a second desk by the window, littered with books, journals, and notebooks—the paraphernalia of a perpetual student. "Yep," he added jovially, "I take an interest in these developments, particularly when the developments are our discoveries of someone else's sophisticated and proven traditions. Ha ha ha!"

"Needles! Instead of anaesthetic?" I mused. I imagined myself undergoing major heart surgery under those conditions and paled at the vision of the doctor lifting out my lungs and, looking up at me, commenting chastisingly, 'Don't forget to keep taking those deep breaths, Mr. Carswell!'

"There is a Chinese tradition I read about somewhere," I said, trying to dispel the ridiculous picture. "Apparently it was common to pay the local physician a retainer, which, when you got sick, stopped until you were well again."

"Uncommon common sense of the Orientals, what? A healthy emphasis on health! If we adopted it here—as if the AMA would buy it!—it certainly would put paid to the opinion that doctors are little more than receptionists at funeral parlours."

So, we struck up quite a positive and trusting relationship.

On a later visit to Dennis, in March 1987, the conversation turned grave.

"Jeff, I am going to recommend that you spend a little time in hospital for us to run a course of extensive tests."

Although I didn't speak, my face must have conveyed my dread. Dennis spoke concisely and clearly, his usual warmth tempered by professional gravity.

"I think we may be dealing here with a variety of cancer."

He looked down at his hands, clasped on his desk in a posture of mock gravity turned real. My eyes followed his, then returned to catch his unwaveringly steady gaze.

"We need a result, Jeff. Even if it is only to exclude finally and definitively this possibility."

He then explained fully the possibility he had lighted upon: what my subtle but perceptible symptoms pointed toward; the nature of the tests; and what would follow if they proved positive. He finished:

"A positive result is hardly welcome; but, in so far as knowing the worst allows you to act accordingly, then it is qualifiedly welcome. Because, Jeff, there is no doubt that you are ill; and my job is to find out with what, and how to treat you from there."

I was shortly afterwards admitted to hospital, where I spent two rather uncomfortable days. There, following an endoscopy and gastroscopy, the truth came starkly to light. I was at a critical stage in the development of cancer of the oesophagus.

* * * * * *

KARL WAS A small, cheerful man, twenty-six years old in 1968. Black-haired, he sported a neat moustache that earned him the nickname 'Half Pussy.' Karl was a blacksmith.

Karl was at Thule to earn money. Being there entailed a number of deprivations, and one of the major ones Karl suffered was separation from his young wife, Marion.

At the end of his time there, Karl returned to Denmark and bought his dream house. He and Marion shared many terrific years together there, until Karl died of cancer at the age of fifty-six.

R.I.P. Karl.

* * * * * *

DR. SHEPHERD LOOKED me square in the eye. I was numbed; a cold, static emptiness filled the space where fear or panic should have been. Sophia, who sat beside me, later confessed that she had half-risen from her seat in shock, only to fall back weakly, choking down the cry that threatened to escape.

"It's not very advanced yet, so it's quite manageable, Jeff. Still," he looked from me to my wife, his gaze steady and professional, "Jeff, Sophia, the earlier we act, the better."

"Act?" whispered Sophia, her voice hoarse.

Dennis looked at Sophia but addressed his remarks to me.

"We will have you listed as an emergency case and get you in right away. Cancer treatment has come a long way over the past ten years, and there is an excellent chance we can contain this, so long as we operate right away."

"But what about the nurses' strike?" Sophia asked anxiously. We were, at that time in the State of Victoria, in the middle of an unprecedented and lengthy health workers' dispute.

"Another good reason for listing Jeff as an emergency, Sophia. The strike hasn't affected that part of the system, thank goodness. Rest assured, there is no problem from that quarter. All you need to concern yourself about," he was addressing me again, "is to prepare yourself for an exploratory surgical intervention within a few days."

I chewed my lip absently. My voice, when I discovered its hiding place, seemed to come from a long way off. I needed to forcibly amplify it from my lungs just so it might sound normal.

"I, er, don't suppose I need worry about not eating anything between now and then, as I can't keep much down now in any case."

"Just keep to what I've spoken about today till you actually go into hospital. We'll guide you all the way through this, Jeff."

"Till you actually go into hospital," I repeated parrot-like, the words flat and hollow. "Till you actually go into hospital."

"Jeff, I'm your medical practitioner. As a profession, we medicos are not given to false optimism. However, whenever it is possible to give an optimistic prognosis, believe me, we don't shy away. From us, bad news is no news; but good news really *is* good news. And the good news is we can contain this, Jeff."

I rallied a little, barely taking in the substance but clinging to the tone of confident hopefulness. "So, this is what shock feels like," I mustered a weak smile. "I don't like it. Not one little bit!"

"Sophia, there's a coffee shop down by the entrance to the park. Have a mineral water together; and don't drive him home till you're quite sure you're both together enough. OK?" Dennis laid a reassuring hand on my shoulder and added, looking at his watch, "In fact, I'll join you."

Downstairs, in the coffee shop, I was still physically benumbed, but I could feel the use of my reason returning, cold and analytical. I began to speak with the calmness of a disinterested observer: "I suppose, when I look at it from the backward perspective, I'll feel relieved that at last I've found out the reason why I've been feeling…" The disinterested observer fled. "…so bloody sick for the last two years. But, just now, I don't think I could give a damn. Something's gone, Sophia, but I don't know what. I have the feeling of having been robbed of something I didn't realize I had till ten o'clock today."

It was as if the colour spectrum had changed. Things formerly out of the range of human vision became visible to me, while others turned opaque, and yet others vanished entirely. I could see the mixture of fear and loving concern in my wife's face, but I could not see the face itself. Neither could I see my glass of mineral water; nor appreciate, except as at second hand, the fact that a moment later I knocked it to the floor where it, according to the best sources, smithereened in a little explosion. I suppose other things happened between that moment and early the next morning, but I do not know what they are.

* * * * * *

BERG WAS ONE of the few who simply could not handle life on the base. He was around thirty when he flew to Thule in 1962 and looked every bit the office assistant he had been. An inordinate, paralyzing fear of flying was perhaps the most memorable facet of his character.

Berg, though a conscientious worker in his new career as a fireman at Thule, never took a risk in his life. Perhaps that explains why he never flew back to Denmark for holidays, choosing the long, solitary confinement of the base over the terror of the ascent.

In 1972, Berg took sick, weakened, and died within a couple of months, from cancer. Only then did Berg fly again: back to Denmark to be buried.

R.I.P. Berg.

* * * * * *

SO, I FOUND myself expecting to spend a joyless Easter in the Royal Melbourne Hospital.

Easter in Melbourne holds none of the echoes of a pagan spring festival celebrating nature's return to life; here in the Antipodes, it arrives in the middle of the slow march toward winter. To have meaning at all, it has to be entirely spiritualized or, as the Australian does with so many inherited traditions, hollowed out and holidayed through.

The troubled grey of a mid-autumn Melbourne sky; the gusting wind that bent the perplexed branches of imported elms and oaks—their almost neon-bright leaves clinging confusedly in the milder climate; the cold squalls that spoil the tennis and golf of even native Melburnians, who have yet to master reading the signs in a city famed for seasoning each day according to whim, not season; all these natural movements seemed less sympathetic to my internal state than stark manifestations of it.

Propped up in my bed, I at one moment wondered if I had been left by accident at the head of a bus queue. Then I remembered that Australians do not queue for buses. The vision of a long line of people stretching from my bed into the grey gloom of the ward came into clearer focus and identified itself as a relentless succession of doctors, interns, and nurses, prodding, poking, and pricking me with a series of gadgets, digits, and whatsits. The very delight of it all palled a little. By the time a stately matron appeared and shaved my stomach in preparation for the intervention, I was thoroughly sated of attention.

Then came the operation itself. It was everything I had expected: traumatic and, afterwards, exquisitely painful. It was an extensive exploration of my middle and upper chest, involving opening up the region near the stomach, which meant the rib cage had to be parted and opened like a wicker gate. Once there, the surgeon peeled off an extensive portion of the stomach's outer layer to reconstruct the region where the oesophagus and stomach meet—a precaution to frustrate the cancerous tumour's growth in the oesophagus itself, where, once established, it would as like as not starve or choke me to death.

If that weren't unpleasant enough, while he was there, the surgeon found it necessary to crush a number of nerves in the oesophagus to assist in the healing process.

I came to in a world of disturbing, swiftly moving shapes and sharply modulating colours. Moment by moment, I made out more, until I saw Sophia sitting by the hospital bed. She looked tired and worn, as if I had been asleep for years and she had waited accordingly, the tedium and the worry each etching their effects. Seeing her there, I felt I had witnessed the worst effect surgery could have on a person. In reality, she had been sitting for hours; I do not know. The flicker of my returning consciousness brought her instantly to my side.

One hand silently took mine; the other brushed through my hair.

I tried to say something like, "Well, if I look half as pale as you do, I think you'd better check my toe for a tag!" Instead, a wave of nausea—in the strange absence of positively felt pain—forced me back onto the mattress as if in a rocket accelerating to five Gs. I could have sworn the room rushed away behind me, dwindling as stars ahead grew and colourfully filled my vision.

The next thing I knew, Sophia was bending over me. "This time, don't try to move or speak, Jeff. I'll call the nurse. She's just left."

The nurse, when she returned, was very businesslike. She manoeuvred me into a sitting position. "Now, Mr. Carswell, are you comfortable? No? How about... now? No? How's... this? No? Well, let's... just... just... ? I tell you what, perhaps you'd be better off... lying flat! No? Hmm. Do you feel like a sandwich? Oh dear, never mind. Perhaps we'll leave you on the intravenous a little longer, shall we?"

By the end of the first week of recovery, I was strong enough to hear *of* food. But several weeks were to pass before I could actually eat any. Even a view of a quarter of a sandwich was often enough to turn me green and send me spinning into a vortex of nausea. Eventually, I could occasionally get that amount down; but more often not.

* * * * * *

ERIK SKJOLDBORG JENSEN hailed from Skagen on the Jutland Peninsula. He was another of those robust country types, his arms and neck burned by sun and wind to the colour and texture of ancient parchment; the rest of his body white and soft, fringed by the intervening area of hot red that separated the two zones.

Erik's perfunctory schooling earned him the epithet 'Erik the Unread' at Thule.

He served as a fireman on the base for five years, returning in 1969 to the family dairy farm in Skagen after his brother passed on following an entanglement with a bull.

Erik died in 1990 of cancer. He was a no longer robust fifty-three.

R.I.P. Erik.

* * * * * *

MEANWHILE, THULE HAD slept on in my memory. It took my mother to wake it, shaking the unwilling recollection from its torpor into the cold, stark morning of sudden realisation. A stream of newspaper cuttings began to arrive from her; underlined, highlighted, and accompanied by terse commentaries: 'Just like you, Jeff;' 'Another one from Thule; a rare skin cancer!'; and 'rashes, loss of feeling, pain in the limbs; sound familiar?'

It all began to sound just too familiar. Thule was shifting its weight forward in the cargo bay of my memory, a restless, unsettling presence.

My mother sent me many articles covering the activities of one particular fellow, a Marius Schmidt, some ten years my senior, who had been a Chief Fire Inspector at the base, in charge of about forty to fifty firemen. He had well and truly caught the eye and ear of the Danish press: 'Radioactivist Prepares to Blast Government;' 'Radioactive Fireman Blows Gaff on Glowing Greenlanders;' and 'Fireman's Shock Waves Shake Chandeliers at Christiansborg.'

Some of the articles contained biographical data about Marius. He had stood with his colleagues by his fire-engine in the mid-afternoon darkness of January 21, 1968, while a fire ball luridly lit up their faces like devils in Pandemonium watching Satan lift himself off the burning lake. He had been there, within four miles of the potent radioactive cocktail as it was shaken and poured out for his consumption.

* * * * * *

FINN PETTERSEN SPENT three years at Thule in the DCC Vehicle Maintenance Department. He was there saving up to open his own mechanic's workshop and service station back home. In August 1966, he was in perfect health.

One of Finn's jobs during the clean-up was to help change the tyres of the vehicles shuttling back and forth between the base and the crash site. Already in October 1968, he was flown back to Copenhagen for an emergency operation for cancer. He returned to Thule, worked out his contract, and left for good in September 1969.

He had scarcely sunk all his savings into his dream workshop when he again became sick with bone cancer. In September 1970, a year after his contract expired with DCC, Finn expired.

He left a widow with three young children and a business that, without him to run it, had to be sold at a complete loss. He was forty-five.

R.I.P. Finn.

* * * * * *

WHEN I RETURNED to work some four weeks after the intervention—there being no alternative—I found I was worn out most of the time. The nausea following even a minimal amount of food was bad enough, but recovery from the exhaustion it generated was impossible, with no opportunity to rest. The resulting chronic tiredness dogged me, making life a misery and effective work a faraway dream.

On more than one occasion, should sandwiches or other refreshments be served at a board meeting—a bi-weekly ordeal at that time—I would be left helpless by a wave of nausea. The profuse perspiring caused intense discomfort, as it was rarely possible to explain to the incomprehending stares around the table why one of their number had turned into a green, trembling waterfall. The sensation of professional disapproval, as if I had broken some code of conduct or been found wanting, was hard to dismiss, despite knowing the truth.

I had just been expressing these sentiments to Sophia. We were on a suburban train bound for central Melbourne. We had brought some lunch, and I was chewing perfunctorily on a triangle of chicken sandwich. Sophia was making a better job of her tomato and lettuce.

"But, surely you can explain that you just feel ill and excuse yourself?" she said between bites. The train had just pulled out of Box Hill, juddering over the switches and out into daylight from the cavernous junction station.

"Sophia, the last thing you think about when your heart starts galloping like a crazy brumby, your face turns the colour of that lettuce, and you feel a steady trickle of moisture run down your sleeve, is what people are going to think. Afterwards, sure, you wish you had had the presence of mind to turn to your neighbour and say, 'gosh, has it become hot in here of a sudden?' But, at the time, all your attention is given to not fainting; and what energy you have left is directed to managing your body under the feeling that it's dying out from under you." I fingered my sandwich. "Rather like what I feel right now."

I could only manage a grimace as I braced for the imminent attack. The train was fortunately just pulling into another station. Sophia and I alighted and spent some twenty minutes sitting on a bench at the deserted minor suburban station while I descended into the nausea and then drew myself back up into the sunlight of relief as the attack diminished. Only then could we resume our simple trip into town.

Suffering, whatever else it may entail, is never dreary or tedious. Boredom is a plain that lies far below the stark, airless heights where you find yourself in the grip of acute suffering. You may well aspire to descend to that calm plain, but only because its comparative tranquility seems inviting from the perspective of one gripping the rocky outcrop in the semi-darkness.

'Anything would be better than this!' you catch yourself exclaiming. Any relief, anything powerful enough to distract you from this intimate, desperate wrestling with an enemy whose weapons are the very bodily organs you are used to calling 'you.'

But the sort of relief available to a person under the sway of strong nausea—the sort we euphemistically call 'relieving the stomach'—was not at my disposal. The operation that was the immediate cause of the nausea had also, incidentally, ensured that I could no longer vomit.

Over time, I learned which foods were reasonably safe and which would almost certainly make me ill. One of the few reliable substances I could safely ingest turned out to be chicken. As a result, my diet became quite restricted, though safer, allowing me to return for long periods to that coveted plain of boredom. After all, even chicken can pall after a week of eating nothing else!

An attendant problem was weight loss. I lost sixteen kilos in four weeks. I eventually managed to contain this by eating tiny quantities over several sittings per day.

* * * * * *

KNUT LILLEBY'S JOB in the fateful period of January to September 1968 at Thule was to assist in keeping clear the scrap yard next to the site where tanks full of snow and debris from the crash site were stored.

During a fairly routine investigation for a hernia as late as 1995, Knut's doctors discovered he was suffering from bowel cancer. Further explorations uncovered a very special, rare leukemia—the sort reserved, according to the same specialists, for those unlucky enough to have lived through something akin to the Hiroshima and Nagasaki blasts.

Knut has been lucky, so far. He is still alive.

Perhaps the Norwegians are a hardier race than the Danes.

But, I do not think so.

* * * * * *

ALTHOUGH I WAS growing accustomed to my new, restricted regime and learning to navigate the treacherous waters of nausea, the leviathan within was not to be mollified or domesticated so easily. In 1990, the beast raised its head again, and I was forced to undergo the same brutal operation in a further, more desperate attempt to cut off the cancer's advance.

This time, the procedure was even more extensive. The incision reached from just beneath my breastbone almost to the middle of my back. The bottom part of my left rib cage was lifted out to grant the surgeon access to undo the previous work and then repeat the grim performance.

The experience was no more pleasant the second time for being familiar—not the three subsequent days in intensive care, nor the massive, constant infusion of analgesics needed to keep the searing pain at bay.

But the pleasure or otherwise of the experience was not the point. The real issue was the profound unease that sets into the bones when you lie in a hospital bed, musing on the nature of the response being leveled against your own rebellious flesh. It seemed to me we were pointing a peashooter at a whale: each time the creature surfaced, we'd fire a round, and it would submerge, biding its time. Sooner or later, the leviathan would realize our tactic for what it was: a scarecrow, a bluff.

This unease deepened into a dark, internal emptiness when I considered—and I had nothing but time to consider—that the enemy was my own body. A further, more terrifying battle was looming on the horizon, one I shrank from in my post-operative weakness: a war against the abysmal divisions within myself.

The fight was not against *myself* as such, but against the fearful temptation to cut my losses, to rally the parts of me that could still be trusted, and to draw myself up in arms against the traitorous cells that were no longer on my side. Just as the operations were meant to forestall a riot of cancer in my body, I now wished to forestall a riot of my own reason should the fear I sensed take hold.

Lying under the white hospital sheet, almost wholly immobile, anticipating the next wave of acute discomfort, I recognized the face of that fear: it was a variety of self-loathing. It was the loathing of health for illness, of the whole for the maimed. I realized that the Jeff Carswell of yore—a healthy, whole, devil-may-care executive who had scarcely known the inside of a doctor's surgery in his first forty years—might not easily tolerate the Jeff Carswell of acute vulnerability and fractured capability.

The immediate battle, however, was not with these imagined two halves. It was a battle for the right to never have to arrive at that desolate arena of self-alienation. I had to fight, there and then, to ensure I would not forever after be my own battlefield. My first tactic was to imagine the cancer as an entity utterly alien to myself. If I saw it as *me* gone haywire, as my own body avenging itself on the hateful world within its reach, I was finished. The cancer would become a form of suicide. My second tactic was to literally take the fight outside myself—to transfer the battleground from the interior of my stomach and oesophagus to the external world of people, events, and causes. I can never count my fortune too highly that such a possibility soon came my way.

* * * * * *

AMONG THE SEVENTEEN hundred or so Danish workers at Thule in the post-HOBO 28 era was an electrician named Mogens Nielsen. Mogens has no memory of being directly involved in the rescue operation or the search for the crew.

Nevertheless, Mogens thought it prudent and just to be a supporting member of the Thule Association. As such, he even underwent a government-sponsored medical examination at the university town of Aarhus (of reverend memory, as will soon be revealed), though he could never recall suffering any symptoms of disease.

He was given a clean bill of health, much to his relief. At that time, he decided to cancel his membership of the Association, though he continued to receive its newsletter. He has kept them all, although he is unsure just where he has them stored.

Then, in the fall of 1993, Mogens visited his doctor on account of a condition so disturbing he feared he would be unable to continue his job as a building inspector and mechanic.

The doctor was sufficiently alarmed to send him to the neurology department at Viborg Hospital for a brain scan and complete examination. All the tests gave the same devastating result. The severity of the neurological damage was outside the experience of the Chief Medical Officer.

The link, the specialists thought, may have been the fact that Mogens had been at Thule in 1968.

Mogens now keeps an hourly record of his activities, just to convince himself of the reality of a recent past that is no longer available to him by the usual means. Should he once forget to keep this log, that period will become a lacuna in his life, forever lost. The afternoon of January 21, 1968, however, remains more than ever deeply engraved on his ravaged memory.

* * * * * *

MARIUS SCHMIDT'S STORY particularly interested me at this time because he had already displayed an uncommon resourcefulness. Many years after the event, he spoke to me about the formative years of the Thule Association and his own health predicaments.

"Twelve years had passed," he said, "since I had flown out from Thule for the last time in 1969, when, in 1981, I began to note an ever-increasing pain in the joints, digestive problems, constant fatigue, and occasional memory lapses—though these latter are a matter of contention, as I have no memory of them. I was put in mind to contact a number of my ex-firemen colleagues from Thule, more, at that stage, just to renew acquaintances than for any other motive.

"I remember getting together with a couple of the guys in that same year, just to chew the fat and relive our youthful glories a little. Ole Petersen and Karl Rasmussen and I gathered at a nice downtown bar in Copenhagen and induced the regressive process with a few good brain cell-building schnapps. Ole, at that time, was living in Slagelse and Karl in Copenhagen itself. I was even then in Korsoer, where I still live. The conversation immediately turned to the characters we had known back then. 'Do you remember Alfred Jensen?' I would say, and Ole would reply, 'Oh, yeah, him, tough as an ox. Died about three years back. Some sort of debilitating disease, stuff in the joints and oesophagus.' 'Aah,' Karl and I would nod gravely. 'But you must remember that little guy with the black moustache?' Ole would ask. 'Oh, yeah,' Karl would reply. 'His name was Per. Apparently the Big C got him a good five years ago.' 'Aah,' Ole and I would nod gravely and stare into our drinks. 'Whatever became of that great big red-headed fellow with a chest like a barrel? Do you remember him, Ole? Used to go dipping in the fiord at the height of winter in the days before the pool was set up,' Karl would ask. 'Oh, yeah, tough son-of-a-bitch. For the life of me I can't recall his name, but I'll certainly never forget that great ruddy grinning face staring at me from the water among the ice floes,' Ole would say. 'Edvard Buganski,' I would put in. 'A Pole, I think. I kept some contact with him, but haven't heard a thing from him in eighteen months.' Alfred was fifty-two, Per Larsen was fifty, and Edvard was forty-six (cancer got him too, I later learned from his widow).

"And so we went on a while, getting deeper and deeper into our cups as the roll of the lost, the dead, and the forgotten grew longer and longer. At one moment in the conversation, I made mention of the pains in the joints of my arms and legs and the digestive difficulties and so on. 'And sure,' I said, 'My memory isn't as strong as it used to be, but at least I'm alive.'

"Each of the other two looked at me and said, 'Me too!' They were experiencing the same symptoms.

"After our get-together, I began turning over in my mind how it could be that so many ex-Thule firemen were either dead of similar diseases or suffering similar symptoms to our own. Some exploration into the yet-complete portions of my memories soon came up with a likely culprit. All the guys in question had been involved in either tackling the fire after HOBO 28 crashed or in the clean-up operation afterwards, or both. It was a shot in the dark; I had no proof. But how else explain the premature wasting and death of men still young and, in their prime, of the best the country had to offer?"

* * * * * *

BOTH OLE AND Karl have since died of cancer; Ole was fifty-six and Karl was forty-seven.

R.I.P. Ole.

R.I.P. Karl.

* * * * * *

"OVER THE NEXT seventeen years," Marius continued, "I gradually built up a register of friends who were ill or who had died.

"Then, in 1988, I began reading in the newspapers about Ole and Sally Markussen. Ole had been a personnel manager in the DCC at Thule at the time of Operation Crested Ice. His health had been deteriorating for some time, which prompted him and Sally to attend conferences in the United States and Holland on plutonium-related illnesses and the consequences of radiation exposure. When in the States, the pair got in touch with an American attorney named Tony Roisman and asked him to represent them in a civil action for negligence and ill-use against the United States government. Tony accepted and traveled to Copenhagen for a meeting with the little ex-Thulers' association that Ole and Sally headed.

"I decided it might be useful to contact Ole, and he provided me with a comprehensive list of Danes—firemen and others—who had been serving on the base at the relevant time. But that was as far as he and Sally were prepared to cooperate with me. Their little association consisted entirely of themselves and a tiny group of ex-Thule employees who all belonged to the same union in Denmark. Their interest in justice did not extend to any other Danes who might have been on the base in 1968 and equally affected, equally entitled to compensation.

"By this time, I had my own vision of how large the question was and what needed to be done to achieve a decisive result. I believed that the larger the association—and there were plenty more ex-Thulers affected than belonged to the Markussens' clique—the louder would be the voice, the more intense the pressure on the government, US or Danish, and the greater the chance of success for all concerned.

"I suggested to the Markussens that we should together organise a meeting of as many ex-Thulers as we could contact for Tony Roisman's visit. That way, I argued, he would see how great a number of people had indeed been affected, and they could get a glimpse in the flesh of the work going forward on their behalf.

"Neither Ole nor Sally showed the least enthusiasm at the prospect of my participation. They behaved in a markedly proprietorial manner toward their association and were not at all interested in expanding it. I felt as if they resented my intrusion.

"Resentment may not be a strong enough word. The part they wished me to play was to go away and not upset their little boat. However, I had other plans.

"Under my sole initiative and at my own personal expense, I posted a series of advertisements in Denmark's leading newspapers, inviting all ex-Thule employees to attend a meeting with Tony Roisman at the 'People's Palace' in Copenhagen.

"I again spoke to the Markussens, as I still believed all should have the opportunity to become members of an ex-Thulers' association, themselves included. My idea of cooperation was stillborn. They just were not interested.

"However, someone was extremely interested in what I was doing. In the time between the posting of the advertisements and the meeting, my family and I were the lucky recipients of several 'tele-offers.' In the peaceful little appendage of Europe we inhabit, it is uncommon to receive phone calls from total strangers promising to fix your club foot or rearrange the ligaments of your knee. But it did happen to me and my intimates. 'Schmidt is to stay away from the meeting on the 4th of January, or else...' was the style of promises made. As unspecified as the threats were, and as Hollywoodesque as the whole incident may ring today, nevertheless, come January 4, I took the precaution of fronting at the meeting place in the company of two generously proportioned, black-suited ex-Thulers whose eloquence was usually tested on building sites and wharves.

"All went precisely as I had perceived it would. At the main entrance to the 'People's Palace,' a rough hand grabbed my arm, and a snarling voice stated the outrageously erroneous opinion that he thought I was not to attend the meeting. Anton and Arne, however, utilizing all the rhetorical devices of the stevedore and the builder's labourer, were no time in convincing him of the error of his thoughts and quickly extracted from him a promise to seriously rethink his position in the time he would have free from physical exertion as he recovered in the hospital.

"Once inside, I took out my knuckle-dusters and took to the members of the private panel then in session. Well, you see, I was upset at them not having reserved a seat for me. Once I had found myself a chair and was seated at the table, I was able to regard the other four members of the panel and was not surprised to see that half of it was composed of Markussens. Tony Roisman made three and Lars Melgaard made four.

"Lars, I later came to discover, was from a lobby group named the Organisation for Information on Nuclear Energy. He had early taken a personal interest in the cause and had been the source of much information for the Association in its infancy, as well as many ideas on strategy in promoting it. To date, Lars's contribution had been one of disinterested self-sacrifice to little effect. But Lars was a battler and an idealist and would not give way easily.

"So, there I sat, grinning like a Cheshire cat, forcing Karl and Lars to actually shift their chairs to make room for me. I pointed out that, were it not for me and my advertising campaign, the large hall we were in would be largely empty. Once that was made clear, both Tony and Lars relaxed back into their chairs while the Markussens exchanged surly glances.

"But they faced a fait accompli; a coup d'etat had been carried out under their crinkled, lifted noses. Voices from the auditorium called for me to be made their spokesman and chairman of the association that represented their interests. I stood and addressed the house.

"'I hope,' I began, no preliminaries whatever—ever my way: direct and blunt. 'I hope you will all take home with you the forms that I have had printed for this meeting, fill them in, and return them to the association president without delay. These forms we will use to petition the US and Danish governments that they extend the statute of limitations, which is due to expire in seventeen days.'

"A buzz of consternation bumbled around the hall.

"'In Denmark, similar to the situation in most countries, there is a statute of limitations on making civil claims in a court of law. That limit is twenty years. On January 21, 1988, the twenty years will have passed. Our time is nearly up.'

"Over the following two and a half weeks, I was full-time receiving and collating the filled-in forms and passing them on to Tony in the US. In the cases of the many more names on the list provided by Ole of Thule survivors who had not attended the meeting, I commandeered my whole family to the task of getting out letters to them, requesting them to fill in the enclosed forms and send them back right away. We all spent an entire day typing up letters and labels, copying forms, folding and inserting contents, and licking envelopes and stamps. The local post office at Korsoer stayed open an extra hour, just for us.

"The response over the next two weeks was unbelievable and meant that the revamped association could put a convincing argument for the deadline of claims being extended; which was duly done. At this early stage, the association already boasted a membership of over 200 ex-Thulers: an increase of nearly 2000 percent."

* * * * * *

WITHOUT THIS QUICK and effective action on Marius's part, the rest of this story would have been one of complete impotence and foolish resistance to fate. As it was, it gave us all a legal context and a flicker of hope; it enabled the true fight for justice and recognition to begin.

Within a few days, Tony had filed a suit in the United States against the USAF "for damages caused by the United States Military in a Foreign Country."

* * * * * *

BETWEEN 1972 AND 1988, Aage Bech was admitted to Aarhus Hospital on many occasions on account of severe pain in his arms, legs, back, and stomach. His condition deteriorated in the middle of 1988 when the pain worsened and he started suffering from diarrhea and weight loss.

In August of that year, Aage underwent his first operation at Sønderborg Hospital, which resulted in such complications that he spent time in intensive care on a respirator.

Three further operations followed between then and 1990. After the last one, the doctors decided to allow nature to take its course, and Aage's family and friends came to say their good-byes.

But Aage just would not let go. In October 1990, he was transferred to Aarhus Hospital for a fifth operation.

At a body weight of thirty-eight kilos and relying on plastic bags to perform the ministry of extracting waste from his body, Aage regrets the time he spent with the DCC at Thule in the late sixties.

* * * * * *

"I WANT TO know more about this fellow." Sophia had just patiently listened to my broad translation of yet another article about Marius Schmidt from *Ekstra Bladet* and was now nodding with quiet enthusiasm as I carefully pasted the clipping into a rapidly growing, battered scrapbook. "I think you should write to him personally, Jeff."

"Yes. Well, so far, our only correspondence has been when I got that letter about the legal deadline, and my reply then was pretty terse and formal. Yeah, I think this guy is really worth cultivating. Remember that bit about... Let's see, where was it?" I started fumbling through the pages of the scrapbook. "Ah, here it is." I raised the book triumphantly and prepared to translate once more the report of Marius' quips about the Danish government not being able to hide a needle in a haystack; only to be confronted with an empty room.

Sophia's voice reached me from the kitchen, "Dinner will be about twenty minutes."

But there was no escape. I wandered into the kitchen and leaned against the fridge, holding my precious scrapbook open and pointing to different articles for Sophia's benefit. "Look at this one, Sweetie. Do you remember this one about that eccentric pair?"

"Do you mind, Jeff, I need the butter."

"Oh, sorry." I shifted clumsily out of the way like an indolent teenager, my train of thought uninterrupted. "This guy, Ole Markussen, and his missus, they're trying to do exactly the same thing as

Marius, except they're going about it like a Pekinese after a semi-trailer. They're yapping about, biting at tyres and ankles; and they'll just end up getting run over and squashed. Why on earth they won't cooperate with Marius' association, I don't know! After all, Marius' group is by far the bigger and must have the greatest clout. I'm worried about this divided attack; this sort of petty grandstanding just gives the government an excuse to ignore us or accuse us of disunity or troublemaking to no purpose. And, should the government ever need to take our claims seriously, they can remove our powerbase, such as it is, simply by recognising this crazy pair as the legitimate representative body in the case. Then, all they need do... "

"Jeff!"

"And look, they're treating the whole thing as a money-raising exercise to fund their trips to America and Amsterdam and Paris and Rome. I mean, whatever their motives might be, their activities could easily be represented as self-serving by a malicious press... "

"Jeff, I know all this." Sophia brought me up short with a wooden stirring spoon pressed gently against my nose. "You've read me that article at least five times now. The question is; what are you going to *do* about it?"

"Er, why don't I write to Marius Schmidt and offer my services as an agitator of complacent civil service behinds?"

Sophia removed the weapon, nodded emphatic and final agreement, and returned the spoon to its demilitarised use.

The idea had already crossed my mind; Sophia's ultimatum-style confrontation simply firmed my resolve. I wrote to Marius that afternoon—a letter which became the beginning of an association that has since grown into a friendship of great warmth and deep trust.

* * * * * *

IN 1967, HENNING Thorup, yet another fireman, was called out for the emergency landing of a nuclear-armed B-52.

So, when HOBO 28 came down the following January, it was not his first encounter with the giant machines. Since November 1964, he had worked as an overseer in the base's power plant. On the afternoon of HOBO 28's descent into Hell, he was sitting in shirt sleeves by the roller doors of the boiler-room, waiting to be relieved by the next shift. He had the doors open to allow the boilers to cool a little.

The explosion that then came was so violent as to smash the door to pieces and jolt the frame out of place by a good foot.

Henning thought a tanker vehicle must have hit the door. When he rushed out to investigate, he was amazed to find nobody and nothing there. Then, the ghostly half-light of the stars and the Aurora enabled him to glimpse the huge black cloud, driven by enormous flames, rising above the fiord. He knew what he was looking at: an aircraft had come down rather clumsily.

Although Henning was not among the firemen who witnessed the spectacle from close up, neither was he ever advised to take any precautions against radiation—to cover himself or stay indoors. Nor was he ever tested, nasally or otherwise.

In 1985, Henning was admitted to Køge Hospital with a blood clot in his left leg. There, it became a matter of some curiosity to a variety of doctors that his legs, from the knees down, carried large red blotches. One professor took a look at them and left, shaking his head. That was the last Henning saw of him.

Blood tests followed without result. Henning was sent home with the message that all was well.

Soon after, Henning's wife started complaining of his breathing and snoring at night. A second trip to the hospital discovered a tumour in Henning's nose. Radiation treatment successfully rid him of the tumour and saved his eye, which had also been under threat. It did, however, leave a rather noticeable cavity in his face.

But by 1995, new cancers had developed. After eight weeks of tests and observation, further radiation treatment was recommended for bone cancer in his legs. Despite that and chemotherapy, the cancers spread to his neck and shoulders.

Henning spoke on the radio about his condition in February 1996, where, having related that he then also suffered from tumours on his ribcage, back, neck, and legs, he expressed his confidence that he would survive his staggering variety of illnesses.

But Henning did not.

R.I.P. Henning.

* * * * * *

SOON AFTER I wrote to Marius suggesting I take a more prominent role in the fight, one of those vaguely threatening things happened that makes you want to run and hide in the back shed a while to think about what it could mean. About a month after the pivotal meeting, while Marius and his ex-Thulers were still celebrating their first steps toward justice, a note, almost as peremptory as an internal memo, arrived from Tony:

To: Mr. Marius Schmidt, Mr. Anders Boelskifte and Other Interested Parties:

Due to commitments both here in Washington and in our Chicago office, which are already severely overstraining our personnel and other resources, we regret to have to advise that the action on your behalf in the US Supreme Court can no longer be pursued by this firm. We regret any inconvenience and hope that your pursuit of justice is not in any way affected by this unfortunate development.

Yours faithfully,

Tony Roisman and Associates

"Looks to me like pressure from above," commented Sophia as I translated Marius's fax—the first of many hundreds—for her.

"Maybe Capitol Hill invoked the 'Divinity Clause' in the US Constitution," I mused in return. "I suppose it's one of those mysteries of human behaviour we'll never explain. I'd like to get Tony in a neglected warehouse some time and see what his version of the matter is then." I clasped my right fist in my left hand and remembered an Aussie accent telling me over the phone, 'Mixing yourself up with cranks and weirdos like Schmidt and those other foreigners…'

"But I am a foreigner," I muttered softly under my breath, dismissing the memory with a scowl and a toss of the head.

"Hmm?"

"Oh, I was just thinking that Marius will have to come up with something pretty good now."

"I reckon so. I just wonder what the Americans are up to. They can't think this will just go away."

* * * * * *

AND IT CERTAINLY was too late to put the lid back on this nasty can of plutonium. One achievement that could not be gainsaid was the enormous amount of publicity Marius managed to generate for the cause, showing even at the start his genius for getting people to point cameras and recorder machines at him. *Ekstra Bladet*'s Per Kanstrup was instrumental in this aspect.

Per took a serious and active interest in the case and made it front-page news, both by his own stories and through the influence he exerted on other journalists across the media by sheer weight of reputation (as well as select words in select ears, of course). Even eight years later, scarcely a day went by without at least one of the country's major dailies carrying a report on the latest developments in the Thule Radiation Victims' Case.

* * * * * *

OLE AND SALLY, meanwhile, sailed on their merry, separate way, keeping their own counsel and preferring to remain aloof from the new, larger association that had sprung from the same bitter root as their own.

Chapter 3: Pen Pals

> That though I loved them for their faults
>
> As much as for their good,
>
> My friends were enemies on stilts
>
> With their heads in a cunning cloud.
>
> *To Others Than You*   DYLAN THOMAS

WITH MY LETTER to Marius began my formal, relentless pursuit of justice. The spurs were my own illness and a cold, simmering anger—a significant component of which was fury on behalf of my hundreds of fellow sufferers, many of whom had already died without ever knowing the true cause of their suffering.

My initial efforts were directed toward a simple, almost naive, end: to inform the relevant Danish government departments, notably Health and Defence. Once they had the facts before them, I reasoned, it would be a simple matter of acknowledging responsibility. There ought then to follow the payment of compensation for pain and suffering, and the extension of practical assistance—financial and otherwise—to those whose lives had become unmanageable.

Oh, happy days of youthful, unreflecting trust! I little anticipated receiving answers whose tenor ran pretty much consistently thus:

Dear Mr. Carswell,

Thank you for your communication of the filth of the dirth. It has been passed on to the Head of Department for his perusal.

However, it appears to me that this is more a matter for the Department of Infernal Retinue and perhaps the Danish Agency for Nubile Synergy. It might serve your purpose better to apply to the National Archives for permission to obtain copies of relevant documents pertaining to other than top security decisions taken at the time in regard to the events at Thule. As you may know, top security documents are classified under the Thirty-Year legislation and will not be available in any case until the year 1998.

Should you in your search come across any information the confirmation of which may be within my department's power to provide, I should then be glad to consider any request you may care to make.

In the meantime, I wish you every success in your undertaking.

Yours faithfully,

Martin Schpoer
For the Minister

And so it went. Letter after letter, thousands in each direction. Theirs informed me, between the lines, that no matter to whom I wrote or appealed, the Danish government was united in its determination to resist and block my progress at every opportunity. They were the last ones I could rely on for support; certainly, no department would concede a mistake or that we had any case whatsoever. My letters, in return, were insistent, needling, and unyielding.

With time, a pattern emerged in the government's responses; to match it, I evolved a return strategy.

First came the initial period of establishing contact: I would write requesting information and assistance, and be gently dissuaded by clones of Martin Schpoer. Next, I would send a letter asking a long range of specific questions and await their replies.

Once I had their answers—which usually came only after harassment in the form of follow-up letters—I would frame alternative answers and suggestions, inviting different approaches. This commonly meant suggesting doing something other than the nothing they had proposed.

The bureaucratic response then consisted of two stages. The first was to ignore me. That tactic never worked because I maintained a constant stream of reminders.

The second stage was to respond definitively in the negative:

Dear Mrs. Cartweels,

I hereby acknowledge receipt of your communications of the fist, filth, silth and stealth of the current month. I am writing to you again at your insistence and regret that I am unable but to confirm our former correspondence; wherein, having considered your requests and heard your grievances, it was our informed opinion that you get lost.

Yours faithfully,
Frida Froegg
For the Cowering Minister

At this, a further stream of letters would flow from my word processor, growing progressively more insistent. I might suggest I was unimpressed with their display of mismanagement and administrative disability. I would underline my dissatisfaction by informing them of a letter I was concurrently sending to the Parliamentary Ombudsman, complaining about their behaviour.

This tactic was particularly alarming to the average Danish bureaucrat, accustomed to the traditional Danish approach to officialdom: for the citizen to accept whatever baloney the officials chose to fob him off with—the 'mustn't grumble' syndrome.

The ombudsman had difficulty handling my complaints and would revert to the old bureaucratic trick of not answering. However, as I had done with the government departments, I would snow the office with reminders and force them at least to break their silence.

I even went so far as to draft letters to the ombudsman for other association members to sign and send. I do not suppose they even noticed that all the letters they got from our members were typed on the same machine; they spent so little time actually perusing them before signing the warrants that condemned them to 'file death.'

Because my work at that time involved a fair bit of international travel, including to Germany, I would often organize to pass through Denmark to visit my family (my parents were then both still alive). So, whenever I had an upcoming business trip, I would let the ombudsman's office know and try to organize a meeting.

Never did I get to see or speak to that gentleman. His bodyguards, sometimes called assistants, were too efficient. The best I could do was confront whichever poor, pathetic lackey was propped up before me with the facts of life.

"Do you realise," I asked of the callow nose-wiper before me on one such visit in 1988, "Are you aware that this file provided by the Department of Health does not contain half the correspondence I directed to it?"

I proceeded to prove my assertion by demonstration, showing him my copies of the letters I had sent and received. I proved that the department had failed to make all the relevant files available to the investigating officer; that they had very efficiently managed to hide the full facts from the very organization delegated by parliament to investigate; and that they had achieved this by mischievously changing file numbers when things got warm, so I would be confused and forced to start over.

He responded by shaking his head remorselessly and answering that he knew little of the matter, but that the guy in charge would be back from a conference in the Bahamas in three days.

I left him with a flea the size of a wallaby in his ear, and another for his holidaying confrere.

I ask myself to this day whether the ombudsman himself was aware of the enormous responsibility being lifted from his shoulders by his underlings as they took it upon themselves to show me the door. Or was he a victim of the bureaucrats' 'need to know' policy: if the minister needs to know, he'll ask; otherwise, tell him nothing. Either way, the ombudsman came across as an incompetent bumbler and makeshift administrator.

I once even went so far as to write to Her Majesty, Queen Margrethe II, whom I had met some years before when I assisted in hosting her visits to Thule in the sixties as a princess, and who was by now Queen of Denmark in her own right.

Of course, I knew such a letter would automatically be passed to the minister concerned, who would have no choice but to respond to a request that came via the Palace. I used this tactic to apply just a little more pressure and to show the uncooperative operatives they were dealing with a case of extraordinary determination.

I was gaining few friends in the administration this way. But by then, I was aware there were no friends there to be made. It became my aim to transform the endemic indifference in these departments into sullen aggravation. And I was making just the enemies I needed, for I knew a hot enemy is less likely than a cool friend to sit on his hands and let me expend my fury on his patient forbearance.

Sooner or later, I would provoke a response of greater moment than 'go away!' and then, once the initial phase of overcoming their bureaucratic inertia was past, I would have them exactly where I needed them: spitting chips and helpless with fury.

Whilst all this was underway, seeing I was in for a long haul, I extended my missive mission beyond Denmark's borders and began sending letters to the American democratic monarchy, notably to three successive presidents: Reagan, Bush, and Clinton. They produced no response of interest.

Unfortunately, I share the all-too-common impression that the American presidency fosters amongst foreigners: that foreign policy and a true interest in the affairs of other nations is, in the average American administration, merely an appendage to the Bureau of Statistics, particularly when it comes time to count where the votes will come from. Otherwise, the president is very much internally focused.

And, as the lack of responses to my letters also proved, so goes the story with the successive First Ladies, be they called Betty, Barbara, Hillary, or whatever.

It may be the pressures of office, or maybe the isolation they suffer from everyday realities by being locked up in their whitewashed cage. I am not sure of anything except that their self-importance seems to grow in inverse proportion to their effectiveness as their terms progress.

The Americans are an honorable people. But, at that time, the US was a definite no-goer.

* * * * * *

SO, FOR THE time being, the Danish government remained my prime target. I found that, in a final desperate effort to shake me off, the department or agency concerned would duck for cover, take to wearing a false beard and glasses, adopt a pseudonym, and refuse to accept any mail or phone calls to its old identity.

I even came to recognise the signs they were about to resort to this expedient by the conciliatory tone that would suddenly replace the bullying and whining in their letters.

It was the afternoon following my return from a business trip to Germany in 1989. I was still only partially recovered from jet lag and was in my study cutting a swathe through the build-up of incoming correspondence with my paperknife. Sophia was as attentive a listener to my running commentaries as a person can be who is half a city away at one of the more exclusive stores. I thought she was out the back, doing the week's washing. I started to giggle at a recent memory wakened by an unsolicited request for moral and financial support from APE: Australians for the Preservation of our Ethos. I dropped it in the bin and shouted to Sophia:

"Oh, that reminds me, dear. I phoned the 'Odd Couple' while I was away. Or, I should say, I spoke to Mrs. Odd. Yeah, the Markussens. Apparently he's really sick now and won't come to the phone for anyone. Blimey, she said little enough. Some strange things, too. She reckons their phone's being tapped! Well, frankly, who's to say it isn't? It just seemed a funny thing to say into a phone that's being tapped. Or so I thought. She mentioned something about an international trip they're arranging; but, could I get any details about it? Not on your life. She wouldn't say where they're going, or who was sponsoring them, or even what the point of it all was. I suppose her closeness could be put down to her fear of being overheard; but, it just seemed to me that she didn't want me to know what they're up to. Perhaps they think it's our association that's bugging them! Anyway, I wasn't getting any sense out of her, let alone any cooperation, so I cut the conversation short and rang off."

I paused to take a sip of my Black Russian and to slit open another letter from Denmark. I started to smile. At the same moment, the front door opened.

"Ah, there you are! Look, Sophia, look what Kjell Sclepp of the Department of Finical Fancies is proposing!" I waved the missive in the air. Sophia, who had hoped to get in the door from her shopping expedition to George's unnoticed, came reluctantly into my study, where I sat smiling over the Danish capability for ducking and hiding. Sophia unobtrusively tucked her shopping bags behind the second armchair.

"An actual proposal, dear? I hope you two will be happy together."

"Ha, ha. Yeah, sure, Kjell and I are made for each other. Look, he's suggesting I organise for all the members of the Association to be medically examined…"

"What, you do it?"

"Yep. And at our own cost; and then the department will make a commitment to consider whether there are grounds for setting up a committee to look into the calling together of a commission to consider the vexed question of investigating liability, whence would issue possible grounds for claims for compensation for lost income capacity to be considered."

"You're making that up!"

"No, really, take a look yourself."

Sophia looked inquisitively at the Danish words, of which she understands not a syllable.

"Hmm, how nice. Sounds like a reorganization and renaming job to me!"

"Of course," I said. "It's as plain as the nose-job on their faces! Besides, I also subscribe to the departmental bulletin. The whole shakeup affects four different departments, with amalgamations mainly but with splinterings here and there. Names, logos, responsibilities, even office sites, are changing. Ah, but look! Now, isn't that handy." I held up the bulletin, opened at page four. "Here is the new address of the assistant secretary for Greenland Affairs' office. I must get a letter off to him congratulating him on the move."

I had to maintain a light touch in this absurd game of cat and mouse, especially as the mouse was several thousand times the size of the cat. But also because I intuited that if they could get me to expend my anger on their deceitful and mean tactics, I would quickly run out of energy for the pursuit of my true object: justice. Rather, my aim was that they should be the ones overcome by anger and start placing false steps.

The suggestion that our members be medically examined, though the bureaucrats were as yet unaware of it, was their first major false step.

For now, though, I was determined that if they placed a maze in my path, I would run it patiently. I would shed not a single tear in lamentation over the perverseness of the obstacle; nor would I bang my head against its walls in a lame effort to bring them down and continue my straight course. I knew where their jugulars were; and, whatever the shape of the terrain I traversed, I would get them. Their obstacles could tire me; but only death would stop me.

* * * * * *

THE PSYCHOLOGICAL PROFILE of the spy must be a curious document. I hardly bother myself over such speculations in the normal course of the day. But the arrival in September of 1989 of a package containing a pulverised egg-timer and a note in pencil, 'Don't let time betray you, boyo,' made me pause long enough to wish its sender madness to the fifth generation. An examination of the packaging revealed the thing had been mailed in North Blackburn, about three miles from my home.

* * * * * *

SO, IN SEPTEMBER 1989, the Danish government acceded to a comprehensive series of medical examinations of the men who had been hounding them for some four years at that stage. Someone, somewhere in the Departments of Health and Social Security, was sick of us—particularly of me—and had weakened to the extent of taking notice.

To what extent the examinations were designed to test our health, and to what extent our resolve to continue the struggle, would emerge in the manner and spirit in which they were eventually conducted.

Several locations were nominated across the Kingdom of Denmark as testing centres. Even Greenland, being part of the Kingdom, was considered. I suppose someone within the Department thought a junket to an exotic location might serve as well as a yearly vacation. Or did the bureaucrats merely want to show the world they were serious about this examination process?

As soon as I heard the decision, I quickly contacted the Department of Health. I requested that, as I would shortly be in Germany on business and intended to visit my family in Denmark, it would be highly convenient if I could be examined in Copenhagen at that time. I would be passing through there in transit to Melbourne. Yours faithfully, Jeffrey Carswell.

My eminently sensible suggestion prompted a reply whose tenor reawakened the sinking sensation I had initially felt at the obstructiveness of the officials, confirming my suspicion of their enduring intransigence.

A roneoed form letter greeted me some weeks later, curtly informing me I should be prepared on such and such a date (perhaps only by luck one that fell within the period I had specified) to travel to a health clinic on the campus of the University of Aarhus, a good four hours' travel outside Copenhagen, on the east coast of the Jutland peninsula.

It is always possible the choice of Aarhus was taken simply out of ignorance of, or indifference to, the degree of inconvenience it would cause: to travel by train with several changes, carrying all my luggage for a forty-eight-hour return trip to Australia, enduring the strain and anxiety of an imminent flight, not to mention the continuing symptoms of my deteriorated health.

In a spirit of magnanimity, the charitable attitude open to me is, I repeat, to believe those responsible ignorant or indifferent. The alternative is to believe them mean and vindictive, malicious and vengeful. Frankly, I hope and believe I was on this occasion the victim of the latter: to be the subject of malice is actually easier to bear than to be the subject of stupidity or heartlessness.

Things got better before they got worse.

I made my long business trip across the United States and Canada to Germany in 1989, concluded my business there satisfactorily, and flew on to Copenhagen. From there, I continued to Esbjerg to visit my aging parents.

From Esbjerg, I phoned the Department of Health, as they had been trying to contact me while I was in the air. I was told the person I needed would phone me back. He did not. In view of the urgency, I phoned back several times, only to encounter the ever more familiar ignorance and indifference of the Danish bureaucrats.

Or perhaps my reputation as the troublemaker from Australia had grown, and having me just a few miles away on the other end of a phone line was too much. I could imagine them including me in their nightly prayers, on the debit side of the divine ledger.

When the young man who had been trying to contact me finally phoned back, he turned out to be a legal representative for the Department.

"Yes, naturally, Mr. Carswell," he commented when I stated that, though I was agreeing to the medical examinations, I would still be pursuing my claim. "By all means. That is your right and prerogative. And, indeed, there is little doubt that there were radiation problems at Thule following the crash."

Interestingly, though hardly surprisingly, ever since, that same young man has expressed a differing memory of that conversation and his final comment in particular, suggesting that either my imagination, my comprehension, or my analytic faculty needed a good vacation.

Loaded down with baggage, the trip to Aarhus was everything it had promised on paper: exhausting, annoying, rushed, and confused. Sitting on my larger suitcase at the station in Fredericia, sweaty, wet from the constant drizzle, and fuming quietly to myself, I knew with a certainty denied me when I first read the roneoed sheet from the Department of Health, that I was being forced into a tiny, enclosed, ribbed space under the spiralling impetus of a great outside agent. (Id est, I was being screwed!)

At Aarhus, I stowed my luggage at the station and caught a bus to the university. Once there, I wandered around the campus until a security man took pity and directed me to the clinic.

As I pushed through the glass doors, the empty reception area was my first taste of the degree to which I was expected and the welcome I was to receive. Some minutes passed before a young receptionist appeared through an inside door and looked not so much surprised as astounded at my presence. She demanded:

"Yes?"

"My name is Carswell. I have a two-thirty appointment with Doctor Kay-Ole Larsen. I have just travelled by plane and train from Frankfurt, Copenhagen, and Esbjerg and am on a seven-twenty flight this evening to Melbourne. I'm a little hot and tired at this moment and little enough impressed as to why Aarhus was selected over the much more convenient Copenhagen. I will not

60

be further trifled with." My voice gathered volume through my minor tirade, and I ended quite authoritatively, "It is now two-thirty-five. Show me to the surgery!"

The receptionist looked at me with astonishment, as if I had threatened to reveal the extraordinary circumstances of her conception. To have a person question the choice of location in a system where medical staff and administrative assistants dictated every detail to their patients was quite extraordinary.

"You must understand, Mr. Carswell," the young lady condescended to explain, "that you fall within our jurisdiction. That is obvious, isn't it?"

"How can that be obvious? I don't know your system as I haven't lived in this country for years. Tell me."

"Well, as you are from Esbjerg, you fall under Aarhus."

I was astonished at the amazing logic that had brought me to this point in space and time.

"Could you not tell," I began, looking at her askance, "From the letterheads and postmarks of my many letters that I live in Australia? Is this not a case of making things as difficult for me as possible?"

I relented a little when I saw the receptionist was as amazed as I was once she knew where I lived. I learned she was only working for the Department for the duration of the examinations and was as much a victim of their incompetence and cold-heartedness as I was.

"Well, we're pleased to have you here on time. We had tried to contact you to come earlier as Dr. Kay-Ole Larsen has to fly back to Copenhagen just after lunch for a two-hour meeting involving the committee responsible for the Thule-related examinations.

"The doctor will see you now. But, remember, he has to leave soon to get to the airport." She advised me and opened the inside door that led to the surgery.

I was getting quite annoyed at this attitude that a meeting in Copenhagen *about* the examinations was a priority before conducting the examinations themselves. "I have an appointment and assume it will take some time to conduct the comprehensive medical examination I have been told I am here for!" I said, and strode through.

It quickly became apparent that the expenditure on these examinations had been checked and checked again on every step until it had eventually been checkmated. To say the bare white-washed room was furnished would be a most ironic use of the term.

Apart from the worn couch, the single plastic chair, and the metallic trolley bearing a small wooden gavel, a stethoscope, and one or two other vaguely medical-looking items, I seemed to be the sole feature there.

Oh, I nearly forgot the battery-operated clock on the wall. But it had stopped at nine-forty-three that morning: or perhaps at nine-forty-three on the last occasion someone had actually been in the room: in 1974.

I had scarcely made myself uncomfortable in the plastic chair and decided against sitting in it for any length of time when Doctor Kay-Ole Larsen bustled in like a matron with a purpose: the purpose being to catch any of the nurses in her charge goofing off. He smiled the wide, insincere smile of the amateur golfer on his day off and greeted me. He looked too young, I thought, to have cultivated the cynicism of the hack, yet there it was.

"Here you are, Mr. Carswell, here you are!" he exclaimed twice over, tautologically and redundantly, as he took a stranglehold on my hand and squeezed it into submission.

" … "

"Just take a seat and we'll take a little ole look at the blood pressure, shall we!"

As I sat gingerly in the chair and exposed my other limb to the ministrations of Dr. Strangelove, I endured a constant flow of aimless chatter.

"You know, you're lucky we could get you in today, Mr. Carswell. I'm due in Copenhagen shortly for a meeting regarding yourself and your Thule colleagues. You're the first of your mob to be examined. We haven't even gotten all the details for conducting your examinations completed yet. There has been so much to do and in so little time! This afternoon the committee really must agree on the paperwork needed. The forms people are to fill in, and those sorts of important issues."

He looked at me gravely as if seeking my agreement. He went on:

"You know, Mr. Carswell, time is a very slippery concept; managing it is like trying to paint a black cat black: not only difficult and dangerous, but pointless!"

I was not only mystified, I was alarmed. I nevertheless managed to nod in dumb assent. The stream of chatter renewed itself:

"We had hoped to have some forms ready for you to fill out; we'll just have to make do with the ol' writing-pad, I guess. Still, we do the best we can, you know. Do you know, the education budget has been slashed year after year in this country. I would welcome a shoestring." The golfer's smile was briefly on show again. "With a shoestring, at least I could tie up a few of these loose ends!"

He had started tapping me about the joints with the gavel at this point in the monologue; so one of the reflexes I had was to grimace in pain on two or three occasions as the hammer came down hard on my kneebone.

Before I knew it, he was scribbling on a pad and announcing that my visit was at an end.

"That's the ol' examination all done, then, Mr. Carswell. I'll just have to write up my findings and submit them to the Department for their consideration."

I would have closed my eyes tight in disbelief except I truly feared that when I reopened them, this unbelievable panabsurdicon would have vanished. My jaw flapped, and eventually speech issued.

"Don't you think it might be useful, for example, to take some blood and urine samples for testing?" I suggested.

"That does sound like a good idea, you know."

"Then do them!" I ground out.

"Mr. Carswell, you seem unaccountably tense. I can barely get this needle into your arm."

As he jabbed me again, I winced in pain and offered the opinion that his observation was a brilliant one that perhaps a lesser physician, or an unseeing flying rodent, might have been in a worse position to make.

"The first case of negative IQ I have ever encountered," I remarked to myself.

I was still rubbing my arm when, his coat on his back, his little black bag gripped in one fist and a large watch in the other, Dr. Kay-Ole Larsen whizzed back through the surgery like the White Rabbit of Alice's adventures and, breathless, offered to share a taxi with me to Aarhus airport.

In retrospect, the major part of the examination actually took place during those few minutes together in the taxi. The White Rabbit quizzed me on my various health problems, on my most recent extensive operation, and on life in Australia. I had the impression, nevertheless, that time was being killed rather than lived and that the Queen of Hearts would soon be shouting after this strange character's head.

The moment we arrived at the airport, he shot off and jumped onto his flight. The last I saw of him were his heels alternately appearing and disappearing under the flaps of his long coat.

After waiting some hours at that dump of a provincial airport that is Aarhus, I settled back in my seat on my flight, my hands behind my head, pursed my lips, and formally declared the episode closed.

It was briefly reopened six months later when I received in the mail an extensive form to be filled in. In the deficiency of the questions asked and the abruptness of the manner, I thought I could see the hand of Dr. Kay-Ole Larsen.

* * * * * *

I HAVE ACTUALLY lost count of the number of times I have been in hospital now; a rough guess would put it at about twenty visits. Every six months, since the first operation until today, I have been required to undergo regular tests to monitor the progress or dormancy of the cancer.

Each time I dutifully present myself at the hospital, I feel like the world's unlikeliest creature: a man on death row who has been allowed parole on condition that he roll up every six months to see whether the decision has been made to administer the inevitable gas this time or not. Each time I walk out again a 'free man,' bound by his word to return, I feel ridiculously elated, as if I have been granted yet another six-month reprieve. I feel almost as if I had gotten away with something, made my escape yet again, foiled the disease and the doctors at a blow, would not return for the next set of tests in six months, as I obviously had this thing well under control. Six months later, I would be back in that twilight terrain of uncertainty and fear and would yet again return to show myself to the 'authorities' for their decision on my future.

These half-yearly visits to the hospital that punctuate my existence have become the incredibly slow swing of an enormous Foucault's Pendulum, under which is inscribed in a colourful mosaic of zodiacal figures and meanings hidden to all but the initiated (my doctors) the fate of this man for evermore. When the pendulum should in its predetermined journey swing over the Crab, the time-bomb tied to my throat in my neat executive's necktie will just explode. Bye-bye blackbird! At that prospect, my mind's eye has me desperately flinging myself onto the pendulum's supporting cable in an effort both to avert the event and avert the inevitableness of the event. 'We can't be as thoroughly and passively predetermined as this damnable machine makes us believe,' I argue, 'And I won't be giving up as easily as that! I'm more determined than that machine is predetermined.'

Each time, after I've been admitted, prepped for the tests, and wheeled into the theatre; after the nurses have done their bit and left me a few moments while the surgeons prepare for their big entrance; I find my thoughts turning with intense displeasure to what is happening to my body and with anger to those whose callous disregard and continued indifference are responsible for me being there.

Then, in my simple way, I wish the roles were reversed, so that I was the one about to operate, even with my limited and only approximate knowledge of anatomy, anaesthesiology, and surgical procedures, on those men and women who have been intent for over twenty years on concealing the truth and closing their hearts to the suffering of myself and many hundreds like me.

The degree to which I could then open the minds to understanding of those concealers of truths and obfuscators of events would be in direct proportion to the amount of suffering they had to undergo under my scalpel: and I would ensure they understood comprehensively and repeatedly.

Gabriel García Márquez, the Colombian novelist, has said of the 'Magical Realism' that critics purport to find woven into his works, that there is no such thing as a special Latin American perception of the real.

Márquez explains that it is everywhere; as bland a statement as a great writer could make, if it weren't then qualified by a further one: it is found in the sense of wonder about the cosmos so alive in Central and South America, a sense that the European and Western sensibility has squeezed out of consciousness. It is found in those things that we immediately understand and recognise in their entirety, even when their terms remain mysteries to us. It is an affirmation of the most primitive of ontologies: I am and it is and, together, we are. We are subjects of magical realism when we are moved by a piece of music, either to tears or to turn it off; and when we derive an unexpected joy from the difficult and back-to-front language of Chaucer; and when an illegible piece of graffiti offends us or pleases us.

My last two visits, in September 1995 and March 1996, to my local 'Police Department Headquarters' in Melbourne's Freemasons' Hospital have revealed to me to an unqualified degree the truth of that first knowledge: I am and it is. I am ill and it is cancer. The dormant, pre-cancerous stage seems to be ending as the Crab starts to stir. The features of the great unknown of the dormant stage have settled into an identifiable configuration; the Great Unknown of cancer.

The image of being tied to a time-bomb often floods my consciousness, and at those times I thank God that I have a fantastic team of doctors looking out for me in Australia, rather than being at the mercy of the incompetent Danish medical establishment who, I feel, would prime the fuse and accelerate the timing device before anything else.

* * * * * *

"THE IMMEDIATE AND closest prospect at this moment is of more corrective surgery."

The words hung in the quiet air of our lounge room, a clinical summary of the fresh, grim reality that had settled over our home. Phillip had taken his girlfriend to Forest Hill Chase to see a film. Upstairs, James was finishing an Australian history assignment on the motivation for Australia's declaration of war on Germany in September 1914—a distant conflict that now felt abstract against the intimate, ongoing siege within my own body. Sophia was on the phone with my sister, Hanne, who had called from Denmark for news of my latest internment. I sat beside her, the receiver close enough that I could easily reconstruct Hanne's anxious questions from the pauses in Sophia's replies.

Sophia answered, her voice carefully modulated but fraying at the edges. "That's right, this time they're talking about something even more extensive." Her voice lowered a little, as if to soften the blow for herself as much as for Hanne. "Yes, quite possibly more painful and more distressing than that second op."

She paused, listening to the distant, sympathetic murmur from across the world. Then:

"Well, I guess the side effects may also be more serious. It may become necessary to remove the part of the oesophagus that is revolting and pull the stomach up into the chest region; simple, straightforward and frightful. So, obviously, that won't help Jeff's digestive problems." A longer pause. "No, well, neither of us much relishes the thought either, Hanne; but it's this or nothing, followed by I can't bear to think what!"

Sophia shot me a glance. I was feigning absorption in the silent, flickering television, my hands clasped behind my neck in a posture of forced nonchalance. My eyes went to Sophia and caught hers. For a moment, we were locked together in that dark, silent place of mutually private anxieties—a landscape of fear, resilience, and weary love that no one else could fully enter. Then the moment passed, and Sophia was talking again, her voice brightening with a practised effort.

"Sure, I'll put him on now, Hanne. Don't forget to send me those measurements, OK! Yes, and tell Flemming all my love. Here's Jeff now."

Sophia handed me the phone, her fingers brushing mine—a fleeting, tactile reassurance—before she marched out to the kitchen, seeking refuge in mundane tasks. A few minutes later, after exchanging familial pleasantries and downplaying the severity with Hanne, I joined her there. The kitchen was a sanctuary of normalcy, filled with the faint, homely scents of cleaning products and the lingering aroma of dinner.

"Coffee?" she asked, not turning from the sink.

"Sure." I sat at the well-worn kitchen table, its surface a map of old rings and minor scars. Sophia poured us both a cup, the steam rising in gentle plumes, and sat opposite me. We were quiet for a while, the only sounds the disregarded murmur of the television in the adjoining room and the soft, rhythmic sipping of coffee—a small, familiar ritual that anchored us against the looming, uncertain storm. The silence between us was not empty; it was dense with everything we had already endured and everything we feared was yet to come.

Chapter 4: Hobo 28 Takes A Dive

In my Eden we have a few beam-engines,

saddle-tank locomotives, overshot waterwheels

and other beautiful pieces of obsolete machinery

Horae Canonicae V: Vespers   W. H. AUDEN

A ROUTINE DAY on the roof of the sky. It is around three thirty in the afternoon on Sunday, January 21, 1968—a time whose meaning is almost abstract, for what is a watch's relation to Greenwich Mean Time in the permanent winter twilight of seventy-six degrees North? The concept of afternoon here is a borrowed fiction, a habit of speech from a sunlit world that holds no dominion over this frozen expanse.

In late January at those latitudes, mid-afternoon possesses the spectral qualities we of more temperate climes associate with the protracted moment the light finally surrenders—when the eye, straining against an ambiguous, grudging gloom that seems less an illumination than a thinning of

67

the dark, reluctantly ceases its effort and relaxes into the definitive clarity of true night. Twilight here is not a transition but a prolonged, denaturing state. It is a veil that strips objects of their familiar qualities, leaching color and dimension, rendering the world outside the window as a canvas of wild, undefined, primitive shapes. It is with a perverse, almost grateful relief that one finally welcomes the arrival of full dark, with its sharp, star-pricked outlines and unequivocal, inky-black bulks. If it is true that at night all cats are grey, it is also true that in this Arctic twilight, all cats, and all other objects, living or inert, become ambiguous, half-formed presences in a landscape of profound uncertainty.

And up here, suspended in the vast, frozen silence above it all, are seven men. They belong to a species evolved to cling to the warm, familiar crust of the planet, to the zones of gravity, breathable air, and communal safety. Yet here they are, defying that pedigree on the very top of the sky, twelve miles above the wrinkled face of the earth, whispering swiftly through the thin, murderous atmosphere at over five hundred miles per hour. Whatever their classified business may be, and whoever in all the world holds the ledger that accounts for their presence—indeed, who sent them here into this liquid cobalt void—they are at this moment at their most profoundly and existentially vulnerable. They are interlopers in a realm that tolerates no permanent guests.

All that surrounds them is enemy. The cold is the primary adversary—an insatiable, disembodied wolf that ceaselessly hunts every calorie of warmth the human metabolism can laboriously produce. You cannot see this wolf, but its presence is a tangible force in the constant hum of the heaters, in the layers of insulation, in the very design of the machine that carries them. It is there, a latent predator sensing the faint infrared signature of their living forms, waiting to draw that precious heat away with a greedy, indefatigable hunger. There is no satiety in its nature; it wants everything. What it cannot claim directly, its lesser minions precede it—the tiny, stinging insectoids of frost that find every microscopic flaw, every imperfect seal. They reach through the machine's riveted metal skin, through the layers of electrically heated gloves and thick fur-lined suits, to slow dexterous movements and numb vulnerable extremities. It is a brutally one-sided siege: the men are prepared, through training and technology, to tolerate a measured degree of this assault for a defined duration; the cold and its minions, however, operate on a timescale of eternity, and they want the men entire.

The cold's intimate companion is the thin, anemic atmosphere at this altitude, which requires the men to exist within a fragile, self-contained bubble of manufactured environment. They must bring their own breathable air, their own pressure, their own pocket of earthly conditions into the void. Have we grown so blasé, so inured to headlines of mankind's technological triumphs over hostile environments, that we forget the swift and murderous consequence of a single failure? A failure that, in the space of milliseconds following a breach, could explosively rip the lungs from a man's chest or freeze his blood in its veins?

Then there are the more abstract adversaries: the altitude itself, a physiological challenge that pounds in the temples; and the speed—a sheer, relentless velocity that transforms their sleek craft into a projectile. These are terrors so mundane in this second half of the twentieth century, so woven into the fabric of high-velocity travel and Cold War posturing, that they are now hardly worth mentioning. And, of course, they have taken all foreseeable precautions. They are professionals. Most importantly, they have the immense, tangible protection of a huge, powerful, and frighteningly potent war machine—a entity whose very existence is a statement of sovereign will.

They are not floating about in any old silver sardine. This is the pride of the fleet, the Silver Ghost of bombers—the B-52 Stratofortress, a design of such rugged and adaptable engineering that it has achieved a remarkable and unexpected longevity, with many airframes destined to fly defiantly well beyond their nominal ten-year life spans and deep into the coming decade. This particular aircraft, the penultimate model before the final H-variant, is a B-52G. One hundred and ninety-three of its kind were built at Boeing's sprawling plant in Wichita, each one a complex tapestry of wiring, hydraulics, and human intention. Capable of speeds around 550 m.p.h., it is, in its first and purest instance, a high-altitude strategic bomber, a delivery system for apocalyptic payloads. On this particular mission—the routine yet taut-nerved Airborne Alert Thule Monitor mission—the aircraft that has drawn our inexorable attention, bureaucratically tagged as HOBO 28 and also known under the call sign Junkie 14, is armed in a relatively conventional manner with four 1.1 megaton thermonuclear devices, each a contained sun of theoretical destruction.

But whose side is HOBO 28 on? The question, on its surface, is simplistic. Obviously, it is on the side of the men flying it, and they, in turn, are on *our* side. That is the clean, binary arithmetic of the Cold War. End of question. Yet this inquiry is less about navigating a moral dilemma concerning a nation's inherent right to defend itself through deterrence, and more a subtle probing of a deeper, more disquieting question: who, or what, is truly in charge? Who is the master, and who is the instrument? It is an intimation, a growing whisper in the subtext, that something critical—some essential element of agency and consequence—is being systematically omitted from the official ledger.

Is it asking too much of words to mean what they purport to mean? To carry the weight of the realities they describe? If we cannot agree on that fundamental contract here and now, then we might as well collectively desist from the fruitless task of reading these squiggles further. Let us suppose, for the sake of narrative, that words can still shoulder their burden. Then, when we employ a phrase such as 'these seven men, indeed all of us in the modern age, are in some profound manner at the mercy of our own technology,' we presumably have a specific and chilling meaning in mind. It reflects a primal human concern, a vestigial fear that, should a specific, unforgiving sequence of mechanical or electrical events be triggered, these seven men would be rendered not just helpless, but utterly transparent to the forces they nominally command—transformed in an instant from commanders to casualties.

So, we have here an aircrew of significant experience, a unit accustomed to strutting its stuff within the immense and rigid framework of Strategic Air Command. They are a coordinated organism, a blend of individual skills forged into a collective will through countless training sorties and drills. However, on this particular mission—a demanding, continuous twenty-four-hour stretch in the sterile, recycled air—the usual complement of six has been augmented by a seventh man, an additional copilot. His exact role is obscured by the characteristic ice-age climate of mental white-out and bureaucratic obfuscation that distinguished the deeper corridors of the Cold War. He may be there to provide mandated crew rest relief, or perhaps he is a qualified pilot on a refresher tour after a desk-bound hiatus. We will never know his precise orders for sure, because in the realm of classified operations, no one will ever tell us for sure. Certainty is the first casualty of secrecy.

For all their collective experience, technical know-how, and martial discipline, we must pause and ask the unsettling question: in this great metal bird, who, or what, is strutting whom? Really.

The B-52 itself is, in a starkly engineering sense, a beautiful machine. Two hundred and four tonnes of beautiful, implacable force, its eight mighty Pratt & Whitney engines delivering a combined thrust equivalent to thirty diesel locomotives straining in unison. But it is, in the final analysis, *just* a machine. As much as its swept wings and massive fuselage might resemble the skeleton of some enormous, primordial animal, it is ultimately merciless and amoral, governed solely by the immutable laws of physics and chemistry. It does not care. It does not judge. It performs—or fails to perform—strictly according to its design specifications and material limits, much as a pen, released from a hand, must drop to the floor. Its actions are not unpredictable in the human sense of caprice or emotion; they may merely be unforeseen, the result of a hidden stress, a fatigued component, or an unanticipated interaction. It neither decides nor feels, neither wins nor loses. It is simply present, or catastrophically not present, at the denouement. Like a capricious and demanding divinity of the modern age, it looks on, impassive, at the intricate activities of mankind and, when the precise, precarious balance tips, it can demand its sacrifice with indifferent immediacy.

The machine, this creation of human intellect and industry, thus holds the power to change everything. In a fleeting moment, through a short circuit, a fuel leak, or a structural groan, it can transform its role from a vehicle of safety and strategic conveyance into the unwitting blade of sacrifice. And the crew, in that same instant, become the necessary vehicles by which that terrible sacrifice is achieved. These seven men, and no others, are thus transformed by the distant, abstract decisions of the rest of mankind into the particular, flesh-and-blood embodiment of a divine exigency. Despite all appearances, despite the comforting glow of instruments and the steady thrum of power, and contrary to the stubborn, cherished belief of the era, mankind here, twelve miles in the alien sky, is no sovereign master. Here, mankind treads a technological tightrope strung over an abyss, and counts the mortal risk on the borrowed fingers of a select few.

And the Russians?

Who?

Oh, yes, the Russians. The ever-present specter, the reason inscribed on every flight plan. Well, on this particular afternoon, as on so many thousands before it, they give the entire tense performance the profoundest cold shoulder. Their interceptors remain in their hangars, their radars perhaps noting the blip with routine disinterest. The ultimate Cold War tactic, it seems, is sometimes not even to show up for the confrontation, leaving the other side to wrestle with the ghosts of its own preparedness.

These seven men are supplied, at immense cost, with every conceivable means: cutting-edge technology, layered defenses, specialized facilities, and clothing woven with metallic threads. It is all provided so that they can venture with a certain audacious *appearance* of security into places which nature, in her ancient wisdom, has clearly reserved to herself—an exclusion zone of extreme cold, thin air, and immense solitude that mankind, with an arrogance bordering on the mythical, now trespasses upon regularly as if with total impunity.

Impunity. Well, no. Not quite. The ledger of nature has no column for political ambition. The sacrifice, when the precarious equation finally falters, will be extracted and honored in full. As we shall now see.

* * * * * *

HOWEVER, IT MAY have come to be, through the intricate chain of command, policy, and fate, there they are. Speeding along in their enormous metallic container, a shape not unlike a grandiose, winged sardine designed by physicists. Outside, the stars are not the friendly, twinkling lights of poetry, but frozen, pitiless eyes fixed to the endless indigo dome of near-space. Beneath them, appearing as little more than a faint, geometric smudge of light against the profound dark, lies a human settlement roughly the size of a small provincial town: some three thousand souls clinging to the rim of the world. Thule Air Base. Though originally constructed with frantic, wartime urgency to accommodate around fifteen thousand, the base has been quietly downgraded since the early sixties, its strategic importance diluted by the shifting tides of the Cold War and the terrifying logic of the intercontinental ballistic missile, which renders forward bomber bases slightly less pivotal.

Apart from its mind-numbing location six hundred and ninety miles north of the Arctic Circle, what makes this settlement statistically unusual for the modern age is its profound gender imbalance: of the three thousand inhabitants, only three are women. Even the legendary Klondike gold rush had its attendant bevies of entrepreneurs, beauties, and determined prospectors of various kinds. What powerful activities, what compelling forces, can tear so many men away from their womenfolk, from the soft comforts of the temperate world, in this advanced day and age? What, other than the oldest and most compelling of human enterprises?

Well, and money.

A great deal of money.

And, of course, there is a war on (and money to be made from it). In fact, there is a veritable menu of wars to choose from in 1968. There is the grinding conflict in Indochina, the frozen stalemate in Korea, the bitter aftermath in Algeria, the recent embers of Suez, the insurgencies in Malaya, Burma, Indonesia: an almost endless list to make the professional soldier or contractor slaver over the possibilities. The one that interests us most immediately, however, is the one most aptly named for these latitudes: the Cold War. But let us be clear: war is war, hot or cold. The temperature descriptor is merely a measure of the immediacy of the violence, not its potential. Just like water and porridge can exist in different states. And, just as some prefer their porridge hot, some strategists undoubtedly relish a more active confrontation. But when the geopolitical porridge is served cold, and that is the only temperature on offer, you take your bowl and you make the most of it. You adapt.

Which leads us to one peculiar, underlying reason why, on this specific Arctic winter's day, a United States Air Force Strategic Air Command B-52G is flying a vigilant, armed mission over the theoretically peaceful, neutral territory of the Danish county of Greenland. And it is the same reason why the settlement below—proudly billed in the USAF welcome brochure as 'The

Air Force's Northernmost Base'—is located with such ostentatious, fortress-like permanence on the edge of the immense ice cap in this remote, empty, and administratively Danish land.

It is a peculiar reason because it is almost one hundred percent certain that, through a combination of bureaucratic inertia, compartmentalized decision-making, and perhaps a little deliberate deviousness on the part of certain top brass in the Pentagon, neither the President of the United States, Lyndon B. Johnson, nor his Secretary of Defence, Robert McNamara—the very architects of the nation's military policy—are explicitly aware that the United States Air Force Strategic Air Command is, as a matter of daily routine, flying continuous, nuclear-armed alert missions *over* the sovereign territory of one of its oldest and most loyal allies, and doing so without that ally's express, mission-by-mission permission. The blanket agreements are in place, but the fine print is written in the opaque language of supreme national interest.

But it makes for absorbing, if unsettling, reflection to go back a little way in time, to trace the catenation of strategic decisions, geopolitical fears, and historical events that led first to the United States establishing a major Air Base at Ultima Thule, the mythical 'last place on earth,' and that subsequently led to the USAF SAC daily infringing, with the best of defensive intentions, the air space of a friendly power. It is a story that begins not with a bang, but with a calculation on a map—a map that, as we must first acknowledge, is often a liar.

* * * * * *

MOST MAPS OF the world, particularly the common Mercator projection hanging in schoolrooms and offices, are liars. That is the first, essential point to make. In their first sin, they either brutally cut up the vast landmass of Asia and Russia into several pieces to fit a rectangular page, fashioning the globe into a distorted animal hide stretched out to dry, or they engage in a more subtle deception: they grotesquely exaggerate the relative sizes of islands and continents the further one moves from the benevolent bulge of the equator.

The effect is cartographic tyranny. On such maps, Greenland appears as a monstrous, icy continent rivaling Africa in size, while Antarctica sprawls as an impossible, white fringe at the bottom of the world. Fishermen, relying on such charts near the poles, would have a jolly good time indeed: there, a humble minnow, drawn to scale, would appear the size of a legendary marlin. Not only is this visually misleading, but it obscures a crucial strategic truth: Greenland, the world's largest *island* (a title it retains only if one demotes Australia to continental status), is—despite the optical exaggeration of most maps—geographically very, very close to the Soviet Union. Or, to be precise, it is as close as it ever was to the beating heart of that rival power: Moscow. Thule Air Base itself is only some 2,370 miles from the Kremlin's spires—a shorter distance than that from Washington State to Washington, D.C. This geographical fact, simple, stark, and irreducible, is the silent, unspoken engine of everything that follows. It is the reason on the map, the cold calculation that overwrites all other considerations of peace, neutrality, or sovereignty. It is the logic of proximity in an age of bombers, a logic that draws a targeting line across the frozen sea and places a dot named Thule firmly upon it.

* * * * * *

IN 1987, A good half-life after HOBO 28 gate-crashed our lives and seeded its invisible poison, I was on one of my frequent business trips to several European countries. As had become my custom, I made a deliberate stop in Copenhagen to visit my sisters, Hanne and Paula, a small tether to a homeland that felt increasingly distant.

While in the capital, a persistent thought crystallized into purpose. I decided to look up the man who had headed the Danish Construction Corporation at Thule during my time there. Niels Kidde-Hansen, called 'Kidde' by all who knew him, was long since retired. He lived now with his wife and a number of lively, spotted Dalmatians in a villa in the quiet and exclusive northern suburb of Vedbaek. I remembered him with much affection: he was a man of warmth and integrity, greatly admired by all who came in contact with him in the DCC for his fairness and his steady hand in that remote outpost.

I rang early one morning from my hotel, the city outside still cloaked in a damp, grey dawn. He readily agreed to an interview, his voice a dry rustle over the line, so long as I understood that, as he was now an old man whose life was complicated by the pulmonal and throat cancers that afflicted him, I should be prepared to cut short my visit at any moment. I saw the condition not as a limitation but as a rallying cry—a testament to the very reason for my visit. I caught a taxi straight over to see him.

We sat together in a sun-drenched conservatory filled with the ghosts of thriving plants, now somewhat neglected. Kidde remembered me well from Thule, having, after all, himself appointed me executive officer. He had been a tall man, wiry and energetic in his prime, and even now, beneath the weight of age and illness, his every slow movement seemed a deliberate, lithe witticism, a conscious economy of effort.

He leaned back in his worn leather armchair and studied the middle distance, which in this case took the form of a small, resilient cockroach traversing the wall. Just the sort of hardy creature, I thought morbidly, that would snuggle comfortably into the cracks of a world at the prospect of a nuclear winter. I noticed that the formidable cigars of his earlier years, once a constant feature, were nowhere to be seen. A nervous, habitual movement of his right hand to rub his lips every so often betrayed their former, continuous presence.

On a low table separating our respective armchairs sat a large, modernist chess set. The board was of beaten and polished brass and steel, and the pieces were of two kinds: one set of clear, hard plastic, and the other of unfinished, earthy terra cotta. The kings stood nearly four inches high, imperial and abstract, and the pawns just over an inch and a half.

"Do you play chess, Jeff?" asked my host, noticing my glance.

"Well, I have played," I answered, feeling suddenly nervous, as if the game were a test for which I was unprepared.

"Good. I have just taken it up in my retirement. A battle of wits to keep the mind sharp, or at least occupied. Do you mind if we play a desultory game as we reminisce? It helps the thoughts to flow."

I said I did not mind, and with careful, trembling hands, he lined up the board between us, the terra cotta pieces placed at my end. I was to begin, which I did by moving my king's pawn to KP4.

"Very regulation, Jeff. I must be so too." He moved his king's knight to KB3. His tone was an admixture of apology and vehemence, embodying that peculiar Danish trait that comes from a fierce, quiet national pride combined with a deeply ingrained suspicion of personal and national insignificance 'in the larger scheme of things.'

But there was no doubting the immense, tragic significance of what he had to tell. One man's pain and death may only have an audience of one, but the audience for this strange, poisoned tale—of decisions made in faraway rooms, of silent flights over frozen seas, of trust betrayed and bodies failing—stretched out to the crack of doom, like the endless line of Banquo's spectral descendants.

"Well," he began slowly, drawing the word out as he studied the board, "The fact of Thule's close proximity to Soviet territory goes a long way to explaining Yankee interest in developing an airbase in such an inhospitable environment. A long way, but not all the way. It might only suggest to the cynical mind the 'why not.' Better the US than the Soviets there. Here, here."

He paused and clapped his large, now-frail hands together slowly like two great pink paws, the sound hollow in the quiet room. "Why should Greenland be the vacuum not abhorred by nature? If we can call fifty years of mistrust and misunderstanding 'nature.' Your move, Jeff."

Kidde sipped at a small glass of schnapps: it was, after all, past ten in the morning. There's an old, half-serious Danish belief that a Dane's blood can freeze or turn to dishwater unless it takes an infusion of alcohol by mid-morning to fortify the spirit against the damp and the gloom. I shifted my king's bishop to QN5, a tentative, probing move. He went on, seemingly fortified by the spirits and the gravity of his own narrative.

"In a manner, I suppose, Greenland fell to the United States in the geopolitical fallout of the War. Denmark, under the terms of a 1933 decision of the International Court of Justice at the Hague, had sovereignty over Greenland. But you know all this from school." He glared suddenly at me, a flash of the old, assessing administrator. "You are a Dane, aren't you?"

I smiled a weary smile and said I had been away for a long while, that Australia had rewired my circuits, and that he would be doing me a great courtesy if he went on, treating me as an eager, if prodigal, student.

The glare disappeared behind momentarily pursed lips. He took my pawn with his knight— a small, early aggression—and continued, his voice gaining a lecturing rhythm.

"So Greenland was a colony of Denmark until, in 1952, it was accorded full territorial status as a province of the Kingdom of Denmark. A noble gesture, on paper.

"Meanwhile, in the fall of 1940, Hitler very kindly made Denmark an irrefusable offer and planted here a puppet government. Berlin became, in reality, Denmark's new capital. In response, a number of Danish diplomats in overseas missions, horrified at the collaboration, refused to recognize the newly structured state. Many sought refugee status in the US, their loyalties torn between nation and principle.

"Among them was a man called Karl Boehm, who, at the time of the invasion, was stationed in Iceland's capital, Reykjavik. He flew to Washington and presented himself to the Danish ambassador there, Henrik Kauffmann. Now, Boehm's cousin was the chief of Danish administration in Greenland. He had made it clear he would not cooperate with the Nazis in any way. So, there we had Kauffmann—a man who declared himself the representative of a 'Free Denmark'—and two cousins from an old, established family that had produced generals, admirals, and diplomats for generations. These men, in what became known as the Kauffmann Agreements, effectively signed over to the Americans the rights to set up air bases and weather stations in Greenland. The stated aim was to help stop the German submarine war in the North Atlantic, which was choking Britain.

"The US was instrumental in keeping the Nazis out of Greenland for the entire war. Hitler would have dearly loved to have Greenland: from there they could have controlled the Northern Atlantic sea routes, which the Allies depended on so much. It could also have supplied an excellent jumping-off point should they ever have seriously considered invading the US. But the Nazis were denied all these possible prizes, partly by the vast, hostile geography, and partly by the American presence, secured in a number of daring B-17 Flying Fortress raids and patrols. The B-17, you see, was a kind of mechanical ancestor of the B-52. They helped secure Greenland for the Allies and at the very least neutralised its potential danger in the hands of the Nazis."

Kidde paused to ponder on the grim irony of replacing one human-made monster with a potential technological one. A flicker of characteristic Danish black humour skipped across his gaunt features.

"The nineteenth-century English poet, William Blake, spoke of a divine symmetry in the universe. Do you like Blake, Mr. Carswell? Do you like poetry? How about science? Philosophy? Religion? Never mind." He waved his hand, dismissing the tangent. "Anyway, it seems to me that modern physics has shown Blake's words to be an apt summary of the congruence of most physical laws, except for those of time and entropy, whose trail only passes one way and always in the direction of greater chaos. Here's a different, more human law: perhaps a satanic symmetry."

I stirred in my chair, not to interrupt but to place my queen at KN4—a potentially bold move, or a foolishly exposed one. I did not intervene in his flow.

"The natural, perhaps inevitable, result of these wartime actions was a post-war alliance between the two countries. Alliance means trust and cooperation, or so the speeches said. Then, after the War, the Kauffmann Agreements were retroactively approved by a grateful Danish Parliament and became an integral, if seldom-discussed, constituent of the broader NATO Agreement. So, in 1951, with pressures on the United States from the Korean War and its swelling role as world policeman in the face of the growing, felt aggression of the Soviet Bear, the Danish and American governments, 'for their common defence,' agreed that the USAF should establish a major, permanent air base at Thule.

"The Social Democrat Prime Minister of the time, H. C. Hansen—you know his reputation, second only in Danish hearts to that of Hans Christian Andersen—was the man who closed the deal with Eisenhower. This was seen, publicly, as a considerable victory for Danish diplomacy: a chance to participate meaningfully in keeping the world's peace, shoulder-to-shoulder with the World Policeman, while ostensibly maintaining the integrity of the Danish Constitution, which explicitly prohibited the stationing of nuclear weapons on Danish soil in peacetime.

"Some unkind, or perhaps merely clear-sighted, minds have since held that the entire NATO Agreement was set up, from a certain perspective, purely to guarantee to the US continued and unimpeded military rights in Greenland. But they were few, and the vocal, hopeful majority held sway in public opinion for the next forty-three years. Whatever else it may have been, Denmark's entry into NATO spelled the definitive end of its historic, cherished neutrality."

Time for another small sip of schnapps and for him to shift his king's pawn to KP3, a defensive consolidation. Then I continued my listening spree, the chess game a slow, silent counterpoint to the history unfolding in his words.

"Life was hard enough subduing the savagery of the German maniac," he continued, a rare rawness entering his voice, "without getting caught forever after between a paranoid and murderous communist juggernaut and a well-intentioned but possessor of enough fire-power to reduce half the globe to a glowing, radioactive ember. After the War, the Ruskies were sitting on our very own Bornholm Island, a mere hundred miles from Copenhagen; and the Yanks were well and truly settled in on Greenland. We were the meat in the sandwich, Jeff. A very small, very nervous piece of meat."

I felt sharply, in that moment, the quintessential Danish suspicion of being insignificant in the great, brutal game of the world outside. Niels downed another small measure of schnapps. If he who suffers, suffers most in the mind, as the saying goes, then it must be a Danish preoccupation to dilute that suffering as much as possible by selectively drowning a few clarifying brain cells in the national firewater.

"What did little Denmark have to offer in a grand military alliance? Two concrete things: base rights on the strategic monstrosity that is Greenland, and control of all ship traffic in and out of the Baltic Sea. That was our dowry. That was our price of admission to the club of the protected.

"So, no surprise that Thule Air Base started full operations in 1952. A sensible and logical consequence of an alliance of trust, we were told. Especially in view of the fact—a phrase we heard so often it became a mantra—that the Americans are an honorable people."

"There was also the unspoken question of military testosterone," I put in timidly, moving a pawn. "The nuclear arms race seems to me a bit like the first lemming going hang-gliding off a cliff without the glider. A thrilling, suicidal momentum."

"Well, yes, there's that too," Kidde went on, a sad smile touching his lips. "It's easy enough now to be theatrical first and reflective second, but I can't get into my head, even now, the sheer madness of that long, global drama we all lived through. We normalized the unthinkable.

"So, there you have things in the 1950s. Fifteen thousand men, a small city, living on the very edge of the planet's viable ecosystem, sustained by an endless chain of supply ships and aircraft. Then, the Soviets, always unpredictable, did something genuinely unspeakable: they launched a manmade object into orbit around the globe. Sputnik."

Kidde gave a short, wheezing laugh at the image in his mind of an artifact of lesser technological sophistication than a contemporary Oldsmobile putting the existential wind up the nation that would, a decade later, put a man on the Moon. I shifted my king's bishop's pawn to KB3, shoring up my own position.

"The whole world got excited over this hundred-pound lump of hurtling metal in October, 1957. But in the Pentagon, excitement turned to cold sweat. It announced, to the Brass, the Soviets' proven capacity to launch missiles—and soon, nuclear warheads—against any target, with ever-increasing accuracy, anywhere in the world. One of their immediate reactions was to intensify its political efforts to ensure its own program would not fall behind; and another was to utilize its current assets to their maximum potential.

"That Pentagon houses a wily lot, Jeff. Don't be fooled. The Air Force had had a lot of highly publicized accidents in its missile and rocket development programs. A test pilot could expect to live only a half-life," he rumbled, appreciating his own dark pun, "and rocket after rocket hit the ground and exploded in premature climax. But, I've often wondered how much of that was theater. It just suited them that the White House and Congress should believe they were struggling, that they needed ever more funds, ever more urgency, to keep up with the Ruskies. The Russians would have had just as many failures, probably more, given what we know now, and suspected then, about the brutal, rushed nature of their experimental military programs. But, of course, the Soviets could and did keep all their failures secret, while at the same time making heaps of propaganda capital out of every Yankee failure splashed across the front pages.

"Out of this atmosphere of panic and opportunity came, within a month of sputtering Sputnik's cheeky orbit, the USAF's 'BMEWS' radar plans. BMEWS," he poetically pronounced it *'Bemuse,'* "stood for 'Ballistic Missile Early Warning System.' Three gigantic, advanced radar stations were planned and put in place: the first at Clear in Alaska (US territory, if you were wondering); the second at Fylingdales in England (exploiting the 'Special Relationship') and the third at a massively revamped, expanded Thule in Greenland (for which our gratitude, they assumed, would be eternal).

"Are you getting all this down? But why am I telling you all this? You've been there. You've seen it for yourself. The four vast screens at Thule, each four-hundred feet wide by one hundred and sixty-five feet high; each one roughly the size of a football field, aimed like accusing fingers at the heart of the Soviet Union." He glared at me again, as if demanding I confirm the monstrous scale. I felt it a good time to put in my own spoken piece.

"Yeah, and don't forget there also emerged from the 'Sputnik Panic' the definitive launch of the United States into the Space Race: projects like 'Man In Space Soonest.'" I sat up a little, starting to draw the memory of the scene in my mind. My hands sketched invisible shapes in the air near my knees as the words followed. "So, between the three of them—Clear, Fylingdales and Thule—even if one was blinded, the BMEWS network swept the entire Soviet Empire. The theory was, if the Soviets launched a missile strike, presumably against the US, the USAF Strategic Air Command would have a good fifteen minutes of warning. Fifteen minutes to get its bombers airborne, to become an unstoppable, vengeful armada, so they could nuke back those who'd nuked them first. It was the doctrine of 'Mutually Assured Destruction,' but with a stopwatch."

"That's about the size of it, Jeff." He laughed, a dry, papery sound. "And the funniest, queerest thing about it all is that, here in Denmark, we were fed a continuous diet of soothing baloney that Thule was purely defensive and meant, above all, to *protect Greenland*. Protect Greenland?" He leaned forward, his voice dropping to a fierce whisper. "For God's sake, protect it from *what*? Polar bears? The Americans were building one of the most powerful surveillance and targeting facilities on Earth in a place that makes Alaska seem a pale, distant second in strategic usefulness, and we were supposed to believe its primary purpose was to defend the frozen, empty miles of Greenland itself. It was an insult to our intelligence, wrapped in the flag of alliance."

"Well," I put in, "We all knew that wasn't true, those of us who'd actually been at Thule. You couldn't miss the fighter squadron, the bunkers, the sense of coiled purpose."

"Of course. Only a blind, autistic corpse could have failed to speculate about all those other secret facilities scattered around the base, or the F-102 fighters sitting alert, or the occasional B-52 visiting on what were called 'training flights.' But, keep this in mind, my friend." He pointed a trembling finger at me. "It was not primarily the Americans who perpetrated this distortion and cover-up of the true purpose of Thule *within Denmark*: it was our own Danish government. For over forty years, our leaders kept that uncomfortable truth from their own people—a truth that any curious American citizen could freely have gleaned by reading any military journal or even popular news magazines like *Life*. Our government knew that Thule was a key component in a first-strike scenario; they knew about the squadron of fighters based there, armed with nuclear-tipped rockets; they almost certainly knew about the nuclear bombs stored there in vaults under the ice. Only we poor, stupid, trusting Danes needed to be protected by our Mummy government from these difficult, frightening truths. It was a paternalistic lie, sold as necessary for security."

"Fifteen minutes," I mused aloud, the timeframe hanging in the air between us like a death sentence.

Again he paused to sip at his schnapps, the liquid catching the light from the conservatory windows. His thoughts, I could see, returned as mine had done to those hypothetical, terrifying moments following a Soviet attack—the blips on the screen, the klaxons, the frantic scramble, the world holding its breath.

"Let's get this clear, Jeff." He began to emphaticize each point not with words alone, but by flicking plastic chess pieces off the board with sharp, irritated filips of his finger. A white pawn sailed across the room. "New York is gone." *Flick.* "Washington is gone." *Flick.* "New Orleans is gone. Chicago is gone. Disneyland is gone." Pawns and a bishop followed, clattering against the wall. "Memphis is gone!! Salt Lake City is gone. Tallahassee is gone." He was breathing heavily now. "But the carbonated inhabitants of those cities will have the cold satisfaction that in a little while, some hundreds of airmen jammed into imitation silver sardines will ensure that Moscow is gone." Now the terra cotta pieces flew. *Flick, flick, flick.* "That Pskov is gone. That Kiev is gone. That Leningrad is gone. That Tomsk, Minsk and Murmansk are gone."

"Well," I laughed nervously, trying to break the grim tension, "All the pawns have gone, anyway. The board is nearly clear."

"Stalemate, Jeff," he said, slumping back, suddenly exhausted. "A bloody, radioactive stalemate."

There was a long pause while we both contemplated the scattered pawns on the parquet floor, tiny symbols of annihilated millions.

"But, let's not be flippant, Jeff." His voice was soft again, reflective. "An attitude of flippancy is one of the great dangers of engaging in the pleasant, academic task of applying twenty-twenty hindsight to what we in the nineties may too easily dismiss as the follies of past generations. It is cheap wisdom. Put aside the magnificent, cruel clarity the telescope of the present throws on the immediate past, and try to call to mind your own childhood's atomic fears—the duck-and-cover drills, the fallout shelter signs. Recall the attendant hopelessness that seeped into every psyche at the time about the safety of the future, a future that might end as close as tomorrow afternoon. In that light, understanding the desperate, visceral desire for posthumous vengeance—for a 'Sunday Punch' that would fly even from a dead hand—becomes an easier, if no more palatable, task. There is, moreover, the lingering suspicion, for we will never know for sure, that the tactic just might have worked: that the Soviet Politburo, faced with the certainty of its own obliteration, might in the event have been sufficiently concerned, might have been deterred. The Cuban Missile Crisis might here be entered as evidence for that fragile balance of terror. But I digress..."

There was a brief pause in conversation as Kidde ran his hand musingly over the few remaining chess pieces on the board, flattening them as if weary of the game entirely. Then, gathering a second wind, he was off again, back to the chronology.

"So, in the Great Mexican Standoff of the fifties and sixties, Greenland became not just important, but indispensable, to the United States strategic posture."

I cut in, steering us back to the central, burning question. "But this still doesn't fully account for the specific flying sardine, HOBO 28, infringing Danish air space in January, 1968. The 'why' of the base is clear. The 'why' of that particular flight, on that particular route..."

"Well," he said, "an appreciation of the *other* major strategic measure the United States government adopted in the wake of Sputnik should help bridge that gap."

"You mean SAC's Airborne Alert strategy. Chrome Dome."

"I mean SAC's Airborne Alert strategy and more. The Airborne Alert was born in September of 1958 under the initial code-name of 'Head Start.' It began as a manoeuvre to test SAC's ability to keep a significant portion of its bomber force continually in the air, a 'fail-safe' presence. But by the time the young, dynamic JFK entered the White House in 1961, SAC was in a position to publicly, almost proudly, announce that a peacetime airborne alert was now a permanent fact of life. The program, by then colourfully and arrogantly renamed 'Chrome Dome,' allowed for a rotation of B-52s, fully armed with thermonuclear gravity bombs, to be in the air on twenty-four-hour sorties. They flew along both the northern perimeter of the North American continent and on southern routes crossing the Atlantic and into the Mediterranean.

"So far, so terrifyingly logical. However, SAC had a little problem, a vulnerability that gnawed at them: BMEWS, and specifically Thule. They felt that Thule's radar screens, for all their size, were a bit of a weak link. Alaska was fine: American-Canadian defence agreements made it possible to run secure, buried cables all the way from Clear to command centers in the US. There were no major communication problems out of Fylingdales in England, nestled among allies. But Thule... Thule was so terrifyingly isolated. They had to run a vulnerable cable along the sea floor to Canada and relied heavily on radio communications that piggybacked, in part, on commercial networks. It was the achilles heel of the early-warning system.

"I'm sure you've heard the old, chilling story about how an iceberg nearly activated WWIII?"

"Oh, you mean the time the undersea cable was severed by a drifting iceberg, and SAC HQ, seeing Thule go silent, thought it was signalling an incoming missile strike and went to a hair-trigger alert?" I recalled the barracks rumor, never confirmed but widely believed.

"That's the one. They all but went to a full red alert; which, as you know, is just a heartbeat, a single misinterpreted signal, from pressing the button. Another story was doing the rounds about then too, Jeff. You may have heard it. It seems that the Russians, in a moment of bizarre psychological gamesmanship, had been quite 'helpful' on one occasion. They informed SAC HQ in Colorado, via a backchannel, that the warning light atop one of Thule's radar screens had gone out. When a baffled HQ rang through to Thule and they in turn sent some poor, frozen technician out in the pitch darkness to investigate, sure enough, the damned bulb had blown. The Ruskies had spotted it on one of their spy satellites and delighted in putting the wind up the Yanks with this playful, yet profoundly threatening, gambit. It underscored the vulnerability.

"So, the wily minds in SAC High Command decided that, as part of the Chrome Dome flights, a specific B-52 would orbit daily *over* the BMEWS radar at Thule itself. It would be a sentinel watching the sentinel. But flying a nuclear-armed bomber on a continuous loop over an allied country's territory required permission. And that's where the sleight of hand came in."

He leaned forward, his eyes sharp. "I guess they thought, 'Gee, with Chrome Dome in place, it would be a pity not to use it for this too, seeing as a B-52 is going to be in the high northern area on a daily basis anyway.' This decision added yet another independent layer of verification to an already Rube Goldbergian system. So, it became possible for that orbiting B-52 to radio back to Washington, in the horrific event of a Soviet first strike that took out the BMEWS site *and* all other means of communication, a final, grim message: that Thule was no longer there. A last testament from the sky.

"Of course, as we only intuited at the time but is glaringly obvious now, the mere presence of BMEWS at Thule was in itself sufficient to make Thule a primary, number-one target on Soviet targeting maps in the opening minutes of any war. We were hosting a bullseye.

"Dandy, hey!" he said with bitter sarcasm. "To this purpose, from August 1961 onwards, one of the airborne alert flights was quietly re-routed onto a three-hundred-mile, bow-tie-shaped flight path directly over Thule. Thus the BMEWS was continually under airborne surveillance from that moment until, in the wake of HOBO 28's unscheduled and fiery encounter with the ice of Wolstenholme Fjord, the entire airborne alert program was finally halted by a furious and embarrassed Secretary of Defence, Robert McNamara, in July of 1968.

"And this minor modification of the approved program," I asked, incredulous, "this persistent infringement of sovereignty, was not considered to be of sufficient importance to warrant the Defence Secretary's *actual* knowledge or approval?"

"They buried it," Kidde said flatly. "They hid it in the paperwork. They delayed their formal submission for budget approval for the Chrome Dome modifications until just two or three days before Congress was due to consider the entire defense appropriations bill. In the pressure and pile of those final moments, a single, obscure sentence noting that a 'minor modification had been made to the Northern Route to enhance verification protocols' was guaranteed to pass unnoticed in the thousand-page document. Sneaky, weren't they? Bureaucratic judo."

I let out a low whistle. "And this went on. For *seven years*." Kidde simply nodded his head, a grim, definitive dip of the chin.

"Of course," he added, the bitter irony returning to his voice, "McNamara, and indeed the Danish government, were also operating under the aforementioned and commonly received principle—the article of faith that smoothed over all doubts—that the Americans, including those ambitious generals within the Pentagon, are, at heart, an honorable people. It's a powerful anesthetic, that belief."

He rose slowly, painfully, and shuffled to the sideboard to pour himself another small measure of schnapps. He did not refill my glass this time; the audience, I sensed, was nearing its end. I rose also, my body stiff from sitting and absorbing.

"But what we *know*," I said, voicing the frustration that had driven me here, "what we feel in our bones and see in our medical files, isn't good enough, is it? Not for them. Not for the courts or the ministries."

He turned to me, the glass in his hand, and raised his other in a gesture that was both farewell and a passing of the torch. "It's what we can *prove* that counts in their world. But, my guess is this, Jeff: your chances of getting anywhere near the actual, documented proof of this truth—the memos, the flight orders, the authorizations that bypassed Copenhagen—are less than the statistical probability of every single molecule in this room spontaneously, simultaneously following the laws of their own natures and deciding to fly out of that window." He gestured to the conservatory panes. "It is the architecture of denial. Good afternoon, Jeff. I have appreciated your friendly visit. My wife will show you out. I must rest now."

And with that, he turned his back, a frail, stooped figure silhouetted against the light, and was gone, leaving me alone with the scattered chess pieces and the weight of his testimony.

* * * * * *

SIX MONTHS LATER Kidde-Hansen was comprehensively gone. He was an old man, and the cancers—those silent, patient invaders born of a frozen sky—were finally stronger than him. I was informed of his death by his wife, who inserted a note telling me of it within the extemporaneous jottings that follow, a final dispatch from a mind that had seen too much:

There is a certain asteroid in the far reaches of the Milky Way that we might call Doubt XII. It is surrounded by the profoundest darkness and vacuum, but paradoxically, it affords the most excellent, unobstructed view available anywhere in space. Such is the human condition. Using imagination, we can project ourselves out to the faint, primordial black body radiation that represents the very end of the known universe, or in time, right back to the singular bang that heralded the start of history itself. But when we try to say what we *know* for certain, we immediately find ourselves reduced, inhabiting only a small, dependable piece of rock. The rest is void. It is on this lonely, metaphorical space rock that I now gingerly manoeuvre, trying to find stable footing.

You could theoretically claim that, if the very top of the American administration—i.e., JFK and later, McNamara—did not know about the specific details of the Thule monitor flights, then it is conceivable that the top of the Danish administration did not know either. But we who were there, we who felt the distant thunder and saw the contrails, we know better than that. They knew alright. They knew and they tacitly accepted it, even though it flew directly in the face of official Danish policy and the proud, repeated assurances given to the Danish people. The vividness of the memory of a drunken Danish MP, the then-Minister for Defence, on a parliamentary junket to Thule in 1967, raising himself from his semi-prone position at a bar to point out to the rest of us the glittering slipstream of the B-52 right then passing overhead, and laughing with a glee born of either power or profound cynicism at God-knows-what aspect of the grotesque situation, will not be erased by so slight a thing as the passage of time. Such moments of unguarded truth happen. But we, the observers, never get near the documentary proof. In the architecture of state secrecy, it is made to be impossible.

It is profoundly uncomfortable on Doubt XII. Cold, and the air of certainty is thin. Facts are easier to recount, a sterile chronology. Between 1961 and 1968, American missile technology caught up with and then surpassed the Soviets'. The ICBM became king. Chrome Dome, with its vulnerable, expensive bombers, diminished in strategic importance daily, and the bloody quagmire of Vietnam grabbed all public and political attention. But Chrome Dome was an empire unto itself. It involved seventy aircraft and two hundred crews, providing good flying hours, promotion paths, and purpose for about fifteen hundred fliers and their support. If the mission was stopped, SAC would have a lot of bored, frustrated, and tetchy pilots on its hands. Worst of all for the commanders, there was the palpable risk that the entire SAC bomber fleet might be cut back in the budget wars. No glorious careers there: trajectories pointed toward the ground, not the sky.

Pilots live to fly airplanes, and the B-52 was a damn good, powerful airplane to fly. There was pride in it, a culture, just as was said of the Luftwaffe pilots who took a fierce, technical pride in their machines. Perhaps they still clutched that pride even when Hitler, in his final, maddened weeks, ordered them to bomb their own collapsing cities. Hence the powerful inertia within SAC when it came to putting an end to Chrome Dome, despite its decreased military utility. Even when a pragmatist like McNamara wanted to end it—seeing it as an unnecessary, heavy provocation to the Soviet Union to endure these nuclear-armed flights every single day of the year—the machine resisted. The US military and its foreign policy makers do not act with one mind. Many fiefdoms, many institutions are involved. But within those corridors, everyone in the know knew. Everyone knew that the official explanation, that Chrome Dome was a temporary, emergency readiness action, was guff. It was a permanent posture, a habit of power.

So, what was left, after all the strategizing and posturing, was just one of those uncomfortable nuclear industry affairs that seem to have only one true, lasting victim: all the people involved. In this case, it was all of us—the aircrew, the firemen, the Danish workers, the silent ice, and the generations to come.

* * * * * *

MEANWHILE, BACK ON the afternoon of January 21, 1968, the commander of HOBO 28, alias Junkie 14, Captain John Haug, has just completed refuelling his aircraft midflight, somewhere over the featureless Arctic Ocean south of Thule and not far from the coast of Canada. The KC-135 tanker from which he has taken on fuel is now on its way back to Plattsburgh base, some 225,000 pounds of JP4 jet fuel lighter. HOBO 28 now carries that volatile lifeblood in its 'wet wing,' a modern design wherein the sealed cells between the spars and ribs of the wings themselves form the fuel tanks. This design, which superseded the older rubber bladder-type tanks, is lighter and holds more fuel—a engineering advancement that on this day will have catastrophic consequences.

During these marathon twenty-four-hour orbits, a man cannot be continually at a peak, knife-edge alertness. Even a top gun needs to take time out to rest, to be at his optimum when it truly counts. As we have been led to believe, the aforementioned seventh crewman is present on this sortie to temporarily act in the stead of whichever crewman needs to take his sanctioned rest.

So it is that, on that fatal day, roughly five hours into their monotonous run, the crew copilot of the aircraft, Captain Leonard Svitenko, has left the cockpit and is taking his crew rest in the lower, confined navigator's cabin. Consequently, he is not occupying his usual seat. In the close quarters, he has removed his heavy flying jacket and placed it down behind his seat, and with it has inadvertently covered a small heating vent.

Shortly after 3:00 p.m., the spare copilot, Alfred D'Amario, stationed in Svitenko's seat, in an attempt to combat the fiendish acolytes of the cold—those insectoid pinpricks that seep through the fuselage—turns the cabin heating up to maximum. Within minutes, however, another crew member, the radar navigator Frank Hopkins, reports in, his voice cutting through the routine hum.

"I can smell something burning. It smells like rubber. Electrical."

Svitenko, roused from his rest, instigates a frantic search in the navigator's cabin. His search uncovers, upon removal of the aforementioned flying jacket from its lodgement over the air vent, a small but vigorous fire at the rear of the cabin. The uncovering, fueled by the sudden inrush of oxygen, proves to be more to the rapid deterioration of the situation than to its correction. The flames, greedy for air, quickly grow, feeding on the freer flow they now receive.

Captain Haug, his voice preternaturally calm, radios to SAC HQ in Nebraska: "Drop Kick. This is Deck Two. We have heavy smoke in the cockpit. We're trying to find out its source. Meanwhile I am trying to raise Thule to get permission to come in emergency style."

Keeping his head, still believing the great aircraft not yet lost, Captain Haug orders the crew to prepare for an emergency landing at Thule. He switches frequencies. "Deck Two to Bean Pole. Do you receive me? Deck Two to Bean Pole. I require emergency permission to land."

No response. The silence is more terrifying than static.

Captain Haug sighs lightly, a sound of profound frustration swallowed by his oxygen mask. He circles twice over the dark, distant geometry of the base, studying the landing lights intently. The code is simple: a slow blink means he can land; a rapid blink means he should move away, that the runway is not clear.

On each desperate pass, the lights blink rapidly, relentlessly.

Someone shouts across the intercom, panic fraying the edges of the words, "Fuckin' hell, we're dying! The bloody extinguishers are out of foam. It's gaining!"

During a third, choking pass over the airfield, the stinking, acrid smoke works its way fully up into the pilot's cabin, rendering the air unbreathable, stinging the eyes, and obscuring the vital instruments.

"Ah, Drop Kick. Deck Two again," radios Captain Haug softly, the professionalism in his voice battling the obvious truth. "We are now on one hundred percent oxygen and the aircraft's instruments are unreadable. I am about to recommend bailout. Over."

With a heavy heart, Captain Haug sets the autopilot and plots a course for it, directing the mortally wounded bomber out to sea, in the general direction of the empty Canadian Arctic; and then gives the order he hoped never to utter. "Prepare to evacuate the aircraft. Eject, eject, eject."

"Hopefully," he muses to himself with a commander's grim calculus, "this way the plane will ditch far out, away from human settlements; and out of the damned environment, too! I don't want to be responsible for the political implications of a nuclear-armed bomber crashing on or near the territory of a friendly power. Better to ditch in international waters." It is his last act of control.

Within minutes of the bailout order, all electrical systems fail with a final sigh, the eight Pratt & Whitney engines cut out one by one, and the aircraft, now a 200-tonne glider, is utterly out of control and directionless, a silent black shape against a blacker sky.

At a unit cost of $8,040,176.25 (in today's terms, more like $32,000,000), the decision years earlier to equip the B-52Gs with individual ejector seats cannot have been made without a certain bureaucratic apprehension on the part of the top brass. After all, it has ever been a powerful, romantic tradition in military circles that a captain does not abandon his ship. But modern war, or the preparation for it, is a calculus. The costs, not always evident on a balance sheet, of training highly specialized personnel probably tipped the balance in favour of preserving this component of the national investment. Apart, of course, from the ever-present desire in every American breast—a genuine article of national faith—to preserve lives where possible, even in the face of great loss of equipment.

For the Americans are an honorable people.

It is never pleasant for a captain and crew to experience the loss of a ship, be it in peace or war. It is doubtful that losing the ship to a misplaced flying jacket can have softened the blow of the loss in this case. The fateful, absurd conjunction of circumstances that conjured up consuming fire out of the atmosphereless sub-zero cold must have resonated with a sickening irony in the hearts of the pilot and crew as they prepared to abandon ship and eject themselves at awful speeds into the forbidding realm of unimpeded darkness and cold.

So the bomber's six sets of ejector bolts are blown, and six parachutes fluff open like strange, pale mushrooms against the night, and six very relieved, cold, and profoundly perplexed airmen begin their uncomfortably slow, blind, and seemingly perpetual descents toward the snow, ice, and rocks below. Uncomfortable because, among other things, in the rushed terror of the emergency, not every one of them has managed to don the appropriate and essential arctic survival gear for a descent into the hell that is the Arctic winter night. Where it is dark, dark, dark; and cold, cold, cold.

"Phew," Captain Haug might have whistled to himself as he floats groundward, the immense, dying silhouette of his aircraft drifting away. "Bye-bye baby. Bye-bye my great grand flying coffin. And what bodies we do have laid out in the bomb bays today!"

Captain Haug is perhaps the most fortunate in that regard, as he has on thermal underwear beneath a winter-weight flying suit. He is also fortunate in that he lands within 600 yards of a heated hangar on the base's periphery, toward which he immediately directs his hurried, stumbling steps, the survival instinct overwhelming the shock.

Alfred D'Amario, the spare copilot, is similarly smiled upon by a capricious fate. Though he only has on a summer-weight flying suit over his arctic underwear, he has had enough presence of mind during the emergency to also snatch up and put on his parka. Having landed without injury, again within the vague confines of the airbase, he walks shivering, a solitary figure, 200 yards to a nearby hangar's promise of warmth.

The radar navigator, Frank Hopkins, and the electronic warfare officer, Richard Marx, fare relatively well. Hopkins escapes the lower compartment with an arm injured by the sea of flames and finds himself rocking uncontrollably back and forth, back and forth like a pendulum all the way to the ground. He calls out into the void, and within moments, Marx appears out of the darkness, disappears, and reappears with parts of his survival kit, with which he attends to the injured man's arm and makes him as comfortable as possible on the ice. They then move off together toward the distant glow of the base and within the hour are located and rescued by a searching helicopter.

The gunner, Sergeant Calvin Snapp, ejects safely and without further physical trauma, except that he has only a summer-weight flying suit over his thermal underwear and, in the violent, twisting exit, loses his helmet and gloves. When he comes to ground, his hands are already too numb, too cold for him to fumble open his survival kit. He decides, even though he is utterly unsure of which direction the base lies, that the best thing is to keep moving, to generate warmth. So he sets out walking into the featureless night. An hour and a half later, nearly spent, he is found by a ground search team and is conveyed, a shivering bundle, to the base hospital.

The fate of the navigator, Curtis Criss, is a little more complicated, though in the end almost as fortunate. Though first out of the aircraft, he is the last to be rescued. On his ejection, his shoulder receives a severe wrench, and it seems to be broken or dislocated. On landing, he finds himself completely lost. Without any idea of direction, he very wisely, as it turns out, wraps himself in his parachute—a makeshift cocoon—and lies in the snow to conserve heat and await the hoped-for rescue. Though he hears the thrumming of rescue helicopters hovering above him, sometimes passing as close as thirty feet, he fails to attract their attention; his flashlight is dead, his voice swallowed by the vastness. Twenty-two freezing, painful, and frustrating hours have to pass before he is finally located by a persistent search plane and carried back to the base hospital. He is lucky, the doctors will say, to lose only parts of his ears and a few fingers to frostbite.

So, all six crew members have ejected safely and... Hold on!

... and have in their several manners...

Hang on. Six!

... been retrieved and saved for next time...

Just a minute. You only mentioned six. What about the other guy? The extra crewman? The *seventh* man?

Well, he is not actually the 'extra' crewman. The 'extra' crewman, Alfred D'Amario, ejected as mentioned above, quite safely. But the crew copilot, Leonard Svitenko. Well, no. He has not been forgotten. He is unforgettable.

As we remember, we left him fighting the growing fire in the lower crew compartment, right above where the fatal ignition started. As we return to him in that final minute, we find him trapped by the wall of flames, prevented from getting forward to an ejector seat—had there even been one allocated for him in that station. Instead, we watch, helplessly, as in a final, desperate act of self-preservation, he turns from the fire, rushes to the navigator's escape hatches in the same compartment, forces one open against the screaming slipstream, and disappears through it into the night at a horrifying, untethered acceleration. When next human eyes meet him, he is beyond cold and fire, and beyond all earthly explanation or recrimination.

* * * * * *

AREN'T CHILDREN GREAT little explorers? They will poke about the oddest corners of their world and bring home the most astonishing, sometimes macabre, objects. Sometimes they don't bring them home but keep them as secret treasures, pieces of a mystery only they own.

A most amusing and instructive incident occurred in Australia a little while back. A group of children in the state of Western Australia—a state of such immense, arid emptiness that beside it Texas looks like a suburban ball park—discovered an enormous, fossilized egg. A dinosaur's egg! Instead of rushing home with it, they very purposefully hid it and then, leaving their parents intriguingly in the dark as to its whereabouts, went on to inform the authorities they had it. Just as well they proceeded with such cunning. The relevant authorities, or irrelevant as they made themselves seem, with all the wit and compassion of the living dead, insisted, with stern threats of punitive consequences, that the kids hand over their treasure immediately, because it didn't belong to them under law; it belonged to the state.

The kids, however, played the curve ball with innate ease. They were quite philosophically willing, they said, to have their parents jailed in their stead for being in possession of a treasure that by law belonged to the whole nation. The standoff made the news. The happy outcome was that the kids, through this clever leverage, rightly ended up with an adequate compensation for their fortuitous find: some $50,000 Australian, according to my memory. Justice of a sort, mediated by the spotlight.

What, then, would be an adequate compensation to the innocent children of the tiny, remote village of Dundas, over the way from Wolstenholme Fjord, who found the helmet of the unlucky Leonard Svitenko a few days after the plane went down? What price for a boy's treasure that is not a fossil from a long-dead age, but a relic from a very recent, very violent death? And why, one must ask with a chill, was it found wet and sticky?

* * * * * *

ALBERT EINSTEIN AND his associates turned our understanding of physics on its head nearly five generations ago, introducing a universe of relativity and terrifying, latent energy.

Four hundred years ago, William Shakespeare shook the English language so severely with his poetry and insight that it has taken all that time to even begin to shake off his influence.

Thirty-two hundred years ago, according to tradition, God took Abram and set him at the head of a family promised to be so numerous they could, theoretically, populate the stars themselves, one to each celestial body.

One hundred and twenty-four thousand years is a long, long time by most human standards of measurement. It is an epoch. It would not have occurred even to the most long-lived stegosaurus.

To a young couple starting out on the exciting, hopeful trek toward family and future, it would not occur to even the most sanguine of them to project their expectations to the end of six thousand two hundred generations, nor to reckon their descendants by then in numbers rivaling the molecules in a single cell.

To the mountains, raised imperceptibly from the seas by the slow, grinding processes of geological tectonics, such a length of time may seem minimal: but the mountains' awareness of time's passing is, I dare posit, at best commensurate with their own slow rate of growth and decline—a geology of patience.

However, counting on the silent, impeccable hands of the atomic clock, measuring the half-life of plutonium-239—which for a curious, exponential reason, we do by halves—that span we can comprehend. We can mark it in chunks of one hundred and twenty-four thousand years.

For it is at the end of one hundred and twenty-four thousand years that we calculate that half of the radioactivity in a given sample of this man-made element will have decayed.

Unfortunately, and this is the cruel, teaching point of the exercise, that does *not* mean that at the end of two hundred and forty-eight thousand years all the plutonium will have decayed. We are not getting off that lightly. The universe does not deal in neat finales.

Rather, it means that another one hundred and twenty-four thousand years' passage will see the decay of half of *what is left*; another hundred and twenty-four thousand years will see half of *that* remnant gone; and so on, literally, ad infinitum, a diminishing but never-ending tail. However, in rough, practical terms, scientists tell us that any place, object, or environment suffering plutonium contamination will effectively be free of dangerously elevated levels at the end of a *mere* one and a quarter million years. A mere geological blink.

Ain't that great? Comforting, isn't it?

But as the crew of HOBO 28, in their varying states of undress, degrees of bodily integrity, and clarity or muddied shock, float toward the soft, dull glow of the ice and unknown terrain below, each becomes an unwitting, privileged spectator to that incomprehensible number of years' future in the making. They are the first witnesses to the start of a clock that will outlast all of human history.

They watch, those who can see, as the mortally wounded bomber makes its final, death plunge. It describes a large, graceful, terrible curve directly over the sleeping Thule airbase, sweeping lower and lower over the unsuspecting community below, whose lives it is about to alter in the next few minutes—and effectively, irrevocably, for the next hundred and twenty-four thousand years. The base lights, from their perspective, wheel slowly.

It somehow conjures a metaphor, if a metaphor it may be termed, of the effects of a black hole, only inverted. This dark, dying object hurtles through space and draws all nearby—the land, the sea, the people, the future—into its grave web of influence. For whereas, once an object has fallen irretrievably into a black hole and passed forever beyond its event horizon, its image is forever engraved thereon, frozen as it was last seen for eternity—a permanent picture of the past— this large, black-against-black celestial satellite instead projects us into a permanent picture of a *future* as determined and set as any past. Between human lives and radioactive half-lives, there is really no competition. The half-lives win, every single time.

In only moments now, HOBO 28 will die. It will not be a silent death. It will be a short, though phenomenally powerful, flash of light and hellish heat as its port wing dips down and touches, with casual violence, the ancient ice of Wolstenholme Fjord. This contact will act as a pivot, projecting the fuselage forward and down into the ice, concertina-ing it as it skids, explodes, and disintegrates all at once into a million smoking, burning, radioactive pieces, scattering its deadly seed across the pristine snow.

What a way to go out. Not with a whimper, but with a world-altering bang that echoes silently down the corridors of deep time.

Chapter 5: A Day In The Life ...

Ultima Thule

Georgics i30   VIRGIL

EVEN ON A major military and intelligence installation such as Thule Air Base, it is not an everyday, routine, or even exactly an expected or foreseen occurrence that a B-52 bomber, loaded with a cargo deadly enough to obliterate Philadelphia, New York, Boston, and most of Maine, should whistle dangerously overhead and proceed to flatten the geraniums (or is it gerania?) by your front fence. But that, given the liberties of comparing our ice-bound home with the average suburban domicile, is precisely what happened in our sleepy hollow at the top of the world nearly thirty years ago. The surreal became real; the theoretical, terrifyingly concrete.

* * * * * *

GREENLAND IS SERIOUSLY, profoundly cold. In the south, it is merely cold. Travelling north, it just gets colder and colder until, by the time you have arrived at Thule Air Base in the northwest, it is a cold of such intensity it feels less like weather and more like a permanent, hostile condition of existence. The winter temperature seldom climbs above -24°F, while the prevailing breezes, usually a biting seven to ten knots, produce a wind chill that can effectively bring the temperature as experienced on exposed skin down to a soul-numbing -54°F—a cold that steals breath and crystallizes thought.

Having arrived at this outpost, though, let's spend a little time there and get to know it a little better, to understand the stage upon which our drama was set.

Thule is located well and truly inside the Arctic Circle, only some eight hundred miles from the geographic North Pole—closer to the top of the world than to any major city. Situated on the rocky shore of the deep Wolstenholme Fjord, it is cradled and constricted on the north by the brooding mass of North Star Mountain and on the south by its counterpart, South Star Mountain. These sentinels effectively form a natural wind tunnel, a corridor to the sea down which blizzards, born on the central ice cap, blow with unobstructed, polishing fury.

Here, day and night are not transitions but starkly separate realms. In the daylight season—also called summer and spring more from a sense of nostalgic habit and respect for tradition than for any perceptible resemblance to those gentler seasons farther south—the sun shines brightly nearly without letting up, a glaring, relentless eye in the sky. Sometimes, miraculously, the mercury rockets all the way to fifty-four degrees Fahrenheit, creating what passes for a heat-wave. If you can find a rare spot out of the ceaseless wind, tucked against a sun-warmed rock, it is actually possible to sunbathe, a surreal experience in a landscape of eternal ice.

At the same time, in the shade and under the buildings, snow persists year-round, ancient and compacted. While snow rarely actually *falls* at Thule itself, due to the dry, coastal climate, it is often blown in in great, stinging clouds from the inland storms that rage perpetually on the ice-cap, with greater frequency and fury during the long winter, or dark season.

There is virtually no liquid precipitation at Thule, with the curious result that rust is unknown. In such low, frozen humidity, oxidation is simply impossible. Metal objects left outside for decades emerge from the snow bright and untarnished. And this despite the fact that the base is built on the shores of a saltwater fjord—a paradox of the Arctic.

This far north, the sun, when present, measures an eccentric, disorienting path across the sky, making nonsense of east and west. As spring feebly bounds into summer, the sun rides the horizon like a skimming stone, dipping briefly below prominences, leaping over depressions, day after day. Over a space of three months, it traces a slow, spiraling path to a modest zenith; from which it declines in a similar, reverse spiral to once more ride the eye's limit before going `walkabout' for another five and a half months of perpetual night.

During these winter and autumn months of constant, profound darkness, the Aurora Borealis—the Northern Lights—puts on a display of such unearthly grandeur that it defies description. It is no wonder the Inuit focused their myth-making attention on them so sharply. Besides the beliefs I mentioned before, it is also held that if you whistle at the Aurora, it will come closer and closer and finally whisk you away into the sky. Conversely, if you bark at it like a dog, you can make it shy away from you.

The Lights are caused when electrically charged particles from the solar wind are funneled by the Earth's magnetic field into the upper atmosphere, where they collide with gas molecules. The wave-like curtains of light that ripple and pulse can simulate the slow roll of a spectral ocean one moment and the rapid progress of a breeze over a field of luminous wheat the next. The color—

ghostly green, bloody red, or pale violet—is determined by the type of molecule involved. Oxygen, for instance, produces that iconic, haunting yellow-green.

As far south as the latitude of New York or Copenhagen, the Aurora is impressive: a faint, beautiful curiosity. Here, at over eighty degrees north, the effect is colossal and deeply unnerving. The intensity of light generated can be comparable to a long, drawn-out series of silent sheet lightnings, illuminating the snowscape in a lurid, intermittent, submarine glow. It is a light that feels alive, conscious, and utterly alien.

The clarity of the night skies, seldom obscured by clouds, makes the display of the Milky Way—a thick spill of diamond dust across the velvet black—and its attendant galaxies another visual feast. This turns to pure marvel when augmented by the full moon, which casts sharp, blue shadows on the snow. Yet, the darkness still reigns supreme. It is a palpable entity. It takes only a hint of light, from the Aurora or the moon, to set the snow and ice glowing with an eerie, almost sub-visual phosphorescence, as if the very landscape remembers the sun.

But, it is still dark. Whatever else may be said about the night season in the Arctic, its beauties and severities; it is, above all and inescapably, *dark*. A darkness that presses in on the soul.

On the base, the extreme seasons had different, personal effects. Some men preferred the dark season, finding its endless night a blanket, a time for interior reflection and respite from the glare. Others, like me, preferred the daylight season, as I found the unrelenting cold and continual darkness a hostile and profoundly disorienting environment, a test of mental endurance.

After the constant, weighty blackness of over five months of night, it was always an intensely agreeable, almost spiritual experience to witness the sun's tentative reappearance. Little by little the days grew longer, as the sun seemed to tease us with its brief, daily epiphanies over the hilltops before retreating again. The first warrant of its return came at second hand: from a hiding place behind South Star Mountain, its first oblique rays would light up like a blinding, frozen diamond the bare, wind-scoured tip of North Star Mountain's peak. Day after day, the line of light would crawl imperceptibly down the mountainside—a light so bright it required sunglasses even in the deep cold—until, at last, the sun itself would crest the opposite peak. There would follow a short, cherished period of familiar diurnal rhythm. After which, the sun would dominate the sky, refusing to set for the next five months, turning night into a forgotten concept.

This time, for me, sun-starved and weary of the gloom, was pure bliss. To see the sun again, to feel its still-weak but undeniable warmth on my face, was a physical and psychological redemption.

* * * * * *

ONE AFTERNOON, BY the clock—though in the mid-dark season, all afternoons were midnight—I was visiting friends who represented a rare fragment of normalcy: they were one of only two civilian couples quartered at Thule Air Base. Asker Lund, the Danish Police Inspector, and his wife, Monique. All other married personnel and their families lived in the separate Dundas Village, some distance from the base on the other side of North Mountain.

Asker, although his official beat included the vast, empty territory from Thule to Dundas and across the fjord to the remote Inuit village of Qaanaq, was nevertheless a plump, genial man. The endless opportunities for arctic exercise seemed to have had little effect on his comfortable physique. He and Monique were a quiet, unassuming couple whose open-handed hospitality and warmth I enjoyed on many occasions, a sanctuary of civilized conversation. On this particular visit, I enjoyed their food as well, a home-cooked meal that was a treasure in the land of mess-hall fare.

The Police Inspector's wife had given birth to a child while they were assigned to Thule. Such an event was, as you will understand on a hardened military base where the three aforementioned American nurses were the only other females, exceedingly rare. The female Greenlanders in the outlying areas would generally look after themselves with traditional midwifery, only coming to the base hospital in case of major complications.

The Inspector was a genial chap, not easily flustered; an ideal temperament for not allowing a serious situation to inflate into a dangerous, panicked one. However, one situation comes to mind in which it was his mere substantial presence, rather than his authority, that ultimately quelled the chaos.

"Last Saturday morning," he began, after we had settled with coffee, "mid dark season and all, some fool Danish clerk from the base's laundry was discovered by his coworkers sitting on his desk, cross-legged like a Ukrainian cobbler, in full suit and tie but conspicuously, puzzlingly, shoeless.

"The other workers saw that something was amiss; even in our strange world, they could see that it is out of the ordinary to start the workday perched like that. So, it was decided that the best course of action would be to have him driven quietly over to the hospital for an evaluation. For which purpose, and to talk him down off his desk, I was called in.

"All went reasonably well up to the point of actually driving the eccentric young rebel over to the hospital. He allowed himself to be gently enough coaxed off his desk and conducted, albeit rather sullenly, to my patrol car. Then the real fun began. Maybe it was that he suddenly found himself unaccountably handcuffed, hands behind his back; or it may have been part of a greater, deranged plan. Probably the former, I dare say. Anyway, once in the car, he transformed into a thrashing maniac and manoeuvred himself with shocking, eel-like speed into a position where he propped himself like a rigid rod between the passenger side door at one end and my poor, vulnerable throat at the other.

"I'd just gotten the car going, you understand. Against all predictions, I found that driving a motor vehicle with my windpipe securely blocked by the grunting, determined feet of a crazy man was hardly productive of feelings of Christian goodwill and forebearance in me; in fact, I all but lost my temper."

"Not you, Asker," I interjected. "You lose your temper! I can't picture it."

He patted his round tummy and chuckled, a deep, rumbling sound. "All but, I said. So, anyway, if I'd been doing any more than the base speed limit of twenty miles per hour, we'd have had a tragedy on our hands. Luckily, though, as I'd barely gotten the car moving, I managed safely to brake with all the ferocity available to me with my rapidly dwindling reserves of air. Then I set about the undignified task of working the podiatrically inclined psycho off my throat."

Monique broke into the narrative at this point, leaving Anders smiling and reflective as she took up the heroic tale with wifely pride. "Having done so, he heaved his considerable self bodily over on top of the struggling and kicking lunatic and by sheer weight of materialistic dialectic—" she smiled at her own phrase, "—after all, he is not a thin man!—subdued him in his controverting attitudes and won him over by squeezing the air out of his lungs. Thus dispirited and deflated, the young man allowed himself to be driven quietly, and much more compliantly, over to the hospital; where he was taken into care by the alerted, and now rather more cautious, medical staff."

"Was this guy on something?" I asked, the obvious question. "Something stronger than the usual Arctic melancholy?"

"Well, it turns out that, after a brisk examination of him and his quarters, the doctor in charge discovered the immediate chemical cause of his peculiar behaviour. Some rather special pills called 'Blue Cheers' came to light, the gift, the patient confessed under pressure, of some well-meaning but foolish friends back in Denmark. They came with strict instructions that they only be taken before a weekend, as the effect takes a couple of days to wear off. He very carefully ignored any and all such instructions, and took some straight away, in the middle of a workweek.

"'My friends thought they might help dispel the gloom of the midday midnight,' he explained, when a little more settled and capable of coherent speech.

"'Hmmm,' said the doctor, grimly. 'Well, they certainly did that. They've also had quite a powerful effect on the physiognomy of our Police Inspector; and he wasn't even taking them!'"

Monique went into quiet hysterics at this, leaving Anders to take up the story again, a tolerant, amused grin on his face.

"So, the offender looks sheepishly at the floor. 'I've never taken them before, you know.' As if that excused it.

"'I'm sure,'" Asker said, taking off the doctor's severe and reprimanding tone perfectly.

"After a pause, the young man had the gall to ask: 'Can I have them back? I, er,... I, rather need them...' A helpless, pathetic grimace accompanied this plea.

"The doctor raised his well-heeled eyebrows at this, backed off a little as if from a bad smell, and called through the curtain drawn round the bed, 'Orderly, see that this patient is given 15cc of pentanol every four hours.' And with that, he disappeared."

"Ah," I broke in, the memory connecting. "So that's the story behind *that* paperwork. The following Monday, a most unusual requisition form landed on my desk requesting me to authorize the shipping back to Denmark of 'Item, one, drug-related lunatic, strait-jacketed and stretchered, to Copenhagen. To be called for at receiver airport.' I remember puzzling over the phrasing."

"Yeah, that's him, all right." Asker nodded, chewing thoughtfully. "A friend called me from Customs in Copenhagen later and told me the rest of the saga."

"You know what was remarkable?" I asked. "Nobody on the medical staff was prepared to authorise for him to be physically restrained in a straitjacket for the flight. None of the doctors on the base, even though they privately felt he should have been totally immobilised during the trip, would sign the authority. The liability, I suppose. So, as the administrative officer, I did. I signed the form.

"And it was just as well I did," I explained. "I arranged for him to be sedated, strait-jacketed, and securely tied to a stretcher in the cargo hold of the fortnightly Scandinavian Airways DC-8. After the normal five-hour trip to Copenhagen, Kastrup Airport was suddenly closed by a thick, unexpected fog. The plane was forced to circle, burning fuel, for two exhausting hours before they could get permission to land.

"So, while they're still whizzing around unwanted and unheeded up there, the young druggie woke up from his sedation. The drugs had worn off. He started yelling and thrashing, trying to free himself. Just as well he couldn't. The crew had enough to contend with trying to land blind in fog without the additional pleasure of a deranged maniac battering at the cabin hatch and threatening, as I heard later, to 'tie their balls to their ankles.'

"The day he arrived back in Copenhagen, the young man's furious father telephoned the head office of the DCC demanding to be informed of the reasons, the outrage, behind his son being dispatched from Greenland like a northern Hannibal Lecter, and so on and so forth....

"Two days later, he phoned again. His tone was completely different. He courteously apologised, saying that he now understood that we had exercised the only option open to us, which was to have sent his son home with all necessary precautions; and that his son was, indeed, in his own father's words, 'as crazy as a chamber pot.'

"So, it seems our young clerk is spending a little time in a mental institution in Denmark, suffering from a severe depression gravely aggravated by the unwise chemical experiment he conducted on himself."

"Better the natural darkness than that kind of internal night," I ventured.

The Police Inspector and his wife nodded in silent, sombre agreement. We all knew men who had cracked under the pressure of the isolation, the darkness, the unnatural life.

Asker, though quite severely bruised around the neck, did manage to survive to debate another day. And, as I remarked to him later over dinner, the traumatic event had not diminished his famous appetite very severely.

"Food, my dear Jeff," he replied, spearing another potato, "has ever been my succour and close companion. And its fidelity was proven beyond all doubt—as if there were any need for it to prove itself!—when it stood by me in my hour of need. While it was not there in its own person, I assure you that young maniac will vouch for the enduring presence and, ah, *gravity* of its sure and lasting effects."

I chuckled, looking over at Monique, who was serving her husband his third generous plate of roast pork and potatoes, and remarked, "You know, Asker, you are the only Don Quixote I have ever known who dispenses with the need for a Sancho Panza by simply becoming his own!"

"Umm?" was the muffled, contented reply from behind a formidable forkful of pork.

* * * * * *

REGARDLESS OF WHICH season each person preferred, the constant daylight in summer and the constant night in winter were always deeply disorienting. In this stark, timeless landscape, the radio became our oracle, our only reliable key to the passing of hours. For example, if you decided to have a snooze on a Saturday afternoon, whether you had slept for a restorative half-hour or for a dislocating six hours was impossible to tell upon waking. No lengthening shadows could whisper that evening was drawing on; no chorus of blackbirds would herald the dawn. Time stood still in the silent, unchanging light or dark while you slept; and only the scheduled news bulletin or music program on the Armed Forces Radio could convince you otherwise. Your watch could tell you the hour from one to twelve; but it was a dumb instrument, unable to declare whether it was AM or PM, whether you had missed dinner or were late for breakfast.

My memory flashes me back to a typical Saturday lunch, the mess hall buzzing with the week's-end relief. Stomach full, the post-prandial lethargy settled upon me. Saturday was our precious half-day off; and on that particular one, all my personal chores were satisfyingly out of the way. The siesta mood came upon me with the force of a command. So, I quietly made my way back to my quarters, moving with deliberate inconspicuousness through the corridors so that no well-meaning colleague would draw me into a conversation that might break the spell. It was so nice to finally snuggle down under the coarse wool blankets with the pure anticipation of a pleasant, uninterrupted two-hour escape. What a great, civilized way to spend a Saturday afternoo...

What?

I jolted awake, my heart hammering. The room was in the same flat, shadowless light as when I'd lain down. I grabbed up the alarm clock from the bedside locker. It certainly had not rung, despite the hour it showed. "Oh, shit! Damn it all." I was horrified, a cold dread spreading through my chest. "I must have forgotten to set the blasted thing." I knew I had been sleepy, but had I really slept for something like a day and a half? Was I now unbelievably, disgracefully late for my Monday morning shift? A wave of professional panic washed over me. I was out of bed like a cork from a champagne bottle, fumbling with my clothes, and rushed out towards my car in a blind, corrective frenzy.

As I hurtled through the foyer of my barracks, I pushed past a number of familiar faces that, in less trying circumstances, would have prompted a nod or a greeting. I barely had time to register their looks of surprise, which then melted into dawning understanding. A hand caught my arm, its grip firm and arresting, finally slowing my urgent, misguided enterprise.

"Jeff, hey, Jeff! It's only seven-thirty, buddy," said Niels Frederiksen, his voice a calm anchor in my storm.

"Yeah, I know that, Niels. And you know perfectly well I start at seven." I tried to pull away, my mind already racing through apologies I'd have to make.

"Seven-thirty, *Saturday evening*, you berk!"

"What? No! What? Seven-thirty, Saturday *evening*? No! What? What? Are you... ? Saturday *evening*?" I faltered and came to a full halt, my face a mask of utter disorientation. The world seemed to lurch. Only by dint of an intense, almost painful concentration was I able to drag back into my memory the simple, recent fact that I had decided to take a siesta on a Saturday *afternoon*. Slowly, like ice melting, the sheer biological unlikelihood of anyone sleeping a solid thirty-six hours straight began to penetrate my panic-addled consciousness. I think I must have gone deep red in the face then, though I am not a man given to easy blushing. Still, it was an immense act of will to believe that my colleagues were not engaged in an elaborate, cruel joke and that it really was, impossibly, still early on the same Saturday evening. I had slept a mere three and a half hours. The timeless light had stolen my sense of duration completely.

I feel the same hot embarrassment now, decades later, at having to confess that that Saturday afternoon was not an isolated incident. The Arctic light played the same trick on me more than once. However, I at least have the cold comfort of knowing that I was far from alone in these temporal errors. Along with the physical hazards of cold, darkness, and blizzards, such *ex tempore* dislocations were a common psychic hazard of the job, and not a few of my compatriots succumbed in like fashion, waking in confusion to a world that refused to declare its time.

"The quicker the passage of time the better" could well have been the unspoken motto of the greater part of the civilian staff on the base, and probably of most of the military staff too. Though I can in no way speak authoritatively on behalf of the latter, I can say that for the Danish civilian staff, the speed with which their contracted time at Thule seemed to pass was a significant factor in their relative happiness, or at least, their lack of despair. I say this because, in most cases, these people were not there for adventure or scenery. They were there simply to earn a formidable, tax-free income away from the temptations to spend it; or to pay off stubborn debts; or some combination of these pragmatic motives. It was no holiday camp, but a lucrative exile.

Because the base enjoyed what could best be compared to diplomatic or embassy status under the bilateral agreements, that meant, for the Danish citizens working there, that after a qualifying period of at least two years, they enjoyed a largely tax-free income. Considering the extremely high marginal tax rates in Denmark at the time, this was a significant financial saving; it made working in that frozen isolation quite a bit more attractive than it might otherwise have appeared to a sane person. The Danish government acquiesced in this arrangement because it enabled the Danish company contracting with the United States government to be more cost-competitive and so reliably win the tender. It was a calculus of national interest.

The company for which I worked, and which employed virtually all the Danes present on the base, was rather inconsequently named the Danish Construction Corporation (DCC). In my time, very little in the way of new construction was going on. A more accurate name might have been the Danish Maintenance, Supply, and Operations Corporation, for that is essentially what we did there. The name reflected the founding optimism of the corporation's creators, who hoped the organization would expand its activities to construction projects elsewhere in the world. It did indeed eventually so expand, but not before it had lost its foundational contract with the United States government for its services at Thule.

By contracting out these support services to a private company, the United States government was enabled to free up its own military personnel for assignments of a more directly martial nature elsewhere, as well as to realize significant cost savings. It had been well established through experience that, because of different work ethics, employment conditions, and incentives, employing Danish civilians where possible on the base was both an economic and an efficient venture. We were reliable, skilled, and undemanding in ways the military bureaucracy appreciated.

The DCC employed some twelve hundred persons when I arrived on the base and had a sterling reputation there for excellent, no-nonsense service. The company's management style was Scandinavian: relaxed but not lax. It paid well and expected the best of its employees, who ranged across the spectrum from professionals—engineers, management staff, doctors—to laborers, firemen, tradesmen, cleaners, and kitchen hands.

On my first arrival, and for approximately my first two years on the base, my living conditions were similar to the majority. I had a small but adequate and comfortable room in one of the more basic, utilitarian barracks. An economy-class airfare to Copenhagen or to the nearest civilian entry point in North America, provided every nine months, was one of the standard perquisites; as was membership of the bustling NCO Club and entry to their dining halls, a social lifeline.

Later, in the post-crash period, I took up an appointment as executive officer in the company's head office on the base. There I was responsible for the secretariat, for the smooth flow of paperwork, and for liaising with the senior USAF officer responsible for the day-to-day management of relations between the DCC and the Air Force. It was a role that placed me at the nexus of the two cultures.

With my higher office, my material privileges were raised accordingly. As executive officer, and later as administrative superintendent, my entitlements included an airfare home every six months, coveted access to the quieter, better-appointed Officers' Club, and the services of a manservant—shared with eleven other senior executives. This invaluable man provided breakfast and lunch, kept our communal facilities in spotless condition, and cooked the meals for any official entertaining we were required to do, a touch of civilized order in the wilderness.

Through this intricate contracting arrangement, the Danish government also enjoyed a significant and steady influx of valuable American dollars into its national coffers, at a time of a high exchange rate and when the Danish economy required constant major infusions of foreign capital to drive its domestic activities and development programs.

So, if the Danish government allowed those Danes who worked at Thule certain lucrative pecuniary perquisites, it must be admitted that they had sound, hard-headed economic reasons for doing so. It was not that they loved us with a greater love than they had for the rest of the Danish population—their subsequent behaviour towards us having left no possible doubt on that painful score. It was that the contract with the US was a reliable little money-spinner, earning the state much-needed foreign currency. We were, in a sense, human exports, sent to the ice to earn our keep and the nation's.

* * * * * *

NO PERSON WAS accepted for employment at Thule without undergoing beforehand a rigorous and comprehensive medical and dental examination. It was the first and most non-negotiable gate.

Employment on the base required that each prospective employee gain a medical clearance stating unequivocally that he was free of any chronic illness or dental condition requiring ongoing or likely treatment. Moreover, these medical statements were not a one-time formality; they were updated every single time we went home to Denmark on leave. We even had to undergo extensive, regular dental checks while on leave, our respective dentists in Copenhagen or Aarhus being required to sign official forms clearing us of any issues before we were allowed to board the plane back to Thule. The system was designed to be hermetic.

All of which makes it not merely disingenuous, but an act of profound bad faith, for any authority to suggest that, at least up to 4:39 p.m. on Sunday, January 21, 1968, we who worked at Thule were in anything but the optimum of health for our ages. We were, by design, a population of the certified robust.

It was not only that the company and the USAF wished to have the healthiest people working for them, to extract the greatest physical and mental return from their human investment, but also a stark necessity: the medical facilities available on the base, while excellent, were not of the kind equipped to care for chronic or long-term conditions. They were for trauma and acute illness.

Not that those facilities and their staff were not of the highest order and capable of the most professional emergency operations: they were. It was simply that the hospital on the base had to be dedicated to the specialized, often trauma-related tasks that might be required at a moment's notice in a very isolated and threatening environment. It was a forward medical post.

Whilst better equipped, better staffed, and certainly less frantically busy than a M.A.S.H. unit, its essential purpose was nonetheless much the same. Between emergencies, life could be pretty boring, even sterile, for the highly-trained medical staff; nothing greater than prescribing for a common cold or a bout of diarrhoea, day after monotonous day, for months at a time. So, there was a grim, professional kind of rejoicing amongst them when, during one summer resupply period, a Danish laborer fell into the deep cargo hold of a ship and suffered serious, complex injuries. Here was a challenge worthy of their skills.

This dramatic incident occurred at one of the most historic and memorable moments of the century. Neil Armstrong was just negotiating his lunar module, the Eagle, down onto the dusty surface of the Mare Tranquilitatis. You must remember the moment: it was in all the papers and even made a spot on the television. I was listening to the crackling, suspenseful report of the event on the Armed Forces Radio, in a temporary hut on the weather-beaten pier, where a Victory ship was unloading its vital cargo of next year's supplies. I had to take other people's word for it later that Armstrong and Aldrin ever actually set foot on the lunar surface, as I became otherwise and urgently engaged at that critical moment due to the laborer's terrible fall. But I do know this: the laborer, after a frantic rescue, was in a coma for twenty-four hours. His struggle was our immediate, human moon landing.

At a later time, another Danish employee, a welder, unfortunately suffered severe internal bleeding from an ulcer and, despite three major, desperate operations over the following forty-eight hours in that same small hospital, died. However, there was no professional rejoicing then, despite the break in boredom the tragic event provided. Only a somber silence.

To have a death in the hospital came as quite a shock to the community because the nature of Thule's setup—its very high health-entry requirements—made the American military hospital staffs' assignments there a peculiar mixture of boredom, paid vacation, and professional limbo. There just was not enough for them to do in the ordinary, grinding course of the day because their charges were, by strict selection, ordinarily so damned healthy.

Consequently, as one of the pre-employment conditions was a thorough medical clearance, any person who was eventually allowed to travel to Thule to work there was in peak health and could be said to belong statistically to the most healthy portion of the human population. The fact that I once belonged so firmly to that robust portion of humanity does not correspond in the slightest with the eroded state of my health at this time. Therefore, logic insists something must have intervened to set in motion the cellular deterioration I have experienced since. Something extrinsic. Something must have happened on that ice.

BESIDES THE STRANGE, psychological oscillating effects of contraction and dilation on the subjective passage of time during the dark season, as I at least perceived it, there were the very immediate, material effects of the extreme cold on the body. Even to go quite short distances in the minus forty-degree air was a sharp, painful experience, a negotiation with an enemy.

While all personnel were issued with heavy, goose-down protective parkas and special, bulky arctic pants, because it was such a hassle to get into the full ensemble for only a short walk, it was customary to do without the pants and just throw on the parka over regular trousers. Consequently, a brisk walk from my quarters to the NCO Club or to the Post Office meant steadily losing the feeling in my legs, a creeping numbness from the knees down. Once inside again, as the frozen nerve endings quickened in the sudden heat, the feeling would return to my limbs with an almost unbearable, fiery rush. It felt like having thousands of hot, sharp needles pushed simultaneously into the flesh. In effect, it was a minor, repeated form of frostbite, the severity of the tingling agony depending solely on how long one had been exposed.

Because of the ever-present, deceptive dangers of the winter cold, very specific, emphatic instructions were always issued to new personnel and visitors: should they be venturing out on foot, under no circumstances should they leave the cleared, gravel-packed paths that linked the buildings like a nervous system. To step off into the drifted snow could mean disappearing into a hidden trench, or simply becoming disoriented and lost within meters of safety.

Unfortunately, one American civilian visitor, a consultant who thought his Texan hardiness made him an exception, was to learn the wisdom of those instructions the hardest way. On his way back to his quarters after a particularly convivial party, he thought he could cheat the cold by leaving the winding pathway and cutting directly across a large, dark vacant space between buildings, reasoning he'd be out in the murderous air a shorter time. He slipped on an unseen patch of ice under the gravel, falling heavily and knocking himself semi-conscious. Only by extreme luck was his absence noted and a search mounted; he was found a few hours later, nearly frozen into a statue. Although he did eventually pull through after intensive care, he paid a terrible price: he lost both ears, part of his nose, and several fingers and toes to the relentless frostbite. The cold took its tribute in flesh.

For those without their own vehicle, a free transit van service for getting to and from work was provided, a heated metal cocoon shuttling through the white darkness.

Later on in my career at Thule, one of the tangible perks of rank was the assignment of a car. I was particularly privileged in that I had the use of one of only three civilian Volkswagens on the entire base: everyone else drove utilitarian US military vehicles—jeeps, trucks, and snowcats. But even having a car, winter travel could still be quite an ordeal unless the vehicle's heating systems were working at full capacity. To this end, every parking space outside every building was equipped with a special, heavy-duty electrical cord socket; via these, a vehicle's block heater and interior heater could be kept running all night, preventing the radiator from freezing solid within minutes and keeping the engine oil from congealing into syrup. Without this simple precaution, the car would be so profoundly cold as to make getting into it a genuinely painful experience. Even through the arctic protective gear, putting your rear end onto a car seat that had been at -40°F for ten hours was a numbing, deeply unpleasant shock, one that made you instantly mindful of the future health of your nether limbs. Then there was the perpetual detail of every exhaled breath creating an impenetrable, instant frost on the inside of the windscreen, so that you had to drive the kilometer or so to work at a walking pace, steering with one hand and vigorously rubbing off the freshly forming frost at each moment with the opposite forearm, a ridiculous and precarious dance.

Another, more pleasant reason for my personal preference for the daylight season over the dark was that in the permanent light, you could see the arctic foxes! These cunning little fellows, with their perpetual, knowing grins and gorgeous cream-colored brushes of tails, were quite delightful to observe from a distance—but for the rabies with which they were commonly infected and which they would readily pass on to anyone careless enough to reach out an unwary hand to them. The rule was strict: if you were bitten or even scratched by one, it was imperative to get the military police to track and shoot the creature immediately, and have its head packed in ice and sent back to a lab in the States for analysis. It was a surreal but deadly serious procedure.

Between every couple of buildings on the base were set large, metal dumpsters where we disposed of our garbage. One afternoon (as determined by social time, not the sun) in the deep dark season, I had skipped outside briefly to empty my small garbage bin into the communal dumpster. In the eerie gloom, faintly lit by a distant security lamp, I made out a lighter, moving shape, sort of hovering there by the dumpster as if lying in wait. A fox! It turned its head, eyes catching the light. It made a sudden, confident move towards me, the cheeky critter, so I dropped my precious cargo of tins and papers and took off for the door. It was like something out of a slapstick cartoon: this desperate figure, arms beating and legs revolving, shooting up the wooden steps to my building, pursued by a luminescent, snapping ball of vengeance. I turned only at the last second to slam the heavy outer door shut on the slithy beast's pointed snout. I drew a deep, shuddering breath of relief in the sudden warmth of the stairwell and made my shaky way to my quarters for a restorative shot of Danish courage: schnapps.

"Whatever else he may have had in mind," I said to no one in particular, refilling my small shot glass, "that fox wasn't out for a kiss and a cuddle!"

My friend Niels, who was visiting, jumped up from his seat, intrigued. "I'll have a look," he said, and went to the window to investigate. He came back a minute later, shivering and rubbing the life back into his limbs.

"No sign of the little beggar," he reported, helping himself generously to the schnapps bottle.

"No, but he'll be back," said Rasmus Lau with a knowing nod. Rasmus was an electrician who assisted in the operation and maintenance of the enormous, vital heating system for the entire base. He was short, sturdy, and moved with a deliberate, powerful lumber rather than a walk, not unlike the character Urko from 'The Planet of the Apes.' Rasmus had a dark, cynical streak in him that was best in evidence in the sly, sideways smiles he would bestow on anyone over five foot two in height. Niels was the other side of six foot and enjoyed the open, innocent wonder of a child even at twenty-six years of age. Somehow, these two opposites were firm friends without ever giving the impression of being a staged comedy double act.

"You know," Rasmus went on, settling back into his chair with a conspiratorial air. "I hate the little bastards, but they can do you a favour now and then." He laughed quietly at his own malicious train of thought.

"What are you getting at, you dark little troll?" asked Niels with a big, confused smile breaking over his good-natured features.

"Oh, I just heard a story last night about three of the new arrivals, you know, those young airmen that just flew in from Plattsburgh on Friday." He stopped and laughed again, shaking his head in disbelief. "God, I don't know what they thought they were up to. A masterclass in stupidity."

"What happened?" I asked, joining in his laughter in anticipation of the tale.

"Just incredible! Apparently, after a few drinks, the three of them managed to entice a fox right into their barracks room, to play with it; or, rather, to torment it, more like. I guess they thought it was a sort of friendly, albino terrier or something. So, there they are, in this cramped room, throwing shoes and boots at this snapping, panicked furball and chasing it in and out and around the beds and the lockers, just infuriating the bloody thing more with every second. Very unreasonably of the fox, under the circumstances, don't you think?"

"Oh, monstrously unreasonable!" the other two of us echoed in mock-emphatic agreement.

"Very unreasonably, the fox finally had enough. It leapt and bit one of them right on the wrist. Sank its teeth in good and proper."

"Ouch! Bloody hell!"

"Not just 'ouch, bloody hell', either," Rasmus continued, his eyes gleaming with the grim lesson. "Do you know anything about how rabies *has* to be treated once you suspect exposure?"

"No," I admitted. "Is there anything that you can actually do about it?"

"Oh, yeah," went on Rasmus, drawing out the suspense. "There is a treatment. But it's not too pleasant. In fact," he laughed with ghoulish delight, rubbing his hands together in dark enjoyment, "it's downright devilish! It's called the Pasteur treatment. I don't know why. Maybe Louis Pasteur came up with it? Except that I always thought Pasteur was a humanitarian, not a sadist. Anyway, it consists of a long series of injections—twenty-three of them, I'm told—administered straight into the abdominal wall, using a needle the size of a small javelin. No gentle sub-cutaneous stuff; deep into the muscle."

"Oh, yuck!" Niels made a horrified, wincing face, instinctively clutching his own stomach.

"And, here's the kicker," Rasmus said, leaning forward. "This wonderful and fun treatment has to be begun *immediately*. You can't afford to wait the days or weeks for the results of the tests on the fox's brain to see whether it really had rabies or not. By then, if it did, you're already dead. It's just too dangerous to wait. So, all three of those geniuses are having to go through the whole pin-cushion schmozzle, right now, on a 'just in case' basis."

"All three?" Niels gaped, his eyes wide. "Even the two who weren't bitten?"

"All three," Rasmus confirmed with grim satisfaction. "Just to be absolutely sure. One idiot bites, all idiots pay. Ha ha ha."

"Poor sods," I laughed, though it was more out of pained sympathy than genuine amusement. The image was too vivid, the punishment too perfectly fitting the crime of arrogance.

"Yeah. Well, they're sore, sorry and bloody stupid; but, at least they'll be alive," Rasmus concluded philosophically, refilling our three glasses. We toasted to that dubious wisdom and continued our soiree, the story adding another layer to the folklore of the place.

For several weeks after my own dumpster encounter, I was extra careful, almost comically cautious, to inspect the surrounding shadows for any sign of my non-amorous admirer whenever I ventured outside, even at high noon in the summer light.

The final, and perhaps purest, reason for my preference of the daylight season over the dark was that in the relentless, clarifying light, the stark, serene, almost abstract beauty of the place was fully on display: the snow a blinding white, the glacial ice a fleshy blue, the open leads in the fjord a blackish blue deeper than the sky.

Yet the dark season has its own severe, unearthly beauty. In the winter darkness, the intense cold freezes the very sea, locking the towering icebergs in the fjord into a still, arrested plain. Whenever there was a party in progress during the Dark Season, it became a bit of a tradition, a dare, to ask one of our junior staff with a vehicle to drive carefully out onto the thick ocean ice to retrieve ice for our drinks directly from the stranded icebergs. The ice so chipped off was millennia old, unbelievably pure, and full of tiny, glittering bubbles of ancient air trapped within the snow as it fell on the central ice cap many hundreds or even thousands of years ago. It also lasted fantastically longer in a glass than anything that ever came out of a modern freezer, cracking and fizzing with a prehistoric vitality.

I recall that on the Fourth of July celebration in 1969, the bartender at the Officers' Club made a show of offering drinks with ice that, he announced with theatrical gravity, had last been exposed to the atmosphere in the year 1776. A typically American touch of patriotism-tinged drama, linking the nation's birth to the ancient ice. We drank to that, the paradox not lost on us.

It occurs to me now, bitterly, that if in two hundred years' time, some future explorer draws a core sample from the ice that fell as snow in January of 1968, it might more appropriately be used to cool a Black Russian than bourbon or schnapps. If, that is, it can cool anything at all, given how metaphorically—and literally—hot it will still be with the plutonium we seeded into it. The thought extinguishes the whimsy.

But under the unimpeded, circling sun of the north, the legendary clarity of the air annihilates normal perspective and gives distant sights that uncanny quality of nearness that belongs more to our dreaming worlds than to waking reality. The inducement is so strong that you feel compelled to reach out a hand, as if you could touch the far peaks of Saunders Island or the distant, sculpted blue cliffs of a drifting iceberg miles out in the fjord.

I can see the dream now, as clear as yesterday. The ice takes on colours not of cold, but of an impossible warmth: the fleshy pink of a newborn, the deep aquamarine of a tropical lagoon, the pure, blinding white of creation itself. Sometimes the glare from the absolute, overwhelming purity of sun on snow and ice seems to be the blinding, untouchable glory of the Creator Himself, a visual symphony of light.

So, whether viewing the world from the rocky prominence dominated by the silent, staring faces of the BMEWS radar, looking down over the steel-blue fjord into which several glaciers calved their fragmentary litter in the form of drifting cathedrals of ice, or from the deck of a small boat on an ocean bluer than any sky, suffering the brotherly, dwarfing protection of the sheer white cliffs of a grounded iceberg, the symphonic modulations of colour and texture that the eye receives invite the imagination to enjoy a sector of the Creator's activities wherein free rein is given to sheer, exuberant, scale-less artistry, unencumbered by the least hint of usefulness to mankind. Unless, of course, with me you account the uplifting, near-spiritual, therapeutic effect of these sights as among the most useful things possible for the completion of the human soul.

Not that we so often paused, in the daily grind, to consciously see such visions then. Beauty was a backdrop to work.

I remember one occasion, on a mid-summer night so clear it felt like day, 'round the midnight hour when the sun hung low but bright. A handful of the senior DCC managers—Niels, Rasmus, Valther Larsen, Gert Jensen and myself among them—borrowed a small USAF landing craft for a unofficial jaunt out onto the still waters of Wolstenholme Fjord. It was to be a floating drinking party; so we were well supplied with cold beer, glasses, and sandwiches; the very icebergs we encountered on our journey provided the ice for our drinks. Thus, if ice were needed at any moment, we simply pulled the landing craft up against a small, stable berg, lowered its front ramp, a volunteer would walk out onto the living ice and simply scrape off a bucketful of crystalline, ancient shards.

Our terminus, our cathedral, was the glacier itself at the head of the fjord, the mother of all the icebergs therein. This absolutely enormous, sheer wall of ice, whose occasional rending explosions and deep, grinding groans were the delivery pangs of her iceberg children, formed the silent, awe-inspiring backdrop to our simple, out-of-hours carousal. We fell quiet in its presence.

Even slightly tipsy Danes were hushed and awestruck by the glacier's face: a pure, towering white, flecked and variegated with all the impossible shades of deep green and electric blue and, most mysteriously, a soft, fleshy pink. The pink was the colour at which I never tired of wondering, it was so unexpected, so warm, so seemingly alive. Beside the soft, welcoming hue of that ancient ice, the pink of the drapes over the window in my study now is as a weak street light is to the full aurora. I could never work out what mineral trace or trick of light produced the pink's origin, nor how frozen water could wear such a human, vulnerable aspect.

I ran across one of the unexpected, tiny delights of the Arctic spring quite by accident on my way to Dundas village during my first summer at the base. The vegetative covering on Greenland's coarse, mountainous sides, where the snow and ice retreats a grudging few inches during the precious daylight months, is virtually non-existent. The bare, rubble-strewn hills can look as blasted and vacant as the craters on the moon. However, as I drove over the pass of North Mountain one late April day, my eye caught a fragmented, secret carpet of tiny, brilliant yellow flowers—Arctic poppies—sheltering here and there in the lee of rocks and south-facing escarpments, clutching life from the thin soil. I was so unexpectedly moved by Mother Nature's valiant, almost defiant attempt at beautifying even this inhospitable corner of the globe, that I stopped the car and picked a small, careful handful of the minuscule, perfect blooms. I pressed them in a book and sent them back to my mother in Esbjerg. She, understanding the sentiment, had them lovingly dried and framed under glass, and they now hang in my home in Melbourne as a fragile souvenir of a stark beauty I am one of the privileged few ever to have witnessed.

Their brief, fierce glory is long gone from the ice: the dead flowers in the frame are poor, faded papery mementos, mere spurs to the living memory: no vital colours remain, no sap. They no longer radiate the startling, hopeful beauty that prompted me to stop and pick them—a beauty that only my memory can now revive. They have followed, perfectly, the natural, comforting round of time, of life and death, of ends and beginnings.

How utterly unlike the radiant, malignant persistence of the poisonous wastes from HOBO 28's deathless and unfading cargo they seem. How unlike the nuclear poison that breaks that sacred cycle. So, not only can I recreate the flower's beauty in the memory, but that same radioactive waste now, were I next to it, would be just as it was then: no decay, no end; just a terrible, silent continuing. Like memory itself, this man-made stuff makes a mockery of the natural passage of time: it compresses eons, annihilates chronology, makes the past permanently, dangerously present. And even when my memory is gone, when my name is dust, it will still be there, as unthinking, uncaring and amnesiac as it is today. But so long as my memory persists, I die a little every day in its invisible, everlasting presence..

* * * * * *

THE ICE-CAP THAT disguises the fact that Greenland is really a series of islands begins only a short, forbidding distance from the base. It is a vast, silent, white presence, a frozen ocean of its own. At the foot of this colossal, creeping cliff of ice that rises uninterruptedly into the mysterious interior, a lonely supply camp was set up. This camp served as the staging point for the remarkable trains that moved supplies to a place called Cape Century—a name that sounded like science fiction.

Constructed some one hundred miles or so in from the precarious edge of the ice-cap, Cape Century was a United States military township literally carved deep into the living ice itself. It housed a population of about three hundred US servicemen and scientists in a world of perpetual, glowing blue twilight. The trains that supplied this surreal installation did not run on rails, but on gigantic, hollow wheels of such a diameter that it was possible for a man to stand upright inside their rims without stooping. These massive, balloon-like tires were essential for safely negotiating the hidden, deadly crevasses that fissured the ice-cap as the laden trains trundled their slow, precarious journey across the blinding white void to the ice town.

Everything at Cape Century, which included a small, humming nuclear power plant buried deep for safety, was built directly into the ice. Even the chapel there, and its quiet decorations of images drawn from the Scriptures, was meticulously carved and sculpted out of the living blue ice walls—a cathedral of transient permanence.

To stand on the surface of the ice-cap itself and to look down into the pure, translucent, fathomless blue under one's insulated boots was to experience a profound temporal vertigo. It was to look directly into the deep past and to lose all scholarly objectivity about it. There, under your feet, was ice that fell as snow while Napoleon gave the Parisians "a whiff of grapeshot." A little deeper, and the ice contained air bubbles trapped within snow that fell simultaneously with the rain that pattered outside a Scottish cave as Robert the Bruce contemplated perseverance in a spider's web. Deeper still lay ice compressed from snow that shared a contemporaneous existence with Nebuchadnezzar as he demolished a troublesome city in the eastern Mediterranean and led its people off to lament by the waters of Babylon. The history of mankind was but a thin, recent layer upon this deep frozen time.

All in all, the experience leaves an impression as deep and as varied in colour and texture as the ice itself—a feeling of profound insignificance and awe before the patient, crushing weight of geological time.

* * * * * *

THE BUILDINGS AT Thule were of a curious, almost makeshift construction, born of necessity rather than aesthetics. The major constraint on the styles of architecture used there, after the obvious one of military economy (it is a military organisation after all, not a spendthrift millionaire's winter chalet), was the permafrost. The ground is permanently frozen solid to a depth of approximately five thousand feet, with only the uppermost few feet—the "active layer"—being subject to the grudging spring thaw. This presented less a problem of not being able to excavate foundations, than a critical problem of avoiding having the buildings capsize, tilt, and sink like drunken ships with the approach of each seasonal thaw that turned the active layer into unstable slurry.

The ingenious solution adopted at Thule was to build everything above the ground. *Everything*: so not only were the buildings constructed so as to sit high on concrete or steel frames, but the frames themselves also sat on broad, heavy footings that rested *upon* the ground rather than being set into it. It gave the base a stilted, provisional look, as if it were merely visiting and could pack up and leave at any moment. During winter, storms of ferocious intensity would come roaring in off the ice-cap and try to literally blow the base out onto the frozen sea. So, the buildings needed to be fixed most securely to their elevated foundations to resist wind speeds of 160 miles per hour and beyond. Not to mention the sudden, hammering gusts that could snap a telephone pole.

Everything means everything: the immense, vital heating system, which was required to keep us alive for the next ten minutes, and the next ten minutes after that, was also built entirely above ground. The large, heavily insulated pipes, wrapped in thick aluminum cladding, ran everywhere around the base like a sprawling, above-ground circulatory system, crossing the roadways by lifting themselves into clumsy, unceremonial arches. The look of the base as a result was quite odd, not to say less than beautiful, though after a while custom bred a kind of indifference and you got used to its industrial ungainliness. From the air, though, the parallel lines of pipes running busily in straight lines and making dramatic, right-angled corners around the square, uninspired blocks of buildings, gave the base an uncanny resemblance to a giant, overgrown electronic circuit board laid upon the snow.

The heating pipes connected into every building, providing very effective ducted heating; although, as always seems to be the paradoxical case in cold climates, the buildings were generally overheated to the point of dryness. I suppose that, as a psychological barrier against the overwhelming cold outside, the thicker and hotter that interior barrier, the better.

The buildings themselves were constructed of a highly flammable, lightweight metallic substance—prefabricated panels. It was difficult not to maintain a continuous, low-level awareness that, in the event of one catching fire, the whole structure would be gone in a matter of minutes, a raging inferno fed by the howling wind. This grim reality was demonstrated to us graphically in a number of the many fire-drills and safety refreshers we underwent, complete with alarming films.

By the time I had arrived on the base in June 1966, the base was already operating on a somewhat diminished, scaled-back basis. Having been constructed in a frenzy of Cold War urgency for a population of around fifteen thousand, it had by that year a resident population of only about three thousand personnel. So, with the population significantly diminished—a reflection of its lesser tactical importance in the age of ICBMs—some of the unused, surplus buildings were designated for live-fire practice. Not many were sacrificed this way, as they were expensive assets; and it was never known for sure that they might not be needed again in a future crisis. But, it was a powerful, visceral rebuttal of any complacency to watch a building exactly like the one you lived in disappear, hopelessly inflamed, in less time than it took to smoke a cigarette. The lesson was seared into us alongside the melting snow.

So, it can be imagined that the most feared scenario for the fire crew—and for all of us— would be a major fire during a peak winter storm, compounded by a failure of the heating system. Which was precisely the orchestration of disasters that did occur one Easter Saturday in 1969. One of those severe storms was whipping the base unmercifully when, simultaneously, the base's heating plant failed *and* the building that housed the library, gymnasium, and bowling alley—a long, low structure over 250 yards in length—burst into flames. Cinders and burning fragments of the lightweight building were whipped willi-nilli about the base by the 120 MPH gusts in a surreal inferno of fire and ice, creating no little danger of other buildings, connected by flying embers, suffering the same fate.

The power of the wind itself was such that it would physically blow a man off his feet. It was shaking the buildings of the base like a locomotive passing at top speed. And out into this freezing, screaming hurricane went Marius Schmidt and his team of firefighters. It was a call to duty that bordered on the suicidal.

Marius, with Joergen Rasmussen, Erik Pistol, and a number of other firemen, manoeuvred one of the towering, three-yard-high firefighting vehicles out of the relative shelter of the fire station and into the buffeting gale. Once the vehicle was clear of the station, gusts hitting it broadside caused the massive machine to shudder and almost stall. The building afire was about 750 yards away. Just 150 yards out, the blowing snow and ice had settled to a thickness of nearly two inches on the windscreen, which rendered visibility a fine theoretical concept but a daydream in reality. The raised gravel road they were inching along had precipitous, unseen drops on either side into drainage ditches, which transformed the possibility of running the huge machine off the edge and overturning it into a certain and present danger.

Marius sat sullenly a moment in the commander's seat, chewing grimly through the stem of his unlit pipe, staring at the white blankness before them.

"Well? What are we going to do now?" asked Joergen, sitting beside him and staring at the obscured windscreen like a perplexed, oversized arctic teddy bear.

"Someone's gonna have to get out and guide the truck through," Marius munched around the pipe stem, his voice calm.

"Yeah, but who?" Joergen looked over at Marius and caught him smiling a stiff, determined smile directly at him. "Oh, no! No! Not fair. It's my turn to drive."

"Mr. Rasmussen. Good man. Thank you for volunteering. Get out of the vehicle. And you too, Mr. Pistol. We need two guides, one for each front corner."

Muttering Danish oaths to themselves about the injustice of rank, the two indicated gentlemen buttoned up, pulled their goggles down, and alighted into the shrieking maelstrom. They were securely tied by strong ropes to the front bumper of the vehicle with enough slack so they could walk a few feet ahead, leaning into the wind, and guide it at a snail's pace the remainder of the distance to the still-burning building, which was only vaguely visible as a dull orange glow through the swirling curtains of snow and ice and black smoke.

Of the four fire engines that set out from the station that day, only three eventually arrived at the fire. The fourth suffered a crippling mishap about a hundred yards from the station. One of the fire fighters found that his window would not wind up; he had wound it down to stick his head out to assist in guiding the truck out of the bay. The pressure of the storm was such that it was forcing the fine, powdered snow into the vehicle through the open window, and the cabin was slowly, inexorably filling up like an hourglass. The firemen were forced to abandon ship. In order to cover the mere hundred yards back to the station safely, they tied the loose ends of their own fire hoses around their waists as lifelines, forming a human chain. Thus they all managed to crawl and stagger back to safety, though not before one of their number, overwhelmed by panic and disorientation, had to be physically assisted—and, when he became a danger to them all, rendered briefly unconscious—and thence dragged back to the fire station.

By which time, Marius and his crew had all but arrived at the scene of the roaring fire.

Once there, having released the "slaves from their bondage at the prow" and unwound the heavy, frozen hoses and trained them on the disintegrating building, the new challenge confronting them was how to put out a blazing fire without being themselves conducted by the hurricane-force wind directly into the heart of the flaming whirlwind.

The only solution, pitiful as it was, was to lie flat under the concrete framework of the building's elevated foundations, at the upwind end away from the worst of the flames, and direct the powerful streams of water upward, allowing the wind to carry the arc through the rapidly collapsing structure. Their impossible job was not made any easier by the later-discovered circumstance that the wooden floors of the gym and bowling alley had been treated over the years with a sealant containing nitroglycerin, a particularly volatile and flammable substance, you understand.

"Yes, I understand," Marius muttered, exasperated, to the universe at large. "Now that the impossibility factor has been raised by a further power of ten, I feel so much more relaxed. Well, at least the booster heater that keeps the water in the truck tanks from freezing into solid blocks is working fine. Small mercies."

The apparently vain attempts by the fire fighters, though not saving the building (which was gone in no time, leaving only the stark metal stairwell and a few twisted, heavy girders), at least minimised the spread of the firebrands and the hazard to the rest of the base. In particular, they saved the long row of buildings directly downwind of the gymnasium: a series of aircraft hangars, the base cafeteria, the chapel, the main dining hall with the adjacent base motor pool and vehicle maintenance facility, a series of barracks used for storage, the main supply warehouse, and the base laundry, to name but a few. It was a desperate, holding action against chaos.

As was the standard drill in a storm of this magnitude, all non-essential personnel had been ordered to remain in their quarters; which was where we all were, listening to the building groan and the wind scream, when we were informed by telephone (thankfully still operating) that a general emergency had been declared on account of the complicating factor of the fire *and* the additional, critical detail of the central heating power having failed. We were ordered to prepare for immediate evacuation to a designated shelter.

A new kind of cold—this one internal, of dread—set in. We all started the slow, awkward struggle into our full arctic survival gear: the heavy, insulated trousers, the thick, down-filled parka, the specially made mittens with wool liners, and finally the balaclava that left only narrow openings for the eyes and a small slit for the nose and mouth. We became anonymous, padded figures.

"This is just great!" I complained to the room at large, my voice muffled by the wool. "I bet there's a whole pack of those bloody vicious foxes out there too, just waiting to get their rabid fangs into us while we're crawling along."

"Don't worry, Jeff," Niels laughed, a hollow sound inside his mask. "We'll just grab 'em by the tails and heave 'em into the fire. A sacrifice to the wind gods."

"Great help that would be, if you get bit in the meantime and have to start those stomach needles before we even get to shelter."

"And, where the hell *are* we going to evacuate to?" mumbled Valther, his words barely intelligible through his balaclava as he adjusted his goggles.

"A very good question, Valther," I said, trying to sound practical. "I suppose the logical place would be to those warehouses to the right of the fire's path, down near the airport. Towards the bay. Maybe the motor pool garage, or else those hardened accommodation buildings just beyond ours here." I gestured vaguely with a thickly gloved arm to where I meant.

We all knew, with a cold certainty, that going out into that storm was a life-threatening exercise in itself, with the wind chill index approaching minus one hundred degrees Fahrenheit. In such conditions, a man dressed in regular clothing would be dead from exposure or cardiac shock in minutes. It meant we would literally have to crawl on hands and knees along the ground, to present the smallest profile to the wind and avoid being plucked up and hurled into the darkness.

Remembering that it is difficult, clumsy work to travel quickly on hands and knees while encased in what was effectively a heavy, immobilizing space suit did little to cheer our spirits. But, by then, even inside our building, with the heating off, the temperature was plummeting rapidly. Our breath fogged thickly in the air, a stark reminder that we would need to have our arctic protective gear on simply to survive *wherever* we were. The disturbing, invasive thought ran through my mind that even in full gear, we would only have a lifespan of a few hours in the iceboxes into which our barracks were being rapidly transformed.

I went back to my small room, my movements slow in the layers of clothing, trying to decide with a sudden, poignant urgency what I should take with me and what to leave behind forever. What would I save from the possible fire that might leap the gap and engulf my quarters? What precious, irreplaceable fragment of my life could I carry in my bulky, gloved hands as I crawled through a storm designed to kill me? The answer, realistically, was nothing. Nothing at all. However, driven by a deep human instinct, I packed together a few pathetic, typical things into a small duffel: passport, birth certificate, bank books, and a handful of prized photographs of family and Sophia. I made my way back to the common area, the bag feeling absurdly light against the weight of the situation.

Just as I arrived back, and much to our mutual, overwhelming relief, the crackling base intercom speaker above the door came to life with an announcement: the emergency situation was being downgraded, the fire was under control, and the heating plant crews were making progress. The immediate order to evacuate was stood down.

Even from under the balaclavas and goggles, the profound relief was evident in the eyes of us all. We began the slow, grateful process of unwrapping ourselves from our survival cocoons, the immediate terror receding, leaving behind a shaky aftermath of adrenaline.

However, from that day on, a subtle change occurred. Most of us kept a small, pre-packed bag in our rooms—a "grab bag"—containing our most important documents and whichever minor, personal keepsakes we felt, in our private calculus, deserved the saving. It was a mute acknowledgment of our vulnerability, a tiny hedge against the vast, indifferent power of the place.

* * * * * *

A NUCLEAR DISASTER of the kind that actually happened—the silent, invisible kind, the kind that contaminates rather than explodes—did not figure in any of our practiced scenarios or private fears. We quite simply failed to imagine it and so were blessedly unable to fear it. Our fears were elemental: fire, cold, wind, isolation. It took fifteen years of creeping illness and buried headlines for that particular, sophisticated fear to obtrude into my consciousness; where it has since set up a permanent advance camp in my mind and refuses, to this day, to be completely dislodged.

But I leap thus into an unknown future in an as yet unknown country. Back at Thule in that moment, the emergency over, the room warming slowly, I regained sufficient composure. The immediate storm had passed. The greater, slower storm was still gathering, unseen, in our very cells.

* * * * * *

EACH BARRACKS BUILDING, being of a standard, utilitarian military pattern, had around thirty identical, spartan rooms to it. However, when the civilian contractors arrived (*id est* us Danes and the four hundred or so US civilians who worked for companies like the Radio Corporation of America), the rigid layouts were quickly and creatively "personalised." Walls were knocked down, rooms were combined, common areas were fashioned from storage closets. Although such arrogation was strictly against US military regulations, the senior US military commanders on the ground were wise enough to realise that imposing such stringencies on skilled foreign civilians, who were not under military discipline, would poison morale and not strengthen working relations. So, they diplomatically demurred, turning a blind eye to our modifications.

In my own case, once I had attained a senior executive position with the DCC, I was moved out of the basic accommodation I described earlier and into a building informally set aside for people at my level. Each of us there had twice the space allocated to our subordinates in the regular barracks. In addition, we collectively removed walls here, there, and everywhere, and set up an extensive, comfortable lounge and entertainment area complete with sofas, a proper stereo system, a bar, and even some carpeting salvaged from somewhere. We were quite elaborately, even cosily, fitted out, quite in brazen opposition to US Air Force regulations. I suppose, in deference to our peculiar position as foreign nationals on what was, technically, our own country's soil, and for the sake of domestic peace and productivity, the authorities preferred to overlook these little misdemeanours. It was a pragmatic, unspoken bargain.

Over a period of time, using initiative and scrounged materials, we even managed to get a number of base-wide facilities upgraded, including several public buildings like the main dining hall. This benefited everyone, and the American enlisted men and junior officers definitely enjoyed the improvements, even when they went well beyond their expectations and understanding of life on a Spartan military base. It added a touch of unexpected comfort to their frozen tour.

In stark, almost absurd contrast to our adapted quarters were the severe and bare cells occupied by the more junior American military personnel. These men usually spent only one year on the base as part of their remote tour of duty. Even the officers' quarters, while better than the enlisted mens', were comparatively spartan and regulation beside our improvised luxury. It is hardly any wonder then that they all enjoyed visiting our much more agreeable, homely environment; which they did as often as invitations could be extended or fabricated. Our lounge became a quiet oasis for them.

The senior American officers were also perfectly aware of the appropriations and modifications that the Danes perpetrated: they regularly attended cocktail parties, dinners, and other functions held in these very quarters. Nor were they the only dignitaries to be entertained there: the base commander himself, as well as visiting generals and congressional staffers, enjoyed our Danish hospitality on several occasions. It is certain that they felt quite relaxed amid these more civilized, less regimented surroundings and were privately glad and even admiring of our audacity in bending the rules; though they dared not do so themselves in their own quarters. They would soon have found themselves arraigned before a military court for "misappropriation of government property" or some such charge.

New arrivals amongst the American military, especially young lieutenants full of regulation, often had some trouble coming to terms with, in the first place, the prominent presence and, secondly, the felt insubordination of the Danish civilians. We were quite disrespectful of the Gordian knots of rules, saluting protocols, and behavioral norms that necessarily govern military life, especially on a closed, isolated base like Thule. However, there was never anything effective to be done about it: we were determined to live as we felt we had every right to, not being soldiers ourselves; and they were free to chafe inwardly or to simply ignore us. The smarter, more adaptable ones soon saw the benefit of a precedent and, in their own small ways where possible, adopted a more relaxed mode of living, at least when off-duty.

Strangely enough, given the above-related circumstances of our comparative luxury and rule-bending, the day-to-day relations between the two sets of nationals were not always entirely harmonious. For some deep-seated cultural reason, many of the Americans seemed to operate from an unshakeable opinion that they represented an inherent elite. I could never quite get to the bottom of its source: whether it was the endemic American military 'World Policeman' syndrome, a residual frontier confidence, or just an exaggerated, unexamined sense of being representatives of a greater, more advanced civilisation than our small, ancient European kingdom.

I still wincingly recall the memory that we Danes were, on occasion, referred to behind our backs, but sometimes within earshot, as "White Niggers." I had, through travel and reading, quite a broad social and cultural understanding and so was immediately aware of the proffered insult's intended sting. But, its power to wound was oddly mitigated upon reflection that America's "Black Niggers" have always in Denmark been appreciated and celebrated as the propagators of two of the century's greatest and most fecund revolutions in art and sport: jazz and boxing—from Louis Armstrong to Miles Davis, from Jack Johnson to Muhammad Ali, just for beginners! The strains of Miles Davis's 'Flamenco Sketches' might come to me from the stereo in our lounge, and I would feel a defiant, proud kinship with the spirit and passion that finds its most direct expression in such unsullied, profound poetry. Their insult, in a way, complimented us by associating us with a culture of immense resilience and creativity.

The latent race issue reached a peculiar boiling point in the long, heated debate over whether the base should finally construct a swimming pool. It came as a real, sickening shock to my Danish system—raised in a relatively homogeneous and tolerant society—when I discovered through the grapevine that a significant number of American whites on base could not, or would not, contemplate using a pool that would also be used by black servicemen. Consequently, for years, there was no swimming facility at all, depriving everyone because of the prejudice of some.

One brilliant, endless summer's day, I was on a visit to Dundas village with Niels, Rasmus, Valther, and a great, red-faced Dane of Polish extraction by the name of Edvard Buganski. We were still without a pool on the base, and the subject arose. Edvard, a man of immense physicality and little patience, decided he was simply tired of not being able to have a proper swim. Right then and there, on the rocky shore, he stripped off his clothes and, with a roar, plunged into the frigid waters of the fjord among the drifting ice floes and bergs. That he did not immediately freeze to death or go into shock can only be put down to the fact that he was built like a barrel, quite a heavy man, and fairly well insulated from the cold by his generous subcutaneous padding. That, combined with the considerable number of courage-building drinks he had consumed prior, must have saved him from the awful, paralyzing cold of the fjord, whose waters never rise above thirty-two degrees Fahrenheit at any time of the year. He emerged moments later, bellowing with exhilaration and turning a spectacular shade of mottled pink, a Viking reclaiming his element.

Thankfully, as time moved into the late 60s, the more blatant racist attitude on base softened a little under pressure from changing times and pragmatic commanders. Finally, a pool for *all* personnel was constructed inside a converted, disused building close to the bay. It was a small, chlorinated victory for common sense over bigotry.

Besides which, in any informal competition for national or cultural superiority, it was needful for us Danes to mention only one loaded word: Vietnam. I do not intend to get into the political whys and wherefores of that unfortunate, divisive conflict here, except to say that its eventual outcome scarcely redounds to the everlasting glory of the Bald Eagle. It is now widely known that the US government was concealing the real human and moral cost of the war even from its own people. But what we can admit to now was strictly prohibited and roundly denied then. Several of the American personnel I met and befriended on the base had come directly from tours of duty in Vietnam, and all were privately, deeply resentful and disillusioned by what their country was really doing there. The body count they had themselves witnessed, they confessed over a beer in our lounge, bore little resemblance to the sanitized, optimistic figures published in *Stars and Stripes*.

This I took hard. It pained me because of a sincere belief I held, and which was constantly reinforced by official pronouncements: that the Americans are an honorable people. The cognitive dissonance was unsettling.

Meanwhile, back in the daily life of Thule, the American non-commissioned officer or civilian sometimes demonstrated his assumed cultural superiority in more absurd, less damaging ways. For instance, when informed by a wine-appreciating Dane that a particular vintage of red Bordeaux is not served chilled but at room temperature to release its bouquet, he might nod sagely, then proceed to hold the bottle under the hot water tap in the mess kitchen, "to get it to room temperature faster." If that were not enough to indicate his confidence in his own ways, his annual "wine sale" should suffice: each year when the new shipment of commissary wine arrived, he would sell off any old bottles left over at scratch prices. After all, the reasoning was clear and irrefutable to him: new is better! We Danes would scour these sales for overlooked bargains, shaking our heads with a mixture of pity and delight at our good fortune.

* * * * * *

THULE HAS a narrow, two-month window during which supply ships can force their way through to the base; even then, ice-breakers are always on tense standby, particularly for the very first and last, vulnerable ships of the season. Consequently, a profound and meticulous degree of long-range planning is required to ensure that such a huge, isolated organism can continue to operate smoothly and safely year-round. Every single item, every spare part and every luxury, has to be ordered with glacial foresight for the ships to haul it north.

Apart from the ancient ice chipped for our drinks and the frozen water melted for washing, everything must be shipped in: all food and consumables, detergents, wheels, tyres, new vehicles, fuel for cars and growling aircraft, Mars Bars, pencils, pocket knives—an endless, vital catalogue of existence.

In my time, we also ordered in sufficient supplies for the silent, outlying areas as well. We supplied the small, lonely Canadian stations in the vast vicinity, and Station Nord, the remote northernmost weather and radio station in the world. In those days, Station Nord was the most important, crackling communication link for all airliners tracing their arcs between Europe and Anchorage and on to Tokyo.

Station Nord lies even farther north than Thule, a deeper scratch on the map. It clings to the north-eastern coast of Greenland and is served only from Thule by air. The flight there and back posed its own unique, formidable challenge.

We must remember that the island of Greenland is essentially a stone atoll cradling a continent of ice. In the earlier days, the flights experienced treacherous problems with the radar, which tended rather alarmingly to ignore the immense ice-cap and register the plane's altitude with reference to the hidden ground itself. The actual ground lies at least five thousand feet below the surface of the ice over most of that frozen mass, a geographic trick which provided some heart-stopping show stoppers on more than one occasion when the aircrew was suddenly, terrifyingly apprised of their true altitude only when the propellers unscientifically took great, grating shavings of the ice.

White-outs of two distinct orders were common: those caused by excessive, blowing snow that erased the world; and those that resulted from eerie interference in the electrical equipment, a ghost in the machine caused by the nearby magnetic pole. Due to these perilous circumstances, the daring flight-route directly across the ice-cap was altered to one that followed the jagged coast all the laborious way round to Station Nord. A little lengthier, but safer and a heck of a lot more tranquil on the nerves.

The principal aircraft in use at that time was the great, grey C-141 Starlifter jet cargo plane. It was my first summer there. I was just hanging around in the dusty office adjacent to one of the hangars, having just gotten the scrawled signatures of the pilots on the documents relating to the safe storage of cargo for the flight. I suppose I was looking out hungrily, wistfully, at the giant, powerful plane. One of the pilots ambled over and, with a big, knowing smile, said, "Wanna join the cargo for a ride?"

"You mean, come with you? Up there? In the cargo hold?" I glanced at the stark, cloudless sky. "Doesn't get a little nippy?"

"Naah! She's heated. C'mon. They'll give us a great slap up nosh up at Station Nord. Real food."

So, I joined them on that bright, deceptively warm, sunshiny day, a typical one for that fleeting time of summer. I sat in the vast, echoing cargo hold right along with the huge, sloshing rubber bladders of fuel destined for the radio station, strapped into a webbed seat against the cold metal wall.

"Well, we'll go quick if we go," I joked, my voice small in the space. "I suppose I can trust you guys to get us there in one piece?"

"Well, heck!" answered the pilot, adopting a thick, theatrical hick Appalachian accent. "I jus' dunno. A-hope so. It's ma first time out, y'all know. Still figurin' which lever is the 'go' one."

But, I felt an absolute, solid faith in the crisp professionalism of the American crew who, I knew with certainty, would not have shifted that colossal aircraft an inch if they had detected any deficiency in it at all. I trusted them all the more, ironically, for having partied till that pale dawn with them in the smoky, boozy warmth of the Officers' Club.

These guys loved their work, especially the particular, precise challenge of flying in the mercurial Arctic; and the C-141 was a true delight to fly, they said, handling like a swallow despite its bulk, even where it offered little in terms of passenger comfort. But, after all, it was a military cargo plane, a workhorse, not a luxury passenger jet. Considering how magnificent and capable this aircraft was, I have often wondered why it was never adapted for civilian use.

I spent some precious time on the humming flight deck and was enabled to observe some of the superb, endless scenery of Greenland's northern coast that passed by beneath us like a slow, beautiful dream. Pure white snow, glaciers like frozen rivers, icebergs calved from nightmares, and bare, black rock may sound a trifle monotonous: however it was the hypnotic monotony of an exquisite delicacy of tone and subtle gradation of hue that kaleidoscopically played the eye's range back to a potent awe rather than to exhaustion.

The flight to Station Nord was quite a long, rumbling one. When we arrived, the crew had to take extra, gentle care in putting the heavy C-141 down on a runway quite blanketed in soft, treacherously obscuring snow. Once down with a final shudder, we were welcomed with genuinely open arms at one of the most isolated communities on earth by some of the most warmly hospitable people you can possibly imagine.

I enjoyed a most entertaining, boisterous interlude whilst the plane was being unloaded of its crucial cargo and the rubber bladders were being slowly emptied of their lifeblood fuel. As it happened, the weather started turning to the bad as we feasted; the light hardening, the wind picking up a keen edge; and we had to curtail our carousing and race the gathering weather home, else we risked being trapped in that whiteness for an indefinite, claustrophobic span of time.

Apart from the critical annual supply mission from Thule, Station Nord got very few other visitors. One other regular visitor, calling perhaps two or three times a year, was the legendary Danish military dog-sled patrol. This patrol, created during the Second World War in cooperation with a desperate United States initiative to wrest control of Greenland from the Nazis, travelled constantly along the brutal east coast of Greenland, a low-tech, flesh-and-blood equivalent of SAC's high-tech Airborne Alert.

Famed as being the longest and most lonely patrol on earth, and its jurisdiction suffering some of the harshest climatic conditions the planet can present to mankind, it is little wonder that it is a fiercely volunteer unit, manned by the toughest personnel from the Royal Danish Military Services. One of the precious breaks from solitude that these volunteers enjoyed was calling in at Station Nord. They would emerge like ghosts out of the screaming blizzards of snow and sleet with their packs of yapping, semi-feral and semi-starved huskies, bringing with them a gust of raw, human companionship in exchange for some stale news of the outside world.

The following morning, they would be whited-out again, swallowed whole as they receded anew into the howling blizzards of snow and sleet with their semi-feral and now semi-well-fed huskies for who knows how many more months of silent, lonely patrolling.

* * * * * *

"THE PRESIDENT'S ON the line for you, sir," said Sergeant Finkle quietly, his voice cutting the thick tension in the room.

"What line, goddammit?" General Burton responded brusquely, not looking up from the storm of papers on his desk.

"Three, sir. It's coded, scrambled and the highest level secure line we have, sir." Finkle paused. "It's a land line. The red one."

Finkle, General Burton's Aide-de-Camp, answered, never waivering in his impeccable military bearing, though feeling keenly the familiar, heated strength of the General's outbursts. A calm man by deep disposition, with the weary demeanour of a seasoned warrior who has faced not only the battlefield decisions associated with the preservation of life at the cost of lives, but also frequently enough in the past the volcano of Burton's spontaneous outbursts, the last few days have tried Finkle's soul to its core.

Evidently, Burton was feeling the crushing pressure. Despite forty years of command experience since Boot Camp, when he became a young platoon leader, occasionally even his iron resolve could weaken. This was profoundly one of those times.

With the Tet Offensive building horrific momentum in Vietnam and Russian subs God-knows-where snooping around in the dark Pacific; and now, to top it all, a Broken Arrow on the top of the world—he was spending more time talking in hushed, urgent tones to the President than to his own, forgotten wife.

Finkle, or the 'Fink' as he had been unimaginatively branded even before he had alighted from the bus that carried him to Boot Camp fifteen years before, nevertheless was not worried about his personal relationship with the General. It was a relationship born out of mutual, earned respect and ten years of shared, tough decision-making in shadowy rooms. Later Burton would wordlessly bring him a bitter coffee or offer him an early night off after leaving a deserted officers' mess; and that slight warmth would be apology enough. Burton, after all, breathed the rarified, thin atmosphere of the highest altitudes, where few of the comforting social amenities were observed closely.

"Yes, sir," General Burton responded into the heavy black phone as if the President was standing, grim-faced, next to him in the room.

The voice on the other end of the phone was clearly, unmistakably the President's, he thought, even as he remained ever suspicious of modern voice links that weren't preceeded by the ritualistic exchange of code words, as in combat.

"Chuck," the President began, the single word loaded with shared history, "We've been through some rough scrapes before, you and I. I want to know it straight. Can we cover our ass on this deal, once the dust has cleared, and still maintain present policy? McNamara's waivering on this twenty-four-hour-alert, Air-Force-in-the-air-at-all-times stuff. It's a damned expensive chess game. So I've got to know from you. You're in the firing line."

General Burton answered his old friend without ever breaking or crossing that invisible line between intimacy and rigid official etiquette which the President himself totally, characteristically ignored. "Frankly, sir, the best things in our favour are the other loud events going on in the world right now. If it weren't for them, we'd be facing one of the worst publicity situations yet. However, there is a brighter side to this screw-up: Railback. You probably remember him. He's a clean-up artist of the highest, coldest standard and has shown virtuosic versatility in similar… incidents in the past, all over the world. He's on site now and will be already getting to the nub of the problem."

"Oh. yeah. I remember him. Hard man. He's defused the political nastiness of a number of incidents in the Third World before this one."

"Greenland's not, er, actually Third World, sir."

"No? Fine! Well, what's his first impression? Does he think we're crucified?"

"Well, sir, if appearances mean anything, at first blush, it's a bad one. A real bad one. But he seems confident that we can damage-control it and keep the fallout within acceptable parameters."

"For Chrissake, Chuck. Cut the military jargon with me, won't you! Keep the canned responses for the media or whatever, OK! Give it to me from the hip. I've gotta know, especially if it gets leaked to the press. The simple question: Have we got live nukes up there that could go off, or not?"

"I beg your pardon, sir. But, I can assure you, sir, I'm not trying to gild the pill, but it's difficult at this early, chaotic stage to make any definitive statements. We're unsure just what went off, but we have had verified multiple explosions. Sir, Railback says the place is, well... black."

"Well, Goddammit, Chuck, its midwinter in the Arctic. Of course its black. I know that much." The President snapped, his temper as ill sounding as it was short. This incident in the middle of bloody nowhere could have fatal repercussions on his re-electability, and he felt the noose.

"Sir," the General interjected slowly and deliberately, the words falling like stones, "Railback meant the ice."

"Jesus!" The President was fully, utterly deflated, the breath leaving him. The implications spread like a stain.

"Sir, I wish to request full autonomy for Major Railback in this matter. His hands, completely."

"Whatever he wants, in that regard, he's got it. You have my authority. White House out."

"NORAD out."

General Burton stood motionless for a few long moments, the receiver cooling in his hand, as if he were interpreting Railback's stark description for the very first time. *The ice is black.*

Burton was not one of those who spent their leisure time tramping over the dazzling, sunlit heights of the Canadian Rockies or whizzing down the pristine slopes of Colorado; he was more likely to sling his rifle over his shoulder and go out to quietly challenge the hog-deer of his native Kentucky woods. But he did know that 'pristine' meant 'unspoiled' and that 'dazzling' suggested a blinding, reflective whiteness. Railback had said the ice was black. The very image was a blasphemy.

He was just forming the word 'black' silently with his lips when he heard from miles away the voice answer the ringing phone. "NORAD. Office of General Burton, sir."

"Give me the General." A sharp, impatient voice spilled out of the receiver.

"Sir, please identify," the Sergeant responded with practiced calm. "This is a secure line, encrypted only."

"I know that. Who the hell are you?" the voice demanded, crackling with static and authority.

"Sergeant Morton Benett Finkle III," the Sergeant stated, drawing out his full name with a quiet pride, as only Fink could.

"Great, a lifer. This is Railback. Zulu Zulu Seven. That satisfy you, Corporal?" Railback asked sardonically, the taunt clear over the miles of wire.

"That was *sergeant*, sir." Fink replied, unblinking.

"That was sergeant, *Corporal*." Railback taunted again, testing the wire, testing the man.

"Railback for you, General." Fink, unamused and unsurprised, handed the heavy phone to Burton.

"Major," Burton said into the receiver as if he would be happier, safer, if the conversation ended right there and then.

"General, sir," Railback said, probing for the mood, for the level of panic in the chair. "We've lost one of the point men." He was never one for dissembling bad news. Only made it worse, he believed. Sugar coated a bullet.

"Like, lost, as in, can't locate?" Burton asked, a thin strand of hope in his voice.

"No, sir. Lost, as in, dead. Definitely a 'cas.' Sir, this place is hot. Radioactive. Plutonium dust spread to the damn horizon. Geiger readings are off the scale, screaming. We're all suited up like ghosts, but these poor native bastards went in unprotected like it was just another day in a snowstorm. Dogs, sleds, the whole sad lot. And the dogs, Christ. They're dying. Two of them just up and died. Stone damned dead in the snow. I need containment, sir. I'm speaking of tight informational containment as well as for the physical contamination. I need delivery of as many lead-lined hot boxes as you can scare up. Have to be resealable. Plan on picking up half of Greenland and shipping it out to God-knows-where, sir."

The conversation paused, the silent satellite link humming with uncomfortable static before Burton finally mused, voice low, "God, Railback, anything upside? Any light?"

"Well, sir, we can sure control the media. There's only one frozen way in and out of here. No ticky, no fly. Almost no radio. And the natives; I don't think they have a clue about the severity, about what this poison is. They think it's a plane crash."

There followed the very hint of a pause, a calculated breath, before Railback delivered the next weight. "Sir, we have a clear reading on what appear to be one or more intact atomic devices under the ice. Deep."

"Good Lord," Burton whispered semi-reverently and semi-expletive-deleted, the pious and the profane crashing together.

Railback continued, clinical. "Readings are too small to be whales and too constant to be walruses or anything biological: they're stationary, metallic. We're continuing to sweep with hand-held sonar, but we're all but certain its the nukes. The upside, if that's them down there, well, they didn't ignite. Didn't cook off. How the hell we're going to get them out, I don't know. Crash trajectory must have forced them into the ice sideways like a bullet into flesh. There's no traceable entrance hole. The ice just closed up again after they'd passed through, healing over the wound. Definitely not rock formations: external readings are too damned symmetrical. Unless new data can rule out our present assumption, it's them. HOBO's precious cargo, or a grim part of it, anyway."

"So far, just the one casualty?" Burton asked, clinging to a number.

"This 'Broken Arrow' is far from over, sir," Railback said, his voice flat and final. "He won't be the last. This is Hiroshima without the people. A silent, white Hiroshima. So far, so good. Trouble is, we're gonna have to bring in people, more bodies, to clean the damn thing up, sir. And ASAP. Every hour this wind blows…"

"What's the progress on the Danish workers? The local contractors?"

"We can mobilise them within a few hours, if the weather holds out, sir. They're on standby, thinking it's construction."

"Alright, Railback. I have some upside for you. The ball's all yours. Run this like you did that final drill at the Naval Academy. Only, this time, for real. No fumbles."

"Aye aye, sir," said Railback, the old phrase feeling hollow.

"NORAD out."

"Thule out."

Autonomy, thought Railback, the cold air biting at his visor. *Just what I've always craved. But, on this one, it's pure autonomy to get my ass in a sling. No matter what I do, this thing can't go well. This has gotta go fast. The quicker the clean up, whatever the cost, monetary and human, the less the spillages from under the lid I'm gonna put on it. No pun intended. This is going to be a silent war, with casualties years from now. Bloodless battles we'll never see, never win. But, we can't just leave it the way it is. We can't.*

Suddenly, Railback barked, his voice cutting through the Arctic stillness, at the closest, shivering airman available. "Get me that Captain Whatsisname on the phone! Now!"

"Captain Burnett? Yes, sir," somebody replied hastily from behind a makeshift desk. "Right away, Major."

* * * * * *

BY THE END of which short, pleasant digression, we have arrived without incident back at Thule in our groaning C-141.

In comparison to the profound silence of Station Nord, Thule felt like a busy, dizzy metropolis. However, it is not a comparison that bears too close an investigation: the Arctic is warm in comparison to the depths of outer space. So, back we slipped into the giddy, artificial rounds of work, sleep, recreation, letter writing, listening to the crackling radio, watching faded films, doing communal laundry, eating and drinking. Because it is possible for even such a variety of activities to take on the monotonous appearance of routine, even, let it be said, of a benevolent prison routine, contact with the rest of the living world became a premium asset, craved and hoarded. This contact came in two precious varieties: communications, electronic, aerial and aqueous; and the rare, actual visitors.

The crucial two-month window was the season when the base also stocked up on vast lakes of aircraft fuel for the civilian airliners that served our island of industry. The United States government chartered planes that served the long, lonely sector between the base and Plattsburgh in upstate New York, operated at least weekly. There was also a precious fortnightly jet service between Thule and Copenhagen operated by Scandinavian Airlines; and, in addition, on the alternate weeks, a jet freight service operated from Denmark. At least every week, therefore, there was a tangible link with Denmark and North America—not counting the unscheduled cargo flights that rumbled in to serve us several times a week.

While the base had a closed-circuit television system, each building having a set and some of the more senior staff having one in their sparse rooms, its telecasts were limited to the popular American sit-coms and other series of the time, beamed in on tape delay. The television carried no news at all; so, we had to rely on the static-laden radio and on newspapers that arrived as historical documents. The radio transmission between the base and Europe in those days was frustratingly intermittent due to technical difficulties, at that date yet to be overcome, posed by the base's disorienting proximity to the North Pole.

An initial, subtle impact on many new arrivals was what I will call 'Information Starvation Syndrome' (ISS). ISS was almost indetectable to the untrained observer. However, its symptoms were a sort of voluntary, painful rationing of newspapers so that they would last out the two long weeks before the next editions arrived. We were always two weeks behind with the news, living in a recent past, and it required a stoic discipline not to voraciously consume all the papers at one sitting, which would leave the sufferer in an aching, wordless limbo for the rest of the fortnight till the next supplies became available. Thankfully, ISS proved itself to be a minor, ephemeral condition related more to the initial trauma of entering the life of isolation and detachment from the rest of the planet than a state indissolubly conjoined to the daily living in that state.

On the other hand, nearly everyone suffered a chronic, gnawing lack of letters in their scurvy diet of the soul. Each employee was issued with a small, private mailbox; and many of us would make it a ritual series of hopeful visits following each landing of an airplane from Europe or the United States, our boots crunching on the ice with a purpose.

It seems odd, now, in this age of noise, the immense value the written word had for us back then in our silent isolation, especially the word that came from our intimates. For now, this day, as I write, I am surrounded by a surfeit of words, a thorough debauch of information: the television bawls, the radio catterwauls and the junk mail piles up, unread, on my desk. None of these can catch my attention or hold the fragile promise of true happiness as did the briefest phone call or a dog-eared postcard from home received while at Thule.

It is to be remembered that Greenland, being an integral part of the Danish state, enjoyed, along with all the rest of the country, the same conditions for its postal service. This meant that Thule was considered a local post office; a simple, profound fact that meant letters to and from the base only required postage at the internal rate, tying us to the homeland with a tangible thread.

When, a little later, the Danish government changed the status of the base, no longer treating it on an equal footing with the rest of the kingdom, and the postage rates rose dramatically, this bureaucratic act was viewed as extremely hostile on the base and caused a deep, lasting resentment. By which may be deduced the quiet, profound degree of importance we placed on these fragile, personal contacts with the outside world we had left behind.

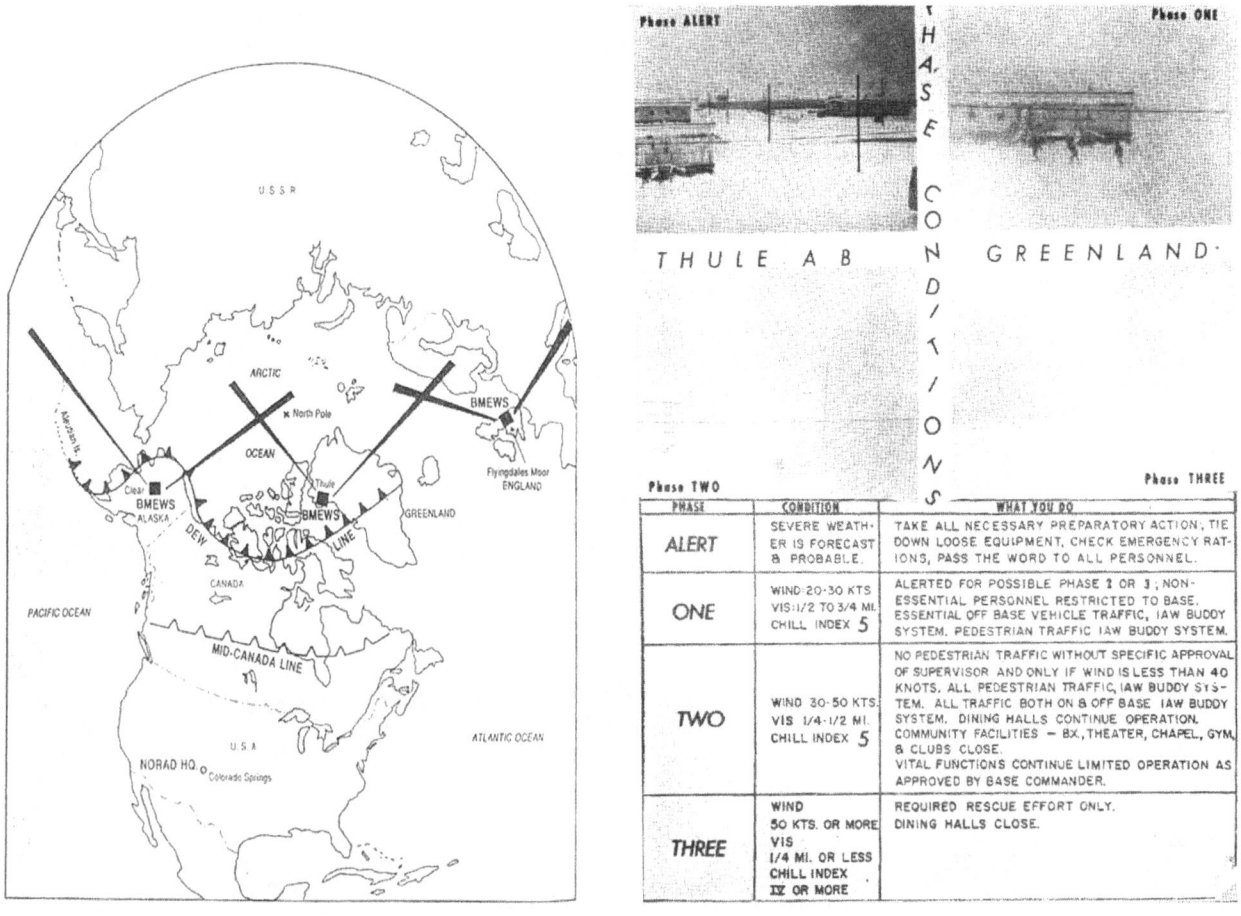

Chapter 6: Crested Ice

> Ibant obscuri sola sub nocte per umbram
>
> Perque domos Ditis vacua et inania regna
>
> (Darkling they went under the lonely night through the shadow
>
> And through the empty dwellings and insubstantial realms of Dis)
>
> *Aenead vi 268*   VIRGIL

AS TO VISITORS, we were quite privileged in the flow and quality of our guests. Obviously, I am not referring to the constant, uniformed ebb and flow of military personnel who were assigned to Thule in what must have seemed a sinecure beside the raw possibility of having their butts blown off in the steaming jungles of Vietnam. I am referring to the remarkable variety and quality of those who, for sundry reasons, were our occasional guests from the wider world.

For example, each year our sleepy hollow image was rudely and gloriously displaced when the United States Air Force held its major military exercises in the area. Thule was an excellent, unforgiving place for testing aircrews and equipment in a very hostile environment. So, the USAF would bring in shrieking phalanxes of jet fighters and the huge, ponderous C-135 tanker aircraft, capable of refuelling them in the thin, cold air; and the people that flew and serviced them would crowd onto the base, making it resemble Coney Island in August. Once installed, they would fly around the clock in the perpetual dark or endless light of the arctic winter.

Besides the training opportunities afforded by Thule, it also gave the Americans an excellent opportunity to remind the Russians, in no uncertain terms, of the existence of a large-capacity air base within coo-ee of their home territory. To a certain extent, it was the very boredom generated by life on the base that made it such an exciting prospect to bait the Russian Bear and risk the holocaust: to provoke that fear and rage in the Bear gave a sufficient adrenaline rush that far outweighed the trivial, abstract possibility of the exercises accidentally spiraling into nuclear hostilities.

High-tension electricity wires buzz less than the base did in the presence of such concentrated fire power and of some of the world's true Top Guns. These guys were, after all, operating the world's most advanced and sophisticated military machinery, and they carried a pretty inspiring, swaggering attitude toward their work and toward life in general.

Not that we harbored any illusions about their common sense, I must add with a wry shake of the head now. The crews were well known as a hard-drinking and hard-living lot. It was not unknown for them to spend the entire night in the smoky haze of the Officers' Club, drinking the venue dry. This manoeuvre was generally followed by a brief, stunned dip into the sheets; after which, despite being, by any normal standard, in no condition to operate even a toothbrush, they would take a heavy, reviving dose of pure oxygen to blast the fog from their systems for the workday ahead, and proceed out on by no means harmless missions at great speeds in great, powerful lumps of forged metal.

I remember one evening, Niels, Rasmus, Valther and I had driven out and sat by the gravel verge, not fifty yards from the end of the tarmac. The C-135 fuel tankers, converted Boeing 707 passenger liners, were, if the possibility could be imagined, even more thrillingly monstrous than the sleek jet fighters. They were used to refuel the fighters in mid-air, and one was taking off over our heads with a bone-shattering concussion of sound that vibrated in our teeth. Loaded down with many thousands of gallons of volatile JP4 jet fuel, it used every trembling inch of the runway and then some to heave its great weight into the thin air.

As it roared by us, we roared back in ineffectual, joyful sympathy. It was a rush in itself then to stroll, huddled together like penguins for warmth, to the very end of the runway, from where this mechanical albatross had just risen heavenward, and to examine the deep, scouring impressions left by its massive tyres in the soft, frozen earth that fringed the runway itself.

"Look!" I joked, pointing at the huge tyre marks that ran on for nearly twenty yards into the dirt beyond the paved strip, "Tracks! I thought I heard the soft, whispering call of the tiny migratory Yankee C-135 Bird."

"What?" shouted Rasmus directly into my ear, finishing off the job the aircraft's engines had begun. "I can't hear a thing you're saying."

"I shouted, 'Would you like another drink?'"

"Oh, I heard that," grinned Rasmus, and we returned, arm in arm for balance against the lingering roar in our ears, to our vehicle and thence to the warm, loud sanctuary of the NCO Club.

Niels was uncharacteristically solemn on the drive back. "The nerves they must have," he mused, "to push that huge aircraft, full of highly flammable fuel, along a runway, in the dark, not knowing how much more runway you have to play with. That is really pushing the outside of the envelope."

The fact that the take-offs of these aircraft, fighters and tankers alike, generated enough noise to make any Judas Priest fan think he was in headbanger's heaven, and that they were going on around the clock, hardly worried anyone on the base at all. We were too taken up with the visceral excitement of so much vibrant, dangerous life going on in what would otherwise be the most tedious, static time of year.

* * * * * *

WHEN, POST-CRASH, I was appointed to a senior executive position partly in acknowledgment of my contribution to the Crested Ice clean-up, it became one of my specific responsibilities to look after official visitors to the base. So, I got close to many of the remarkable guests we hosted over some five years. These included some very high-level American politicians (just below the President, in fact), a vast assortment of generals and admirals and whatnot in both the United States and the Danish military, and Danish politicians on earnest, fact-finding missions.

Memories are powerful presences. Those times at the absolute edge of human habitation are so vivid that I often feel I could reach out and caress them. I am not a nostalgic man; nor do I consider myself in any degree a royalist, but, before all the visitors we had, and supplying some of my fondest memories, come the Danish Royal Family. Members of the family were quite regular guests at Thule, including the now Queen of Denmark, Margrethe II, then heir to the throne; and her husband, Prince Henrik.

If, in certain sectors of the English-speaking world, royalty is falling somewhat into disrepute (the negative public perception in the United Kingdom of the dismal private lives of Charles and Diana and Andrew and Fergie; and the republican hullabaloo convulsing my new home, Australia), in Denmark things are quite, refreshingly different. I am not alone in finding the Danish Royals nothing less than genuinely charming. And the most charming of them all, in my experience at Thule, were the brother of the then King, Prince Knud, and his wife, Princess Karoline-Mathilde. They were real gems, genuinely compassionate and unpretentious. A couple you would quite happily mix with and talk to for hours. And the same can be said of their children and spouses.

Their visits generated something of a giddy, party atmosphere among the Danes. Just such an atmosphere that I suppose prevailed in the warmth and comfort of the ballrooms, bars, and staterooms on board an unsinkable ocean liner, while outside the waves beat equally against the ship's hull as they did against the unimaginable bulk of an undetected iceberg. But the merriment's abrupt end need not be felt before its time.

It was summer 1970, and one of the royal family's visits was in train. I was in charge of settling certain of the arrangements for the official reception. HRH Prince Knud was given into my personal charge for the evening.

Also present was the highest-ranking Danish military officer in Greenland, Rear Admiral Bjoern Olesen. The Rear Admiral was the nearest I have ever encountered to a living caricature of the aging seaman: very tall and thin and of a noble bearing and understated presence of authority. From the peaked cap of office down to the permanent, horizon-searching gaze, he was holus-bolus taken from *Boys' Own*. A caricature, yes, but a seemly and worthy one. He spoke not a word the entire evening.

Nor scarcely did HRH Knud. Although, his reticence was a species of royal articulation all its own.

"I have been given to understand that Your Royal Highness is under instructions from his doctors?" I enquired a little nervously of the formidable Knud.

"Hmph!" accompanied by an impatient and ambiguous nod, or was it a shake?, of the head put me entirely at my ease. Despite which dissipation of my anxiety, I broke into a minor sweat. On I went:

"I believe he is not to drink more than one beer at a sitting?"

"Hmph!" seemed to indicate both assent and an emphatic end to our extended and informative exchange of views on the Prince's health. Luckily, at that moment—for the Prince seemed intent on making his way over to the drinks counter in defiance of his medical advice and my will to curtail him—the bell rang for dinner.

It is not to be thought that our dinner parties, particularly in view of the sorts of guests we had on this occasion, were crudely got-up affairs. Quite the contrary. Our parties and functions were always planned well ahead and always with the degree of sumptuousness to which the guests would normally be accustomed. We would have special food items flown in from Europe: fresh seafood, venison, pork, crisp salad ingredients and so on; as well as lots and lots of fresh flowers to adorn the tables.

On this occasion, with the Prince and Princess present, we had ordered in even more flowers than usual. So the tables, as well as the reception areas and the Royals' own accommodation suites, were decked out in all the cheerful colour of late spring and high summer in any of Copenhagen's more delightful and well-tended public parks.

In nothing could we be faulted: the uniformly accoutred waiters, the crisp white tablecloths, discreet candelabra, correctly placed wine glasses, printed menus and calligraphed place cards, our best reserve silver cutlery; and, of course, the pièces de résistance, the fresh flowers enlivening it all. The sheer contrast of this sea of colours with the stark, monochrome environment outside was enough at times to make even the most hardened male officers pull up short in astonishment. One of my greatest quiet pleasures came from observing the surprise and delight that succeeded each other on the guests' faces when they entered the dining hall and were thoroughly, happily disappointed in their pessimistic expectations of a plain setting and a dull dinner. The preparations would have done the *Titanic* proud, while our blissful lack of awareness of the near future's bright gifts lent our little barque navigating the arctic darkness an additional, uncanny similitude to that fateful ship.

Although it was the case that the dinner guests were sometimes all and always nearly all males, the effect on these males in the almost exclusive company of males, many of whom had been on the base for a considerable period of time, of these vivid reminders of home and civilisation was quite powerful. Nor, among the staff who came time after time, was the effect lessened by familiarity. Rather the poignant poetry of the created environment was augmented manifold against the stark and cruel background of the obsidian `no-home' outside. I suppose in some ways our activities resembled the forbidden night-time soirees the inmates of boarding schools sometimes indulged in. Or, perhaps, the simile of a jailhouse festivity serves to draw the picture with greater, if sadder, precision.

And the food itself, on these special occasions, was always of superior quality and preparation. Usually we offered four courses: an entree, a light soup, followed by something like saddle of venison with Waldorf salad as a main; and sweets.

I confess to a certain abuse of power in relation to the main courses, in particular to the venison, which I would sneak onto the menu as often as I felt I could get away with it. For I was the person responsible for arranging all the details of these receptions; and, if my memory serves me rightly, I did indeed ensure that the menu always contained something that I particularly enjoyed myself. Being also in charge of compiling the guest lists and of settling the seating arrangements, I was in a position to induce and enjoy the degree of comfort or discomfort I believed to be the just deserts of whomsoever fell under my eye.

In order to succeed in this part of my job, it was necessary for me to know pretty well every person in a senior position on the base, which in itself was quite a task; and one on which I rather prided myself. Admittedly I seldom wielded this special power in a wanton manner, as is evidenced by the fact that the record shows that sauce bottles were never exchanged in anger at my tables.

My father was a man who made it his special duty to warn his children against the corrupting influence of power. I am sure it was his felt presence that drew me to use my power well, even in such constricted, peculiar circumstances.

In fact, I was accustomed to use my power for good rather than for evil. I earned some genuine appreciation from younger officers whom I would strategically seat beside high-ranking visitors. It was not unknown for them to seek my advice, their faces pale with anxiety, before being thrust into their first such social engagement with senior officers, generals, admirals, and royals.

My aplomb in handling the intractable Prince Knud will explain why I was so sought out.

"If Your Royal Highness would be so pleased as to take his seat here." I indicated Prince Knud's place. The waiter pushed in his chair for him. I took my own and, in some alarm, having taken a moment or two to settle, noted that the Prince was already being served his first, foaming beer.

"Hmph!" sounded a note of deep satisfaction this time. He looked at me squarely and said, "cheers," holding his half-emptied glass aloft.

"Er, cheers!" I echoed with a suddenly dry mouth and grabbed for my wine glass: which raising to my dried lips I found to be yet empty and which nevertheless in a panic I lay against my lips and tilted. I simultaneously felt three things: my face redden as no wine reached my lips; my dry lips stick well and truly to the edge of the glass; and Prince Knud's eyes harden on me in mild, regal amusement. I was all confusion till:

"Hmph, hmph, hmph" and a firm, friendly clap on the back restored all things, and I was able to unfix the glass and lower it to the table with a wry smile of relief. I looked around the table and the face of the Rear-Admiral caught my eye. He had looked up from his soup at me, I suppose, but it seemed his sight was fixed still on some distant horizon. The unworthy question briefly came to my mind, '*was his glass already empty?*'

Despite the comraderie that had sprung up between us on account of this shared absurdity, I warned the Prince that I took my duties seriously and, a little later, when I noticed him blithely about to crack open a second tube, I could not but intervene.

"I do believe that Your Royal Highness is about at his doctors' recommended limit," I gently suggested. "And I'm sure they were not arbitrary in setting that limit for his health's sake."

He looked at me less gently and convinced me wordlessly that, *au contraire*, precisely what he needed was another drink; and another after that; and after that, yet another. Yes, I could see his side of the argument, and he had convinced me *in actu* of the merits and justice of his position.

I again looked in the direction of the Rear-Admiral. His gaze had not shifted since last time, and I felt uncomfortably that he looked like he was on lone for the evening from a taxidermist's.

Prince Knud, once I realised the futility of attending to limits set on his royal will by others, was a real charmer, and a gentleman who made you feel easy in his company. Which is some feat for a man whose entire vocabulary, it seemed, was recapitulated in the sound, 'hmph!'

He was, in addition to his other ranks, a full admiral in the Royal Danish Navy, thanks in part to his military service and in part to his being the King's brother. None of this, as I am sure you have understood, intimidated me in the least.

With Knud's wife, HRH Princess Karoline-Mathilde, I was quite a favorite. On this particular occasion, when I was to wrestle with the Prince over the beer and wine glasses, she had subtly drawn my attention to the presence of her royal person when I entered the dining area of the Officers' Club by yelling and waving her arms about at me.

"Oy! Hey! Look, over here! Here we are!" I sidled up to her and expressed my relief that at least she had foreborne to whistle at me.

"Whistle? What sort of uncultivated barbarian do you take me for?" she enquired rhetorically.

"Why, my dear," chafed her husband, who stood by, uncharacteristically voluble, "he takes you, I dare say, for exactly the barbarian you are."

At which witty retort the Princess gave Knud a gentle tap on the chest with her lightly clenched fist and, before he had recovered, led me off to inform me of the impossible task I had before me, of which I have already related the issue.

I got to know Princess Karoline-Mathilde quite well over the course of the next couple of years, organizing several official receptions for Prince Knud and her.

On another occasion, I was informed at very short notice of an imminent visit from Prince Knud and Princess Karoline-Mathilde, on this occasion accompanied by their new daughter-in-law, the Countess Anne Dorthe of Rosenborg. The young Anne Dorthe had been a commoner and sold flowers until her marriage not long before to the Prince had transformed her into a fairytale princess (or, rather, countess, the official title awarded her on marrying into the Royal Family). She was on her first official visit with her in-laws. Because her husband the Prince was unable to be with her due to his commitments as an officer in the Royal Danish Military, it was decided the newly-created Countess should travel with her in-laws on her own.

She was as yet new in her official responsibilities and was very nervous about the major official dinner in the private dining room at the Officers' Club. She was given into my charge for the evening.

At first, she was as nervous as a finch in the big cat enclosure at the zoo. But, as time wore on, she relaxed a little, especially as she was sitting directly opposite Princess Karoline-Mathilde, whose occasional encouraging smile gave her courage in an unfamiliar situation.

She was a pleasant and astute young lady, scarcely touched by her sudden removal to the dizzying heights of aristocratic society. At one moment she observed to me, softly, "I see that you've hardly touched your red wine."

"Well, you see, Countess... " I began, and stopped when she giggled behind her hand.

"Do excuse me," she laughed, putting her hand lightly on my arm, "I'm still not quite used to being addressed in such a manner. `Countess!' Really! But, please do go on." I felt pleased that she was so open with me, and I said I guessed it must be a difficult transformation to achieve. "But, as I was about to say, you're wrong in a small detail," I finished.

"Oh, what detail?"

"Well, you see, I haven't touched my red wine at all. I don't drink it. I prefer white wine altogether, and I have arranged it with the waiter so that he merely fills my red-wine glass at the beginning of the evening, complying with etiquette, and then the rest of the evening just discreetly replenishes my white wine as necessary."

The Countess quickly leaned in and whispered to me, "Can I confess that I'm not overfond of red wine either. Do you think... " and looked pointedly at her own full glass of burgundy. I put my finger to my nose in comprehension and immediately and quietly arranged to have her white wine replenished as per my own clandestine system.

One of the HRH's daughters stays particularly in the memory: Princess Elizabeth. She was very down to earth, even a little bit wacky, if I can use that epithet without disrespect to a Royal personage. I feel sure she would not be personally offended by it: quite the contrary, indeed. She enjoyed, as she herself declared, getting away from the media limelight that plays so hard on public persons these days, and just letting her hair down a little. Reasonable enough, it seems to me!

Princess Elizabeth was, frankly, no beauty pageant winner: however she made up for that lack by possessing in profligate abundance those qualities that the beauty queens only sham to own: compassion, intelligence, tenderness, wisdom. She had enough grit to put her beliefs into practice; and actually worked for her living as an archivist in a library in Denmark. She had also worked in the Danish embassy in Washington for a period of time. Whilst there, she had won the reputation of being very easy to get on with and of being a real team player.

"It helps me," She claimed somewhat obscurely on one occasion.

"Helps you what?" I thought to myself, as I awaited the explanation, "*Put some little thing aside for your old age?*"

She could see the vestige of the malicious reflection flicker across my face and continued. "Sure, like I need the money! No. What I mean is that it helps me avoid the trap of otherwise indolent Royals: going around the twist."

I could not help laughing at that, both because it amused me and because it seemed wise (I mean of her to work, not of me to laugh—Oh, what malice!).

In that brave new world that was Thule, she really enjoyed herself.

She maintained her own informal style of court, and avoided as much as possible the pomp of the official diplomatic travelling status. It was not beyond her to take off for Qaanaq, the Inuit village some miles to the north of the base, and just disappear out of the sights of both the paparazzi and royal exigencies for a while. Besides, she was so much loved there, that the people would have protected her from any intrusions and kept her safe from all prying eyes.

There was never a hint of frivolity on the part of the Royal Family in this freedom. It just happened that the isolation and remoteness of Thule made for a pre-cultivated spirit of intimacy and joviality that would elsewhere be the height of indiscretion; but there was transformed into immediate comprehension, in the best two meanings of the term: understanding and magnanimity. Again the similitude to the *Titanic* comes to mind: when a restricted and special space is shared with utter strangers, it makes for a species of instant intimacy that elsewhere would not happen and would not be tolerated if it did.

Of the small number of local Greenland VIPs who found their way into our special functions, Egon Hansen, the station manager at Dundas, the village across the fiord, and his wife, Else, are a couple I recall with particular affection.

Although Dundas was off-limits to the greater part of the inhabitants of Thule, even the civilians, I was one of the privileged few who, because of our seniority and jobs, were allowed to visit it.

Dundas township hugs the foot of the very distinctive flat-topped Dundas Mountain. During the Winter, it is accessible via the ocean ice, while in summer the only way was to follow the winding road up the slope of North Star Mountain and down again on the opposing slope. So, ironically, the winter route is the quicker of the two, though not as spectacular as the summer one. From North Star Mountain the views across the fiord and toward the glacier where the great bergs were born is truly breathtaking.

The village consists of an elementary school and a few small, brightly painted buildings occupied by native Greenlanders and Danish expatriates in official capacities with the communications station there or with the Official Greenland Trade Organisation. Back then, Dundas relied almost entirely on the base for its provisions, as well as for hospital facilities and the television system.

And, yet, despite its obviously deprived condition, Dundas had a comparatively homey, human feel to it: there were wives and families, children and dogs, of which we knew nothing in the monastic world of Thule.

This couple became my good friends then and remained so till Egon's death. Else still is. They had spent virtually their whole working lives in Greenland and had been posted to Thule at about the time of the crash. He was a tall, slim man whose face bore all the marks of many years exposed to the arctic climate: principally in its sun and snow-darkened complexion and in the deep furrows that attend on years of squinting and frowning out the relentless cold. They were then in their early thirties and had already sent their children off to boarding school in Denmark, as only the most basic level of education was available in Greenland itself.

Else is a petite, attractive lady with a friendly, open face. Being one of very few women in the entire region and the nearest proper hairdresser being several thousand miles away, she was forced, like the other ladies in the area, to look after her own coiffure, and to make do for our official functions without recourse to those run-of-the-mill conveniences such as dress shops and perfumeries that are available in civilised climes.

Being invited to an official reception at Thule was not for her or the other women of Dundas the unmixed blessing of cultivated proceedings which we, in our arrogance, believed we were bestowing upon them. Nor was the discomfort confined to the women; the men, too, often felt themselves quite out of their depth and unprepared for the sort of company they were bound to encounter, in particular just after their being appointed to senior positions at Dundas.

Well, just imagine for yourself, if you can. For the entire year you can spend weeks without seeing virtually anyone apart from your spouse, perhaps a neighbour or a trader, nary a visitor from Thule, save the odd Inuit hunters passing through on trade.

131

Next moment you're seated at a polished table with the Heir to the Throne of Denmark; or the befurred and bejewelled wife of a three-star American general; or a Republican senator from Delaware on a fact-finding mission. As you mumble and stumble through your evening in a kind of exquisite Hell, at least you can be secure that your single, slightly wrinkled frock is free from the incursions of moths: creatures too wise to follow man this far north just to harass his poor wife!

Despite all this, I often noted to myself, observing the behaviours and attitudes of the several classes of guests, that those whose social graces, natural elegance, honesty, and naturalness were greater, were those same simple souls from the windblown, snow-whitened, tumbledown village of Dundas.

But, today, all of this has already gone. On reflection, it was often our friends from Dundas who were the more elegant and entertaining guests, despite their personal discomfort. They demonstrated, with quiet grace, that it takes more than the latest fashions and most expertly coiffured hair to bestow true quality on a person: nor does the absence of these accoutrements take it away. And long before the passing of the next one hundred and twenty-four thousand years, so will the Danish Royal Family have gone, as will the nations we know today have gone, and even this arctic coastline will have altered beyond our limited, loving recognition.

* * * * * *

FINALLY, AMONGST OUR guests from time to time were Asker, the Danish Police Inspector and survivor of the 'Blue Cheers' episode, and his wife, Monique; Jens Zinglersen, the local manager of the Danish Greenland Trade Company and his wife; and Commander Poul Moelgaard, the Danish military liaison officer.

Jens usually managed to impress—or, more accurately, confound—those at table with him by his exaggerated and rather Pecksniffian manner. He seemed to enjoy causing them to wonder at his vast, self-proclaimed knowledge, especially when compared with their own, of all the intricate workings of that remote region of the world and of his own central, indispensable part in them.

The entire North Western region of Greenland was, it seemed, under his special, proprietary care, and an appreciation of this state of affairs was of the first importance for his fellow guests to grasp. Jens was given to tapping the side of his nose at whoever he was directing his ironical sallies, as a signal of their supposed mutual comprehension, and to winking his eye at whoever might have been overhearing his conversation, just in case there remained any doubt as to the playful, mocking nature of his remarks.

Jens' wife was, in contrast, a woman refreshingly down to earth. Whenever we had this couple over for a function, I would somehow find myself gracefully foregoing Jens' self-burlesquing records of outstanding achievements and content myself with the simple, genuine conversation of this charming lady. As much as for any other reason, it was just that I have always preferred dialogue to monologue, colloquy to soliloquy. Unfortunately, Jens seemed to be prolific in the latter and quite miscomprehending in the former, especially when the person of his interlocutor tended to interfere with his seamless flow of mock self-absorption.

Jens' company was enjoyed best from a safe distance, from where you were enabled to observe with detached amusement the palpable discomfiture of the poor guest upon whom he had decided to visit his never-ending, looping humour. The liaison officer, Commander Moelgaard, appointed by the Danish government to coordinate matters of mutual interest between the government and the United States base authorities, was one of his favourite targets, and their verbal encounters became quite popular spectator events.

Where Jens adopted Pecksniff as a kind of mock self-idol, Commander Moelgaard had no need for an idol and no place for such mockery. The Commander operated with a stark, literal earnestness; he had little feeling for the subtleties of language or irony and opined that the issue of their little social debates—on whether commerce or the military was of the greater consequence in that strange hub of human endeavour that was Thule—was a matter of the first importance. Jens just enjoyed himself and, in the process, provided some welcome entertainment for the rest of us.

Given Jens' habit of irresistible ribbing of Poul on every possible occasion, the incident in which Commander Moelgaard got to know my immediate supervisor at the time, the cigar-puffing, table-thumping Torben Staehr, is even more memorable on account of Jens' uncharacteristic forbearance from joining in; he allowed the incident to develop free of his usual acerbic, satirical intervention. He seemed to intuit, with a rare social tact, that the event was Dickensian enough without his deliberate elaborative input.

This contest issued in the fall 1967 confrontation that has gone down in our small history as the 'Bunfight at the Thule Corral.'

The Officers' Club was the scene. Pre-dinner drinks were being drunk. Pre-dinner talkers were talking in their clustered groups.

Jens had collared a couple of junior American officers who were blissfully unaware of his fame and peculiar facility, and was harassing them for their country's restrictions on whale blubber imports, for which—by his blustering manner and grandiose gestures—it was evident that he held the pair personally responsible, at least by proxy.

"Ah, you Americans," he declared, "you are all for free trade so long as it does not interfere with any of your precious markets. And how could it? You are far too large to be endangered in any part of the world by any serious competitor. But, the moment a little country like Denmark— a prosperous, diligent, self-effacing and honest people—wants to break into your market with a product of the first-class order, such as is our excellent whale blubber, *bang!*, down come the restrictions and it's, `Sorry, but what would we *do* with your whale blubber?'"

"But, surely," put in one of the poor, captive lieutenants, "surely there are no actual restrictions on such an import."

"Perhaps it just is that whale blubber is in... little demand," ventured the other, his voice trailing off into incredulity.

The Dane, at this valiant sally in defence of the Stars and Stripes, knowingly tapped his nose twice and, with a gentle smile of forebearing pity, launched into a full and complex critique of the fluctuations in the arctic fox fur market and the alleged American conspiracy to deflate it in favour of New Mexican gila monster gloves.

Commander Moelgaard, meantime, had found himself the centre of a small but rapt audience of acolytes (I stood unadmiringly by), whom he entertained with stories and anecdotes that seemed always, inevitably, to spiral in upon himself at some crucial stage in their telling. It was always at this point in the narrative that the narrator would pause portentously and mutter some dark intimation that to continue might entail a grave breach in the Official Secrets Act.

It is, on reflection, funny—in a grim way—how little sense people have of impending disaster. No matter how close you get to the future, its specific shape always just defies our efforts to grasp it. Its sense continues to defy precision until the moment is literally, violently past.

So, how could our earnest liaison officer have foreseen the disaster that was to shortly overtake our idyllic, insulated cubby-hole? And, really, it is just as well; for, if we could see into the fullness of time of such events, we would be paralysed by the vision. Time carried life on that evening inexorably toward the precipice and let out not a single hint of its hidden, dreadful offerings.

Even so, I cannot help but feel that we do hold some collective and individual responsibility for the future. For the event that was about to flash so powerfully over the helpless inhabitants of Thule was in a great degree manmade. Or was it that only the ingredients were manmade and the disaster itself divine? However we may construe the event, our utter ignorance of it does not entirely exculpate us from some censure. The gathering darkness outside, in some unfathomable way, seemed to penetrate our minds and leave us powerless, vulnerable, and ignorant, unaware even of our own profound ignorance.

One tale Commander Moelgaard retailed that night involved, from what we could gather over the very complicatedly blocked communications channels the liaison officer customarily used—a verbal system he employed, it seemed, so as to avoid being traced, no doubt, or at least, to avoid being *followed*—... Where was I?... Oh, yes. Well, it appeared that certain unspecified lobbies had gained certain ambiguous rights to certain vague privileges with regard to usage of certain channels of communication which were already being used to their ultimate capacity and whose unrestricted use by uncleared personnel was an affront to authority, a fault in security, and a downright danger to the functioning of the base, and that he felt it his solemn duty to investigate the matter and report to the base authorities, whose trust he knew had, from former dealings with them, and, but no, to say more would perhaps be a lesser wisdom...

As a result, all of us found his manner not only a little opaque, but inconsequential in the extreme. Whatever may have been his aim in all this circumlocution, it is certain that the looks of general confusion and thinly-veiled annoyance on the faces of his audience gave him a peculiar delight. Perhaps he mistook them for signs of awed, acquiescent approval of his double nature— both importantly connected and admirably discreet.

It came out a few weeks later that this little ditty was, in fact, all about the rights we Danish civilians had won to use the United States military postal system. Through this minor concession, we were able to send and receive letters via New York in between the regular, slower mail from

Copenhagen. We were also able to shop much more cheaply through the mail-order catalogues from the States. This was an arrangement that the Americans themselves were quite happy with for their own practical reasons: levels of manning, extra income, and so on. But our own busy liaison officer saw it as a threat second only to the USSR itself; and, no doubt, if he had been able, he would have trained the whole of the BMEWS early-warning system on the heavy canvas bags of the U.S. Post Office, searching for signs of incoming Danish propaganda and coded missives.

I was glancing at my watch from time to time, as I was to call the party together to make its way into dinner at the appointed hour; a movement which caught the Commander's eye every time. He indicated that he had noted my poor attention to his account of an adventure with a couple of drunken clerks discovered playing poker in one of the hangars about a week earlier, by shifting his lower jaw to one side, projecting his tongue into his cheek, and pausing mid-story until I should have been regained, fully and chastened, to attention to his person.

I was not the only one less than impressed with the liaison officer's peculiar ability to obfuscate the simplest verbal interchange. I spotted my supervisor, Torben, puffing vigorously on his cigar on the fringe of the group and growing redder in the face by the moment. I retreated a few yards, positioning myself to quietly observe the impending action.

"I *what the heck* are you getting at, man?" Torben's voice cut through the murmur. "You talk like the CIA had an operative in your underwear."

"Have we been introduced?" the Commander stopped short and pulled himself up to his full, affronted height.

"I should say not," Torben chuckled out, at each word issuing a further puff of smoke markedly into the face of the Commander, before turning and moving off to find another drink.

Moelgaard turned a mottled red and muttered, "Eternal vigilance," with a mysterious and self-impressed look on his face, as if he had just uttered a profound and original maxim.

"Well, gentlemen," I said at five minutes to seven, clapping my hands softly, "Time to move in to dinner," and quickly moved off with some relief to herd the other scattered knots of guests toward the dining area.

The Commander released the remainder of his bewildered hostages and seated himself at his assigned place at the table. He was alone, as, unfortunately, his wife had some time before taken off with the previous Police Inspector. This occurrence had occasioned no, or little, sadness among the rest of us, sad to say. However, there he was, settling his drinks orders with the barman, as Torben reappeared in the company of Jens, who was still seemingly browbeating the poor Yanks about their mediaeval banking and financial practices. Jens sat down a couple of seats up from the Commander and, taking a big, satisfied breath, smiled broadly. He dismissed his young proselytes with a wave. "Well, it's no longer in your ball park, boys. Someone else will be calling the shots soon. You mark my words. Keep an eye on the Japs! 1985 at the latest."

A mere amateur in predictions of a financial nature, it is a real pity Jens did not apply his prophetic ability to military matters. We could have done with some accurate prognostications of our near future at that time.

Torben sat down directly opposite the liaison officer and puffed a final, defiant plume of smoke at him before extinguishing the offending cigar in a nearby ashtray. The drinks waiter had arrived and was doing his job, i.e., waiting. Commander Moelgaard perused the drinks menu with great deliberation and looked up at the waiter to order. The waiter, however, was unaccountably occupied in communicating some trivial matter to Mr. Staehr.

"Well, I suppose it is of no consequence," the Commander sighed with eyes rolling dramatically around the gathered company, allowing his menu to fall limply into his lap. "This far away from the centres of higher cultivation and etiquette." When piqued, he often resorted to speech in such a manner and with such a recondite vocabulary that made it appear he was running on rhetorical tracks only roughly parallel to—and in the same general direction as—the rest of mankind. As enervating and endlessly annoying as it was to have to discover the trail through the jungle of his inflated mannerisms and wearying approximations to sense, the reasonable man could, with effort, usually understand him.

The waiter, however, reasonable man or not, had not registered the comments wafted his way, and merely continued scribbling the last part of Torben's order on his pad. He then turned his peremptory attention to the Commander. Unfortunately, the latter was still rolling his eyes like a minor, afflicted female character in an Edith Wharton novel.

"Does sir perhaps require some water?" asked the waiter, uncertain whether he had a case of a minor fainting fit on his hands.

"I would value rather more your benevolent ear," the Commander enunciated coldly, "when you have clearly placed yourself at table for my benefit, than that you lean over me and bestow such etiquetteless attentions—quite out of order—on a guest clearly down-table from me!"

The waiter, it turned out, was not a reasonable man: but neither was he a stupid one. He spotted the impending explosion in Torben's florid face opposite and, with a hasty, 'certainly, sir,' made for the safety of the kitchen; where he spent the rest of the evening judiciously juggling a succession of plates and trays to the ocular satisfaction of his harassed supervisor without actually venturing out into the dining hall again.

Torben Staehr, meantime, suppressed a strong desire to rise and rearrange the liaison officer's teeth to a position closer to his digestory tract, and instead turned to his neighbour—a slight, slightly-built Danish clerk from the shipping division, at `High Table' for the first and likely last time, who visibly shrank into hopeful invisibility—with the retort, "I'm taking the Chardonnay with the trevally. However, you may prefer, with *others*, a pot or two of cooking sherry."

Commander Moelgaard was on to his feet in an instant. From between tight, pale lips he let it out that he found the quality of the service only surpassed by the quality of the *guests*; which drew from Mr. Staehr an inconsequential comment on a natural history documentary he had recently seen, wherein were highly commended the eating and sanitary habits of the much-maligned swine. Which interesting aside had the startling effect on the Commander of causing him to remark, when his coughing fit of indignation had ended, that pigs are fine beasts, but that he would let them dine with their own. At which point he moved off with great dignity to seat himself at another table; thereby causing a considerable consternation for me, as I had to hastily reposition twelve people to accommodate this idiosyncratic and unauthorized, although personally satisfying, realignment of social forces.

We are such civilized creatures, we humans, even when it comes to our little altercations; but especially, and most bafflingly, when we get hold of nuclear weapons.

* * * * * *

ENTERTAINMENT ON OUR little, calamity-bound asteroid was a bit of a hit-and-miss affair. Bands would often be flown in from the United States and Denmark to attenuate our deep well of boredom. This was the era of the go-go dancer, and more often than not the bands would be accompanied by such glittering, gyrating artistes. Apart from the solo dancing of these lithesome ladies, there was partnered dancing little enough, for obvious reasons: no matter how close we might grow to our fellows as colleagues and friends, and no matter what may or may not have gone on in the closets, none of us felt much like going up to Lars or Niels and requesting the pleasure on the dance floor.

Some of the lady artistes, on the other hand, were able to significantly supplement their wages—till such time as their extracurricular employments should be discovered by the vigilant authorities; at which point they would find themselves unceremoniously expelled from the base on the first available flight out.

Under the banner of the USO, major shows would sometimes come to the base. That old stalwart, Bob Hope, a superb entertainer—as if it needed to be said—was just one of the great acts to play the northernmost theatre on earth in those years.

But things were not always as racy as that on the base. Often, nothing more exciting than getting from one's quarters to the dining or recreation facilities without being frozen into a tingling human popsicle was on offer. Or perhaps it was being stopped by the Military Police for exceeding the speed limit for wheeled traffic on the base. Anything over 20 miles per hour would see you severely chastised by the competent officer and fined a not-inconsiderable amount of American dollars.

Drink-driving was an offence dealt with with even greater severity; but, as I was in a quite senior position, I never took the chance and, if I had been drinking on any occasion, I would always avail myself of the free base taxi service and arrange to have my car picked up the following morning from outside the club rather than from my quarters. Later, I learned that junior staff closely watched how their seniors behaved in this regard and took their cue from them. So, I am glad to relate that, if ever I had to discipline another for a drink-driving related offence, my own clean slate was probably known to that one, which perhaps made the medicine slightly less bitter.

Or maybe the evening's diversion was negotiating the temperamental clothes dryer. The dryers in the base laundry—where one would spend spare time, the room being particularly warm and a welcome break from the boredom of paring one's nails—generated a phenomenal level of static electricity. To touch one of them unawares could deliver a quite painful, snapping jolt. The way around this minor inconvenience—which, to have lived in the memory some twenty-seven years, cannot have seemed so minor at the time—was to walk quickly up to the machine and, in a swift, sweeping motion with the hand, touch it so rapidly that there was only a very limited, buzzing sensation from the electric shock. It could not be avoided altogether; but it could be controlled, a small mastery in a world of vast, uncontrollable forces.

Our lesser, constant entertainments were a movie theatre, a library, a gym, a ten-pin bowling alley, slot machines, billiard and pool tables, shuffleboard, and so on.

Ten-pin bowling turned out to be one of the most popular of all pastimes on the base. Teams were formed and a trophy heatedly contended for among Americans and Danes alike, the crash of pins a satisfying sound in the sterile silence.

The movie theatre caused a little friction between the Danes and the American base authorities. Late on Saturday nights, the theatre would show Danish-language films, a concession to those Danes whose English was not sufficient to allow them to enjoy the American films without considerable, wearying effort.

When the idea was first mooted, of showing some Danish films for this purpose, there were major, pearl-clutching concerns on the part of the Americans. In the 1960s it was a well-known misconception that all Danish films were of an explicitly sexual nature. In fact, while it was true that you were more likely to encounter scenes of nudity in a Danish film of the time, the greater part of these films were no more risqué than the contemporary American product. Permission was only granted after a great deal of earnest discussion within the social club, as well as careful 'socializing' of the proposal to convince those concerned that morale and morals would not be adversely affected among the Americans if such films were shown.

After all the hullabaloo, it never ceased to be a source of somewhat dry amusement to us Danes that often there would be more Americans than Danes attending these sessions, sitting dutifully through films of which they understood not a single word, just for the fleeting thrill of a few seconds of naked female flesh.

The Danes, on the other hand, would probably be off at one of the clubs, or have gone bowling, or be in the gym. Coming from a culture in which there was, in this respect, significantly less restriction than among the Americans, the slightly 'blue' movies held less attraction to the Danes for being 'blue' than they did to the Americans for simply being *movies*.

The cultural ambivalence of the Americans toward nudity and the like was expressed again when a base commander once tried to ban *Playboy* magazine from the local shop. The uproar that ensued among the American personnel included even letters of complaint to politicians back in the States. This attitude—that at one and the same time wished to prohibit all displays of moral impropriety of this type, and that nevertheless flocked to see light-blue Danish movies—remains to this day a mystery to me. I am not sure that it is mere hypocrisy; but it is certainly a profound uncertainty, a conflict in the soul.

It is strange how, on the other hand, they never expressed any such uncertainty about the absolute rightness of risking blowing up the entire world in defence of freedom.

Perhaps the answer is that they went to see the Danish movies just to be sure that they were as morally reprehensible as they believed them to be! The same logic, I suppose, that applies in the bleak rejoinder, *'don't knock nuclear war till you've tried it.'*

* * * * * *

MEANWHILE, THE ORDINARY chores of existence—working, shopping, washing, ironing, cleaning, eating and drinking and the rest—were liable to fill a considerable portion of the average day. Time was not the precious commodity it is in, say, the Big Apple; time became rather our opponent in a quiet contest between a man and his own ingenuity in getting it to flow with greater speed past him. The man was Achilles and the tortoise was time; the prize, time past. The future was only of consequence once it had been achieved and safely possessed in the form of memories—of tasks completed and recreations fulfilled.

The working day for myself and most of my countrymen was from 8.00am to 5.00pm, Mondays to Fridays and 8.00am to 12 noon on Saturdays; though it was seldom a burden to work a little longer. After all, what else would one do? If you kept busy with work and a good mixture of the entertainments and diversions outlined above, life could feel pretty close to normal, though infinitely quieter and more repetitive than life in what we called civilization.

My own work involved overseeing all aspects of cargo handling in and out of the base. Early in my career there, part of my job was to ensure that cargo movement details were correctly recorded. That meant that, in all weathers, I had to trek across the exposed tarmac from my office to the main hangar, which served additionally as cargo and passenger terminal.

Later, around mid-1967, once I had been promoted to assistant supervisor, I was enabled to enjoy watching from the comfort of my heated office window as one of my underlings rushed across that freezing, wind-scoured expanse in the depth of winter, muttering under his breath imprecations upon my name and upon those of all wielders of unchecked, petty power.

I hope he included in his silent prayers those who were, at that very moment, about to let a far deadlier power roll out of their hands, as it were, and splash down upon him and upon all of us: the power of the atom; the particle, the ion, the alpha, beta and gamma ray, the maverick neutron to whittle away, silently and invisibly, at the very substructure of our bones and blood and flesh.

Because, it was right into the middle of this staid, steady, sober, and not to say mundane, jollity, that the United States Air Force—Strategic Air Command—sent the spawn of the devil, in the form of a hundred-and-twenty-four-thousand-year sardine-can explosion.

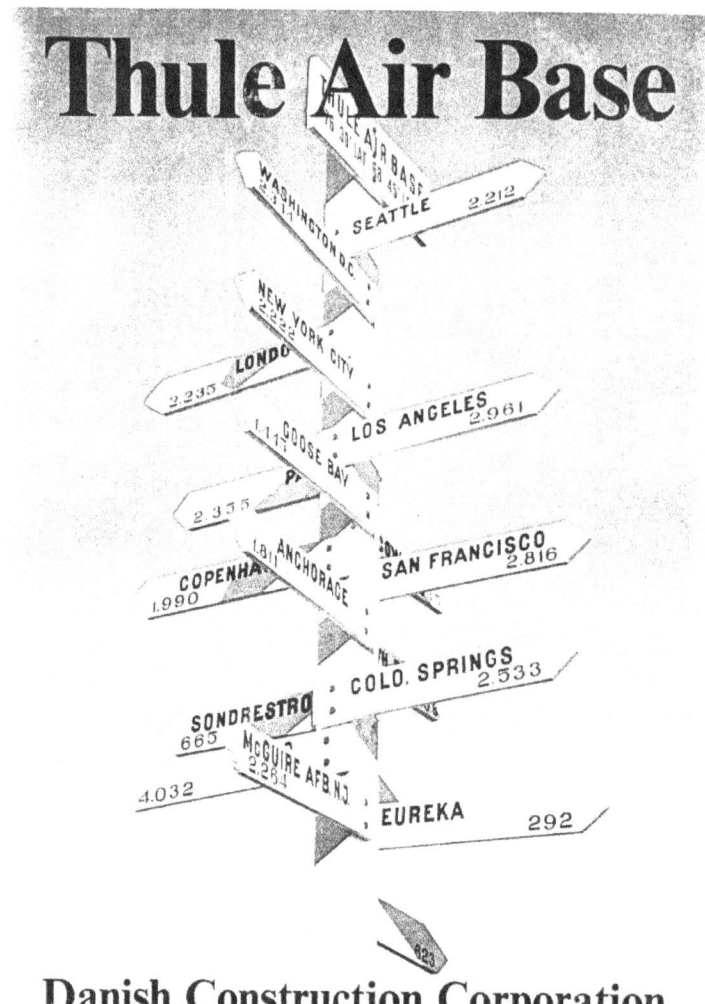

Danish Construction Corporation

Chapter 7: First We Take Washington ...

> Grave men, near death, who see with blinding sigh
>
> Blind eyes could blaze like meteors and be gay,
>
> Rage, rage against the dying of the light.
>
> *Do Not Go Gentle Into That Good Night*   DYLAN THOMAS

ABOUT TWO YEARS after having made his unwelcome acquaintance at Aarhus, I thought I had flushed the oily presence of Dr. Kay-Ole Larsen quite out of my life. It was not to be. A full, frustrating year had passed since he had knocked my knees and tapped my chest with his cold instruments, and now, according to the crisp, official report that appeared in my letterbox, it came to light that, in doing so, he had miraculously failed to find any signs of cancer in me whatsoever.

Sophia had settled behind the desk in my study to listen to my halting translation of the dense Danish document. When I had given her its sterile essence, she grimaced in a fresh wave of discomfort and frustration, her knuckles whitening as she gripped the edge of the desk.

"So, where to now?"

"We fight on. It's as simple—and as infuriating—as that. We *know* this report is a worthless, cynical piece of baloney. You remember what I told you about Larsen's examination at Aarhus? You remember what I said even back then? It was an elaborate and dirty cover-up, a pantomime. I knew it as such straight off, and I'd mentally dismissed it before I'd even arrived back in Copenhagen."

I fanned out the clinical pages of the report before me as if exposing a crime scene photo.

"Look at this thing. These bureaucratic idiots haven't even *included* me in the final conclusion. I'm a ghost in my own medical record. And they only conducted about thirty examinations in toto. A token gesture. Besides which, where they do deign to mention me, they reckon they found me 'quite healthy.' There's not even a footnote in here to the effect that my Australian doctors have not only diagnosed me but gone so far as to perform essential, preemptive surgery. And if I've told them these facts once, I've told them enough times for it to sink into even the thickest of skulls. But they consistently, deliberately, ignore me."

"At least they're consistent," joked Sophia uneasily, a weak attempt to lighten the leaden atmosphere.

"But, I'll tell you what," I continued, my voice rising, "If they imagine I'm going to run skulking away in shame because they made me a victim of that fool doctor in Aarhus, well, they really have mistaken their little black duck! If they think that now we'll just sit back feebly and fold our hands in our laps, after four years of fighting, after surgery, after trusting—naively—that they might see their way to doing the right thing by us... and instead, in their snivelling, petty stupidity, they fob us off with smears and distortions. If they think this mean, authoritarian behaviour is a legitimate way of handling the claims of angry, broken people, then boy, have they miscalculated! ... "

Sophia's smile grew grim, a thin line of resignation. "Well, Jeff, you've pretty well summed up all the reasons why you *should* throw in the rag... "

I heard her words, but steamrollered straight on over her, propelled by a furious energy.

"I've fought too long, Sophia. I know I'm right in this; and all this disgusting, paper-shuffling rigmarole has only made me all the more determined to fight to the bitter end. I'm determined to find out what's *really* motivating this stone wall of an attitude."

I flung the report vehemently onto the desk, the pages scattering.

"These lackeys, these so-called professionals; doctors? They're just quacks on the government payroll. I'd like to know how qualified medical practitioners—people who have taken a solemn oath—could let themselves be so pressed by a government that they'd falsify medical reports? I mean, this is really worrying, sinister stuff. This is corruption and dereliction of duty at the highest levels! You know, doctors take oaths, and so do politicians, about serving honesty and truth and protecting the weak, and here we have them behaving like a pack of schoolboys shoplifting in the local candy store. I'm damned if I can work it out. I'm entirely in the dark, and the dark is where they want me."

"My God, Jeff, you're right," Sophia cut in, all of a sudden on her feet, her eyes wide with a dawning, alarming vision only she could see. A distinct, electric change had occurred in the atmosphere of the room.

"And the question becomes, then, *why*? Why would a government instruct its own doctors to falsify examination results?"

"They're bastards!" I suggested, perhaps unhelpfully, my fist clenched on the table.

"Well, we know that!" Sophia laughed, a short, sharp sound. "But, I think it's more specifically, more chillingly, because they have something to *hide*."

"Except for me and my monkey," I chimed in, again rather unhelpfully. "That's no news, Sophia. It's what all the fight's been about: getting them to recognise what happened in Greenland and that they have to take responsibility for the consequent health problems of the men who were used so meanly. We were used like convenient slaves, or as if we were French Foreign Legion volunteers who had joined up in search of death. Is that what a government's for: to sacrifice its own people in some ridiculous, expedient notion of the 'greater good'?"

"I don't mean *that*, Jeff," she said, leaning forward, her voice low and intense. "It just looks so peculiar, so *extreme*, that a government in its normal operations would go so far as to deliberately erect this sort of elaborate smoke-screen just to avoid paying out some compensation. It wouldn't *like* making such a pay-out, and it would certainly try to wriggle out of it: but the means they've adopted are as extraordinary as they are clumsy. This is an action born of desperation and fear. It's beginning to look like a sustained, high-level cover-up of some sort. They have something big to hide, and they're scared you might stumble onto it if you persist. This farcical examination result they gave you is just the nose of the walrus. What's still under the water must be as big and as ugly as the rest of the beast."

"Well," I muttered, running a hand behind my head, the fatigue of the fight pressing down. "If they're so worried about something really bad coming to light, why not just pay us off? We'll get our pictures in the papers, we'll go away; and that will be that. As it is, they run the real risk of us digging deeper."

"Because.... " Sophia stretched the word out in deep, probing thought.

Suddenly, I was alerted to the shape of what she was uncovering. I finished for her, the word dropping into the quiet room like a stone. "The Yanks."

Sophia smiled, a triumphant, grim flash, and sent the flats of her hands banging down on my desk. "Jeff, you've got it."

I jumped to my feet, a jolt of adrenaline-fueled excitement cutting through the weariness. "Yeah, yeah, the Yanks. So, tell me about our 'friends' over the ocean."

"Yes, in just a sec. But, getting back to the geniuses in—where is it, the Parliament Building?—Christiansborg, and what you said before about how their behaviour is only likely to cause you to dig deeper. You see, Jeff, they've misread you quite comprehensively. They should have sized you up better than they did before sending you off to Aarhus on that wild goose chase."

I unfolded my hands from behind my head and leaned forward in my seat, the puzzle pieces beginning to align with an awful, clarifying click. Sophia's words seemed to rush now, the logic becoming terrifyingly clear.

"After all the letters they've had from you! But, why? Why have they pushed you so far that you've effectively been forced to purify your resolve and fight on for the sheer, naked justice of the cause? To fight on for the single reason that the fight is morally right?"

"God, Sophia, that's it," I breathed. "After all, we're talking in the main about functionaries: people just carrying out instructions from on high. You've seen how often these middlemen change names and offices and duties. In other words, those higher up, who don't change quite so often, must have had my letters passed to them repeatedly by a series of uncomprehending lowly Bjoerns and Larses. They got tired—I wore them down. And then, when I was getting too close for comfort to something they preferred remain buried, they panicked. So, instead of continuing to ignore me, they mistakenly thought they had to *do* something. Unfortunately, they treated me, and my colleagues, like fools. Question: Where do you hide a dead body? Answer: On a battlefield. They tried to put us off the scent by waving a blood-soaked handkerchief under our noses. By changing from passive obstructionism to active deception, they made their worst nightmare come true. Instead of causing our brains to reel with sensory overload, they've just alerted us to the existence of darker, more obscure motives."

Sophia relaxed back into her chair at this stage, a big, knowing smile on her features. I took my cue from her and allowed myself to sink back a little too, the initial fury settling into a cold, focused determination.

"Yees," I went on slowly, measuring each word. "And we were supposed to play along with the farce and maybe accept some kind of pathetic, guilt-ridden payout as a reward for getting off their backs. Instead, like the hardheaded, honest idiots we've been, we've played with a straight bat; and, again, like the hardheaded honest idiots we are, we're only now becoming aware that they have exposed a flank to us. The Americans, you say?"

"The Americans, I say!" she affirmed, her eyes sparkling with the chase.

I pursed my lips and contracted my brow, the old obstacle rising again.

"But that's a path already unsuccessfully trod. Remember the Roisman affair. Marius already had gotten a case underway over there that went suddenly and inexplicably awry."

"Yeah, yeah, I know," Sophia answered, waving a dismissive hand. "But, I don't mean you should pursue a *legal* case in the US, but a *moral* one. A public, moral crusade. And that moral case will inevitably have repercussions in the places you want it to: in Denmark, and especially in the marbled halls of Christiansborg."

"Hmm," I mused, scratching my head. Then it hit me. I sprang to my feet as if ejected from the chair, crying out:

"The Americans don't want a certain series of questions to be asked. Or rather, the Danish politicians don't want the Yanks to be *asked* a certain series of questions in public!"

"Right on the button!"

"Because, if there should be any sort of in-depth inquiry, judicial or otherwise, into this affair, eventually someone will ask, 'What was a B-52 with a live nuclear payload doing over sovereign Danish territory?' Because, according to the most fundamental legal precept the Danes have, it should not have been there at all. It was an article of faith!"

Sophia leaned in, picking up the thread. "And look, Jeff, you remember you told me about all those restricted facilities on the base? And all the B-52s that landed there in your time. The ones that Marius secretly took pictures of. It's not as if the bomber that went down was the first one you'd encountered. It was just the one that *failed*."

"Yeah, that's right," I said, the memories vivid. "They'd come in at odd, secretive times and be surrounded by a knot of ornery Marine types with hair-trigger tempers, just in case one of us curious Danes should see the stupid thing. Sort of holding hands in a ring so we couldn't see what they had behind their backs. Pathetic! Now, what do you reckon all that clandestine traffic was about? A jamboree? I don't think so! But, they couldn't stop Marius with his little 8mm camera tucked under his coat. Ha!"

"Exactly," Sophia finished, returning to the main point with precision. "It was all, as the Americans themselves would heartily agree if caught, thoroughly *unconstitutional*! That is, against the *Danish* constitution, not theirs."

"Well, I don't know that it's explicitly *against* the constitution," I put in, lawyer-like, "But it certainly contradicts every public platform, every promise, of every party that has put up candidates at any election over at least the last forty-five years. It's a betrayal."

"But, in any case," I said, making myself explicit, the conclusion now inescapable, "The cover-up of our radiation claims is just the visible part of a much greater, deeper cover-up. One with serious international relations implications. We're not just fighting for compensation; we're accidentally poking at a secret treaty, a hidden agreement."

"And, what's more," said Sophia, excited now, "you must have been getting too close for comfort. They could feel you breathing down their necks and thought perhaps you were on the very brink of their dark, dirty secret."

"We weren't," I mused, almost to myself. "But now," I added, scrambling up out of my chair like a man with a new, galvanizing purpose, "Now that we know that we were poking around in the closet just inches from the family skeleton, boy, are we going to rattle dem bones! It's time to go explore America!"

* * * * * *

BACK IN MY study a week later, the scattered report now a symbol rather than a setback, I set about preparing a formal submission to the board of the association. Based on my thinking through the issues with Sophia, I had solidified a new conviction: I needed to take the fight beyond the fjords and the parliament, to the international arena, namely, the United States itself. I proposed a dramatic departure from past, circular efforts—an entirely fresh, outward-looking strategy to counter the Danish government's cynical and ultimately foolish dismissal of us.

I would take our story to the world and force it to sit up and listen.

Being recognised by this time as a de-facto member of the board on account of my relentless letter-writing, and having a sharper command of English than anyone else involved, not to mention a stubborn streak of strategic planning—and knowing I could rely on the unwavering, if weary, support of Marius in particular—I was able to convince the Board of the stark necessity of my plan. A major charitable foundation in Denmark, moved by the injustice, was compassionate enough to put up the essential funds.

So I proposed, planned, and would execute an intensive, literally running tour of the United States, specifically targeting New York and Washington D.C. The objective was threefold: to alert the United States, in particular its politicians and relevant lobbyists, as well as its general public, to the fact of our existence and our plight; to uncover any available documentation on the running of Thule Air Base and specifically on the crash and the chaotic clean-up operation; and to contact, if it existed, any brother organisation on American soil.

I suppose most of us have had the experience of setting out with boundless enthusiasm on a Sunday afternoon to put together a set of modular bookshelves, only to find halfway through that the Phillips-head screwdriver you thought was in your toolbox has been on loan to your brother-in-law in Sydney since June of 1985.

Whether you are assembling furniture or planning a tactical incursion into the heart of a superpower, it is essential to have the correct tools, materials, and personnel. I planned, with a dose of naïve ambition, to take the United States by storm, and I did not intend to go off half-cocked. Nothing was to be left to serendipity, though serendipity (and a good screen-play) had been the fictional Ruritanians' best weapon; nor to a blind trust in the services of doubtful allies.

My first move, then, was a reconnaissance mission to the United States' Consulate General in Melbourne. The plan: to draw up a list of key government officials, senators, and members of Congress who might be willing to meet us and lend their voices in the centres of power.

So, along I trotted to the imposing US Consulate General on St. Kilda Road, a pleasant, tree-lined boulevard in the great garden city. I made my way past the long, patient queues for visa applications, passed through the heavy doors into the building itself, and went up to the top floor.

The security measures grew more palpable, more imposing, the closer I got to the inner sanctum. On my arrival at the top floor, a stoic security guard watched my every movement as I was ushered through a sterile clearing zone, past a gauntlet of humming metal detectors, and finally into the hushed, carpeted world of the consulate itself.

The transition from the ultra-pacific, sun-dappled world of downtown Melbourne to this sealed region of quiet suspicion and controlled distrust was quite bizarre, jarring. But, given the American experience of terrorism in many parts of the world, it is not to be wondered at that they should be so carefully, coolly vigilant, even in benign Australia. The price, I supposed, that is paid for being the World's Policeman.

When I finally found the library, I was beset not by suspicion, but by friendly and overwhelmingly helpful staff who supplied me with complete, weighty directories of all senators and congressmen, and of every newspaper and TV and radio station in the vast country. My problem then transformed from one of scarcity to one of selection from this sheer, embarrassing richness of targets.

I chose a version of the dartboard method, within certain strategic guidelines. I copied out the details of names I recognised from the news and threw in a number of women members for good measure, a calculated gamble. Thus, I chose, as it were, a mixture of high profile and potential compassion. I guessed that, if the men were too hard and gung-ho to give me a hearing, I might, just might, be able to touch the hearts—or the political instincts—of the women.

* * * * * *

NONE BAR TWO of the males ever replied in the long run to my meticulously typed letters, and those replies were long delayed, perfunctory, and from junior staff rather than from the members themselves. None of the women replied at all. None of the major media outlets showed even a flicker of interest. But, I've lived with disappointment for a long time now; it is an old, familiar companion.

* * * * * *

NOR DID I fail to attempt to directly engage the interest of the mighty American media in our obscure campaign. I wrote to all the major newspaper, radio, and television companies based on the Eastern Seaboard of the US, both to their distant head offices and, where they had them, to their powerful Washington D.C. branches.

I received not one single reply.

Not a solitary one.

Their uniform, echoing lack of interest astounds me to this day. I do not know whether to put it down to an invincible parochialism or to a profound inability to recognise a hot, human news story when it is handed to them on a platter. It must be a case of the latter, as the parochial attitude would only apply where there was no direct American interest. But, the fate of the hundreds of US servicemen sacrificed to 'Project Crested Ice' should surely rule out that cosy conclusion. Which only leaves a staggering, institutional stupidity and a negligent, unforgivable ignorance of their own field.

Sad, really, and bitterly ironic. Given how fundamentally honorable the American people are, that they should be served so poorly, so passively, by their own Fourth Estate. The silence from across the ocean was, in its own way, as damning as the lies from Copenhagen.

* * * * *

THE PLAN I devised I carried out entirely on my own initiative and under my own steam. The part played by the Association ceased at giving me carte blanche; the whole of the actual, grinding work I did myself, late into the Australian nights and in the cold, pre-dawn hours.

What drove me was a cold, burning determination to win, to show the inert, smug heaps of Danish officials and scientists and politicians that they were not invincible; that their paper fortress could be breached, that they would be found out. I swore to myself, staring at the silent phone and the empty mailbox, that I would prove the old saying 'the truth will out' to be more than mere words. It would be a weapon.

* * * * *

A MELBOURNE-BASED ANTI-NUCLEAR group, hearing of my quixotic mission, supplied me with a long, crumpled list of lobby groups in the States potentially interested in our obscure, frozen cause.

To these, over the next few months, went a relentless round of over one hundred letters, faxes (that modern miracle), and expensive, static-filled telephone calls. My study became a command post, maps of Washington and New York pinned to the walls, a world time zone chart taped above the desk.

My initial contact was always a carefully crafted introductory letter outlining the salient, damning elements of our cause and asking, with a politeness that belied my fury, whether it would be useful and convenient to make personal contact when I visited the States in the near future.

My first, unexpected hindrance—a lesson in the surreal—came not from malice, but from my dealings with that very special, anarchical universe: the American Civil Service.

One very early morning in December, the air still dark outside my window, I was trying to get on the phone a senior official in the Department of Energy with the sublimely unlikely name of Jeremy `Stonewall' Hodson. The sun had not yet set off the alarm of the morning chorus, so I sat and carefully sipped my orange juice as the long-distance connection whirred and clicked through. I needed to assess in advance the effect each sip was likely to have on me so as to avoid the sudden, familiar onset of nausea—a lingering guest from my own body's betrayal.

"Good evening. Department of Energy. Mr. Hodson's office. Maggie speaking. How may I help you?" rang a female voice composed of the culturally ingrained, omnipresent American cheer, modified by the personally furnished vexation of someone taking that five-to-five call after a slogging day at the word-processor.

"Yes, good evening," I replied, my own voice sounding thin and distant across the Pacific. "My name is Jeff Carswell and I'm calling from Melbourne, Australia. Is Mr. Hodson available, please?"

"I'm sorry, Mr. Hodson has left for the evening," came the crisp answer, though the voice seemed to subtly add, *'But I'm still here, working my ass off and talking to some foreigner from Austria or wherever.'*

"Would you ask him to call me back, please? It's rather important."

"Certainly, sir. What name was it? And your number?"

I gave them, patiently, and added, "Could he ring me either early morning his time or late evening mine? Because of the difference in our time zones, those are the only windows where we are mutually available."

"Certainly, sir. I'll see that he gets your message. Thank you for calling the Department of Energy. Good evening," she purred with practiced, terminal insincerity, and rang off.

I then took the receiver away from my ear and rubbed the side of my head with slight, gathering irritation.

A day passed. Another. Another. A full week had gone, and I felt the aptness of Mr. Hodson's nickname. He was stonewalling me, or his system was. I rang his office again. This time, late evening my time; early morning his.

"Good morning. Department of Energy. Mr. Hodson's office. Maggie speaking. How may I help you?"

I explained again who I was and was perversely relieved to hear Maggie say, "Oh, yes, Mr. Carswell. Mr. Hodson is available now. He was wondering what your call was about."

"Well, why didn't he call me back... " I began, when I was abruptly put on hold and subjected to the ultimate American Persistence Test: five solid minutes of the insipid, saccharine melodies of Station WZIT.

Finally, salvation:

"Hello, Mr. Carswell? Jeremy Hodson speaking," came the voice of my rescuer from WZIT's rabid, LSD-inspired disc-jockey.

I had just set about explaining my reason for calling—the words rehearsed in my head for days—when those familiar, fateful words sliced in:

"I'm sorry, Mr. Carswell, I have been expecting an urgent call this morning, and I think that's it coming through now. May I put you on hold?"

"I'd prefer you didn't." The psychedelic torment of Station WZIT rose in me like an aural hallucination. "Could you call me back in a few minutes? My number is... "

"Oh, I *have* your number, Mr. Carswell. Maggie gave it to me after you called last week."

He rattled off my number correctly, excused himself with bureaucratic smoothness, and rang off.

I made myself a little more comfortable in my worn dressing gown, took a sip of my now-cold coffee, decided I'd better make a fresh one, then thought better of it—or was lazier—and sat back to await `Stonewall's' promised call.

It was twelve-forty in the morning. I nodded off for a few minutes in the chair and woke with a start to see that the clock now read one-fifty-six. I yawned, the taste of stale coffee in my mouth, and wondered about Mr. Jeremy `Stonewall' Hodson: how he might have earned his unoriginal though colourful and seemingly appropriate nickname; and how he would look with a paperclip piercing his tongue.

I reached for the handset with a weary sense of déjà vu.

"Good afternoon. Department of Energy. Mr. Hodson's office. Maggie speaking. How may I help you? Oh, yes. Mr. Carswell. Mr. Hodson was just speaking to me of you, and he said to tell you, should you call back, that he won't be available the rest of today. Could you try again tomorrow?"

A note of raw exasperation may have entered my voice. "Why didn't he call me back just now? He said he would."

"Well, Mr. Carswell," she said, her tone frosting over, "you may not be aware that you are in Australia. The time difference, you see. Call again tomorrow. I'll leave a note that he should expect your call. Goodbye." *Click!*

"?????"

Only after a number of equally frustrating and fruitless communications with several other government bodies—none of whom answered a single one of my faxes or returned a phone call—did the penny finally drop, revealing the meaning of Maggie's convoluted statement. It seems that American government officials, in a staggering display of petty bureaucracy, often lack the simple authority to make international phone calls or send international faxes on their own initiative. An astonishing truth I still find difficult to believe.

Once I knew that critical, absurd detail—which incredibly none of the officials I spoke to had ever bothered to mention to me, an astounding defect in people who otherwise impress the world with their remarkable capability for *expressing* themselves!—I was able to plan my strategy around it. I would ask when such-and-such an official would be available to speak, and then, with the patience of a sniper, tell them I would call back at that exact time. Or I would send a fax telling them *when* I would ring and ask them to confirm all arrangements by mail—throwing the bureaucratic ball neatly back into their court.

Into my mailbag consequently began to arrive classic examples of correspondence that made my Danish experience of officialese seem like a dream run in comparison. One such masterful missive came from Tara O'Toole, M.D., M.P.H., Assistant Secretary, Environment, Safety and Health of the Department of Energy, Washington D.C.:

"Dear Mr. Carswell,"

Wrote Tara,

"Congressman Miller has passed your letter on to me. Unfortunately, we are not at liberty to release to you the information you seek. The records you ask about are controlled by the Department of Defence. If you have not already contacted them, I strongly suggest you do so. They will also be able to advise you further about policy changes that have occurred in regard to the release of information.

"I may, however, suggest that you write to Ms. Nell M. S. Hayes, Defense Nuclear Agency, Public Affairs Office (FOIA), Room 113, 6801 Telegraph Road, Alexandria VA, 22310-3398, Phone 703-325-7095.

Yours Faithfully,
Tara O'Toole"

Or, consider the elegantly deflective note Denise B. Higgin, Chief, FOI and Privacy Acts Branch, Reference and Information Management Division, Department of Energy, Washington D.C., sent me:

"Dear sir,

"Re your note of the 21st inst., I advise that the following is the correct person to be briefed in this matter:

"Gloria Inlow, Albuquerque Operations Office, PO Box 5400, Albuquerque, NM, 87185, Phone 505-845-4173.

"Yours Faithfully,
Denise Higgin"

Denise did, however, perform the most powerful act a civil servant can: she activated a file and allocated a file number; in this case, no. 94061620DR.

Whoa. Pat my wrist. Now we're really cookin'. A number in the machine.

But, despite the smokescreen of unctuous dissipation that emanated from the Department of Energy, it was from the office of Congressman Miller, chairman of the Committee on Natural Resources, that I finally received some real, proactive help in the person of Heather Gangaro, Miller's executive assistant. She wrote to me herself, a human-sounding letter, and explained that she had herself encountered similar institutional obstructiveness and that any and all information on the Thule matter that had ever been forwarded to Denmark had been promptly, and suspiciously, buried in their archives.

Heather was the single, shining exception to the obstructionist rule followed by most American bureaucrats and was genuinely helpful in suggesting and establishing contacts for my trip.

It was a hectic, disorienting two or three months, during which I would stumble into my home office around four in the morning, the world silent, to ensure I could catch people on the eastern seaboard of the States before they left for home. Other days, I would call from home late at night, my voice husky with fatigue, to catch people in other time zones, in Chicago and San Francisco, their daytime voices bright and jarring against my darkness.

It grew to be quite a complicated logistical puzzle, especially as Christmas was rolling up—the time when the States effectively shuts down for a month—and I was planning my visit for the following February and March, threading a needle between holidays and congressional sessions.

But slowly, like Rome abuilding (or more accurately, like ice forming), in spite of all this first-class officialese and obfuscation, a tentative schedule of meetings started to form. Eventually, I was sufficiently confident that I had enough quality meetings organised to make the arduous trip worthwhile; among them, a pivotal meeting with a key advisor to the American Secretary of Energy, who had as one of his labyrinthine responsibilities the oversight of the United States nuclear arsenal. Mr. `Stonewall' Hodson, Heather Gangaro and their ilk had turned out to be quite helpful, in their way, once I learned the cardinal rule: never, ever expect them to return an international call or fax.

Just three days prior to my scheduled departure for the States, with bags nearly packed, I made a breakthrough. A chain of letters to successive lobby and interest groups, each suggestion leading like a reluctant clue to the next, eventually led me to Greg Maas, an ex-US airman who was in the fragile, early process of organising an association of ex-Thulers in the States. Greg became my man in Chicago, a voice from the other side of the same haunted ice.

* * * * * *

GREG HAD BEEN sent to Thule shortly after the crash to participate in the grim clean-up operation. He had recently undergone extensive, gut-wrenching surgery, which had involved the removal of his stomach and other precious, internal parts of his body. He now needed an elaborate system of external plastic bags as aids to basic digestion, a constant, physical reminder.

Greg's wife, Jan, a sharp-eyed and fiercely loyal woman, had been the one to make the chilling connection between Greg's time at Thule and his rapidly deteriorated health. It was around that time that disturbing reports were circulating about an experimental program in United States hospitals that had used innocent patients without their awareness or assent as radioactivity guinea pigs, and she was quick, and horrified, to note the ghastly similarities between those cases and Greg's own medical history.

So, putting two and two together, she convinced a reluctant Greg to ring a lawyer. The surreal result of the sum was not four, but a deep, chilling suspicion: something was profoundly fishy.

A quick worker, even in his weakened state, Greg charmed his way onto a local current affairs program on Chicago TV and told his story—a story that could have been my own, or Marius', or that of any one of the gaunt members of our Danish association.

"Do you believe, Mr. Maas," asked the interviewing reporter of Greg in his first, nervous appearance, "that the military authorities who sent you to Thule in the wake of this nuclear disaster knew of the potential dangers to the health of you all?"

"Well, I reckon they *must* have," Greg said, his Midwestern accent softening the damning words. "But they sure didn't say so to us at the time. Or to me, in any case. I guess it's *possible* they didn't really know back then just what effect that kind of radiation can have on a man's body. I dunno. But I reckon it's more likely they knew and just kept good and mum about it. Whenever the question of danger came up, it was easy for the brass to put the wind up the GIs, who were hardly in a position to answer back. They relied on saying little enough, and even that little was more than enough to shut down questions. And, you know, with Vietnam hot as hell, what GI was gonna ask a whole bunch of questions about an assignment to a US base in a *non-combat zone* just to shovel a little ice and snow?"

The finishing credits had not ended rolling before the station's switchboard lit up. Three calls came from viewers in the area whose stories, they attested, had just been recounted by Greg. They, too, had been at Thule in 1968 for the clean-up, and were now suffering a similar litany of strange health problems.

There developed over the following weeks, as that and other interviews were progressively screened across several states, something of a Pied Piper Effect. More and more ex-Thuler servicemen came forward, men who were displaying various stages of deteriorating health from an unlikely, horrifying variety of rare cancers and allied diseases—a medical pattern emerging from the statistical noise.

"Well," mused Greg, on a later program out of St. Paul, "I just reckon you'd have to say that the US military was a heck of a lot more cunning and a helluva lot of powers of ten more underhanded than we've given them credit for so far."

"How do you mean, Greg?" asked the host, Arlo.

"What I mean, Arlo, is that the evidence—what we've been able to track down so far—is mounting that a deliberate policy was adopted. They brought in servicemen for the clean-up from a large number of different stations, all over the world. Scattered them to the winds beforehand. The intention, it looks like, was to make it more difficult afterwards—maybe impossible—for any of them ever to have enough contact with other ex-Thulers to be able to notice that too many of their buddies were going under with the same strange diseases. It was a dispersal policy."

"But, since I first appeared on Chicago TV a few months back," he continued, a note of grim triumph in his voice, "we've had such an incredible response from a growing number of isolated and sick ex-Thulers that we've just set up a body to represent them. We're planning actions, all the way to the Supreme Court if we have to, in an effort to gain some sort of justice. Some sort of acknowledgement."

"What membership do you have so far?"

"So far, there's over seventy of us. From a clean-up contingent that numbered somewhere between 600 and a thousand, that is quite a few. A statistically terrifying few. In addition, I have been in contact with the families or widows of some dozens of other men who have already passed on from some very nasty diseases. They didn't just scatter us; they buried us, one by one."

"Thank you, Mr. Maas, for your time this afternoon."

"Thank you, Arlo."

"And now, folks, following a few words from Andy's Hardware and Manchester Supplies, 2A Main St., St. Paul, our major sponsor, I'll be back with the incredible and moving story of Jack Donnelly and his faithful packhound, Matador, who found his way from New Mexico all the way back to St. Paul: the dog, that is; where Jack had lost him in the desert, hunting ocelots. That coming up next ..."

* * * * * *

I ARRIVED AT Chicago-O'Hare on a freezing cold but clear day, the kind that bites any exposed skin. The dusty, faded-blue sky was distant and held promise only of more snow to come; the waters of Lake Michigan, visible from the descent, snapped symbolically at the heels of the city that cowered under its blanket of frost, shivering and breathing shallow plumes of steam.

I was met by the American association's lawyer, Larry Leck, who drove me in his large, warm car to my hotel in the looming city. On the way in, he made great, efficient use of my very short time in Chicago—less than a day—to discuss the issues we had in common, his voice a steady, rumbling presence.

Larry is a big, heavy-set man of Polish extraction, with a solid, reassuring bulk. His demeanour was generally solemn, as I guess becomes a highly competent lawyer such as he is, whose work on behalf of the less fortunate from the old Eastern Bloc has taken him as far as conferences in the White House, where his advice is, he told me modestly, highly regarded and sometimes even taken.

"Mr. Carswell," he drawled. Or it seemed to me that he drawled, used as I had become to the truncated twang of the Australian accent. "So glad to finally have you on board. You've been in the vanguard of this fight for some time now, they tell me."

I had imagined him, from our phone calls, to be somewhere between the slick consultant of *L.A. Law* and the world-weary pleader of *Night Court*. He fell, in person, somewhere between the unobtrusive, moral authority of a Jimmy Stewart character and just about any decent, grounded adult in a story by Ray Bradbury.

"Nearly eight years," I answered, the number sounding even longer spoken aloud in this foreign context.

"Now, that's persistence!" and his entire body and face transformed as he laughed the open, delighted laugh of the open Mid-Western Plains. "That, I fear, is exactly what we're going to need heaps of here too, in the States. Oh, we've got a case. Yeah, oh yeah. Don't doubt it. Trouble is, you see, we've got to deal not just with the White House, but with those boys in the *Pentagon* with enough brass across their shoulders to put the Salvation Army to shame and more brass in their faces than Midas had gold at his fingertips.

"They're death to deal with, Mr. Carswell... "

"Please; Jeff," I said. I was warming already to this expansive, direct personality.

"They're death to deal with, Jeff. They'll hit you with the patriotic bit as hard as they can and swear black is blue that whatever they did, they did for `America.' You ought to be *glad* they care enough about America to test the missile that's just obliterated your home on the outskirts of Las Vegas—and if you complain, you're a damn Communist Internationalist Anarchist; and they'll start a file on you and *find* the evidence to back their claim, sooner or even sooner."

He laughed heartily again at his own dismal portrayal of the fearful powerhouse and stuffy conscience of the world's great moral leader. "Or else they'll take the Fifth Amendment faster than a Kentucky man'll take a fifth of bourbon."

"But, you'll fight on, surely," I insisted, needing the reassurance. "This opposition is all in the future at this stage."

"Sure we will," he answered in that semi-sarcastic, utterly noncommittal tone that Americans have perfected, and which means they intend to do just what they say.

"And they think the English have cornered the market on irony," I mused aloud as the giant, black Sears Tower loomed out of the pale, snow-bearing sky like a cold monument.

We arrived at my hotel, where I met Greg Maas for the first time in the flesh.

He is physically a man of medium stature and thinning, greying hair. A long post-Thule career in sales has given him the gregarious, open personality required in that misunderstood undercast of society. But his warm, hand-shaking exterior barely covers the deep well of sadness and bitterness he carries on account of his sickness. His 'sewerage system,' as he calls it with bleak humour, is a series of plastic bags clipped to his belt. He is America's equivalent of Marius—the driven, wounded heart—and has been the sole, tireless reason for there existing any ex-Thulers' association on this side of the Atlantic.

As we spoke over coffee in the hotel lobby, the uncanny sensation grew that we each knew the other's story at least as well as each did his own. It was as if each was describing his experiences of being shipwrecked on the same, totally uninhabited desert island, years apart. One of us would tell how, one day, he had scratched a series of lonely verses in the sand on the beach, just to the left of a series of rocks he had dubbed the 'Midget's Causeway'; and the other would counter, his eyes widening, by telling how, one day, on the beach, just as the tide was on the rise, his attention had been captured by curious, as he had supposed, natural 'hieroglyphs' etched into the sand, perhaps by crabs, only to watch them dissolve in an instant as the waves flowed over them. This all occurring within a stone's throw of the rocks *he* had named 'St. Paul's Piles.'

"There was one guy in the Non-Coms' rec area who would *always* put 'I Feel Good' on the juke box," I said, smiling at the trivial, vivid memory. "Boy, I was sick to death of that damn song by the end of 1968."

"Yeah," said Greg, a slow grin spreading across his face. "That was me."

"Get out of here!"

"I still love James Brown."

"And I *still* can't stand him!"

We talked on into the Chicago night, filling out the perspective of our sometimes telescoped memories with the advantage of the triangulation offered by the other's story. It became clear that, on no few occasions during that surreal summer of the clean-up, we had been in the same crowded, noisy rooms, had perhaps even passed each other a tool or shared a grim joke.

"True life previous lives!" quipped Larry, as he finally grabbed up his bulky coat and looked pointedly at Greg. "Let's let Jeff recover from his jetlag. He's earned it."

"Hey, Jeff," Greg said, turning to me. "Listen, I'd love to have you along for an interview I'm doing in the morning with ABC TV Chicago. The effect of someone with your experience and credibility—with your history and, on top of it all, being a *foreigner*—could be immeasurable. It lends weight, you know? Makes it an international thing, not just a bunch of disgruntled vets."

"Sure, a pleasure," I said, though privately sceptical about how effective I, with my Australian accent and complex story, could be on fast-moving American TV. But I knew we had nothing to lose, and any crack in the wall of silence was worth pursuing. "I want to do anything at all that might advance the cause here. It's still early days for you, and the more airing you can get, the better."

"By the way," put in Larry, pulling on his gloves, "Could we get together before the interview, just for a bit of a chinwag? Any advice you can give us—strategic, legal, tactical—from your long campaign would be most useful. Whatever it may be! We're learning as we go here."

"I'd be delighted," I said, feeling a sudden, unexpected sense of purpose. My years of frustration might actually be of use to someone else.

"Great, Jeff. How about I call in for you at seven, and we'll taxi on over to our offices and then on to the studio for the interview? We'll grab breakfast on the way."

When the interview was screened in Chicago the following evening, the viewer response was the same powerful one that Greg was becoming used to, yet still grateful for: even more new contacts with ex-Thulers were established, lonely voices finding a chorus.

That same afternoon, with a handshake that felt like a pact, I flew out of the biting Chicago cold to New York, where I was to rendezvous with Marius and his wife, Christel—bringing the fight full circle, from the ice, to Denmark, to Australia, and now to the very doorstep of the power that had set the tragedy in motion.

* * * * * *

JONAH HAD FEWER problems with the whale than I have had over the past few years with Airline companies. This time, it was the heavens themselves that threw the flight-plans of every carrier in the States into chaos and threatened to do the same to my meticulously, desperately tight schedule. The snow that had been a promise in the sky the previous day was now a thick, silent blanket on the ground. Chicago-O'Hare was virtually closed down as the swirling snow reduced visibility to a ghostly, impenetrable invisibility.

I was struck by the bitter irony of seeing my first decent, heavy snowfall since leaving Thule in 1971 and being immediately threatened by it. The memory surfaced, sharp and cold: how careful you had to be walking about up there following a snowfall to avoid slipping; and that losing your footing on the ice was called being 'bitten by a snowflake.' I felt I was being devoured by an entire blizzard of them at that moment as my precious, irreplaceable time dripped by, second by frozen second, outside the huge, fogged windows of the airport where I was helplessly, infuriatingly trapped.

Fortunately, through a mixture of pleading and persistence, I was able to have my ticket endorsed to fly out on the only airline that was still braving the elements. I was not, however, the only desperate soul in the terminal; and I was to pass seven long, unhappy hours waiting in a snaking, shuffling queue until a flight became available, my feet aching, my anxiety mounting.

When I had crafted my schedule for this trip, I had made every minute count, each meeting a domino in a precarious line: and now, here I was, caught out by Mother Nature, whose mercurial vagaries I had simply, stupidly failed to factor in. I had lived too long in temperate Australia. There, the only thing that ever closes the airports is a national celebration over winning the America's Cup. I was not even able to leave the queue to go find something to eat, for fear of losing my hard-won place. It was a miserable and clawingly anxious wait, a period where I truly feared that all my intricate plans would unravel before they'd even begun. I was anxious, too, over how Marius might handle things in New York if I failed to turn up. He was not a patient man.

Marius is a great publicist, a born campaigner: but I had my specific strategies and talking points worked out, and I doubted he could step into my proverbial shoes at the drop of the proverbial hat for all the delicate meetings I had lined up. Besides which, his English language skills were on roughly the same level as his quantum mechanics skills: you had to hear them to disbelieve them.

However, it all panned out in the end; my purgatorial wait concluded and I bid an indifferent, relieved farewell to the limbo of Chicago-O'Hare and finally boarded my delayed United flight to New York, my body stiff with tension and fatigue.

I was undeniably excited to be descending into the 'Big Apple,' even though I was pretty sure I was going to see very little of it beyond hotel rooms and taxis during my visit. But, just being in the world's most talked-about, most loved and loathed city sent a shiver of raw vitality through me, cutting through the weariness. I was looking forward to my single, frantic day there with a kind of grim exhilaration.

Marius and Christel met me in the marbled foyer of my hotel the following morning. He was buzzing with a business-like, nervous energy.

"Jeff, thank God you're here." He grabbed my arm and practically pushed me towards the elevator, his grip tight. "No time to chat or relax. Our first guest has already arrived. And I haven't the foggiest idea of what to *say* to him. My English has… deserted."

"Is that the guy from World Uranium Hearing?" I asked, pulling off my gloves and rubbing my hands across my cold-numbed face, trying to summon some alertness after the freezing New York air.

"Yeah, Glenn Alcalay. I've just sat him down in our rooms with a glass of schnapps. He doesn't seem to understand too well anything I say to him. He just smiles and nods."

"Well, maybe if you had a few more words of English and less of German in your conversation, Marius…?" put in Christel, teasingly but with an edge of genuine concern.

Marius grumped at his wife, a familiar sound, and stared fixedly at the ascending numbers in the elevator for the rest of the short trip up, his jaw set.

Glenn Alcalay was an exceedingly sharp and dynamic personality, whose knowledge and quiet wisdom on cultural issues—particularly of the way in which an entire people's way of life may be silently, irrevocably warped by radiation—was immense and immediately apparent.

"Mr. Carswell, er, Jeff," he said, after I had outlined our story to him with as much clarity as I could muster, "I know exactly where you're coming from. And, believe me, these are the issues of the future. It's not just that people are losing their health and dying as a result of radiation exposure. Which they most certainly are; but that's only the visible, personal part of the tragedy. As long as the exposed survive—that is, until they finally die of the effects—they exert a profoundly disturbing, erosive effect on those they live with, particularly those who depend on them for their own physical and cultural survival."

"We're talking in the main about pre-technology cultures here; and it's no joke to have, say, twenty percent of your hunting population dying, and until they do, either being rendered infertile or experiencing birth defects that ripple into who knows how many future generations. There is, as it were, a critical mass of devastation that a culture can bear: exceed that mass, and the culture just kind of implodes. The people might continue on, perhaps even in the same place. But their life will bear no resemblance to what their forebears had known for centuries. Even physically, the generations can become stunted, rickety and weak.

"Look at the inhabitants of the Marshall Islands, especially Bikini and Rongelap. It's the end of those peoples *as a distinct culture*. As you may know, some of these peoples have been evacuated from their ancestral islands and will never, ever be able to return. Island paradises turned into permanent death camps. It's similar in its destructive scale to the Plague in thirteenth-century Europe, or introduced syphilis in sixteenth-century Mexico. Or, another good example would be the effect on the psyche and social fabric of France and Belgium from the devastation of the Great War. No one has fully counted that cost yet. Cultures can just… disappear, as if they'd never been!"

"Well," I replied, feeling the weight of his words settle on our own, smaller struggle. "A lot of what you say would, I think, apply to the Inuit of Greenland. You realise they were used—unwittingly, unprotected—in the initial search for the crewmen and for sensitive parts of the bomber."

"Yes, indeed, quite right," Glenn nodded, his expression grave. "The proof of the pudding is in the death of the guest! A very black pudding indeed. But also, and this may well be more disputable, people usually can't see the mortality of their own culture even when they can see their personal mortality staring them in the face.

"And this is all the truer the grander and more omnipresent the culture is. It's a sort of collective, unconscious bargain with the Almighty: 'OK, so I may die, but this *thing*—this nation, this way of life—must not die!' In other words, the incredibly rich and developed culture that came up with the bomb and nuclear energy has yet to truly confront the fact that radiation does not die. It will outlive the next step mankind might take on the evolutionary scale, *should* he and she be around to take it. The afflicted individuals fade out of the picture as the gigantic, geological scale of what we're dealing with comes into terrible focus. The day may come when the collective voice ceases to speak for the person and speaks only for its own perpetuation: and it in turn will say something like, 'OK, so I may die, but this *thing* cannot die!'"

I was at a loss to respond adequately, the philosophical enormity of it momentarily silencing my more immediate, political anger.

Glenn's face had worn an intense, almost ecstatic mien till this moment. He now let it relax into a gentler, more mundane smile and said, the shift jarring after his previous rhetorical flights:

"I can tell you, Jeff and Marius, our organisation will give you all the support we can muster in this country. It is *precisely* to make people aware of the very real and dastardly effects of radiation poisoning on very real people like yourselves—and, by extension, themselves—that we exist.

"I don't know whether you realise it," he added, leaning forward, "but you're actually in a slightly better legal position than the US servicemen involved in the clean-up."

"How do you figure that?" I asked, surprised.

"Well, GI Joe, when he signs on the dotted line, signs an awful lot of the very things away that he is ostensibly signing up to defend. One of them, often, is the right to seek certain types of compensation from his employer, Uncle Sam. There are formidable legal barriers."

"You're kidding. How the hell can that be?" I was freshly outraged, the injustice deepening.

"You explain the contradictions of a great culture to me, Jeff. I don't know, frankly. War to protect peace, oppression to ensure freedom. It's got me beat. The law is a strange animal."

I could not nut that one out, so I filed this new, galling layer of injustice away and forced myself back to the practical point of our being there.

"Well, Glenn, what we need principally at this stage is just what you say: to reach as many people as possible. The fact is, this is, at its heart, an issue of simple justice. This country has exported plenty of great things over the years; but it tends to export its blind spots and injustices along with them, and then just shakes its head piously over the terrible injustices elsewhere in the world. Sure, the injustices are in the world: at the same time, there is no disputing the US's part in putting them there.

"The ironic thing is that the Americans, individually, really *do* care about justice. The difficulty arises when that care becomes inextricably tangled with the 'American way of life'—as if, not only is justice every American citizen's birthright, but that the American birth is the formal *cause* of justice in the world; and being, by definition, local—an American can only be born in America—true justice can therefore never fully exist outside America's sphere. It's a paradoxical solipsism."

"You know, I agree with you wholeheartedly," Glenn nodded, a wry look in his eye. "But it has been America's profound, if flawed, belief in its ability to *spread* justice that has led it to assume the role of World Policeman. Unfortunately, and often all too truly, the perception of what that means in practice is that America turns into a rabid interventionist acting primarily in its own interests. What America needs to do to redress the balance—and I suppose the UN is potentially the forum for it—is to somehow also learn to play the role of World *King*. A ruler, not just a cop. After all, *de regis clementia est*—from the king comes clemency."

"Phew!" interjected Marius, who had been following with intense concentration. "Is need more or less America in der *welt*?" His passive understanding of the language was, thankfully, fairly accurate.

"Well, Marius," answered Glenn, turning to him with respect, "The fact is that there is plenty of America in the world already, and more where that came from. I guess I'm a pretty firm interventionist myself, when it's right; and that role doesn't in the least preclude mediation and clemency. The wisdom of Solomon lay in his statecraft, not in his domestic arrangements, which were, frankly, a dog's breakfast.

"But," and Glenn smiled the smile of self-awareness, "this is a pleasant, academic pastime: fixing up America's foreign policy over coffee. For the time being, I would just repeat my wholehearted support for you and your association, Marius and Jeff, and I'll get onto the job of telling your story to the widest audience I can reach. We have a number of newsletters and specialist journals that will take such stories, as well as contacts with some daily newspapers and lesser state TV networks. Through all the different media available to us, we can potentially reach an audience numbering in the tens of millions."

"Phew!" went Marius again, his eyes wide. "This really is America! Well, I prepared am for do any interviews you to set up for us. I speak, Jeff translates, yes?"

"Sure thing, Marius. I'll get back to you as soon as I have a word with a few contacts. Oh, yeah." He held his hand up as if to physically balance his thoughts. "By the way, if you are interested, I might be able to organise for you to talk with Warren Nelson, Congressman Dellums' Chief of Staff. Dellums heads the Congressional Defence Committee. Would such an encounter be of use?"

"Would it ever!" I gaped, feeling the first real jolt of strategic hope. That was a direct line into the very machinery we needed to influence.

"Right. Consider it a priority. I'll get on to it then."

Glenn shook our hands firmly, his grip conveying a sense of shared mission, and we parted in uncharacteristically high spirits, the cold New York day feeling suddenly brighter.

* * * * * *

THAT SAME SATURDAY afternoon, the three of us—Marius, Christel, and myself—flew, using different airlines as a hedge against further cancellations, to our final and most important strategic objective: Washington D.C. The heart of the beast. If we could make even a faint scratch on the consciousness of Washington, the rest of America might, we dared hope, eventually follow like dominoes.

Our first manoeuvre, once in the zone, was to reconnoitre and photograph the iconic instalments and facilities, to get our bearings in this city of power.

So, despite the biting, freezing conditions, our Sunday was spent as tourists in the Mall and West Potomac Park; gaping up at the majestic dome of the Capitol, researching the vast halls of the Library of Congress, judging the austere façade of the Supreme Court, investigating the hushed galleries of the National Gallery of Art and the Smithsonian, ogling the White House from the distant Ellipse, staring in solemn silence at the Lincoln Memorial and the stark needle of the Washington Monument and the perfect reflection of each from the foot of the other, contemplating the eternal flame at the Tomb of the Unknown Soldier and the simple, powerful grave of the better-known JFK in Arlington National Cemetery, taxiing up the Rock Creek and Potomac Parkway past the imposing John F. Kennedy Center for the Performing Arts to the infamous Watergate complex; and finally, wandering dazed and sombre along the stark, black granite wound of the Vietnam Veterans' Memorial.

Did the Phoenicians, the Gauls, the Nubians, the Ethiopians, the Celts, the Goths and other awed foreigners gaze with the same struck awe and paralysis of the critical faculties at Trajan's brand new column celebrating his conquest of the Dacians, as we foreigners did at that grand, sweeping gesture of public keening—that imposing, polished stone record of name after name after name? Poignant is not an adequate term: *devastating* almost reaches it. Christel would not walk down the sunken causeway with us, preferring to wait, arms wrapped around herself against the cold, at one end while Marius and I inched haltingly along the relentless roll call of a sacrifice that no one in America had been able to properly acknowledge before this cenotaph was erected in 1987.

Afterwards, though none of us noted it until we were back in the taxi, we returned to our hotel in a shared, heavy silence. The monument had spoken a language beyond politics.

From the jungles of Vietnam to this polished wall of grief in the capital: that was America all over, it seemed to me. A nation forever wrestling with the consequences of its own immense power. *Sunt lacrimae rerum*—there are tears for things.

* * * * * *

MONDAY MORNING, AND the birdies are singing somewhere under the grey sky and the telephone lines in our hotel room are humming. Marius and I, fortified by bad coffee, are mentally preparing for our encounter with Richard Christian, the associate director of the American Legion, when the phone rings with a jarring shrillness. Christel has appointed herself our private secretary for the duration and takes up the apparatus.

"Jeff," she says, her voice tight, holding out the handset for me. "It's Melbourne. It's your office. They have received a message from the Secretary of Energy, Hazel O'Leary: she is unable to see you! A cancellation."

The wry, bitter thought instantly crosses my mind that, on the only occasion when an American civil servant *finally* phones me back in Australia, I am inconveniently in a position to taxi down and speak with him in person, but the person at the top has vanished.

"What a way to start!" I slam down the handset, the plastic cracking against the cradle, and thump discontentedly around the cramped room. I grind my teeth in pure frustration and then, forcing calm, ring through to the hotel reception to get me the Secretary's Chief of Staff on the line. At that moment, the full, crushing enormity of the task ahead weighs on me like a great, cold rock on my shoulders. Only the white-hot consciousness of the anger I feel, of the sensation of my personal time and our meagre funds draining away, supplies me with the raw impulse to go forward and take the next step; the first step in yet another frustrating series.

The voice that answers, I discover, belongs to Hank, the Chief of Staff's secretary.

"Hank," I say, gathering myself up, injecting a tone of reasonable urgency. "My name's Jeff Carswell, and I've come all the way from Melbourne, Australia to meet with the Secretary of Energy, and now I understand she is unexpectedly unable to see me. I wonder would it be at all possible to arrange a meeting with Dan Reicher, her Chief of Staff, in her stead? You see, I'm on a very tight schedule; in fact, I'm only in the States for a very brief stay and I doubt I'll have the opportunity to return within the foreseeable future. I know that if I can have just a few moments with your boss, even that may be valuable time spent. Otherwise, I'll be going away from Washington quite empty-handed. I've travelled literally half way 'round the world for this meeting, which was to have been the most significant of my entire trip."

"You're from out of town, then?" Hank asks, his tone bland.

I hold the phone up before my eyes and blink in sheer disbelief. Hank's flat, scratchy voice continues, and I put the handset back to my ear while a wearying, familiar heaviness droops my shoulders down again.

"That's a joke, son!" Hank abruptly assumes the exaggerated accent of Foghorn Leghorn and gives a short, hollow laugh. "Mr. Carswell, I'll have a word with Mr. Reicher. We weren't expecting him in at all this morning—he's hurt his leg rather badly over the weekend, skiing in Colorado, and is heading into hospital this evening for surgery—but the Secretary wanted to see him briefly, so he's dragged himself in anyway. I'll speak to him immediately for you and get back to you, if you'll give me your number."

Just moments later, Hank is again on the line, a minor miracle of efficiency.

"Does eleven o'clock suit, Mr. Carswell?"

"Yes, perfectly." I reply and, hanging up, breathe out a huge, shuddering breath of relief. "All is not yet lost, Marius. We live to fight another hour." *'Till the next absurd setback,'* I muttered silently to myself.

"Well, come on," I add quickly, grabbing my coat. "We'd better be on our way to our first rendezvous. We can't be late. We'll see you this evening, Christel."

On our arrival at the swank, sober offices of the American Legion, the associate director greets us and shows us into his wood-panelled office with great, formal civility and watchful attention.

"Gentlemen. Can I offer you tea, coffee? Something to warm you up."

Richard Christian is a greying, distinguished man of about sixty with a gentle, superficially solicitous nature.

"Please, tell me more of your story. I was quite… astounded by what you outlined in your letters to the organisation."

Marius, much to my open-mouthed astonishment, seizes the initiative and launches into one of the great, impassioned spiels which he seems to command at an instant, his limited English no barrier to his fervor. I decide, for the moment, to remain unobtrusively in the background, resting my elbows on the arms of my leather chair and pressing my index fingers lightly against my lips in a thoughtful pose. I have not yet fully accounted for my allowing Marius his head on this occasion, especially in view of his independent and wildly idiosyncratic—not to say often incomprehensible—approach to the English language... But I will. I will.

"Mr. Christian, just over twenty-six years ago, at height of Cold *Krieg* with Sovietski Union and Hot War with Vietnam, Operation Chrome Dome was set functioning by the United States Air Force Strategic Air Command. This operation... "

162

"Marius is a great story-teller," I muse internally, settling back to observe the tale unfold, despite the car-crash of his grammar.

" ... B-52s day and night, around the clock, cover entire planet in web of security... "

"Mr. Christian seems to wear his patience rather near to the surface," I think, observing him cross and uncross his legs, alternately sitting back in his high-backed chair and leaning forward, and continually interlacing his fingers into a prayerful gesture with a steeple, in unconscious imitation of my own attitude. Then, glancing at me, he quickly unravelled them again. I wonder whether he can sense the depth of the horror and the cold anger we have carried into his comfortable, insulated offices.

"...some *millionen* fragments boiling *mit* plutonium and tritium and uranium. Fire ball thrown up colossal was and *ich*, as chief fire officer, was immediately in scene; or, at least, on edge of ice where bomber went in... "

"I think Mr. Christian could wish Marius further," I note, seeing further, unmistakable indications of unease in his gestures. He is now rubbing his palms on his trouser legs and smiling a weak, fixed smile. Now he is picking invisible fluff from his tailored jacket. I decide the moment for intervention has arrived.

"So, as you can well understand, Mr. Christian," I say, smoothly cutting in, "we are concerned to reach as wide an audience as we possibly can in this country, which we do hold ultimately responsible for creating the situation that led to the current widespread suffering amongst our members and, we believe, amongst those of the emerging association here in the States. Which must be of particular concern to the American Legion, as undoubtedly there will be ex-Thulers within your own vast membership."

"You may well be correct there, Mr. Schmidt ..."

"Carswell," I correct him gently but firmly.

"Er, Mr. Carswell. Yes, it is most likely. And clearly yours is a great cause, an admirable struggle for justice against such immovable objects as politicians, bureaucrats and twelve-star generals who eat, sleep, work and recreate within the five walls of the Pentagon. However," he paused, choosing his words, "I'm just unclear as to in what *practical* way we can lend you assistance."

"I can make it clear," I clarify, leaning forward. "You could arrange to publish an article on the subject in your magazine. I understand it has a readership of some hundreds of thousands. I'm certain that many of your members would be most interested—perhaps shocked—to discover that there may be a specific, hidden reason for the unusual health problems they undoubtedly suffer; and here it is. All you need do is supply the basic facts of when, where, what; and then provide the telephone and mailing address of the ex-Thulers' association in the States and ..."

I started to feel a fragile hope that we could be at a genuine turning point. But, when he cuts me off, I am hardly surprised by the refusal. What surprises me, chills me, are the actual words he uses to frame it.

"I'm afraid that, as good as it sounds, that is just not possible."

"I'm sorry?" I ask, needing to hear the bureaucracy articulated.

"You see, Mr. Carswell, and Mr. Schmidt, the association just does not exercise any control over the editorship of our magazine. We pride ourselves—we *like* to think—that it is free of interference from the boards and various lobby groups within the membership and can pursue its independent publishing role. It's a matter of principle."

"Am I to take it," I ask, my voice growing cooler, "that the world's largest organisation of ex-servicemen and women has no say, no influence, in what goes into its very own, flagship organ of publicity?"

"We pride ourselves on allowing it complete editorial independence," he asserts, and indeed there was pride—a bureaucratic, sanctimonious pride—in his voice."

"Could you not, in a personal capacity, write the article yourself and submit it to the editorial board? Surely they would view it favorably, seeing as though it would be of at least passing interest to almost all ex-servicemen; and of major, life-altering interest to any of them who served at Thule in the late sixties!"

"As a senior board member," he said, drawing himself up slightly, "I am not in a position to be able to do so, I'm afraid. My position would be compromised by allowing myself to become the mouthpiece of an organisation whose growth has been initiated outside this country. Don't misunderstand me. I sympathise greatly with your plight. I just cannot take the side of your specific organisation and remain a neutral and disinterested board member. It's about perception."

"Well, once again," I said, trying one last, pragmatic appeal, "may I just remind you that it would be on behalf of the many *American* servicemen who served at Thule that you would be acting; not on behalf of the Danish association? It's your own members you'd be helping."

"I'm sorry, I just can't see my way clear on this. Which doesn't mean that *you* can't submit an article to the editors yourselves. That avenue is always open."

"Yes, I understand that. However, we were rather hoping that you, given your standing, might be in a position to help the chances of such an article being published, to give it a… nudge."

"And that, gentlemen, is precisely the position that is simply untenable for me. I'm sorry I can offer you no other help. I can only recommend, once more, that you suggest to the board of the American Ex-Thulers' Association that they submit an article of the type you've outlined. Perhaps it would then be viewed favourably by the independent editorial board. Beyond that, I cannot presently make any promises, I'm afraid.

"However," he concluded, rising to signal the end of the meeting, "I do wish you the best of success in your enterprise."

Out in the damnedly cold Washington air again, the imaginary birdies had stopped singing and my ears were ringing with the hollow, polished sound of his refusal. We walked to our next rendezvous in two solitary, parallel silences, the snow crunching underfoot. We stopped briefly at a sterile coffee shop to try to defrost our spirits with scalding liquid. But time and the brutal temperature of the coffee were against us, and we went back out into the political cold unfortified and even more profoundly depressed than before. The corridors of power, it seemed, were lined with closed doors and principles that served only those already inside.

* * * * * *

CHRISTEL, HAVING SPENT the morning waiting by the silent phone without a single call to divert her boredom, is just making her way down to the hotel restaurant for a solitary bite to eat and a reviving coffee. When she arrives at the head of the grand staircase that leads down to the opulent foyer, a man of about forty emerges from behind a nearby pillar as if conjured from the shadows. He is dressed in the nondescript uniform of faded jeans and a thick, warm lumber jacket.

He folds his newspaper with a sharp crack and roughly pushes past Christel, as if there were a dense crowd to be negotiated. There are, in fact, only three other people on the entire staircase. Christel gives him a look of frowning perplexity, fully expecting an apology. After all, the Americans are famously an honorable people.

"Patient research leads to greater understanding, doesn't it, Mrs. Schmidt?" he says, his voice a low, rapid monotone. His breath smells of stale coffee and cigarettes. "Especially cultural researches. They are the safest by far. Do you understand me? Go visit the Smithsonian, Mrs. Schmidt. Enjoy your researches, Mrs. Schmidt."

The ominous and unmistakable character of the repetition of her name drives its meaning home to Christel's awareness immediately. The jowled, unshaven face is uncomfortably near to hers for only a moment. Despite her shock, she reaches out her hand to the retreating figure, her fingers brushing the coarse fabric of his jacket.

"Who do you think you are? Answer me, you rude man!" But he tears her hand roughly from his arm and is gone, his movements swift and practiced. Her heart is thumping a wild rhythm against her ribs and her hand shakes visibly. She watches him saunter unconcernedly down the vast foyer, through the heavy brass doors, and out of sight onto the crowded, indifferent boulevard. Christel, her appetite vanished, turns back towards the sanctuary of her room, forgoing lunch and coffee. There she locks the door and waits, trying to still her trembling hands, for the return of her nerves and of her husband and myself.

* * * * * *

"LET'S HOPE THIS one's a bit more cooperative," Marius remarked brightly between puffs of frozen breath, his spirits seemingly recovered from our earlier, crushing failure.

"We're late, we're late. We must hurry. We are late." I misquoted Lewis Carroll as I pushed Marius bodily before me through the morning-tea crowds of the civil service centre in L'Enfant Plaza, the downtown heartbeat of American power. Our next rendezvous was with a couple of representatives of the Center for Defence Information.

"Well, I just hope that our first encounter with the American military establishment was not typical," I said. I knew even as I spoke that I protested too much. The word 'hope' leaps too easily to the lips of those whose hope has long since soured into weary apprehension.

"I can hardly get over that last fellow," observed Marius, shaking his head. "He was like an old rooster with clipped wings, flapping uselessly around an empty pen."

"Yeah," I added, glibly, "Paper authority over nothing!"

I might have added a few more colourful epithets but, for the sake of propriety in this formal city, I only thought them.

"No guts, no sense, no balls!" Marius declared suddenly, his voice carrying more than I would have liked.

I stopped short in the pedestrian traffic and just looked at him with eyes wide, then we both broke into unseemly, tension-relieving laughter. Marius brought us both back down to reality as we approached and entered the cool, quiet foyer of a very modern suite of offices.

"These men we're meeting are ex-military, are they? Captains Carroll and Bush?"

"Well, actually, they're Navy, and one is an admiral and the other a captain, but in the navy, whatever your actual military rank, if you have command of a ship, then you're called 'Captain.' It's a title of command, not just a rank."

We asked at the polished information desk for Admiral Carroll and, being told that we were expected (a positive note, at least) and asked to wait, I continued my impromptu lesson in American military etiquette, nomenclature and procedures. I was quietly pleased that I had done a little background reading on the subject over at the Library of Congress the day before. To cross these particular cultural lines, you need to develop a few anthropological skills.

"And, if you're in charge of a whole fleet of ships, then you're called 'Admiral.' Roughly equivalent to a general, I gather. At least, I think that's right. I'm sure that's what the book said. One of the fellows we're meeting today was first officer on a nuclear submarine."

"Yeah? So, he's had some personal exposure to these issues, then!" quipped Marius, unable to resist.

"You could put it like that," I grinned, though the joke felt thin.

Almost immediately, a very big man, not fat, just imposing in stature, in his late fifties, with a portly and starboardly bearing that spoke of a life on decks, entered and introduced himself.

"Good afternoon, gentlemen," he shook hands with each of us, his grip firm and dry. "I'm Captain Bush. Unfortunately, Admiral Carroll cannot be with us today and sends his sincere apologies. However, I am fully deputised to stand in for him and to report back should I find there is anything of particular interest in what you have to tell me. Shall we go up to my suite?"

We arrived at our destination: an attractive, understated consultancy suite, and were shown into a small meeting room furnished comfortably with wood-panelled walls, maritime paintings, occasional tables and deep, comfortable easy chairs. I shot a glance over towards Marius. He was fidgeting uncomfortably, out of his element. I felt my own internal optimism droop. Our host went on.

"As you may well understand, Mr. Carswell and Mr. Schmidt, an organisation of the size and global importance of the US military is not unfamiliar with individuals and groups who bear grievances against us. Some ex-guerilla from El Salvador stubs his toe on a rock while on holiday in Valparaíso, and we get stuck with a writ from some smart attorney in New Mexico. But, that is the price we, the defenders of peace and prosperity, pay in the modern world with its vast and incredibly fast network of information. We learn to live with it. We even learn to use it to our own advantage, when we can."

I was on the verge of pointing a sardonic thumb at this personification of Uncle Sam's Little Helper and asking Marius, *'Is this guy for real?'* when he looked me directly in the eye and said, his tone shifting from bureaucratic to blunt:

"You look like the spokes-bloke. So, speak! Tell me your story."

As I spoke, relating our whole sorry saga in as clear and brief a way as I could muster under the pressure of his interrogating gaze, his eyes, deep and dark in their sockets, never wavered from my face. I felt quite isolated and laid bare under the glare of his spotlight attention, a specimen under examination.

Throughout my monologue, which he interrupted from time to time only to ask for crisp clarifications on points of fact or dates, the Captain seemed gradually to unfreeze, like the reputed frog of scientific myth which, being extracted from an icy state, returns to life and movement as warmth is restored to its body.

I ended, "So, Captain, the reason we have brought our grievances to Washington is more a tactic to pressure our own government to own up to its complicity and wrongdoing than to solely blame the United States military for its undoubted part in the affair. Although, by no means can we simply exonerate them either. But, it is probably more the job of the emerging American ex-Thulers' association to bring direct pressure to bear on that particular point."

The Captain began slowly, deliberately. He seemed to dip into a private store of memories and convictions not often shared with people outside his immediate military circle.

"You may or may not be aware of this," he said, his voice lower now, "but in my time, I served aboard some of the United States Navy's most sophisticated nuclear submarines, both Nautilus and Polaris classes. Since retiring, neither I nor my doctors have failed to notice the… coincidence… of my many years' service and the significant health problems I now suffer. Of course, I use the term 'coincidence' with heavy irony."

He went on to detail the specific cancer he battles and added, a note of grim resignation in his voice:

"There is no doubt in my mind that my condition, however you may choose to describe the medical connection, is a direct result of my prolonged exposure to radiation over all those years. And, I might add, there is no shortage of unofficial documentation of similar cases among my former colleagues.

"Although," he finished, a wry, tired smile touching his lips, "Getting the official clearance to see that documentation? Well, put it this way: if there's a snowman in Hell, maybe, and only maybe, he has that clearance. For all the good it would do him in that climate!"

He shook his head very slowly and blew out a deep, weary breath.

"And you men were directly, massively exposed to the raw stuff! My God! No wonder you're suffering!" He exhaled another deep breath and, after a weighty pause, said:

"I will take your case up with Admiral Carroll. I have no doubt that he will be totally with you, as I am. And, should you ever need my personal support, for instance, as an expert witness in any legal action you might pursue, I will be most willing to lend my considerable weight to your cause."

He shifted his considerable frame in his chair as if to physically underline his words. "I have some experience in such matters, having appeared on behalf of a number of complainants already, with a measure of success. I have also testified as an expert witness before parliamentary committees and similar tribunals in Germany, Denmark and Spain, advising on the inherent dangers of nuclear power and naval reactors."

Out again in the icy streets, hurrying to our next meeting, I remarked to Marius, my spirits lifted, "What an ally to have on the inside."

"You said it!" Marius agreed, his step lighter. "Better an ally like that than an enemy. He has seen the beast from within."

* * * * * *

"C'MON, C'MON, C'MON." I literally pushed Marius into a rapid trot toward our next destination. The Physicians for Social Responsibility had, at the time of our visit, as its chairman Peter Tyler, a key figure in the Defence Lobbyist Group.

When we arrived at their offices, puffing like steam trains, Peter himself invited me to address one of their regular meetings that very morning. So, there I found myself moments later, standing before some sixty or seventy intense, intelligent members of one of Washington's most respected and powerful lobby groups.

"We can only give you about a minute to make your point, Mr. Carswell," said Peter, not unkindly. "We have quite a packed agenda to get through this morning."

I raised my eyebrows, grinned an artificial grin of understanding, and said, "OK. A minute it is."

After I had spoken for ten minutes, carried away by the attentive faces before me, I could see that my points were being received not just politely, but with intelligent engagement, signaled by the nodding of several heads and the deepening concentration in many gazes. After my impromptu presentation, several members came up to me personally and offered their support, handing me cards and making notes. I left them with raised eyebrows all around when I casually mentioned that I had secured a meeting with Dan Reicher, the Secretary of Energy's Chief of Staff. To the Washington health policy lobbyist, he was a glittering, elusive prize; and Marius and I left there that morning wearing, in their eyes, the subtle glow of unlikely champions.

We had, it seemed, achieved a small access that was their constant professional ambition.

I, on my part, treasure the memory of having been privileged, if only for ten minutes, to address such a decent, honourable and effective group of people. It was a small island of sanity.

* * * * * *

OUR NEXT DESTINATION was the National Security Archives, whose offices were only a short, brisk walk away for two people whose spirits were now cautiously high. This time I had no need to push Marius to hurry: he was as impatient as I was to get there. I suspect he had been infected by my own renewed sense of urgent purpose, not to mention the underlying anxiety that never fully left me.

We arrived at the address we sought. The building had an aspect you might have called unassuming had it not been such an act of quiet presumption for it to exist at all in this city of grandiose statements. It was a terribly Kafkaesque monolith, instantly reminding me of my youthful reading of *The Castle*, that story of mindless, distorting, horrifying bureaucracy. But, we were not to be so easily dejected after our recent encouraging experiences. In we went, pausing only to note the drab, functional interior of the lobby and the presence of a young lady whose red nose and watery eyes told us from a distance that she ought to have called in sick that morning.

The groaning elevator carried all three of us reluctantly to the fifth floor, the aforementioned young lady sniffling and sneezing unashamedly the whole way, a minor symphony of misery.

We scrambled out of the elevator all at once, bumping into each other and offering muttered apologies simultaneously. I, for one, could see little use in spending the next four days nursing the beginnings of a Washington cold. We headed for the dust-filmed glass doors that displayed the name of our destined organisation, only to repeat the bumping and apologizing affair of twenty seconds prior.

Inside the offices, our eyes, I guessed, were the only things that had swept through there in a long time. Filing cabinets covered every square foot of floor not occupied by desks or chairs. The walls were a chaotic tapestry of charts, tables, maps and posters covering a huge range of subjects: from global warming estimates to the end of the century, to the NBA's new season fixtures; from a detailed contour map of the Mariana Trench, to a classic black-and-white David Redfern shot of Miles Davis at Fillmore.

Finding what might serve as a reception desk was like hailing a cab at night with rain on your glasses: an exercise in hopeful failure. Eventually, a young man with kind eyes took pity on our confused hovering and hailed us over to his paper-strewn desk.

When we arrived there, the sneezing young woman from the elevator was already in whispered conference with him.

"Hold just a mo', Sheryl. Hi there, can I help you gentlemen?"

"My name is Jeff Carswell. I am the President of International Relations for the Danish B-52 Crested Ice Disaster Thule Radiation Victims' Association. And, this is Marius Schmidt, our Chairman..."

"Oh, yes, yes, we've been expecting you," the young man said, his face breaking into a warm, genuine smile. "You're here on behalf of the ghosts of Thule. Glad you could make it. I'm Steve. We spoke on the phone a couple of times, I think, Jeff. And this is Sheryl, our legal beagle. She's come in today despite being under doctor's orders to spend a week in Bermuda, just so she can lend her expertise on any points of law that might be useful for you."

We shook hands all around, laughing a little awkwardly over our previous elevator encounter.

"Look," Steve began. He was quite an animated fellow in his late twenties, casually dressed in jeans and a sweater, but with an air of self-possession rare in anyone under forty, and almost as rarely authentic in anyone over. "Your story, Jeff, just about knocked me out. Sure, I knew about HOBO 28. It's my job to know these things. I spend my days researching them. But, boy, some of what you told me on the phone! The sheer, breathtaking cynicism of it! The US military's, the Danish government's, the American government's too. It just blew me away. All of us here, in fact. It's just the kind of secret that could, if you think about it, blow away the whole human race."

He looked at Sheryl, shaking his head at the marvel of human moral obtuseness. Sheryl, despite her cold, took up the baton with fierce intelligence.

"My guess is that, before any other consideration, the best way we can assist you is to simply open our files. Let me introduce you to a couple of our archivists. They'll be able to help you identify and locate exactly what information you might need, if it exists. Because, if it exists anywhere in the public domain, it's likely here. We make it our business to see that the Freedom of Information legislation in this country is a truly democratic and candid instrument of the citizen's right to know. Sorry if I sound a little like a textbook," she said, sniffling, "but I don't do this job just for the money. I have a real stake in the good functioning of this society, and I want my knowledge to make a difference..."

Sheryl pushed open another set of doors and beckoned us through, still talking rapidly, where we met the two archivists whose time for the rest of that afternoon she put entirely at our disposal.

It is seldom in this life that the sensation of complete and utter vindication visits a person. It is the common lot to struggle through life clinging to more or less likely, more or less useful versions of reality, often in the face not only of a diffuse feeling of the world's indifference, but of a very specific and concrete opposition.

'Such is life!' quipped Ned Kelly, the notorious bushranger, police killer and nationally celebrated folk hero, underdog and Irish self-styled political idealist, from the scaffold at Old Melbourne Jail. Well, no, Ned. That was *your* life! The life that is summed up in a throw-away line is a thrown away life.

But, no! Wait! Surely we cannot dismiss this issue as surreptitiously as Ned dismisses us, his audience, from his biography.

Perhaps so; but as Ned dismisses us mighty summarily, we can never know more than just enough to keep the legend alive. The truth dies with the man.

It might at least be said that Ned found his specific opposition; in which case, in some grim manner, his was a life well spent, if spent all too quickly. Ned forced his life into a shape, and considered that, in his death, its meaning was recapitulated.

But whatever else we may decide about this gigantic, ambiguous figure, it is certain that Ned Kelly never knew the profound vindication of his position in this life that I knew on that grey afternoon in Washington D.C.

We sat ourselves down at a vast mahogany table large enough to accommodate a state dinner for twenty and I began sifting through the huge, towering pile of documents, memoranda, grainy photos, faxes and photocopies that Sheryl and her helpers placed before us.

My first, overwhelmed thought was, *'My God, look at all this paper. Where do I even start?'* But, as I laid my eyes on the first few documents, documents that explicitly corroborated my long-held view of the secret political manoeuvring behind the events at Thule, a sensation washed over me. It was as if a dark, sooty smoke that had covered and obscured every visible thing in my universe for years was suddenly sucked eddying and swirling into the ground in less time than it takes a gnat to blink. What I had believed to be true, what I had fought for so many lonely years to have recognised as true, squared perfectly, devastatingly, with the facts.

Because, here, in my own trembling hands, I held the irrefutable evidence. The facts themselves.

I looked up at Marius at one point from a photocopy of a memo from the Pentagon to the White House. In it, mentioned as a matter of routine and as something not worth bringing to the personal attention of President Johnson, was the fact that a B-52 was regularly, *id est* daily, diverting from its assigned course to fly over Danish territory, *id est* Greenland, *id est* Thule, *id est* the BMEWS station, without the express permission of the Danish government, *id est*, in a democracy, without the permission of the Danish people.

"This is dynamite!" I said, my voice hushed, my eyes glistening with a fierce excitement. I turned my head to Sheryl, who was watching us with a satisfied look. "How did you manage to get this stuff?"

"We asked for it," she said simply, shrugging.

"You asked for it," I repeated in a flat monotone of disbelief. Then, emphasising each word as if tasting them: "You. Asked. For. It."

"That's right. That's what we do. We keep a watchdog's eye on the politicians on the perch and the military wallies on the leash, just so people like you can come and access the information you have a right to anyway, without having to run the brutal gauntlets of the Pentagon or the White House mailrooms."

"Would I," I continued slowly and deliberately, needing to be certain, "Would I, not being an American citizen, have the right to access this information directly from those sources, as you have done?"

"Yes, of course. You only need to know how to apply for it. But, to be able to apply, you first need to know that you *can*. And that is the subtle feature of the Freedom of Information Act that makes governments feel easier about it: most people simply don't know they have the right; and then they have to discover the how and the where. So, organisations like ours exist to make sure the Act isn't just a paper tiger. Around the clock we request information in areas we feel may sooner or later be of significant public interest. And we have a very good strike-rate, as you have witnessed today."

"So, the Danish government or its agencies could easily have gotten this information at any time?" The implication was staggering.

"Of course. As a matter of fact, much of the documentation you have before you was originally gathered by Doctor Scott Sagan for research. He included a chapter on the Thule accident in his new book on nuclear weapons risk analysis. Which, by the way, has just hit the bookstores. If you can manage to get a copy, I would highly recommend it. In addition, when we ourselves uncover information that may be of interest to allies and friendly foreign powers, we often contact relevant government bodies in that country and offer it to them. I'm afraid, in this particular case, your Danish Departments of Energy, Foreign Affairs, Defence and the Office of the Prime Minister simply failed to respond. They weren't interested, it seems."

"I'll bet they weren't," Marius exploded, his face flushing. "That's your responsible and compassionate civil servant for you! Protecting their own hides."

"Yes, but we've got them now," I countered, the weight of the paper in my hand feeling like a moral weapon. I held up the damning memo. "With this short and curt memorandum, we've finally got them by the short and curlies!"

At that, all three people present laughed, more in shared triumph and, in the case of Marius and myself, profound relief, than at the feeble humour of my pun.

On our way down to the group's own small bookstore, where we did indeed lay hands on a precious copy of Dr. Sagan's invaluable new book, I remarked to Marius, my voice thick with emotion, "Finally. Finally, we have found some disinterested fellow human beings with compassion and the power to help. Thank God. We are not alone in this fight after all."

* * * * * *

DASHING OUT OF the Archives on our way to our improvised, crucial meeting with the Secretary of Energy's Chief of Staff, copies of at least one hundred thoroughly incriminating documents tucked tightly under our arms, I felt as I'm sure Woodward and Bernstein must have felt after their clandestine meetings with Deep Throat. We were no longer just petitioners; we were now armed with hard evidence.

In the taxi, weaving through Washington's late afternoon traffic, we had to cover a fair bit of town in a short time. I recalled with a pang that we were on our way to see the Chief of Staff; not the Secretary herself. Still, even the acuteness of that disappointment could not dampen the fierce, buzzing energy in my spirit. The information we now possessed was a tangible weight, a weapon. We could, I dared to think, almost bring the Danish government to its knees with it.

I mentioned this happy, heady fact to Marius, but, being too busy adjusting his tie and patting down his unruly hair in the taxi's window reflection, he scarcely heard me and just muttered a non-committal 'hmm.'

When we arrived at the monolithic Department of Energy building, the reason for Marius' frantic preening became manifest: the television crew from the Chicago station was already waiting for us on the sidewalk, their camera a dark eye pointed our way. I had quite forgotten about their planned coverage. They wanted to film us arriving at the offices, which we had to do twice, walking back out and then in again, before they were happy with the result on film. It felt absurd and theatrical.

I grew a touch concerned when a couple of uniformed security figures detached themselves from the shadowed facade of the building and ambled, after exchanging brief, disapproving looks, over towards the film crew.

One of them, the elder statesman of the pair, drew himself up and thrust his hands into the front of his belt, in that universal braggadocio's way of making it known one is armed, and spoke, much to my alarm, directly to Marius.

"Here, what's all this? You can't go taking videos around federal buildings like this. Move along, please, or I'll have to confiscate your equipment."

Whatever Marius said then, no one in this life will ever know for sure, certainly neither Marius himself nor the flustered security guard. Whatever it was, delivered with Marius's characteristic booming confidence and Danish accent, it had a semi combustible effect. The middle aged uniform turned a bright terra cotta colour and gave Marius a sharp, warning shove in the chest.

"Just move along, smart ass."

At this, Marius executed one of his most sublime diplomatic manoeuvres ever: he uttered no verbal reply, but took a smart, decisive step straight backwards and vanished through the spinning leaves of the revolving door into the Secretary's offices, with me whipping in behind him like a shadow.

Inside the hushed, marbled lobby, we just leaned against the cool wall for a moment, our hearts pounding, and laughed silently, enjoying the dumb show through the glass as the TV guys outside tried to reason with and cool down the overheated Federal officer.

"I'm happy enough to get the coverage," I panted to Marius, "but sometimes, your methods get just a little out of hand."

Marius just grinned wider, panting all the harder, and hurried us up to the vast, polished reception desk, our moment of rebellion over.

Our meeting with the Chief of Staff, Dan Reicher, was scheduled to last only a few minutes: a poor consolation prize for the absent Secretary. Half an hour later, this young, dynamic attorney had shown us exactly how he had earned his reputation as something of a crusader for groups and individuals like ourselves, victims of accidental radiation exposure or of unethical experiments.

He had, as we knew, hurt his leg badly days before while skiing in Colorado and was due to be admitted to hospital that very afternoon for surgery. Despite the pain and the impending operation, he had agreed to meet us and, in fact, had interrupted a high level briefing with Hazel O'Leary, the Secretary of Energy, to do so.

He asked several penetrating, intelligent questions about the precise location and circumstances of the crash and about the spectrum of problems we had been facing, both the insidious health issues and the maddening wall of bureaucratic indifference. Feeling emboldened by our earlier find, I commented that the American military seemed dangerously irresponsible when it came to "bandying about its nuclear weapons." At that, Dan put up a hand, a wry smile on his face.

"Mr. Carswell, I don't doubt for a moment that you've been fobbed off with officialese and balderdash. But, I must correct you on a small, crucial detail of fact: the nuclear weapons the U.S. Military 'bandies about' do not actually belong to them. They belong to us. To the Department of Energy."

I creased my brow, utterly bewildered. "What?"

"Yes, that's right," he said, leaning back in his chair. "The most devastating weapons of mass destruction on the planet today, as much as George and Bill might go on about Saddam Hussein's little armoury, which is more a powder room than an arsenal, are in the capable hands of the United States Department of Light Bulbs and Donkey Engines. We make them, we maintain them, we own them. The military just borrows them when needed."

"Isn't that a bit like keeping kerosene in a soft drink bottle?" I asked, my mind struggling with the absurdity.

"It keeps all nuclear related functions under one roof," Dan shrugged, though his eyes were sharp. "And, after all," he added, grinning wickedly, "the military are the last ones you'd actually trust with nuclear weapons, aren't they? Too trigger happy."

"They're the ones who would drop them like flapjacks on innocent civilians," I retorted, the image of Thule's blackened ice flashing in my mind.

"Admittedly, Mr. Carswell, admittedly. Which is precisely why the custodial responsibility lies here."

"So, so..." I stammered, unable to fully comprehend the staggering import of his words. "I don't know what to say!"

"The dividing line for responsibilities in this country is not strictly drawn between peace and war. We have not found that to be a particularly useful division. A more pragmatic one is the divide between the provision of a capability and the wherewithal to use it. Nuclear weapons belong to the former category, and defence to the latter. We provide the sword; they decide when to swing it."

"It sounds awfully cynical, but I don't think you mean it to be," I queried, trying to read his face.

"Well, without the freedom guaranteed by the presence of an invincible military, no service, however benign, can be efficiently provided. So no, I'm not being cynical, Mr. Carswell, but I am being a little sardonic and brutally pragmatic. If you can understand this peculiar schism in the American mind, your visit to Washington will have been most fruitful. And in all of that," he said, rising carefully, favouring his injured leg, "I wish you every possible success."

He shook our hands firmly, his grip both an apology and an encouragement, leaving us admiring and profoundly nonplussed at the same time. It was a masterclass in the surreal logic of power.

Although, to date, Dan's specific promises of further information and direct support never fully materialised, the mere fact that I had managed to get face to face with a man of his seniority and personal stature did immeasurable wonders for us in terms of credibility and publicity back home.

Still, I thought as we left, had he kept all his promises, that would have been rather nice too!

* * * * * *

AT LAST, THE evening drew a close on a long and intensely draining day. We had a quick, quiet dinner and retired to the dimly lit bar of our hotel, which boasted a sombre view of the lit up, geometric bulk of the Pentagon across the river. We settled in for a few drinks, preparatory to a sleep we had profoundly earned. I became concerned when I noticed Marius start nervously adjusting his tie again and brushing invisible lint from his jacket with his hands.

"Marius, what have you done now?" I asked, my suspicions instantly aroused. "You know I wanted to keep a reasonably low profile here, at least until we're ready."

"I called the local Danish news hounds when I had a spare minute today," he said, not meeting my eye, "and... Oh, here they are now!" he finished abruptly, his face breaking into a radiant, practiced smile as he rose to greet the approaching contingent of journalists and cameramen. I looked helplessly at Christel.

"How does he do it?" I asked her, genuinely mystified and exasperated. "We've been running all day."

Christel spread her hands in a gesture that was half shared puzzlement and half mute apology for her husband's relentless zeal.

"Well, in any case, I'm not up for this at this time of night," I said firmly. "I'm off to bed. Marius, see you at seven sharp tomorrow!" I called over the gathering noise. He gave me a distracted thumbs up without looking and was promptly swallowed for the third time that day below a sea of microphones and bright lights.

Christel drew a deep, tired breath. "Me too. I'm absolutely pooped."

So, we left Marius in his absolute element, already holding forth, and made our way towards the elevators and our much desired rest.

In the elevator, Christel laughed softly and said, "It is something of a masterstroke, don't you think, though, Jeff? The publicity."

"Oh, yes," I conceded, the fatigue making me generous. "As a matter of fact, I do. Marius is a natural force with the press. He speaks their language."

"It's a skill that many people in our association just don't appreciate at all. The publicity angle of this whole trip can't be overstated."

"Absolutely," I agreed. The doors opened on our floor. "You know, when Hanne first encountered Marius, she was quite overwhelmed by his ethos of 'communication at all costs.' And she's no slouch herself when it comes to that sort of thing; she was a union rep for a long time and knows the importance of good communications." I hoped that might mollify Christel, and perhaps myself. In truth, Marius's media habit had me quite worried. I knew the wildfire properties of a poorly managed news story, and felt that even a little prudence often goes a long way.

We were making our several ways down the quiet corridor to our rooms. Christel paused, her key in her hand, and sighed heavily. "Jeff," she said, her voice low, "I had a very strange encounter today." She then told me of her Chandleresque confrontation on the staircase.

I was stunned into a thoughtful, cold silence. The adrenaline of the day drained away, replaced by a slow chill. "The skunks," I finally muttered. "Have you told Marius yet?"

"I'll tell him when he comes up. I just didn't want you to hear it first from him tomorrow morning. What do they want, Jeff? And who the damned hell are they?" She had paled, and let out a brief, stifled sob, then steadied herself. "I'm OK. I guess it means they're scared of us. We're getting under their skin."

"Yes," I answered, the pieces fitting together with a grim click. "And that we're getting too close for someone's comfort. The Archives today... it proves we're on the right, dangerous track."

"This whole business has been such a great strain, Jeff." Her voice was thin with weariness. "What with Marius's illness, and all the work he's poured into the association, and the sheer injustice of it, and now these vague threats. It's a bit much at times, you know. It really is."

"Yes, Christel. I know."

She looked at the patterned hotel carpet for a long moment, then replied softly, "Yes, I know you do, Jeff. But is it worth all this? The harrassment, the intimidation?"

"What else do we have, Christel?" I said, my own frustration surfacing. "We're between the proverbial rock and the hard place. Whether we lie down quietly on that hard place and die, or whether we chance being crushed by the rock, they are going to outlive us; at least Marius and me. The cancer isn't taking a holiday."

I was shaking my head vehemently now. "I for one am going to chance the rock. And I think you know Marius is the same. If these cowardly idiots imagine that by making us even angrier with this sort of cheap, theatrical prank they'll make us give up, then boy, do they need a lesson in human psychology. It has the opposite effect."

Christel had regained some colour. She shook her head in a mixture of exasperation and resolve and gave a quick, nervous laugh. "What can I say? You're right, dammit. I suppose I'm just so worried about Marius. He has such a high public profile now. It makes him a target."

"That's probably his greatest safeguard," I put in, trying to believe it. "They won't touch him while the press is recording his every move and word. I'm probably in more direct danger, in a way. After all, the press don't even know I exist. I'm the quiet one in the background."

Christel started to speak, "You're right, at that..." when a hotel security guard appeared at the turn in the corridor and proceeded towards us, his shoes silent on the thick pile. She started violently, put a hand to her heart, and then gave me a big, embarrassed smile. "My God. I'm just a scared little mouse, aren't I."

"The hell you are," I said with feeling. "You're the one holding everything together."

"Good night, folks." The guard touched the brim of his cap politely as he passed us. We bid him and then each other a good night and made our separate ways to our rooms, the cheerfulness forced.

I dreamed, among other chaotic things that night, of committing Marius to a quiet sanitarium and of watching him go 'cold turkey' after three days of no interviews, no media attention, and no flashing cameras. He twitched and paced in my dream, a lion in a cage.

Meanwhile, downstairs in the glowing bar, Marius carried on as usual with his media feast, his voice a steady rumble, his laughter ringing out the refrain of a man who had chosen his battlefield and would not, could not, retreat.

Chapter 8: Project Crested Ice

Truth, of course, must of necessity

be stranger than fiction, for we have

made fiction to suit ourselves.

Heretics   G. K. CHESTERTON

I DREAMED TOO that I had just gotten my various domestic duties out of the way on the permanently dark Sunday afternoon of January 21, 1968 and had snatched a short half hour nap. This time I had set my alarm, and so avoided the confusion of appearing to reappear Rip Van Winkle-like after an uncounted absence. It was time to head for the NCO Club where everybody who was anybody, Danish civvies and American millies alike, congregated in Thule.

I negotiated the killing, dry cold of the space between my quarters and the club and underwent the unbearable, fiery discomfort of the millions of pinpricks in my legs that told me feeling was returning to them after the minor dose of frostbite they had suffered in just those few minutes.

"Ah, here's Carswell!" cried Rasmus. "Let the celebration... continue." he ended with a laugh, raising his glass to his lips. "Oh, Eddie, Mr. Carswell's usual, if you please."

"Certainly, sir. And, what is Mr. Carswell's usual?"

"A finger of schnapps, thanks, Ed," said Rasmus with a wink.

"Make it a Black Russian," I corrected, settling onto a barstool. And added, "Celebration? What celebration? What have I missed? What are we celebrating?"

"Why, the fact that you've arrived, my dear old boot," laughed Rasmus, clapping me on the back.

"A finger of schnapps, eh, Rasmus. Or, perhaps a snap of fingers!" joked Valther, simultaneously illustrating his words and spilling a good measure of his own drink.

"Perhaps," I said, taking the proffered glass from the barman. "Or perhaps I'll just drink it."

The feeling in the club on a Sunday afternoon was always heightened, a collective exhalation. It was a place where the buzz of comradeship and strained human intimacy sounded loudest at Thule; especially on the remainder of the weekend before the grinding round of work began again with Monday morning. That day was one such Sunday; a Sunday with the promise of a Monday like all the others we had experienced for months and, in some cases, years before. A predictable, monotonous future.

It did not matter how close we got to that future, what was waiting there, as imminent as it was at that very moment, remained hidden, its own timely revelation. Much the same way that an iceberg reared up from the North Atlantic and bid the Titanic a sudden, fatal 'good evening,' what happened next showed us that the Monday to be ushered in by that Sunday was not to be a typical one. It was to be the day the world changed.

It was getting on to four o'clock. I was just raising my Black Russian to my lips when the glass was violently snatched from my hand by an invisible force and the whole building shook with a deep, groaning violence, as if shaken like a large matchbox in an immense, angry hand. Considering that the building was a great elevated concrete bunker, designed to withstand anything the arctic blizzards could muster against it, whatever had shaken it had to have been of extraordinary, unnatural force.

It shook the building and it shook the entire base down to its foundations;

It shook our lives right out of the safe, dull grooves they would have undoubtedly followed otherwise.

It presaged the sinking of the lives of a great number of those present into a cold sea of pain of unmeasured depth.

It presaged the dropping of many more of us into the long night of premature death.

It presaged the endless decline, decay and silent extinction of the family lines of many of the men there present on that innocent afternoon.

Without us taking a single step, the future had taken us all by the hand and firmly ushered us into another room in the house of life: from a pleasant, warm sitting-room, we were shoved into a windowless torture chamber.

We were dead men: we just did not know it yet. The sentence had been passed; the symptoms would simply take years to manifest.

"My God, Carswell," spluttered Valther, reeling as if he were drunk, "Where are your manners?" He stared at the spilled liquor spreading on the bar.

The rest of us were struck speechless and gaping, frozen in our poses.

"What the fucking hell was that?" exploded Rasmus after another moment of stunned silence. No one among us was in any position to answer; our only response being to continue our earlier action of looking at each other in shared, dawning shock.

This we did till finally we came to our senses and were able to observe the general chaos that babbled and swirled around us. Heavily clothed and agitated figures blundered in and out of the club doors, letting in gusts of deadly cold. They were U.S. Military Police, their faces grim behind frost rimed balaclavas.

"What's happened, Rob?" asked Gert, when he recognised one of those ominous figures as a friend from the base gym where they worked out together.

The figure came over clumsily to our knot and put his thick gloved hand on Gert's arm. "I wish I knew, buddy. But I reckon it's something I can't even suggest to you foreign civilian nationals! You know the rules."

"You mean, the Soviets.... a strike on BMEWS?" Gert's voice was a whisper.

"!!" Rob just backed off shaking his head, his eyes wide behind his goggles. He replaced his balaclava with a practiced jerk and was gone, back out into the swallowing cold. A white faced Dane, whose name I never learned, who worked in the loading area of the port, rushed up to our group, his breath coming in clouds:

"They reckon there are missiles right now headed straight for New York and Washington! Holy shit! What the hell are we going to do? This is it!"

"Look, stupid," broke in Valther, grabbing the man's jacket, "if the Ruskies had just dropped the big one on BMEWS, where the bloody hell do you think we'd be by now? A puff of radioactive dust!" He turned wildly on Gert. "Well? Wouldn't we have been obliterated by a whirlwind of radioactivity by now? We're four miles from the damn station!"

"No, man," cut in a large, swaggering Afro American sergeant, who had sauntered up to my side as if drawn by the panic, "It was an earthquake. I ought to know. When you spend as long as I have in California, you get to know the signs. I reckon that one was strong enough to rupture the whole mother of a heating system's piping. Shit, man, we'll be frozen to death inside three hours; every last mother of us!"

As he wandered off to spread further his version of the good news, I could swear I saw a brief, grim grin distort his sour features. My relief at his mundane explanation was only temporary, however, as one of my own colleagues from the freight handling centre rushed up and asked breathlessly, "Have you fellows heard? My God! Apparently there's been an explosion in the aircraft fuel dump and the whole damn lot's gone up. A chain reaction!"

180

"Now that really is good news, ain't it?" put in Gert, his sarcasm brittle with fear.

"Well, hell, if that's all it was, then it's not so bad." there was a desperate plea in Rasmus' voice, a need for it to be something ordinary, something containable.

"Yeah, except that the explosion ripped a colossal crater in the main runway," the breathless Dane finished, delivering the final blow. "We're completely cut off from contact with the outside world. No one in, no one out."

"Enough!" I said, rather more vehemently than even I expected, slamming my hand on the bar. The noise cut through the babble. "So far just about every possible act of God and man has been made responsible for that… that *thing*. Well, I've had quite enough. I'm going back to my room. Whatever it was, what with the permanent darkness and the killer cold out there prohibiting any personal investigation, I'm happy to wait for an official version. But, if you want to know my view," I said, pulling on my parka, "I reckon an aircraft has crashed and exploded on the fiord. It's the only thing that makes sense of that kind of impact."

Out in the devil's domain again, on my solitary way to my quarters, I felt a deeper, more profound threat and uneasiness all about me, beyond the mere physical cold and darkness. Crossing the frozen, gritted pavements to my building, the eerie presentiment solidified into a cold certainty: I had not been far wrong in my guess. The air itself felt different, charged with a secret.

Working as I did in the freight handling section, which was likely to be called upon to provide transportation of some sort in any major emergency, I knew I would probably be summoned. I had figured I would be most easily found in my quarters. But, I knew no more than anyone else what had really happened and was as surprised as the next guy when, back in my sparse room, listening in on the military radio band, a terse, official announcement was broadcast: a B 52 Stratofortress had crashed and immediately disintegrated, not four miles away, on the sea ice of Wolstenholme Fiord. Notices were also issued that all personnel should "keep a sharp look out for anything unusual around the buildings of the base: debris or crew members," for example.

"So," I reflected aloud to the empty room, "the crew's missing; that means they must have had time to bail out; and, if any of them has survived the crash and the descent, we're now their last best chance of surviving the infernal cold of the arctic winter." A grim race against time had begun, though for whom, I did not yet know.

Over the radio it was being suggested in constantly repeated, calm announcements that it was "a very serious situation." I could have guessed that much all on my own. There was, however, no suggestion whatsoever that the emergency involved nuclear fallout or that there was any danger to our persons. The word 'nuclear' was conspicuously, absolutely absent.

As the evening wore on, undoubtedly, elsewhere on the planet, twilight drooped into blackness and the daytime denizens of those zones made way for those of the night: here, however, the moving hands of the clock only contributed to enhancing the dreamlike, suspended quality of the boredom and anxiety that set in during those dark hours. Each tick sounded like a solitary drip of water from an unfathomed, poisoned reservoir; and each successive announcement over the radio sounded more and more like the small, controlled dribs of information that are let slip discreetly to draw one's attention away from the deep, silent well of ignorance and danger you sense somewhere out there on the ice.

I sat by the phone, willing it to ring with orders, with explanation, with truth.

During the night, the level of activity on the distant airstrip was quite out of the ordinary, a continuous roar and whine against the usual frozen silence. This extraordinary movement of who knows what number of people and machines onto the base did nothing to put me at my ease. Until the next morning all I could do was lie awake and surmise why it was that the calm, uninformative reports over the radio were so utterly incommensurate with the night long, uninterrupted howl of landing aircraft outside my thin window. "One thing I know," I wryly told myself in the dark, "It won't all come clear in the morning light. They're bringing in an army."

I scarcely dared to surmise what was truly going on out there on the ice and in the hangars, and yet the temptation to guess at the unknown was irresistible. I found my mind running on the spot, so to speak, trying to dredge up a likely scenario from my limited knowledge of the facts and my reading of the alternating information flow and information freeze over the crackling radio.

"Well, I don't suppose we're in any direct danger," I reasoned, "otherwise they would have started evacuating us by now. So I guess the large number of incoming flights is for some other purpose than to get us to safety. Unless ..." My blood seemed to freeze in my veins at the thought. "Unless the Yanks just plan to leave us here, to contain the story.... But, no. That's madness. The Americans are an honorable people. They wouldn't just run away and leave a whole bunch of allied civilians to die up here. Would they?"

"What could it be, then?" I muttered. "They said the bomber disintegrated. Blew up. *Kaboom!* What's left to worry about? Unless the damned thing was carrying some special payload, like atom bombs or something. After all, that's why they've got the damned things in the air all the time: so they can bomb the shit out of the Ruskies should they poke out their tongue in this direction. No point flying around if you can't get the bastards when you want to. But they'd never fly them over friendly territory armed, would they? It's against every agreement..."

I sat by the silent phone, the unanswered question hanging in the cold air.

But morning did bring something, if not light: it brought the grim certainty that neither I nor my Danish colleagues knew *nothing* of the true magnitude of the disaster in our front garden. The base was suddenly awash with U.S. military personnel, mostly young, low ranking men, hundreds upon hundreds of whom had been flown in through the endless night from locations all over the United States and the world. I noticed, with a pang of something like pity, that a high proportion of these GIs were Afro Americans; and I noticed that quite a few of them must have been dragged out of their beds the previous evening from military installations as far afield as California, Hawaii and the Philippines, because they were still wearing tropical issue thongs, thin tee shirts and shorts under their hastily issued parkas.

They were ludicrously, tragically ill prepared for stepping off an aircraft into minus forty degree conditions. I watched from my window as, from one of the final flights to arrive in the eerie grey dawn, a knot of chattering, nervous GIs emerged from the innards of a groaning C 141. All were Afro Americans in this group. As I looked on, a particularly tall, gangly individual caught my eye: in the first place because he was extremely voluble, gesturing wildly to emphasise his words, paying no attention to his new, lethal environment; in the second place because he wore an unbuttoned Hawaiian shirt open to the navel; and in the third place because, the moment his boots hit the tarmac, he doubled up as if punched, clutched his arms around his torso, and scuttled across the ice like a crab, howling a string of curses that were ripped away by the wind.

"Ha, ha, ha!" laughed Rasmus bitterly, who had appeared beside me. "Fuck, the poor son of a bitch had probably never seen snow before, let alone felt this. Probably never been out of Louisiana."

They came from Vietnam, from Spain, from Germany, from Turkey, from Cuba and even from bases in Central America. Those who had been flown in directly from the steaming jungles of Vietnam understandably felt, at first, they were on a bit of a holiday mission. Away from the constant dangers of being sniped at or mortared, cleaning up after a mere plane crash in the empty Arctic was, in the timeless words of one Private First Class Toby Jogues of Omaha, Nebraska, "a piece of cake." They would learn.

* * * * * *

IT WAS ONLY much later, not until 1994, in fact, when on that investigative visit to the States, that I found out the chilling truth. The Pentagon had enacted a deliberate, calculated policy of bringing only a small number of men from each of a large number of distant, unrelated locations to work on whatever had to be done in the wake of the crash at Thule. It was not logistics; it was a strategy.

In 1994, sitting in a cheap motel room, I put two and two together and they made a critical mass. There was a silent, devastating explosion of comprehension in my brain. "Let's see," I thought, my hand trembling as I wrote it down, "hundreds of low ranked, likely lowly educated soldiers, certainly none of them doctors or experts in nuclear matters, a disproportionate number of them Afro American, drawn from dozens of isolated posts all over the world, not knowing each other; and then being sprinkled back to those same far flung corners afterwards, never to see each other again! Hmmm! Amnesia by separation. GI Joe goes home. Forgets Thule. Thinks it was just another cold, weird job. Contracts rare cancer ten years later. Shrugs his shoulders. Thinks, 'That's life.' So much cancer about, specially when you start to spend time at a VA hospital. Dies. Never suspects the statistical impossibility, never connects his illness to the throats of ex Thule guys dying in Akron, St. Louis and Seattle. How the heck would he? He never saw them again. He was alone." In 1994, with this realization, I felt physically nauseous. It was a policy of deliberate obscurity, a guarantee of silence.

But, back in 1968, I knew none of this. I merely sat by the phone in my room at Thule, a dumb organ in a body that was being systematically poisoned. What else could I have done? Back then I knew only what my fevered, anxious brain could surmise on the basis of an official information drain.

* * * * * *

THE FIRST THE larger world, the world outside the high walls of the U.S. military complex, the world that sometimes makes itself felt inside there only when it becomes expedient to invade some foreigner's little independent tinpot regime, the first that world knew of the nuclear disaster at Thule was through a confused, routine radio communication between Station Nord and a Scandinavian Airlines DC 8 en route to Tokyo via Anchorage. The crew was mystified and then deeply alarmed when asked to confirm by the isolated operators at Nord that a B 52 strategic bomber had crashed near Thule with a number of hydrogen bombs on board.

"Station Nord, could you repeat? Did you say a bomb's gone off at Thule? Over."

"No, SC12, we are asking you. Haven't you heard anything about a bomber going down there? Can you confirm? Over."

"Are you on the level, Nord? We've heard nothing about any bomber. What can you tell us? Over."

"SC12, just that. That is the rumour. We were hoping you could confirm that a B 52 bit the ice down there? We've been hearing some pretty creepy whispers on the Danish net. Over."

"We've heard nothing on this, Station Nord. I would suggest that, in the absence of independent confirmation, you treat this as either highly confidential or as a malicious prank. Either way, your best policy would be not to spread the rumour any further by asking every aircraft that happens by whether World War Three has broken out. You'll start a panic."

"Roger, SC12, sorry to trouble you. Over and out."

What a profound pity that the Scandinavian captain's natural caution won over natural curiosity; otherwise, the truth might have burst into the wider world much earlier and might have prevented the Danish and American governments from so effectively conspiring to censor the thing from the very first moment. As it was, it became impossible for the embattled Danish Social Democratic government to keep a lid on the story over a very sensitive weekend: the weekend of a general election. It was a government in serious trouble and little needed to be exposed to the worst political disaster imaginable. However, a rough justice was done in any case; and the socialists were heaved out of office by an electorate that only came to hear of the censorship under which they had been placed by those "trusty" politicians some days later, the betrayal tasting all the more bitter.

One of the first things to go, unsurprisingly, was our open communication with the outside world. Putatively on account of "all the phone lines being needed to direct the operation," all of a sudden, Danish civilian personnel were no longer privileged to use the military telephone system. We were cut off, silenced.

I sat by the useless phone.

As it was, wild rumours still spread out there which, in the absence of any accurate information, created terrible, gnawing concern among families and loved ones back home. One particularly vicious rumour came as a result of a sensational newspaper story some days after the crash. Having decided that their own carefully garbled version of events was preferable to the uncontrolled garbled version being whispered about, the military authorities, in connivance (the only descriptive term that actually accords with the truth) with the Danish government, decided to have a hand picked press contingent flown in to Thule to 'see for themselves.'

The gentlemen of the press were treated to a comfortable, indeed euphoric, flight north; after which, filing off the aircraft, we watched dumbfounded as they proceeded directly, under escort, to the Dundas Telegraph Office to file their pre approved, sanitised stories back home. Thence they proceeded in a neat Indian file to the warm Thule Officers' Club to make further "investigations" guided by the old dictum *in vino veritas.*

As a direct consequence of the contrived conviviality meted out to them, at least one of the thoroughly lubricated reporters concocted a story that had the entire personnel of Thule evacuated to the secret, underground Camp Century. Though how between three and four thousand persons, with provisions, could have been transported a hundred miles across the treacherous glacier in sub zero conditions was left romantically unexplained. The story also glossed over just how those three thousand something people were surviving in an installation built to accommodate barely three hundred. I suppose in the story they, I mean, 'we', were just thankful to have escaped the nuclear explosion that, apparently, had quite obliterated Thule!

That such a wild, frightening concoction might provoke profound anxiety among the families and friends of men on the base, especially given that Thule was now incommunicado from the moment of the crash, all phone lines being reserved for military use only, seemed to be of no concern to the concocter or his minders. Panic back home was a small price to pay for narrative control.

While the press contingent was thus pressed together in the Officers' Club, it was thought expedient to hold a swift press conference there; in the course of which the journalists were told by a straight faced officer that, "for the time being, there was little danger of radiation exposure." I assume that what they meant was that they *hoped* such to be the case, in the absence of definitive proof to the contrary. It was a hope dressed as a fact.

By these means, as Colonel O. J. Sundstrom, the Team Chief for Project Crested Ice, was to report smugly in the USAF Nuclear Safety journal, in the Jan/Feb/Mar 1970 issue devoted to the Crested Ice debacle, did the U.S. successfully counter 'these erroneous and misleading stories.' The well oiled junket parties I witnessed he described blandly as 'numerous on the scene briefings and tours conducted by the On Scene Commander and his staff.'

All this expensive theatre, just to counter the nasty 'fictions' that dared to compare Thule to Palomares (where, of course, nothing in any way similar to Thule happened only a B 52 Stratofortress exploding in midair and dropping four nuclear bombs, contaminating the Spanish countryside. No, nothing at all like Thule, where a B 52 Stratofortress exploded on ice, scattering its nuclear cargo. Completely different).

Even the devil, it seems, has his smooth talking apologists.

I continued my vigil by the silent phone. Finally, it rang. It was Rasmus.

"Carswell, have you been outside? No? Well, you should see what they've been up to in the night. It's incredible. I don't know how many new, flimsy accommodation huts have been jerry built out there on the ice. A whole temporary town. I've also heard from a reliable source that Major General Hunziker himself and a whole bunch of other big boy types have flown in to implement a Broken Arrow operation."

"Broken Arrow?" The term was new, ominous.

"Yeah. That's the top secret military code word for the emergency operation that comes into effect when they have a nuclear weapons accident on their hands. The real thing. It seems they always have these expert 'Broken Arrow' teams on standby, men who could be gathered together and flown into an accident site in a matter of hours to assess the damage and to decide on cleanup procedures and so on. They're here, Jeff. They're all here."

"Did you say *nuclear accident*?" I gulped, the word finally spoken aloud between us.

"Nuclear weapons accident. Yep. We're right in the middle of it, Jeff, old boy. And they're not gonna let us out of here for a good long while. We're part of the scenery now."

"What in God's name do you mean by that?"

"I mean, we're gonna leave here eventually like innocent lambs, parroting tales of how squeaky clean SAC is, and how safe it is to eat a little plutonium for breakfast. We'll be the living proof nothing was wrong. They'll see to that."

"I don't know what the hell you're getting at," I snapped angrily, my fear turning to rage, and smashed the phone set down into its cradle. But I did in fact have more than an inkling of what my foresighted, cynical friend was getting at. He was describing our future: usefulness as uninformed witnesses, then silence.

But it was seven thirty, Monday morning. The weak, unseen sun was somewhere below the horizon. Time to leave for work, to join the great, hidden machinery of the cleanup. The phone had given me my orders after all.

* * * * * *

RAILBACK SLUMPED BACK into the overstuffed commandeered chair in his newly acquired office at Thule Base Headquarters. He had taken it over from some poor, self important slob as a matter of course, a simple necessity. It was not that Railback imposed his will on people with malice; he just had a long history of taking on impossible projects and was constitutionally, ruthlessly accustomed to getting his own way by the most direct means possible.

He did not exhibit the usual military social graces associated with tossing those of lesser rank out of their offices. Or, for that matter, with tossing anyone of any rank out the door if by doing so the desired result was achieved. In reality, he more *squeezed* than tossed them out. They would arrive for work and find that there was simply no longer physical or psychological room for them there. Nobody in their right mind really wanted to be Railback's bunkie; and few bothered to complain to higher authority, knowing instinctively it would be futile.

At six feet five inches, 225 pounds of hardened muscle and with a thirty two inch waist, Railback was an imposing, almost sculpted physical figure. He had been described early on in his Marine career at Boot Camp (Marine Corps Recruit Depot, San Diego, California) as a 'special order private.' This literally meant that his measurements pressed at the outer limits of the clothing manufactured for the average Marine, requiring specially ordered uniforms. If the Marine Corps general issue clothing, which fit 99% of all recruits, was akin to buying 'off the rack' in civilian life, Railback was the man who always went under the tailor's scissors to get fitted out in the Corps' finest. Needless to say, Railback had to be the only raw recruit who looked as impeccably tailored as the Drill Instructors, because his uniform fit him like a second skin. When Railback put on his cammies, he looked less like a grunt and more like he was off on some lethally expensive African safari in a Dior creation.

In most situations, the mere possession of such a formidable physique was sufficient to avoid violence. It was a deterrent worn on the outside.

The Drill Instructors, of course, loved to torment recruits like Railback. On his very first day at Boot Camp, Railback's diminutive but terrifying Drill Instructor screamed out in the time and use honoured manner of his species at the terrified line of young men, "Who here *thinks* they're the biggest, baddest motherfucker in this here platoon?"

Then, whipping around to face the poor fool who had the audacity to step forward and respond, "Sir, Private Railback *thinks* he's the biggest, baddest motherfucker in this here platoon," the DI would pause like a cobra about to strike.

This particular DI, perfectly positioned to administer a couple of quick, debilitating groin kicks, as he had done many times before in Kendo Karate on his way to earning a Second Degree Black Belt, could only stop and openly admire the superb, sculpted human form standing ten paces away. He quickly responded, "You know what, Private? I think you probably *are* the biggest, baddest motherfucker in this here platoon. Now, why don't you just step your ass back in the ranks. Private? OK. Now," he bellowed, turning back to the others, "who thinks they're the *next* biggest, baddest motherfucker in this here platoon?"

Suffice it to say, Railback was an instant legend and learned a crucial lesson: while his diminutive DI had a dark sense of humor, he was absolutely nobody to screw with. The DI promptly demonstrated this by dropping the two eager pretenders to Railback's throne to their knees in a matter of seconds, a blur of efficient violence.

Railback's Boot Camp fame preceded him to every duty station he ever went to. He was instantly recognizable: a hero to some, a tantalizing target to others. Anyone who set the Marine Corps rope climb speed record dressed out in full pack and combat gear, as Railback had, never using his feet, just sheer arm power, had to assume demi god status in an institution fundamentally driven by physical accomplishment.

Such early tales, buttressed later by Railback's Silver Star, Purple Hearts and battlefield commission to First Lieutenant, still circulated in many Marine Corps beer halls throughout the world's ports of call. What truly set Railback apart from the common herd of Marine Corps hulks was his mind: he had earned himself a college degree with a double major in history and philosophy. This intellectual edge had seen him caught in the top 1% the Marine Corps took from the draft during Vietnam, a thinking man's warrior.

His historical perspective, often causing him a certain amount of intellectual turmoil as he judged the success of all present day operations by how they would be viewed in the future, nevertheless was no barrier to his acting decisively. He could wear the future like an uncomfortable jacket, so long as it stayed where it belonged: in the future; and did not interfere in the brutal necessities of the present, except as a silent warning. He realised that this Thule 'Broken Arrow' was in every sense an 'historical event' in that it was big, it mattered and it would have long range, invisible consequences. The warning he heeded was to make the future historian's task as difficult as possible by ensuring the records were cryptic, few, and deliberately contradictory.

Yet, Railback's toughest critic remained Railback himself. He was blessed, or cursed, with the gift of instantaneous strategic thought. He claimed that his uncanny ability to make the right decision under extreme duress came from being one of a tiny number of black students in a highly visible, athletic and academic, middle class Chicago high school where he became adept, as a matter of mere daily survival, at reading threats and acting quickly. The distinction between 'war zone' and 'peace zone' meant nothing to him. Life was a perpetual war zone. Only his private thoughts, when not in specifically combat mode, isolated him from that environment. Thule, for all its frozen silence, was just another battlefield.

"Captain Burnett, reporting as ordered, sir," a voice brought him back from that place of mental and personal abstraction.

Railback looked up to see the under average height, pasty white skinned, balding, semi out of shape Air Force Captain whom he recognised from earlier in the day, attempting to stand to a semblance of attention before him.

"Never make it in the Corps," Railback thought quickly, instantly putting himself ill at ease. He wondered whether he would get the required speed and ruthless efficiency out of this Captain Burnett, who looked more like a harried accountant than a field commander.

"Jesus, Captain! Where the hell have you been?" he barked, not bothering to mask his irritation.

"Well, sir," Burnett began, his tone deceptively calm, "we've had a bit of an unfortunate incident here that you may or may not have heard about. A plane crash or something. And then some sonofabitch Marine, important as all outdoors, threw me out of my own office. So, it took me a bit longer to figure out how to get to the head from my new digs and then back to here, sir," said Burnett, only accenting the closing 'sir' ever so slightly, a needle in the word.

"Dammit, Captain," said Railback, a slow, broad grin spreading across his face despite himself, "Are you smart assing me?"

"Absolutely, sir," Burnett responded, still counterfeiting attention as well as a flyboy ever could manage.

"Well, then, maybe we ought to go do a little ice fishing together, eh, Captain? See what we can catch."

"That's a roger, Major," Burnett said, his mouth held firm, but his bright blue eyes dancing with a cunning light.

Railback jumped to his feet and extended a large hand as Burnett continued, "You know, sir, we're going to have to put some type of fluorescent orange vest on you out there on the ice, so we don't lose you. You blend in a little too well with the scenery, sir." He gestured at Railback's dark skin.

"Keep it up, Captain, and we might just get to like each other after this whole mess is over," Railback said, the challenge accepted.

They shook hands, a firm, assessing grip, and left the commandeered office together. As they walked, Railback once again heard his grandma's old advice in his ears, from long ago Chicago courts: "When you snag a rebound, boy, you hold that 'rock' high above your head. That's how you stay in control. You bring it down, some little guard is gonna steal it from you and take control of the whole game."

"This guy is shrewd," Railback thought, eyeing Burnett. "He's the man guarding the northernmost point of U.S. defences. As long as he's an ally, we'll be okay. But he wouldn't be up here if he was a fuck up or disloyal. I wonder who he's reporting to directly in D.C. or NORAD? I wonder if he wants control of the game? Hell, I wonder if he's already got it and is just letting me think I do?"

"We've been doing a bit of fishing out there already, Major," Burnett said, breaking into his thoughts as they hit the blistering cold outside. "Maybe you'd like to see what we're catching?"

Burnett looked even paler than the white skin on the backs of his hands, a man stretched thin. The ever perceptive Railback offered, "When's the last time you actually slept, Burnett?"

"Oh, it's been a while, I suppose, sir. Nice thing about the Arctic this time of year: you never have to worry about night coming to tell you to fall asleep. We just sleep whenever we get an opportunity, if we get one. The sun doesn't care."

"Is sled the only way in to the site right now?" They were walking quickly, leaning against the inertia of the dense, killing cold.

"That's affirmative, sir. We can get part way to the edge of the zero line on our tracked vehicles, but we're still unsure how far from the actual crash site the ice is fractured and unsafe for heavy tonnage. Until we can get a true engineering estimate, it's hard to tell what it will hold and what it won't. But, we've been looking for a volunteer to see how close we can get a Weasel. How much do you weigh, sir?" Burnett asked, a flash of mischievous survival humor in his exhausted eyes.

Railback just shook his head abstractedly without looking at Burnett, a ghost of a smile on his lips.

"You get many visitors up here, Burnett?" Railback asked, changing the subject.

"No, sir. Not the social season."

"I can see why," Railback whispered, shaking his head slightly at the sheer, brutal emptiness. "You know, Burnett, we're going to need proper roads into the site; as close as we can get to the hole in the ice. In the meantime, can we put choppers down out there?"

"We tried it, sir. And it was a no go. The skids just sink into the pulverized, oily slush. I've got the Inuit hauling out sufficient timber planks to construct a makeshift landing pad, sir. Should be in use within the hour. I've also already put in a call to NORAD for use of their specialised engineer quick response team, which has been scrambled and is due here inside twenty four hours, fully equipped." Burnett again revealed his foresight and competence.

"How about land line communications to the site as well, Cap? Radio frequencies won't give us the security we need if anyone's listening, and we have to assume they already are."

"Yes, sir, we're on it. We've got a local hunter, named Ululik, pretty handy guy, on that. He started to run some cable as of zero dark thirty this morning from the back of his dog sled. A few other natives are in there giving us a hand, too, collecting wreckage, that kind of thing. Actually bringing pieces out on their sleds." Burnett's voice was matter of fact.

Railback was quietly impressed. "Maybe we can control this game together after all," he thought. "I always did work the inside better when I had a smart point guard on the perimeter."

He spoke out in feigned astonishment. "Jesus, Cap, what took you so long to get this thing organised? Air Force bureaucracy hold you back?"

"Well, sir, as you can imagine, we are fairly autonomous up here at the edge of the world. But, then, I suspect you know a thing or two about autonomy yourself, sir."

"Did a little research on me, Captain?" Railback asked, his eyes narrowing.

"Just cursory, sir. Had to know who was stealing my office."

"I'll bet."

"I did some time in the Pentagon myself. Before this… exile."

"What, four to eight and you're out on parole, now?" Railback could be as sardonic as the next man, perhaps more so.

"Something like that, Major. Only, now I'm on the outside looking in, I find I can still get information from the Pentagon without having to go back inside the building. Useful contacts."

"Shrewd," Railback thought. "Very shrewd, and connected. A dangerous combination."

Burnett allowed himself a thin smile. "Another primary concern, Major: that's one seriously hot zone in there. If we've had natives in there already, and we have, we're going to have to make a contamination sweep. And without setting off any alarm bells in the local population. It may be too late for some of them already." His voice betrayed a grim resignation.

Railback was off making mental checklists that just seemed to appear in his mind unbidden. "Do we know who and where they are? Have they discarded clothing? Have they eaten with hot utensils? You know the drill, Captain. The hot particle game."

"Sir, the good news and the bad news is it's not the Inuit way to discard *anything*, ever. If clothes are hot, they'll still be being worn. If they've eaten with hot utensils, they'll still have them in their huts. Why would they throw them away? What would they know of 'hot' in this sense? So, even though these guys are as good as dead walking, at least we won't have to go scouting over a thousand square miles of ice for those particular hot items. The contamination is sitting in their villages."

Burnett's voice was flat, clinical, but his eyes showed the cost of the calculation. Railback knew he was right. It was a brutal arithmetic.

"We have neither the manpower nor the political inclination to take on that task just yet, sir. It'll just have to wait. And, hell, how, on the one hand, can we sweep the villages and remove clothing, sleds, dogs, basic survival tools and so on with the explanation that these are now deadly possessions, and, on the other hand, encourage the locals and the natives to give us a hand cleaning up, with the assurance that there is no risk to life? We can't. The two facts are mutually destructive."

"Christ," Railback thought, a cold admiration cutting through his fatigue. "Burnett's a smart boy. He's hit on the fundamental contradiction right at the black heart of this matter. Our job, my job, is to lock up Frosty the Snowman because he's started glowing in the dark. No more, no less. And pretend we're not."

"Shit!" he spat out the word between clenched teeth, the frustration visceral.

Burnett glanced sympathetically at the big man wrestling with the impossible. "Medical personnel will be here ASAP. And we'll use them as the information conduits, the friendly face. But, by the time we got enough 'moon suits' up here to clothe all the workers, we'd have radiation flowing all the way down Canada to New England. The clock is ticking the other way."

"OK, Cap. Point taken. Ultimately the villages, the people, will be your look out. Mine is containment and clean up of the primary site. We split the headache." The lines of responsibility had just been drawn up and tacitly agreed on between the two men in the frozen alley. As tragic as it was, both had agreed on the cold priorities. Survival of the mission over the individual.

"Meanwhile," Railback suggested, realising he had no need to *order* Burnett, the understanding was already complete, "let's get some suits and a sled and get out there. I need to see the beast."

The pair had arrived at the low, humming barracks that was serving as the nerve centre for the operation and were struggling out of their stiff, arctic overgear.

"Telephone for Major Railback." The voice crackled over the intercom speaker. "Telephone for Major Railback. Secure line."

"Where can I take it?" Railback asked Burnett, shrugging off his parka.

"In that conference room, sir." Burnett pointed out an open door that gave access to a soundproofed room furnished with the familiar long, grey military table surrounded by metal framed chairs in perfect, sterile alignment.

"Secure?"

Burnett nodded once. "Scrambled. Best we have."

Railback went into the room and noticed the single black telephone and squawk box gracing the centre of the bare table; the only amenities in that stark, war ready room.

"Railback," he spoke into the receiver, his voice echoing slightly.

"Please stand by for General Burton from NORAD," a crisp voice came from the phone.

"Is that you, Finkle?" Railback asked, recognizing the sergeant's tone.

"Yessir," the voice responded quickly, sounding as if it wished it had been faster in transferring the call to General Burton's office.

"Don't you want my identification on your encrypted line, Sarge? Zulu Zulu Seven?"

"We have voice authentification on this line now, sir," Finkle countered with almost too much military efficiency, a slight defensive edge in his voice.

Railback let it go. Finkle was probably okay, or the old man would have sent him to Adak, Alaska, moons ago. He waited.

"Railback." Burton's voice sounded almost breathless, as if he had run to the phone down some long, Pentagon corridor.

"Yes, sir."

"We have another problem brewing up in your neck of the frozen woods." He was calmer now, the professional taking over.

"Oh?" Railback enquired, his mind bracing. He wondered how the heck it could possibly get any worse.

"We've been tracking a Russian sub, known to NATO as a Golf II class, code named K129. We believe it's ultimately heading for the Pacific, northwest of Hawaii, but its present course is… curious. We are unsure of its precise location right now and have strong reason to believe it will be investigating HOBO's crash site. It's turning toward Greenland."

"Jesus!" Railback muttered, the implications immediate. "To locate and maybe recover downed nukes?"

"Precisely. Until we can locate it again and determine its intent, we're disinclined to send the *Halibut* up to give you a hand recovering our own nukes. That sub is top secret itself; and we believe the Ruskies know nothing about its capabilities yet. We want to keep it that way. Besides, since its conversion from a cruise missile sub to one designed for deep sea covert operations, *Halibut* doesn't have the kind of armament necessary to defend itself against a Golf II if the shit hit the fan. And we've ruled out the *Glomar Explorer* platform not only because we're unsure it can even get to the site through the ice, but because it's being tracked by any number of private groups and foreign intelligence agencies. Nothing could be done without the entire world knowing almost immediately."

"Fine," Railback replied, already running a myriad of potential scenarios through his mind instantly, like a computer trying to crack an encrypted message. "Give me the mini subs, then, the ones *Halibut* carries. We can maybe use them from the ice edge." He still had not entirely digested the ominous data about the K129 lurking somewhere under the same ice. "I'm not sure we can pull the nukes up even if we find them. And, God knows, with the tides and shifting ice, who can say we'll even find them now. Maybe the best tomb for them is the mud under the arctic ice. Let the sea bury its own secrets."

Railback had one more, crucial question for General Burton. "What's Golf II carrying, sir? What's in its tubes?"

Burton paused for an inordinate amount of time, the secure line humming with hollow static. "About 2.4 megatons of explosive payload across three ballistic missiles," he said finally, matter of factly, as only a seasoned war veteran could, envisioning the absolute horror such weapons could deal out. "We'll keep you apprised on the sub. You focus on the ice. NORAD out."

"Thule out." Railback placed the receiver back in its cradle with a soft, definitive click. He sat for a moment in the silent, grey room. Not just broken arrows on the ice, but a lurking bear under it. The game had just expanded, and the stakes had been raised to unthinkable levels. He took a deep breath, stood up, and went back out to find Burnett. There was work to do, and now they were racing against two invisible clocks: one of radiation, and one of geopolitical disaster.

* * * * * *

MONDAY MORNING. ON my arrival at work, a little before eight, I was presented with my first direct task in connection with the disaster of the previous day. The surreal had become routine with shocking speed.

"Carswell, we've got a stiff for you to wrap up."

With these blunt, unceremonious words was I requested to prepare the paperwork covering the shipment back to the States of the body of the crew co pilot, Captain Leonard Svitenko. My colleague, Niels, said it as if asking me to file a cargo manifest for spare engine parts.

"His body was recovered during the night. They reckon it's best to ship it back to the States straight away. Get it off the base."

"Why the rush?" I asked, my mind still clinging to a semblance of normalcy. "It's not as if it's going to go putrid in the midday sun. There is no sun."

"Geez, Carswell, have some respect for the stiff, will you?" Niels said, though his own tone was purely practical. "No, the colonel reckons its presence might be a… distraction. Bad for morale. The critical issue is elsewhere."

"Which is?" I asked absently, searching for the appropriate morbid forms in the metal stores cabinet. I sat back down at my desk, the cold metal of the chair seeping through my trousers.

"'Recovery, if possible, of the nuclear bombs and any other sensitive fragments from the wreck.' is what it says on this little internal memo, Jeffie boy." He let the flimsy sheet of paper drop onto the desk before my downturned eyes. It fluttered like a dying bird.

We both read the stark words. He whistled softly, and I echoed it, a low, two note sound of dread. *Nuclear bombs*. There it was, in typescript. The unspoken fear made official.

Such was my first personal role in an affair that at the time seemed, on the surface, just a little unexpected although perversely welcome excitement at a normally quiet and boring time of the year. I did not know then, could not have known, that processing that paperwork was also my own quiet death warrant, a guarantee of future, unsought and vicious effects on my health and my very life. I was signing my own future away with each triplicate form.

The building I worked in was quickly transformed into the frenetic transfer point for all transportation to and from the crash site. At that early stage, less than twenty four hours after the bomber went down, transportation still meant Inuit dog sled, a scene from another century. No one had definitively found out yet whether helicopters could safely land at the fragile site; nor whether a road route could be blasted and levelled for the tractors and trucks and waves of personnel required for the monumental clean up.

A number of military police were stationed at our doors, to keep a check on who went out to the crash site and, more importantly, to make sure they all came back again. Besides being a crude system to ensure the safety of those moving about the hazardous site, it was also a blunt security measure, in view of the catastrophic cargo the bomber had been carrying. Check Point Charlie, as we fondly and ironically named it, was manned twenty four hours a day by bored, cold GIs with clipboards and suspicious eyes.

Eventually, because of a severe shortage of space on the overwhelmed base for the swelling emergency team, part of the main cafeteria, with its adjoining storage rooms, was hastily converted to their use as a planning and staging area. The smell of coffee and frozen food began to mix with the odor of sweat, anxiety, and wet wool.

As the days passed, more and more personnel arrived in a steady stream to assist in the clean up, and we settled into a grim, emergency routine. One of the first items on the grim agenda was to establish the thickness and stability of the ocean ice at the precise place of the crash and the possibilities of establishing some sort of semi permanent camp there. The Danish Construction Corps foremen assisted with their local expertise, and soon, several flimsy, transportable Jamesway huts were erected directly on the ice at the site. One of the huts was designated to serve as a makeshift eating enclosure for those working in the frozen hell. Although the personnel were allowed to take soup and hot chocolate and coffee on the ice, these meagre meals were to be prepared back on the main base, on account of the 'dangerous situation' out there.

I, for one, have never been able to account for the glaring, monstrous inconsistency in this specific circumstance, unless it be that, given the belief that plutonium is only dangerous when ingested, the authorities were aware *at least* of that particular danger and so took these specific, minimal measures to protect people from it. They knew enough to keep the food preparation away from the dust, but not enough, or not enough that they cared, to keep the *men* away from it.

Let this point not pass us by: if my interpretation of this circumstance is correct, then there is in it an implicit, damning admission of the known danger of radiation poisoning from plutonium ingestion. This is not a trivial, academic point: its full, tragic importance would only be clarified in about twenty seven years, around the time the last victim of that ice would take his final meal. The future was writing itself in our contaminated bones.

But, nuclear waste, like nuclear war, cannot be knocked until you have tried it. And, once you've tried it, you will never eat anything else again. You will simply cease to be.

* * * * * *

ALLAN NIELSEN HELD the illustrious title of General Superintendent of Roads and Grounds. As such, he was the man in charge of delivering the crucial, referred to expert opinion regarding the safety of the ice for heavy vehicles.

"Well, Supremo," I called to him as he entered the office a couple of days into the strange, post crash time, alongside Valther, "How's the ice? Can we all go skating now without dropping through to China?"

"Skating!" laughed Valther, looking hard at Allan, his eyes wide with incredulous admiration. "You could bloody well build a Gothic cathedral on that ice, if you wanted to! A solid block!"

Allan stroked his chin thoughtfully and attempted, unsuccessfully, to abolish a half smile of pride from his weathered features. "Well, not quite that solid," he began modestly.

"Well, a six lane motorway, in any case!" Valther came up and sat on the edge of my desk, almost gasping in his excitement. "Do you know what this Jack Brabham of the snowplow has just done?"

I indicated that I most certainly did not.

"He's only just taken the blindfold test for the craziest bastard on the base. And passed with flying colours!"

"It's always nice to have your hypothesis verified by the empirical data," I smiled, crossing my arms and settling in for the whole story.

"Yeah, well," Valther looked at me a little askance, but the story was too good to hold back. "Anyway, so Allan is out checking the equipment this morning, having a look at the heavy machinery and the trucks and whatnot. He casts his eye out over the permanent darkness toward where the plane went in and says, casual as you like, `About time we had a closer look at that ice.' And, next minute, before you can say 'hypothermia,' he's revving the guts out of a D6 snowplow, inching it gingerly down the ramp onto the ocean ice itself. The bloody ocean!

"'You coming?' he shouts out to me over the roar of the motor, like he's asking if I want to pop down to the shops."

"And you replied?" I enquired, already knowing the answer.

"And I replied, `You gotta be kidding! I'm not paid to be a human icebreaker!' So off he goes, at the break neck speed of about ten miles an hour, straight into the black hole of Greenland. One minute later, and you couldn't even see his tail lights in the dark. Swallowed whole."

"My word," I said, shaking my head. "This is exciting stuff! A one man polar expedition."

"There's more," persevered Valther, refusing to be stung by my sardonic jibing. "He's not out there two minutes before there comes this snowburst down the valley from one of those inland blizzards, and next thing you know, this silly bugger is completely lost on the ice. No visibility, no landmarks, nothing! Ha, ha, ha!"

Valther pointed his finger accusingly at Allan, then raised it to cover his own irrepressible grin. "He was flying blind and totally directionless, just a big metal beetle in a bowl of milk! Ha, ha, ha."

I was open mouthed at this point. "So, let me get this straight. You're trekking along at ten miles per hour over ice whose thickness and safety you were literally guessing at every moment, and you were caught in a total white out? A *white out* on *black* ice?"

Allan merely joined his hands as if in prayer and answered with a quiet, matter of fact tone, "I just lost my bearings totally. Couldn't see the caterpillar tracks of my own tractor, let alone the ice or where the bloody heck I might have wanted to go. He, he." He laughed a modest, nervous chuckle. "I can tell you, the sound of ice groaning and cracking under you under those circumstances is enough to put God back in your life in a hurry! And, on top of that, I had no idea when I might not reach the limit of the safe ice and just kind of... slide gently off the end into the inviting, freezing depths of the Arctic Ocean. A very final test."

"You utter loon!" I let out with a semi quashed laugh of disbelief. "So, how the hell did you get back? Divine intervention?"

"I just followed my instinct and used my knowledge of the ice. I felt fairly sure I could describe a wide semicircle blind, so that's what I did. I kept the wheel at about the angle that I thought should take me in a loop about five hundred yards across; and, when I guessed I was facing back towards shore, I just straightened her up, and a couple of minutes later, I nudged her gently back up onto the ramp. Heart going like a jackhammer."

"You think that explains it?" I asked, my voice thick with incredulity.

"No," he replied, without a moment's hesitation, the smile gone. "It was mainly bloody good luck. And a very thick sheet of ice."

* * * * * *

THE SAFETY OF the ice having been thus definitively, if recklessly, established by Allan Nielsen's madman survey, a proper highway was constructed out to the crash site. The outward and return lanes were built some hundreds of yards apart in the interests of basic safety. An excessive concentration of traffic over any one section of the ice could cause stress fractures to appear, so it was deemed wise to ensure that vehicles moving in opposite directions were kept well apart to minimize the collective risk to persons and expensive equipment. In addition, a third, standby lane was constructed so as to allow for one lane to be always 'recuperating,' as it were, while the other two were in service, a lesson in Arctic logistics learned the hard way.

A roped off area on the stained ice grimly indicated where the plane had gone in. All that was visibly left was a sinister litter of tiny fragments, the biggest pieces being the three massive engines that had survived relatively intact. The greater, more chilling evidence was the long, narrow stretch of blackened, filthy ice that betrayed where a significant, fiery explosion had occurred. It looked like a wound.

It was over this blackened ice, which looked like the northernmost stretch of some damned Route 666, that the young, base grade military personnel flown in especially for the task were set walking, shoulder to shoulder in grim lines, heads down, picking up every last twisted remnant of HOBO 28's shattered hide. They moved like ghosts in the halogen light, placing fragments into bags with tongs.

All of these interesting, contaminated remnants were then removed back to a 'Top Secret' designated building on the base where they were examined, where possible, identified (most were no more than unidentifiable shards of burnt metals and composites) and carefully packaged up for shipment back to the United States, to be buried or studied in some desert facility.

* * * * * *

THE 'PRESS GANG,' as we unkindly called them, the journalists, were not allowed any closer to the actual site of the crash than about three hundred yards distant, held behind a second cordon. My first time out on the ice I travelled in a truck with one of them, a pale faced man from a Copenhagen daily. Our vehicle was a heavy, groaning snow truck and I must confess to feeling a tad concerned the entire way over the thickness of the ice, the tide movements and whatnot. However, we made it out without mishap, the ice groaning ominously but holding.

He was quiet, almost reverent, out on the ice, his breath pluming in the freezing air. On the way back, after a long silence, he turned to me and said shakily, "That scene back there is the most unsettling, most bleak evocation of Hell I have ever experienced. And I covered the war."

I confirmed his feeling with a solemn nod. "It's like a black hole in the world," I commented. "It's emptier than empty, just a sort of... negation. An absence that feels heavy."

I was righter than I knew. It was a void into which only the damned reached and from which none truly escaped. The grim and nervous demeanours of the military personnel, the darkness only pierced fitfully and poorly by a few sputtering electrical halogen lamps running off a chugging donkey engine, the crunching, squeaking sensation of the contaminated ice underfoot, the light breeze that multiplied the effects of the cold by a factor of ten, the unnatural, apocalyptic vision of blackened ice, all together were eerily reminiscent of the Inuit legends of the lower world, of a weakened sun and moon, of deep caverns and eternally unhappy, wandering spirits.

* * * * * *

WITHIN A FEW days, it became clear that the specialists in the field of shipping highly dangerous artifacts that I would have expected the U.S. military to immediately bring in, given the grave, unprecedented situation, were simply not going to appear. We were the specialists, by default.

Instead, Torben Staehr, my slightly officious, middle aged Danish supervisor, who enjoyed pungent Havana cigars (much to the chagrin of some of the more chauvinist American officers), and hero of the 'bunfight at the Thule corral,' wandered haltingly into my office behind his customary acrid smoke screen on the fourth day post crash. In as offhanded a manner as he could summon, puffing furiously, he said:

"Mr. Carswell, er, Jeff, as you are alone at the moment I'll take this opportunity to advise you that, if you are prepared to do so, the American military authorities would be very pleased if you could assist them in the sensitive area of the movement of dangerous goods from the site. It seems that you are the only person on the base with the requisite formal experience and expertise. The Chief Engineer has personally asked that you be involved."

He replaced his cigar in the corner of his mouth and puffed hard, like the little train who thought he could.

I was astonished, but nonetheless found my tongue to ask a few pointed questions.

"When you say dangerous parts, do you mean very heavy scraps of fuselage, or wing ribs with sharp edges, or grimy engine casings? Things that are mechanically dangerous?"

"Well, no, Jeff. I gather they mean something more... inherently hazardous than that."

"You gather ...?" I pressed, my skepticism rising.

"Look, Jeff, you know the Americans," he said, waving his cigar as if to disperse the awkwardness. "Sure, sometimes they seem to be wandering about like headless geese, and they have that annoying attitude that if they don't have the biggest and the best of something, then obviously that thing's not worth having; and probably should not be on the face of the earth in any case; and is probably responsible for all the political and social problems of the place that has the thing. But, basically, they're our allies. Our friends. We have to help."

"Jeez, Torben, if ever I need a character reference, you'll be the last one I'll come to. Are you suggesting I simply trust them; or that I just throw them a bone? Why not just tell me straight what it is that's so dangerous that they want *me*, a Dane, to help them collect? Why won't *you* tell me?"

Staehr puffed and went red around the collar.

"Well?" I insisted.

Staehr puffed and went redder, a slow burn of embarrassment and frustration.

"They haven't told *you*, have they!" I realized with a sinking feeling.

The other man puffed and relaxed a little, the truth now out. "It's sensitive material, Jeff. That is all that the general, the colonel, and the captain with whom I met permitted me to pass on. 'Sensitive material requiring expert handling.'"

"You mean, that's *all* they'd tell you." I retorted, the anger bubbling up.

"Mr. Carswell," he said, polite as ever when cornered, "you are becoming tiresome. You are behaving as if *I* were keeping something vital from you."

"I'm just a little worried that *they* might be keeping something vital from *you*! Look, a blinking great B 52 explodes on the ice, and now you're telling me that I'm requested to help ship dangerous debris from it back to the States. What do you *think* I think? That damnable machine almost certainly had hydrogen bombs or some such killer stuff on board. Don't you think I have a right to be concerned about what I might be touching out there? Just how dangerous could this 'sensitive material' be?"

"Precisely, Jeff." He spread his hands in a generous, disarming gesture that felt utterly hollow. "Just how dangerous could it be? Don't you think it would have been brought to my immediate attention had there been any extraordinary danger? Don't you think I have already keenly interrogated our American friends on just these points?" (He had not, of course! I could see it in his evasive eyes.) "Look, we're responsible adults here, Jeff; we realize there are certain dangers in many things we have to do as grown men. You're being requested to assist in an organisational and personal capacity. They don't have their own experts on the shipment of dangerous cargoes with them and, having heard that you are an expert, they prefer not to fly any in. I guess that makes sense: why involve more people in this than absolutely necessary? That's all. But, of course, if you don't feel sure you're up to it, well, you've every right to refuse. I just hope you can explain to the Yanks why you chose to hold up these urgent works needlessly while they find someone in the U.S. to do your job."

"Let me get this straight," I said, leaning forward. "The U.S. military, the most powerful and technically advanced on earth, wants a Danish civilian shipping clerk to coordinate their most sensitive activities in cleaning up after a nuclear armed plane crash. Doesn't that strike you as even a little bizarre?"

"No," he said flatly, avoiding my gaze. "It's pragmatism."

I watched him puff away into the further corner of the office, retreating behind his smoke screen.

"No," I echoed, the resignation bitter in my mouth. "No, it doesn't, does it."

* * * * * *

"PENTAGON, SPECIAL OPS research, this is Captain O'Hayer. How can I help you, sir?" Railback heard his old buddy answer the phone with familiar, rapid fire efficiency.

"Railback here."

"Say, Major, how's things up in the eternal darkness? Long time, no hear, only about twelve hours ago. At least this time you called me during working hours. No shit, thanks." O'Hayer said in his staccato, machine gun type speech. "What's up now? I assume this isn't a social call. Though, unlike you, I can make dinner at any number of decent seafood restaurants near the Hill tonight. Did you meet our miracle fly boy? Is he still breathing? OK?"

"That's affirmative," put in Railback. "Say, O'Hayer, how come I haven't heard much stink about this crash back home? What's going on out there in that fine, wider military world that I might not know about up here at the top of the world, that's taking the heat off this little problem? I've gotta know if I should get close to this Burnett if he has something to offer, or distance myself from him and let the heat fall where it will. No pun intended. I'd like to make some rank out of this and not be the designated goat. What's the skinny?"

"No pun intended, none taken. Your secret is safe with your old buddy. But, you know, you must have heard about this little skirmish in Vietnam that's all the news these days? Khe Sanh is under siege." O'Hayer tempted Railback with just enough to pique his interest so that he could show off his insider knowledge.

"OK. Out with it. Tell me all you can in four minutes. That's all I've got before Burnett'll be turning up to take me on a sleigh ride through the snow. So save some of it for later." Railback knew this show off side of his old friend well.

"Oh, I'm cut to the quick! A time limit on brilliance! Well, really ... Anyway, early January, as near as we can tell, between eight and thirteen thousand NVA regulars crossed onto southern soil on a mission from Buddha, marching toward Khe Sanh. As you know, it's our northernmost Special Forces Camp supporting missions into Laos and anywhere else in Southeast Asia for that matter. We figure the Cong are a little pissed off about all that activity of a non tourist nature in areas they want to control. Tet's in full force and the fighting at Khe Sanh is plenty ugly. NVA has been fragging the shit out of the place, inventing a new dance called the 'Khe Sanh Shuffle,' which the leathernecks practise on a regular basis, ducking for bunkers.

"Even on the same date that your little hoe down in Greenland began, your Air Force pulled the Tigerhound Project out of Khe Sanh. Tigerhound's been there since January '66 trying to help 'Westy' figure out where the bad guys were. We had some pretty good air reconnaissance for a couple of years. We bombed areas as far as twelve miles inside Laos with Air Force, Marine and Navy fighter bombers. Hell, Westmoreland could call B 52 strikes with our recon, you name it, we bombed it, and Tigerhound was the table setter.

"Well, I guess those ground pounders are on their own now. Only thing saving a lot of their asses is that underground med evac centre. It's now the ultimate bunker for the combat ops centre or we'd have a few more body bags to evac.

"It's not pretty, but it's definitely taking the heat off you guys. You get the feeling the news is all about the party on Route 9 in Vietnam instead of the one on Route 66 in the good old USA. Hell, Hills 881 North and South and 861 are honeycombed with Charlie. One of the last assaults came from 861, got within thirty yards of Khe Sanh perimeter. VC want Khe Sanh to be another Dien Bien Phu. But, the 1st Battalion, 9th Marines, you know, 'The Walking Dead,' say they're going to hold their sector, The Rock Quarry, 'until Hell freezes over and they skate on it ...'"

"Thanks, buddy," Railback cut off O'Hayer, who was off on a runaway tactical explanation.

"Yeah, no problem. Hey, don't forget when you make chief of staff, give your old Irish buddy some plum assignment over there in Belgium with NATO, will you?" O'Hayer closed.

"I can do that," Railback said, a ghost of a smile on his lips.

"Hey, Major, remember that guy Geoffrey? The spook you pulled out of that firefight in Laos last year."

"Yeah. Vaguely."

"Well, there's a lieutenant in Khe Sanh right now that's damn glad you did." O'Hayer, an expert at extending conversations, continued.

"How so?"

"Geoffrey came running off one of the hills into the base with this lieutenant on his back and about a million rounds of ammo, just a skip in front of Charlie, and that's what was left of his platoon after they got bushwhacked trying to retake the lookout. Saved his bacon. Said he owed it to the big Marine who got him out of Laos."

"Thule out," Railback said, cutting the connection. He needed to think.

Jesus, Railback thought, hanging up the phone, Khe Sanh, Laos, the Arctic Circle: were the core problems really that different? Containing chaos, managing disaster, saving what you can, burying the rest.

He paused and remembered infiltrating Laos himself, watching the relentless building of the Ho Chi Minh Trail, the troops and supplies in Laos threatening the guys now dying at Khe Sanh. *One tactical nuke and that trail is gone.* And now, that same potential saviour, that same destructive power, is the enemy under *this* ice. What's the diff? Impossible to draw a clean analogy between Vietnam's conventional hell and this frozen, silent mess. Lives are always lost, but entire continents could go under with nuclear arrows, broken or unbroken, falling to earth. He wondered what had happened to that man Geoffrey after all.

"Don't moralise!" he chastised himself sharply. "Focus and get the job done. That's the only morality here."

"Major."

Railback jerked his head up to see Burnett already dressed for the deep cold, holding out a pair of bulky Air Force 'bunny boots' and a thick, anonymous arctic parka.

"What, don't I get one with real wolf fur inside the hood?" he asked good naturedly, which probably made Burnett immediately suspicious of his motives.

"Negatory, Major. We reserve those for visiting VIPs and senators. You just get the standard issue ghost."

"You just keep trying to get on my good side, Captain, and I may just include your name in my report. In the 'adequate' column." Railback responded, pulling on the stiff parka.

* * * * * *

A FEW DAYS into the post crash hullabaloo, I was called in by Puffing Billy to a meeting attended by all the supervisory and higher administration staff of the DCC. The purpose was to formally welcome a coterie of scientists who had newly arrived at the base. Present also were the base Commander, our good friend the liaison officer Poul Moelgaard, and a number of other unfamiliar, stern American military faces. Among these was one face that stood out on account of its smooth, hardened planes and because, even though this face belonged only to a major, even the sandy haired, normally composed Colonel Dresser seemed to defer to him subtly. It was the Afro American Marine I had noticed before.

The meeting was limited to Staehr introducing the newly arrived scientists by name and obscure reputation, at which each one nodded at us wearily or stood clumsily for a moment or seemed utterly oblivious to the proceedings (one of them, a man with a soft felt hat that constantly circled between his nervous hands, could have been at home in bed speculating on the transit of Venus for all the impression the formalities appeared to make on him). We offered polite, confused applause and were profoundly thankful to be allowed out of the stuffy room without further fuss or long winded speeches. Niels, Rasmus and I escaped and headed straight for the club for a fortifying drink and a bite to eat.

"What in God's name was all that about?" Rasmus asked, downing his schnapps in one go. "A welcome party for eggheads?"

"Rasmus, you are too much of a cynic," said Niels, ever the reasonable one. "They just wanted to introduce us to some people who are going to be doing important scientific investigations connected with the clean up operation. They need to know who we are, we need to know who they are. It's coordination."

Rasmus scarcely seemed to hear Niels. "How about that character in the pink socks, eh? What do you reckon his special field is? Neon ankles and their after effects? Ha ha! Or perhaps he's an expert in colourful hosiery under extreme cold!"

"I'm just a little worried about why they need so many specialists in nuclear type matters," I put in, my brow furrowed, ignoring Rasmus's foray into absurdist humour. "That's what they are, you know. Health physicists, radiologists. Not road engineers."

"Well, they've got to make sure it's safe to be working around all this burnt ice and debris, don't they?" replied Niels, his voice calm. "I'd certainly like to be sure of that. Wouldn't you? I don't fancy glowing in the dark."

"Yeah, I guess so. I guess that's it," I agreed, trying to sound convinced. "I just hope they actually *do* let us know if there is some danger. Truly let us know."

"Pah!" Rasmus lowered the empty shot glass with a sharp crack. "Sure they will. And, then they'll let us all go home on a nice, long vacation, and when we get back, it'll all be nice and safe again. The magic cleaning fairies will have been. You are a dreamer, Niels."

"You are too much of a cynic, Rasmus, my friend," Niels clapped his friend on the back, causing him to spill his fresh drink down his jacket. "The Americans are an honorable people. They wouldn't lie about something like this."

"Yeah, but these scientists are *Danes*," Rasmus shot back, mopping his front. "Our own countrymen! And you know what *they're* like! Masters of saying nothing very carefully."

* * * * * *

I HAD ARRIVED at Thule back in July, 1966, employed on a simple three month contract during the hectic summer supply season; the precious window during which ships are able to batter through the ice to the base.

At the end of that period, I was invited to take a new, indefinite contract. I did so for two reasons: the income was quite good, much better than in Copenhagen; and I was fishing about for something new, having just left a travel and shipping agency partnership in Denmark. The future was unsettled.

"A few more months in the Arctic wouldn't be such a bad idea," I thought, "And it will give me time to decide on where I'll finally settle: Canada or Australia." I was thoroughly bent on emigration, on a fresh start under a sun that actually set.

Because of my previous experience with the Lauritzen shipping company, and being a fully qualified shipping broker, I had been placed in the freight handling section; and, from junior shipping officer, I was promoted in mid 1967 to the position of assistant supervisor, freight handling. It was a job I took seriously.

I was young and conscientious then, and, I suppose, a little credulous, like most of those working on the base (it was, after all, something of a young man's society, a suspended adolescence in the ice). My fellow workers and I never supposed we should read the official silence of the base authorities as anything other than how they clearly meant us to read it; 'If there were any real dangers, well, of course, they'd tell us, wouldn't they!' we innocently reassured each other over beers. Trust was the currency of the realm.

Sometimes the bigger the lie, the greater the silence that conveys it and surrounds it. Some lies leave you speechless; some take away the very faculty of comprehending speech; and some leave gaping, festering holes in your future. Perhaps, just as we find it difficult to see where life has been in the shrouded remains of our mortal coil, the biggest lies of all lie so shrouded in strategic silence as to seem never to have been uttered at all. The absence of warning became the warranty of safety.

It did not occur to us, not in our wildest, most paranoid dreams, that the United States military in the first instance, and later the Danish government and its scientific community, might remain in mendacious silence about something that touched those concerned in their very cells, in their future children. They did not lie to us with their words, at least not at that early stage; rather they allowed their silence to lie for them, a lie of omission. It was what they failed to say, in effect, the cavernous spaces between their few, careful words, that held the greater, fatal meaning for our fates: they could not even bring themselves to the stoic and yet candid despair of Pontius Pilate, 'What is truth?' They left it up to us to guess that a truth worth the asking about might be being deliberately, coldly withheld from us. We never asked.

It was not until 1994, on my visit to the United States when I met up with Greg Maas, the president of the U.S. Ex Thulers' Association, that I discovered a slightly different, more active strategy had been used with the American GIs assisting in the clean up. The strategy for them was not just silence, but active distortion and cynical underplay.

The young GIs were told that yes, there was radiation around, but only "low levels" of it, and that "a little radiation would do them no harm." They were even "respectfully" informed that yes, they *might* experience some temporary infertility problems; but that this effect would be short term and that they would be perfectly able to have children later on. It was framed as a minor, transient inconvenience.

The same ancient, cynical wisdom told the authorities what would be the general response of the young soldiers to that news: amusement, indifference, and even perhaps a feeling of 'how convenient.' We are dealing, after all, with very young men; some just in their teens, away from home for the first time. What true comprehension were they going to have of the nature of the irreversible risk they were being asked to take? What eighteen year old male, full of life and immortality, seriously wonders about the children he may or may not have in four or five years time? Moreover, as soldiers, they had been rigorously trained to do what they were told without question, even at the immediate risk of their lives. And, besides, they trusted their superiors, their *American* superiors; and, remember, we all believed the Americans were an honorable people.

While the authorities could afford to be offhand and misleading with the GIs, fobbing them off with distortions and half truths, with us Danes, their allied civilians, it was judged better, safer, not to allow the dangerous spectre to be raised at all. They trusted us kooky, compliant Europeans to just get on with the job without asking awkward questions: which is precisely what we did. We, in turn, trusted them to keep a professional look out for our welfare: which is precisely what they didn't. Not in any meaningful way.

On one slate, a *tabula rasa*; a clean, ignorant surface. On the other, an indecipherable, lethal doodle: a Yankee doodle that spelled our doom.

* * * * * *

SO I WAS more than placated. Open-mouthed, I accepted the US military's request to assist them in handling the most dangerous parts of the aircraft debris, to ready them for shipment back to the States. Not until years later did I look back and see a young man breathlessly joining the queue to become a victim.

Having been requested in this indirect manner, in effect by my employers, I could hardly refuse. Besides, I was excited by the sudden frenzy of activity around me and wanted a piece of it; and I was, as a young man of twenty-four, professionally flattered by the suggestion that I was the only competent and qualified person on the base to do the job. Touch a young man's pride, and he is unlikely to heed any warning voices. Not even the faintest suggestion that he might be risking his own extinction will reach ears so deafened by hubris.

So, I went to the building with the 'top secret' designation that served as the storage depot, and I actually felt proud to be admitted. It was thrilling, being ushered into a top secret sector positively bristling with armed escorts and boiling with high-ranking brass.

I was soon apprised of the material I was to help recover. In the first days after the crash, after the crew had been accounted for, there was a frantic search for the most critical parts of the hydrogen bombs and the most sensitive parts of the aircraft. These were the dangerous parts I was to assist in shipping back to the United States.

Two American officers greeted me: a full colonel and an Air Force captain. The colonel did most of the talking.

"Mr. Carswell, if you are not already aware, I must inform you of the significance of the 'top secret' designation of this hangar. It means that only cleared personnel may enter. Practically, for you, it means that as this place is off limits to nearly everyone on the base, including the Danish labourers who would normally handle such materials, you will be asked to fill that role. I have other affairs to attend to, Mr. Carswell, so if you have any questions, the captain here will deal with them."

He saluted, shook my now-limp hand, and strode off behind a great pile of drums in the centre of the hangar.

The Air Force captain was pleasant though businesslike. He shook my hand and introduced himself as Captain Marc Benjamin. He was a large man, tall and solidly built, and clearly respected for his professionalism. A respect I was to come to share.

"Well, Mr. Carswell," his Nebraska accent rang musically, "here we have the most severely contaminated parts that have been located, all containered-up." He indicated the sealed drums behind which the colonel had disappeared. "When the transport arrives, we'll call you. In the meantime, here is some paperwork." He grinned and handed me a wad of forms. I took them with a disappointed glance from him to the papers. "We'll call you," he repeated.

So I learned I was to be one of the privileged few to manhandle the drums of radioactive debris onto a pickup for transportation.

The following day, our C-141 jet freighter flew in. It sat there with engines running while a general, whom I had not seen before, pointed out six drums and said, "These will do for this flight."

I stood waiting nearby with Captain Benjamin and the Colonel. We four were the only ones present. I was nonplussed. "What about the rest?" I asked to no one in particular.

Benjamin replied to a question I had not asked, "Not this load, Mr. Carswell. Too dangerous. Shipping any more than four to six drums on a single flight would expose the crew to too great a concentration of radiation during the trip."

I nodded a superficial comprehension. Only now, with the greater wisdom of fifty-two years, can I explain why that comment did not set off alarm bells.

My logic must have run thus: because they had drawn my attention to the danger of long exposure, I must not be in any significant danger from a short exposure; having been so frank about the long-term dangers, they would have told me had it been otherwise.

Besides, here were a general, a colonel, and a captain, all doing exactly what I was doing.

I was reassured.

Seldom had I worked so closely with men of such rank. The three Americans bodily assisted me; huffing the general, puffing the colonel, and sweating Captain Benjamin, as we loaded the drums onto the pickup once I had completed the documentation.

We all rugged up in our arctic gear. Captain Benjamin jumped into the pickup, with the colonel and me beside him, and out we drove onto the runway where the C-141 waited, engines running, rearing for takeoff.

The three of us then, the General having retired to the Officers' Club, struggled in our thick protective clothing and somehow managed to transfer the drums from the truck to the C-141's huge cargo hold. There they were secured on their sides, as far from the crew as possible. "They look quite forlorn," I thought. We drove back to the base in an oppressive silence.

Only since has it become clear that it is the intensity of exposure, as much as, if not more than, the length of exposure, that determines the effect on the body.

And this cargo was hot. Very, very hot.

And I had been as close to it as the mere thickness of a metal drum and a pair of arctic gloves would allow.

Still the alarm bells stayed silent. My trust in the system and those running it allayed my fears. If I was a little annoyed at the manual labour, the feeling of being taken into the confidence of our powerful allies, the Americans, overrode it.

Afterwards, back in the comparative warmth of the hangar, Captain Benjamin turned to me.

"Jeff, can I invite you to the Club for a drink?"

"You certainly can, Captain Benjamin," I smiled with relief.

Some twenty minutes later, leaning back in an easy chair and taking a sip of his bourbon, he turned his easy smile on me.

"Call me Marc, Jeff." One thing I like about the Americans is their easy hospitality.

"Yes, of course, Marc," I answered.

"You do know what you've just done, don't you? What you've just become?" he asked slyly.

I nearly choked on my bourbon and blenched.

"Don't panic," he guffawed. "What I mean is, you are, to my knowledge, the first foreign national who has ever carried in his hands an American nuclear bomb; or at least, the remains of one."

"I'm ... honoured," I said. And I meant it. At the time. I remained thoughtful, handling my bourbon with caution.

Then I asked, "What were they so worried about finding out there? The bombs? Have they found all the bomb parts?"

It was Marc's turn to choke. "Jeez, Jeff, do you think I'm going to know that?" His forthrightness impressed me.

"Well, you know ..." I smiled.

"Do you think I'd tell you if I did know?"

"It'll go no further," I promised.

Marc finished his shot and ordered a second, and a Black Russian for me. Then:

"It's no big deal. Just that the Pentagon's paranoid about secrecy."

He paused and leant forward, his arms curled around his glass. "They were anxious to secure the top secret documents and maps that indicated the targets for their payload, in case they got orders to fly to Russia."

I silently considered this, nodding as if in comprehension.

"A young airman found them yesterday. He's now been flown back to SAC HQ for a full debriefing."

"They'll have his trousers," I joked uncomfortably.

"And all that's in 'em. The silly dope panicked when he saw what he had, and realising they'd never believe he hadn't looked, destroyed them. Drink up, Jeff. There's work to be done."

He clapped my shoulder and we left the club.

* * * * * *

THE FOLLOWING DAY, the four of us repeated our task of loading drums onto a pickup, driving out to a roaring C-141 and securing them in the cargo bay. The day after was the same, and the day after that. The fourth day saw the last of the drums off to its interment in South Carolina. With a mixture of relief and satisfaction, I watched the C-141 lift heavily off the tarmac, then turned with Marc towards our by-then routine watering hole.

* * * * * *

ONCE THE MOST dangerous items had been shipped, the clean-up operation began in earnest. The Tank Farm, set up in an unused corner of the base, consisted of numerous twenty-five-thousand-gallon containers for receiving dangerous debris and contaminated snow and ice.

The months passed. As summer approached, the containers were systematically filled and sealed. There was a race against time, as the clean-up needed to be completed before the summer thaw melted everything into the fiord, losing any chance of containment. 237,000 cubic feet of ice and snow had to be shaved off the surface of the ocean ice. This ice formed the bulk of the material to be shipped.

Besides the Tank Farm, there were scattered special containers of varying sizes. In my continuing role, I was the only non-American allowed near those areas. I was too busy to ask further questions about the dangers, and they were too busy to answer. There were no specific warnings, so I assumed I ran no special risk.

My days were spent moving around the huge containers, checking they were properly sealed and labelled. In a few cases, unstable materials caught fire during loading, releasing dangerous fumes we were not told about.

As spring wore on, the ice in the containers melted and leaked a radioactive cocktail of sticky mud and slush onto the ground. Day after day, I walked in it.

I had been appointed liaison officer for the DCC to the 'Clean-up Task Force,' about twenty-five men flown in from New Mexico and Texas in May.

About three days after my adventure with the drums, and the day after the Task Force arrived, I was out with my clipboard when an unusual sight caught my attention I gave a double take and, having spotted Marc Benjamin among the small knot at a small distance from one of the tanks of contaminated debris, I went up and spoke to him.

"What's all this?" I asked, a little ruffled, pointing with my clipboard at the men milling about the tank in outfits that I thought might be useful for doing a space walk. Four guys with clicking boxes also came within my ambit query.

"The question you asked and the one you want answered aren't the same, are they?" replied Marc, whose face offered only the reassurance that the sight of men checking the tanks in heavy protective clothing and men checking them with Geiger counters was as unsettling to him as it was to me.

"Are you thinking what I'm thinking?"

"If you're thinking, 'Does it ever rub off?' then, yes, you are, Jeff."

One of the guys wielding the Geiger counters approached me and ran his probe quickly over me. It clucked like a mother hen. My jaw dropped.

"What the fuck ..." I began.

"Shit, Sarge, we've got a live one here!" let out the geiger accountant with a wry smile, and moved on, shaking his head.

* * * * * *

THE PACE OF work was hectic. The job had to be done by mid-September, with no room for negotiating changes to the deadline. This was for two reasons: the ice needed to be scraped before the spring thaw set in and melted it all away. The ships needed to be loaded and on their way before the fall saw the ocean freeze over once again and trap them at Thule till the following spring.

As nearly all the men involved were very young, in their teens or early twenties, they were strong and fit and up to the long hours, freezing cold and hard yakka. They did get exhausted from time to time. But, I suppose that is understandable. It was hard work they were doing. Or maybe it falls within the confines of likelihood that the effects of radiation exposure were playing preliminary havoc with their bodies already.

Luckily, the deadline was met and, by mid-summer, it was all over. The last tank of contaminated material, decorated on its circular end with those fulsome words of wisdom from 'Loony Tunes,' 'That's All, Folks,' was loaded on the last ship en route to somewhere like the desert of Nevada to sit snug and smug in the sand and leak out its deadly cargo for the special consideration of future generations. With it went the Task Force, and with that, went the many good friends I had made: among them, Marc Benjamin. We'll meet again!

* * * * * *

BACK AT THULE, we had one final, overwhelming wave of visitors: a massive cargo plane shuddered onto the runway, disgorging a fleet of miniature submarines and their skeleton crews.

One afternoon, Niels, Rasmus, and I idled on the weather-beaten pier, speculating. "What on earth," Rasmus wondered aloud, "could those tiny things possibly be hunting for on the fjord's black bottom?"

"Well," said Niels, with a shrug, "Official line is they're checking for debris that might have slipped through the ice."

"Yes," I murmured, more to myself than to them, my eyes locked on the dark water slapping the pilings. "Yes, they've given us a lot of lines by now, haven't they?"

"What are you hinting at, Carswell?" Rasmus pressed. "You don't believe them? What's your theory?"

"I believe they're looking for something, just as they claim," I said. "And I believe they're *up* to something, which they do not claim. I'm learning to read their silences as clearly as their words."

"Hmmph!" grunted Rasmus.

"Hmm?" queried Niels.

I turned to face them.

"You've got a properly malicious grin on your face," laughed Rasmus. "What's brewing in that thick skull of yours?"

"I think it's time we showed our maritime guests some genuine Danish hospitality. Come on!" I took off at a brisk walk toward the quay, where one of the midget subs, having just broken the steel-gray surface, was wallowing home.

That evening, in my modest quarters, I played host to as many submariners as I could lure to a small, impromptu party. After loosening them up with American beer and bourbon, I applied the decisive tool: the Danish 'truth serum'—schnapps.

"So, tell me, admiral," I playfully addressed a flushed midshipman in the chair opposite, "What's the real quarry out there in the fjord?"

"The fjord? Oh, right, the bay."

"Yes, the bay," I laughed. "What's the true story? Don't look so offended. We know you Americans never tell foreigners more than you think they absolutely need. We know the CIA is just a publicity firm for the American art of staying quiet."

The midshipman swelled with outrage. Fortunately, his pride was wounded precisely where I had hoped—in his national honor. So he spilled. After each staggering sentence, he would drain his shot glass. After each empty glass, a colleague or I would thoughtfully refill it.

In three explosive minutes, before four mortified shipmates dragged him away, he confessed. The mission was to locate and recover one item: one hydrogen bomb, intact, unexploded, property of Uncle Sam, which had sunk to the fjord's depths. Confirmatory signs had been found, but tidal currents had apparently moved the bomb from its resting place. Despite an extensive search, it remained lost.

Presumably, to this very day, that fourth bomb lies on the bay's bottom, within arrow-shot of the base itself!

Oh, splendid. Isn't that just perfectly peachy?

* * * * * *

CAPTAIN MARC BENJAMIN, shortly after his return to the US, was transferred from Fairchild Air Force Base in Washington to Offutt Air Force Base at Omaha, Nebraska. It was there that I visited him and his family during my annual break in May 1969.

Marc is a substantial man, softly spoken and fundamentally warm. If one person could embody an entire nation, like the Ancients' idea of a champion—a figure feted and granted privileges far beyond the ordinary warrior—then America could do far worse than revive the custom and name Marc Benjamin its Modern Champion. Not to fight in some archaic duel, but to be sent into the homes of both allies and adversaries alike, to show by quiet example the depth of American hospitality, the generosity that exists far beyond the uniform and the headline.

It is a great pity that such an institution will never be. It would have shown the world the hidden, warm life of a people too often seen only in camouflage, blurred by the fog of war.

At the time of my visit, Vietnam was about to erupt into a white-hot fury, whose brutal glare made the dull, radioactive embers of our Greenland incident seem a forgotten ghost.

My flight to Nebraska took me via Montreal to Chicago, then on to Omaha. To combat the travel boredom, I had bought a copy of *Time*. That issue featured a chronicle, with photographs, of every American soldier killed in Vietnam during a single week sometime earlier. Seeing those faces, names, ages, and hometowns—all those ordinary 'grunts' who would never have grandchildren, never feel the complex pains of return, never even sow their wild oats—I closed the magazine. I laid it gently on my knees and rubbed my eyes. The cabin had grown unaccountably foggy, even at 10,000 feet.

Our innocent reminiscing over our shared duty now seems heartbreakingly naive. Neither of us had the slightest inkling of the secret, sub-cellular sapping underway within our bodies. I have kept in contact with Marc since, and discovered, surprise surprise, that he too suffers a range of peculiar ailments, not entirely dissimilar to my own, nor to those of many of my former colleagues.

A few days into my visit, Marc informed me I had an invitation to accompany him onto the base, to meet some of the higher command. Apparently, Marc had told them I was one of the Danes who had helped, especially during the Thule clean-up. I found myself shaking many braided, beribboned hands, introduced as the 'Saviour of Operation Crested Ice.'

From Marc's home in Nebraska, I travelled on to California for a few days. I managed to visit Vandenberg Air Force Base, to see Senior Master Sergeant 'Mickie' Thompson, another American I had met during the clean-up.

Vandenberg was then a main portal for Vietnam. As my bus pulled into the base terminal, I thought sadly of the faces in that *Time* magazine. With a jolt of grim recognition, I realized I was now looking at the faces destined for the next such article, and the one after that, and the one after that.

After a pleasant dinner with Sergeant Thompson and his family, I was on the bus again, leaving. As the ill-fitting uniforms and cropped heads of the draftees—*Time*'s future column fodder—paraded past the high wire fence, I reflected, "They had better at least win this bloody war. And quick."

* * * * * *

IN THULE ITSELF, in the lull immediately after the clean-up toward the end of September 1968, a profound anticlimax settled over me. The adrenaline had faded, leaving only the bleak promise of the normal, interminable winter routine.

While I later heard that several Danes who assisted were rewarded with special payments, that was not my experience. The Danish Civilian Contractor company did receive a significant premium for its cooperation, but little of that trickled down to the workers, and none reached me. What I gained was a heightened profile within the company, which, I am sure, accelerated my promotion to senior management.

After September that year, I became an Executive Officer in the DCC. I remained at the base until July 1971, when I left to forge a new life in a new New World, and travelled to Australia, which, like Peter Allen, I to this day call home.

So closed to what I thought was an eventful chapter of my life. I was wrong. It was reopened many years later, when I was forced to count the cost of those six weeks in 1968, not in memories, but on the fingers of pain and lingering death.

Chapter 9: Science Attains Maturity

but the weeping man, like the earth, requires nothing

An Absolutely Ordinary Rainbow　　LES MURRAY

RISOE IS A LITTLE VILLAGE that serves as home to and gives its name to the Danish Atomic Energy Commission's Research Facility. To the public eye, it stood as a modest citadel of reason and national progress. To those familiar with the quiet currents that flowed through its corridors, however, Risoe was a permanent, low-frequency blot upon the Danish scientific conscience. It was an organisation perpetually and shamefully diverted from its noble charter by the blunt instrument of governmental will, its purpose softened into complicity by the obedient silence of the men and women within its walls. A place built for asking questions, it had perfected the art of providing convenient answers.

Its founding charter spoke in lofty terms of keeping Denmark at the vanguard of atomic research, of pioneering original inquiry, of vigilant monitoring for radioactive peril. In sober reality, it had long since been moulded into the state's chosen instrument for a very different task:

the white-washing, the distortion, and the quiet disavowal of any atomic truth the government deemed too inconvenient, too complex, or too frightening for the public to grasp. Its laboratories were less for discovery than for the manufacture of reassurance.

On the chill morning of January 24, 1968, however, Professor Otto Kofoed Hansen, Director of the Physics Department at Risoe, entertained no such corrosive thoughts. He moved through the pre-dawn darkness of his home with a focused, practical energy, packing a small bag for the five-and-a-half-hour flight to Thule, to which he had been summoned with only as many hours' notice. His mind, a precise and orderly mechanism, was already aloft, turning over the sparse facts of the crisis. He believed—with a scientist's innate, perhaps naïve, faith in the integrity of his summons—that he had been selected for his expertise alone.

Professor Kofoed Hansen believed he was flying north to assist in a genuine, independent scientific investigation into the wreckage of HOBO 28. He believed his task was to help ascertain any Danish casualties, to evaluate any threat to Greenlandic and Danish personnel from radioactive materials now adrift in the polar atmosphere. He believed he would be working alongside Henry Gjoerup, Per Grande, and Professor Joergen Koch, in full cooperation with the SAC Disaster Control Team. Together, they would apply objective rigor. They would measure, they would calculate, they would trace. They would determine, with scrupulous honesty, the true level of contamination and chart its probable journey on the Arctic winds. For the good Herr Professor was a renowned expert in turbulent diffusion, in the secret, swirling pathways of airborne contaminants. He was a man who trusted in the clarity of numbers and the sanctity of a well-run process.

His colleagues at Risoe were not the only ones to have noted, time and again, the Professor's singular, almost devotional single-mindedness. The trait had been etched into his character from the beginning. His paternal grandmother had observed its first glimmers with a mixture of awe and vague disquiet. She had once watched the three-and-a-half-year-old Otto spend an entire autumn afternoon in their garden, utterly rapt, tracing the drunken, spiraling descent of individual leaves from the maple trees. He did not merely watch; he documented, scribing intricate, mud-based notations on the ground with a twig, his baby face a mask of profound concentration. To her alarm, she perceived his scrawls were not random, but a crude yet coherent record of patterns, of trajectories—an attempt to predict the unpredictable.

"The child is obsessive!" she had confided to his mother later, her hands fluttering to her chest. "He doesn't play. He audits. He plays as if he's trying to catch nature herself in an error."

His mother, wiping a porcelain plate with a slow, deliberate cloth that evening, had simply smiled. The sound was warm, a gentle counterpoint to her mother-in-law's fretful energy. "At least he's not pulling wings from butterflies or burying the neighbour's cat," she had said, her tone laced with a quiet pride. "I'd say he's just exploring the world with every fibre he has. Wondering, powerfully. Perhaps he simply believes in making an honest use of his time. And he remains a cooperative soul. He did, after all, dry all these dishes without a single complaint."

Over forty years later, standing in the bureaucratic echo chamber of Risoe, the Professor still held to that boyhood principle. To him, *to cooperate* was an active verb of integrity, implying the coming together of independent minds in mutual respect for a shared truth. And he carried another, related belief: that the Americans, their allies, were fundamentally an honourable people. They would, he was sure, have no reason to obscure the facts of a terrible accident.

This reputation for principled clarity was well-established. He was the co-author, with J. Thomas, of a pointed 1960 paper examining the profound safety issues inherent in a nuclear-powered naval fleet. In it, Kofoed Hansen had expressed deep reservations about floating such vessels in an enclosed, fragile sea like the Baltic. His colleagues often smiled and suggested this stance was merely the sentimental anxiety of a dedicated sailor—a man who had, after all, piloted his own small yacht across the choppy waters to Karlskrona in Sweden more times than he could count. They saw it as a lover's protest, not a scientist's warning.

But his argument was colder and harder than sentiment. He posited that even a minor incident, one causing no measurable radioactive release, would seed a psychological catastrophe. The mere spectre of contamination, the chilling whisper of *what if*, would be enough to poison the region's fishing industry for a generation. He argued that the public mind, when confronted with nuclear energy, operated on a different calculus, one where doubt had infinite weight. And this was all before one considered the sheer, concentrated folly of placing hundreds of potential critical masses of the most toxic materials known to man into the confined and stormy waters of a shallow sea. It was, he maintained, a real and monstrous danger, waved away with inadequate data.

All this was well known within the muted halls of Risoe. And Professor Hansen knew it was well known. A flicker of this understanding—cold, clear, and brief—may have passed through his mind as he accepted the mission to Thule. Perhaps they needed a man known for his obstinate commitment to truth, a credible face, when a real nuclear accident demanded investigation. The thought was there and gone, dismissed as unworthy. He was a scientist, and he was needed.

When he clambered up the metal steps to the military transport plane later that day, swaddled in a heavy wool topcoat, a thick scarf, and his favourite soft felt hat, he presented a figure of quaint, academic vulnerability. He was oblivious to the faint smiles of the hardened air crew and other officials. He could not yet fathom the profound, physical hatred of the cold that awaited him, a cold that would make his careful preparations seem laughable. Luck, or bureaucratic necessity, would provide him and the others with proper Arctic survival gear upon landing at Thule. But the penetrating cold of the Greenlandic winter was merely a physical foretaste, a literal chill, of the glacial, bureaucratic reception his final report would eventually meet. That report's fate needed to be kept frozen, locked in perpetual ice, for its conclusions would quickly be seen as politically putrid if ever exposed to the normal temperatures of public scrutiny.

In the meantime, on the fractured ice of North Star Bay, Professor Kofoed Hansen's investigation began with a stroke of personal fortune. A friend of his mother's, a senior police inspector from Copenhagen, had been visiting the Thule base at the very moment of the crash. This man, along with the base's permanent constable, Inspector Flemming Skov, would become the Professor's most crucial and credible eyewitnesses. They were gold, untouched by the coming machinery of obfuscation.

On that catastrophic afternoon, the visiting inspector had been taking coffee in the home of his colleague. Skov's house was perfectly, almost theatrically, positioned on a rocky rise overlooking the sprawling base and the vast, iced-over expanse of the fiord beyond. The two men could not have had a better vantage point if they had been issued tickets. They were front-row spectators to Armageddon.

Five days later, one of Professor Kofoed Hansen's first acts after landing in the howling, surreal whiteness of Thule was to be driven up to that very house. He sat in the vehicle beside his mother's old friend, the cold seeping through the layers of his newly issued parka, feeling the immense, silent weight of the landscape. Even in full Arctic regalia, the cold was a shocking, living entity. He had, out of some stubborn attachment to normalcy, kept his soft felt hat on beneath the fur-lined hood.

At about 2:30 p.m. on January 29, a time when the sun was a mere bruise of suggestion below the horizon, the three men stood with Mrs. Skov on the frozen patio of the house. They looked out into the deep, blue-black gloom of the perpetual Arctic twilight. Darkness was not an absence here, but a presence—a heavy, velvety dust settled over the world by a neglectful hand. The silence was profound, an auditory void that pressed against the eardrums. Into this void, the distant, frantic activity on the ice far below was rendered a silent, ghostly pantomime—tiny, illuminated figures moving against an impossible darkness, like damned souls labouring in a frozen circle of hell.

A profound and unsettling feeling settled over Professor Kofoed Hansen. This desolate quiet felt like a premonition, a held breath before a cosmic verdict. The frantic yet soundless struggle on the ice seemed to pull at him, willing him down into the dumb show, to become another masked player in a drama whose script was already written elsewhere. He felt, for a terrifying moment, complicit in a vast, unspoken conspiracy—a conspiracy not yet articulated, but known in the gut, the way members of a secret priesthood understand their vows without hearing them spoken aloud.

With a sharp, physical shudder, he threw the feeling off like a shawl of cobwebs. He turned to his companions, his breath pluming in the stagnant air. He felt suddenly ashamed, as if caught in a private act of voyeurism.

"A simple, practical task," he said, his voice firm against the silence. "Can I ask each of you to write down, independently, exactly what you saw when the bomber came down? Every detail you can remember."

The two policemen, solid, reliable men of fact, nodded. They would do it. Mrs. Skov politely declined; she had been in the kitchen, tending to her daughter and the evening meal, a guardian of domestic normality against the apocalyptic backdrop.

The statements they produced were dry, unadorned, and therefore devastating. Each man wrote that the monstrous sound—a thunder born of earth, not sky—had brought them running outside. Each described an enormous, lurid fireball, a wound of violent light tearing open the Arctic night. It was, one wrote, like seeing the lid blow off a subterranean world. A spiritual Pandemonium made briefly, terribly physical. And crucially, identically, and independently, they both affirmed the conflagration had raged for approximately twenty minutes.

To Professor Kofoed Hansen, holding the two sheets of paper that felt heavier than lead, this single fact was a key turning in a terrible lock. A twenty-minute, high-temperature inferno involving the materials known to be aboard HOBO 28 was not a contained event. It was a volcano. It meant the plutonium, the uranium, the myriad toxic alloys—all of it would have been vaporized, pulverized, and lifted into the air on the thermal column of its own annihilation. The minor firestorm it created would have acted as a bellows, scattering the poisonous essence of the bomber across the ice, the sea, and the relentless wind.

There would be no resurrection for HOBO 28 from this pyre. Instead, a different, more spectral entity would rise from these modern phoenix ashes: a ghastly, invisible sprite of lasting spite, an undying nemesis forged in that instant. It would haunt its makers, binding them in a silent, endless pact with the consequences they sought to bury. This poetic, bleak thought drifted through the Professor's mind as he stared at the blunt prose of the two policemen. One had noted, *'The fire was very high, perhaps over one hundred yards, and lasted twenty-two minutes.'* The other stated simply, *'The huge fire took at least twenty minutes to extinguish itself.'*

"No prosecutor in the world," Kofoed Hansen murmured to himself, the words forming little clouds of finality in the cold air, "could wish for more credible witnesses." Their value was incalculable.

The conclusion he drew was immediate, and it settled in his stomach like a stone. Pending the physical confirmation he would now seek on the ice itself, they must operate on the assumption that highly radioactive debris was scattered over a vast area. The contamination would be widespread, it would be variable, and it would very likely have reached the very edges of the base itself.

* * * * * *

THE NEXT ITEM on the Professor's agenda was the detailed physical investigation he needed to carry out so as to place his anecdotal knowledge on the firmer basis of scientific data. He required numbers, measurements, the hard currency of his profession. Yet an unexpected obstacle now sat drinking his whiskey.

Back down the mountainside at Thule and inside the barracks building assigned him as his laboratory-cum-living quarters once more, he was surprised to find an unknown figure lounging in his easy chair, long legs stretched towards the stove, calmly helping himself to the Professor's own bottle.

Kofoed Hansen stopped in the doorway, the frigid air clinging to his parka. He returned the American's wide, toothy grinned greeting of 'Howdy, pardner!' with a nonplussed grunt. The scene felt absurdly staged.

"Hey, buddy. Help yourself to a drink. You must be Coffered Andersen."

The American was on his feet and reaching out a great raw hand to the Professor. The Professor took the proffered paw and found himself bodily dragged down, as if by a drowning man, into the other armchair in the room. A glass of liquor was thrust, sloshing, under his nose.

"We're gonna be pardners, pardner," continued the Southern drawl, a sound utterly alien in the Spartan Danish quarters. "I'm Wright H. Langham, Group Leader of Biomedical Research at Los Alamos Scientific Laboratories. Born and bred in Amarillo, Texas in the good ol' US of A."

"Otto Kofoed Hansen, Risoe, Denmark," replied the Professor, his voice tight. He was struggling to reconcile this caricature—this lanky, grinning apparition straight from a Hollywood western—with the reality that the man was, ostensibly, one of the foremost American experts on plutonium. The disconnect was jarring.

The next thing Kofoed Hansen noted was that the still-smiling Langham had somehow folded his great frame back down into the armchair from which he had emerged and was simultaneously expostulating fiercely and despatching glasses of liquor freely. The formalities, it seemed, were now considered complete.

"I guess we can have a little ol' look out there tomorrow, the two of us, pardner. Though I'm darned if I can see what all the fuss is about."

"A B-52 loaded with hydrogen bombs smashes to smithereens on the ice and you wonder why you're here?" The Professor furrowed his eyebrows, his intellectual superciliousness a feeble shield against this onslaught of folksy bravado.

"Jeez, fella, it ain't as if the darn things went off, for Chrissake!"

"No, well, you have a point there. We can be thankful for that in any case," Kofoed Hansen conceded, the words tasting flat. "But still, there's bound to have been a significant amount of radioactive debris scattered around out there."

Langham's smile vanished as if switched off. "So what?" For a moment the edges of his lips reached sourly towards the floor, revealing a different man beneath the grin.

"Well, it could prove a health risk to the men on the base and to the native population nearby, for a start. Not to mention the environmental risks, to the food chain and…"

Langham had straightened his legs out before him, poked his thumbs into his belt and leaned well back in his armchair. His gaze searched the room with a theatrical hint of displeasure, dismissing the Professor's concerns.

"Are we all out of whiskey, then?" He asked inconsequentially, sucking at his gums.

The Professor calmly took the opportunity to bide his time, to observe. "There's another bottle in the kitchen."

"Great mother! Then we can spend the rest of the evening here together, getting to know each other." The return of Langham's smile did not put Kofoed Hansen any more at his ease; it felt like the baring of teeth.

That night he recorded in his diary his meeting with Langham, the pen pressing hard into the paper: 'A cross between a latterday Jeckle and Hyde and Doctor Strangelove. An outrageous confrontationalist and scientific fundamentalist.'

Kofoed Hansen was scarcely surprised, then, a couple of days later when he and Langham came to address in a professional context their scientific difference of opinion. The two were looking over some analyses of ice and soil samples taken from the crash site and from the base. Kofoed Hansen made some comment to the effect that he considered it incumbent on the scientific community to ensure the safety of nuclear technologies before they should be introduced into industry and so on. One of those sighing emissions of frustration at mankind's scientific hubris.

He looked up from his papers in surprise at what sounded like a wild boar someone had kindly released in the room. He had hardly been aware that he was being overheard even though he knew that Langham was in the room.

"Don't tell me you're one of those pussy-footing soft-science nancy-boy wimps who are scared of a little harmless radiation? Nuclear science is entirely safe for energy production, specially when compared to coal. Look at the emissions of gases into the atmosphere even now from coal-burning power stations. Don't you agree that they are contaminating the atmosphere?" Langham snorted out his words as if each one was a challenge to a duel.

The Professor agreed quietly that they did and shifted his soft hat to the back of his head. He returned his eyes to his work, as he assumed that, with his acknowledgement of agreement, the intrusive conversation was at an end. It was not.

"And I'll tell you something for nothing," continued the irrepressible Langham, a evangelist for his own dogma. "Not only is nuclear radiation not harmful, but mark me, it won't be long before medical science puts it to work as it has done with X-rays. Let me show you something."

Langham stood up from the desk and sauntered over to a set of flasks which contained the samples of fused ice from the crash site. Taking up one and unscrewing its top, he proceeded to demonstrate the harmlessness of radiation by performing a personal though uncontrolled experiment on himself: in the dedicated tradition of Doctor Jeckle, he ate a mouthful of plutonium oxide-covered ice.

"That," he declared vehemently, licking his lips and baring his teeth in a grimace, "That's what I say to the leftie punks who go on and on about radiation as if it posed even half the dangers to civilisation that communism does."

"Well, I'm not in a position to declare on political matters," the Professor replied evenly, though a cold knot of disbelief had formed in his stomach. "But I don't think we can be as sanguine as you appear to be about the risks to health of radioactive substances."

"Get real, buddy. You're more likely to die under a bus or from smokin' cigarettes than from hangin' 'round some little bit of ol' pitchblend."

"Perhaps Marie Curie should have taken up smoking."

"Ha!"

Kofoed Hansen could only shake his head, a gesture of profound professional and personal dismay, and turn back to his analysis. Langham shook his own head and threw the Professor a look of pure pity and disdain, as if viewing a child afraid of the dark.

Langham hoped by his little experiment to convince the more conventional and staid Danish Professor of the innocuousness of plutonium. While most would join Professor Kofoed Hansen in a kind of horrified admiration and stupefaction at the amount of ideological dedication that must be achieved in order not only to defy fashionable hypotheses, but to run in the face of well established scientific opinion, few could bring themselves to believe in Langham's view of plutonium. Nor, indeed, could the Professor. He just hoped that Langham would go away and leave him to get on with his investigations in peace.

The last we hear of this character, in an update to Kofoed Hansen's diary made in 1987, is that, within ten years of his plutonium snack, Wright Langham was dead: killed in a plane crash.

R.I.P. Wright H. Langham.

* * * * * *

JUST ONE WEEK after his arrival at Thule, Professor Kofoed Hansen was on his way home to Copenhagen, his studies completed and his report, a damning collection of facts and figures, under his arm in a slim zippered briefcase. It was ready for Professor H. H. Koch and the other honorable *illustrissimi* at Risoe.

Kofoed Hansen was flown back to Copenhagen via New York. At every stage of his journey he was accorded the status of a Three-Star General, a treatment so lavish it curdled into unease. As he made his way onto the aircraft that was to take him on the first stage of the journey, from Thule to Plattsburg in upstate New York, the crew and the other passengers lined up for him like a guard of honour. The silence of their formation felt less like respect and more like a ritual.

On a refueling stop at a military base in Canada, he was met by a waiting limousine and driven to have a solitary, awkward breakfast with the base commander. On arrival at Plattsburg, he was again chauffeur-driven towards JFK Air Terminal. Halfway there, the driver pulled over to the side of the desolate road where another car idled, and this car carried the by now wide-eyed Professor, a specialist in turbulence and airborne contamination, the rest of the stretch to the airport. Scandinavian Airlines had reserved him one of their best seats for the flight across the Atlantic.

All the time the Professor gripped his leather folder under his arm, its contents feeling heavier with each superfluous courtesy.

The stupefied Professor spent some two or three minutes of every hour of the eight-hour trip staring in disbelief at his reflection in the mirror in the aircraft's toilet. His hat looked and felt quite real, but the face beneath it seemed that of a stranger caught in a slow-moving plot. During one such interval, he looked down at the image of the leather case caught in the mirror, momentarily frowned, then shook his head dismissively at his own creeping paranoia.

The Americans are an honorable people (and so are the Danes).

But still he could not resist the temptation to re-run his extraordinary journey in his imagination, where each time it became a little more imbued with a sense of something very awry, of an undefined external threat. On a final replay, the threat was at saturation point, and, as he watched himself in his mind once more board the aircraft at Thule, he could have sworn that the guard of honour was actually a protective barrier, that each heavy greatcoat of military and civilian personnel alike bulged with weapons and that those weapons were not to defend the good Professor, but to ensure he did not make a break for it.

"Ridiculous!" he snapped under his breath at his mirror self on another of his visits to the back of the plane. "Am I to become paranoid at this age? Just because the Americans take good notice of me and treat me like a VIP?"

But the Professor was not to be entirely convinced by his own reassurances. When the mental re-runs subsided, there still remained in the scene a figure among the lined-up civilians whose solemn demeanour and intense scrutiny of the Professor left him with a lingering, acidic unease. His disquiet was scarcely lessened when, returning to his seat, he saw that same solemnity and intensity turned and staring at him from under a porkpie hat just four seats forward from the back of the plane. The man did not look away.

He was met on arrival at Copenhagen by Dr. Koch's personal driver, Sonnesen. His persecutor—or perhaps just a fellow traveller—seemed to hand him on to Sonnesen like a baton. Though he may just have said 'I beg your pardon' to Sonnesen in English out of mere politeness, having bumped him quite accidentally as he made his way through the airport exit gate. However it was, Sonnesen whisked him away, straight to the Danish seat of parliament at Christiansborg. The directness of it felt like an arrest.

This did nothing, however, to dispel the sense of unreality which had begun to cling to the whole affair like a persistent odour. The good Professor braced himself for the terrible moment when Dr. Koch would greet him only to exclaim 'but there must be some mistake!'

But the feared moment never came, as on his being deposited at the Danish Parliamentary Offices, it soon became unmistakably clear that there had been no horrible and humiliating mix-up. Dr. Koch greeted him by name and introduced him to a small select coterie of Danish and US big nobs, boffins and sundry big-guns. In a shuddering discord, the Professor noted the presence of Wright Langham among them, smiling like the neanderthal who has just convinced the tribal elders to introduce the wheel only on condition that it be square.

In his diary, the Professor reflects in passing that this was the only time in his life he was allowed into the United States without a visa and arrived back in Denmark without having to go through Immigration and Customs. The observation was noted with dry irony, a tiny flag planted in the narrative of his own compliance.

For two weeks following his triumphal return, Professor Kofoed Hansen was allowed to cool his heels and dispute within himself the motive behind this unprecedented and alarmingly good treatment he was suffering at official hands. He was left in such profound peace that he began to fear they had forgotten all about him and his report. Even the memory of the suspicious character on the plane faded. And after the first few times, when he had wondered vaguely what it was, the little click whenever he picked up the phone no longer even registered in his consciousness. At the end of that time, he was invited by Dr. H. H. Koch to attend a politico-scientific assembly in Copenhagen with 'Our Dear Friends,' the Americans.

Or it might be better put that he was invited not to attend.

"Click! Professor Kofoed Hansen," began Dr. Koch, his voice smooth as polished stone. "Would you be available for a little informal briefing session tomorrow, Wednesday, before the plenary session on Thursday?

"Yes, of course, no problem at all."

"Good! Shall we say eight-thirty?"

"Fine."

"Good!" Without a pause he asked, as if he had been leading up to it all along, "Oh, by the way, do you mind bringing any notes you may have that went into your report? Oh, and any relevant empirical data and any samples you may have brought back with you?"

Kofoed Hansen frowned at the telephone handset, remembered the click, and then replied with careful neutrality, "Well, if you've read through my report..."

"Yes, of course I have. Most thorough and complete. We were all most impressed."

"Well, I would have said preliminary and as yet incomplete. But, however that may be, if you have read it through, you would have to surmise that the last thing I would be doing would be bringing back souvenirs from the crash site. As for my notes and the rest, well, I'll see what I can hustle up of them. They add nothing to the conclusions I've already drawn in the report."

He put the handset back in its cradle slowly as if it were a delicate piece of porcelain. Having done so, he removed his soft cloth hat, folded his arms, cocked his head on an angle to one side and contemplated the part of the hall where the walls met the ceiling. He was trying to imagine the scene the following day in Koch's office. He shook his head with a look of cold comprehension on his face, and made his way to his study where he keeps a largish safe, to retrieve some somethings from it.

To the carefully circumspect phone call he makes a few moments later we are not privy.

* * * * * *

AT EIGHT-THIRTY THE next morning, Kofoed Hansen was let into the head of Risoe's office by a Koch who wore the insincerest mask of welcome since Clytemnestra smiled at Agamemnon after ten years away at Troy.

Inside, the Professor's eyes adjusted to take in a semicircle of solemnly composed faces and insignia. They belonged to the ubiquitous Wright Langham, two members of the American

Atomic Energy Commission, a fellow Risoe scientist and two US military types, their uniforms crisp, their eyes impassive. Opposite to the horseshoe of inquisitors a single lowly straight backed chair awaited the Professor, a stark island in the spacious room. But, the faces fell to pieces and the insignia stirred crazily when our canny Professor introduced to the unexpected assembly his secret weapon.

"Doctor Fortinbras has kindly consented to lend us his expert opinion in relation to the data and notes I have put into his hands." Kofoed Hansen smiled the teeth out of his head as he noted the looks of consternation that came and stayed for the rest of the interview on the faces of all present. Langham chewed his cheek in silent fury and the brass rattled into a stiff silence. No one cried out *touché*, but Kofoed Hansen knew that he had won a significant, if minor, battle. He had brought with him Risoe's own leading expert on meteorology, a man of unimpeachable reputation.

Still smiling with a fixed, almost manic serenity, Kofoed Hansen steered himself to the lonely chair and, sitting himself in it, looked about him. Defiantly out-smiling the diorama of grouches, he asked, "Could another seat be provided for Dr. Fortinbras?" and sat fingering the brim of his soft hat, a humble prop in this theatre of power.

Dr. Koch redrew his smile, a strained etching on his face, for Dr. Fortinbras and had a chair drawn up for him with a stiff wave.

"Dr. Kofoed Hansen," Koch began shakily, the script already fraying. "You know everyone here present, I believe."

A single, slow wag of the head said yes he did.

"Having, er, read your report, which, er, was, as I intimated before, thorough and, well, er, well-received, we have come to the conclusion that, er, given the, er, supporting nature of the work done at Thule by the experts in weather conditions and atmospheric motions, it might be as well to present your conclusions to the full session, er, in conjunction with theirs. Drs. Langham and …"

"Um, no." said the Professor shortly, the word cutting the air. "And Doctor Fortinbras agrees with me."

"Um, yes. Yes, I do." Fortinbras's voice was calm, pedantic. "Having looked at the data and done a quick, perfunctory analysis of it, I feel that Doctor Kofoed Hansen's results deserve to be heard in isolation from any other so as to circumvent the danger that it may get conflated with other material and its relevance go unnoticed. Or it may simply get accidentally overlooked in the piles of material through which the sessions will have to wade in coming to any decision regarding appropriate action in this situation."

Doctor Fortinbras spoke as if rehearsed in innocence and candour. He did not smile, but rather looked askance from time to time at his colleague's inexhaustible, unforced mirth, a beacon of quiet defiance.

"Very well," Dr. Koch conceded, looking daggers at Kofoed Hansen then blanchemanges at Fortinbras. "But I do hope you won't unnecessarily delay this most urgent task by presenting us with speculative hypotheses and premature conclusions."

"Ask Doctor Fortinbras. What would you say I had to offer? Just facts and hard scientific analysis?"

"Just facts and hard scientific analysis." nodded Doctor Fortinbras, his tone leaving no room for debate.

The American brass jingled angrily and muttered something ungraceful under the scraping of chairs as the meeting adjourned, its purpose thwarted. Langham failed to notice the Professor's outstretched hand as he chewed his way past him out into the corridor, a storm contained in a lean frame.

That evening, H. H. Koch spoke again at length on the phone with Professor Kofoed Hansen. To what was said, once again, we are not privy. All that can be reported is that Koch's insistent wheedling and persuasive tone, a blend of flattery and veiled threat, eventually gave way to a tone of grim satisfaction and that the Professor came away from the conversation patting his pockets and frowning as if he had lost something valuable but he was not sure what, or perhaps as if he had just traded it away.

* * * * * *

SCIENTISTS FROM DENMARK and the United States have been meeting for the past 2 days for discussions of the technical questions arising from the B-52 crash at Thule, Greenland. The meetings continued the close cooperation which has existed since the time of the crash. Scientists of both nations have worked together at the scene of the crash and participated in the gathering of scientific evidence. The scientists reviewed the considerable progress which has been made at the site in collecting aircraft and weapons parts. Contaminated material will be removed from Greenland. They also assessed the extent to which radioactivity was released.

"It was agreed that under present conditions the radioactivity spread in the area is not a hazard to people or biological species, nor is any hazard foreseen for the future. Nevertheless, an effort will be made to remove the main part of the radioactivity which is on the ice. The conclusions of the scientists regarding the absence of hazards to the biosphere will continue to be examined in detail. Further supporting evidence will be accumulated through an extensive program of data gathering."

The press release fell limply from Kofoed Hansen's hand onto the desk. It was three days after the private meeting with Koch and Uncle Sam's brass band had taken place. The words were a masterclass in bureaucratic alchemy, transforming danger into diligence, concern into cooperation.

"Reads like something the Supreme Soviet might have thought up," exclaimed the surprised Dr. Fortinbras, peering over his glasses.

"Hmm," mused Kofoed Hansen, the sound hollow. "And no mention of, how did Koch put it?, 'the tremendous work of Professor Kofoed Hansen, who has made a contribution on the Danish side of fourteen men.' It seems they've put the kibosh on me in any case." He had not mentioned to Fortinbras his second, longer phone conversation with Koch, the one that had secured his muted compliance.

"Do you really feel that way?"

"Well, where are my concerns expressed here?" Kofoed Hansen asked, a little peeved at his total failure to influence the eventual outcome of the two-day meeting. After all, at the meeting he had been feted and attended to as was his due as a major, albeit dissenting, contributor to the proceedings. It had been a pantomime of respect.

"There's a pretty big 'nevertheless' there, you know. And that's entirely due to you."

Fortinbras took up the sheet of print and searched it. "Ah, yes. Here we are. 'Nevertheless, an effort will be made to remove the main part of the radioactivity which is on the ice.'"

Kofoed Hansen shook his head slowly and pursed his lips. His soft hat circled in his hands like a cat settling itself, a familiar comfort. "The radioactivity that is no hazard to people or to any biological species will be removed from the ice. Well, isn't that dandy! They'll remove that totally harmless stuff and bury it in concrete and metal containers deep in the mountains of South Carolina. Just to make doubly sure that that harmless stuff will never harm anyone again. They might by the same logic lock up Boffo the Clown in Alcatraz and melt down the key, just to be sure he'll never kill again." His analogy was absurd, and it perfectly captured the absurdity he felt.

"Quite so. It is not a satisfactory outcome by any means, having seen your data and considered your conclusions. But, at least a clean up will be effected."

"Yes, but just how useful will that be? After all, a good deal of the fragments are at the bottom of the fiord. And, frankly, I don't see how they're going to recover that stuff. Not to mention the contamination that's spread over the entire area in the fire. It's a farce." He became suddenly quite animated and flung his hat from him. "A bloody farce."

He felt as suddenly a twinge of remorse and recovered his hat from the floor. He dusted and smoothed it as he continued in his more customary steady tone, the anger subsiding into a weary ache. "I just hope they do the clean up efficiently, without putting the soldiers involved too much at risk."

"I hope so, too," added Fortinbras quietly, the shared dread hanging between them.

His anger returned, this time directed inward. "All I did there was sit and not disagree out loud. I could have made a greater difference. I could have insisted on the strength of my own doubts."

The two men sat in a deep silence for some minutes. The silence penetrated the room like shafts of crystal and entered into the hearts of both. Kofoed Hansen recalled those moments on the rise above Thule, the premonition of complicity, and his lukewarm attendance at the Risoe meeting. A heavy weight moved to rest on his chest. He recalled the final, persuasive call from Koch and sank deeper into his chair, diminished.

"You know they've set up a committee to continue to advise the Americans. Both H. H. and Joergen Koch are on it. Along with Lassen and Gjoerup and a few others."

"But you're not, right."

"That's right. Nor is Per Grande. Perhaps he didn't turn out to be reliable either, when it came to downplaying the health risks. So they've put Juel Henningsen there in his place. I'm not saying Henningsen is a conspirator, by no means. But he hasn't been out on the ice at Thule."

The Professor ended, once more a little heated, the bitterness rising like bile. "He's a mushroom. Kept in the dark and fed on bullshit. Just a bloody mushroom. And so am I."

It was not a pleasant feeling for Professor Hansen to be so clearly aware of how he had been swayed from his course by Koch's deft manipulations, and to know, with a sick certainty, that he would not act otherwise even now. The single-mindedness that he had early accepted, on the assessment of his grandmother and of many others over the years, as the most intimate and defining part of his personality, seemed a paltry, brittle thing to him when he contemplated his lack of courage to stand loudly and vocally by his scientifically quantified conclusions. The boy who tracked leaves to catch nature in an error had grown into a man who sat quietly while truth was buried under an avalanche of polite, agreed-upon lies.

"Just a bloody mushroom," he muttered again, the words barely audible, a confession swallowed by the silent room.

* * * * * *

PROFESSOR KOFOED HANSEN'S brief emergence from 'Boffinland' lasted about two months, after which period he disappeared quite from view. Apart from a trip to Spain to confer with colleagues there on the subject of an accident similar to that at Thule over the little fishing village of Palomares, he was not to trouble the public or scientific conscience again until April 1987. He retreated into the silent work of routine, a man who had glimpsed the machinery of power and found his own hand resting on a lever he was not permitted to pull.

The Professor did not enjoy the rest of the years in between those two dates. The quiet was not peaceful, but heavy. In the meantime, he had been struck down by prostate cancer in 1972, with a cruel repeat in 1978. Operations on each occasion seemed successfully to stem the cancer's growth, but they were invasive, draining affairs that left a permanent mark on his vitality. Besides the cancer, he was suffering from a constellation of ailments: high blood pressure that thrummed in his ears, vision problems that blurred the pages he loved, a tendency for angry lesions to develop on his legs, a difficulty walking that turned each corridor into a marathon, a high level of fatigue that sleep could not touch, persistent digestive problems, and an extensive and comprehensive so on. His body, once a reliable instrument, had become a site of revolt.

The manner in which the good Doctor made his reappearance was through additions to his diary and a report he wrote in the same year. He was spurred to the task no doubt by the common human desire to achieve a scrap of immortality through bequeathing to tomorrow some valuable artifact, and specifically to redress the wrong he had done so many years before in a moment of moral cowardice and failed to undo in the following nineteen years of silent complicity. The ghost of Thule had grown solid within him, a malignant companion to his cancers.

He commented in his diary that Thule had returned to the field of public debate, shaking off the ice of two decades. This time it was a big news story because one Marius Schmidt had raised an association of Danish ex-Thule workers, civilians, that claimed that its members were suffering what looked unnervingly like the long-term effects of radiation exposure. He noted, with a scientist's chill, the similarities of symptoms reported by them and those he suffered himself— the fatigue, the lesions, the systemic failures.

Nevertheless, and this is another big nevertheless in view of the Professor's lifelong attendance to fact and hard science, he attributed his own deteriorating health to the simple, banal fact that, as he put it, 'I am not that young any longer.' It was an excuse offered to himself, a statistical refuge for a man who dealt in probabilities.

He spoke, in the next part of his diary, none of which was ever meant for publication, at some length of reasons for retaining a certain 'doubt' over the causes of his health problems. The word hung on the page, heavy with unspoken certainty.

One reason for 'doubt' was the stark fact that his colleague and leader of the expedition to Thule for those few weeks in 1968, (and brother to H. H.) Joergen Koch, had died in 1971 from prostate cancer. A coincidence, perhaps. Another reason, or better, series of reasons, for 'doubt' sprang from the eerie similarity between his symptoms and those of people like the members of the Thule Association. Patterns were emerging from the noise.

Professor Kofoed Hansen spoke of 'doubts' where the layperson would be tempted to speak of certainties. That is because he was a scientist, a 'brilliant' one, as he was reported to have been described to the United States military establishment all those years ago at the height of Project Crested Ice, a 'brilliant but eccentric and unreliable scientist.' We are left to guess for ourselves how a brilliant scientist can be labeled 'unreliable;' could he have been a perilous dinner guest, or maybe he was forgetful of the important familial anniversaries? Or perhaps he was unreliable in the only way that mattered: he was unwilling to bend his conclusions to fit the preferred narrative.

But, anyway, as a brilliant but unreliable scientist, he had to speak of 'doubts' because he was dealing at the moment with anecdotage, not hard evidence with controls and strict statistical analyses. These were 'doubts' that issued from the life-long habit of good scientific scepticism, not from pusillanimity. Yet the distinction felt thin and academic in the dark of night.

Back in 1968, Professor Kofoed Hansen had made a choice in the full freedom of his powers and knowledge and health. Now, he was in an inexorable decline toward death, his freedoms shrinking with each laboured breath. And as his freedoms to choose evaporated in the stark realities of impending death, so did his protective carapace of 'doubt.' Doubts are the luxuries of the idle and the healthy. The dying deal in sharper currencies.

So, he asked himself the unscientific though philosophically sound question, 'Who should benefit from the doubt?' The only answer he could arrive at, echoing in the hollow of his conscience, was that the many men who worked on the clean up at Thule and who now suffered symptoms similar to his own should be the beneficiaries of the 'doubt.' The doubt should shield them, not their powerful employers.

When the diary continues, it lets surface a deep vein of cynicism, apparently mined from a deep and long-safeguarded motherlode. With reference to the proposed medical examinations of the ex-Thulers, it says:

'I don't believe any honest statistician will deny that the results of the planned health examinations will leave any doubts. As a result it must follow that the debate will continue like that between Per Degn and Erasmus; and the audience, including Maren Hansen in the pond, will probably agree with and support the loudest though least scientific. So why waste the money in the first place, why throw the money out the window? Let us agree and accept that in Denmark today it is the professional liars who have the power. Let's throw in the towel and conduct an opinion poll to decide what the democratic majority believe. Should the probably drunken, syphilitic and tobacco-damaged slobs from Thule in 1968, who claim they have suffered, be believed or not? Tell me what you think, Mrs. Hansen? And you, Mrs. Koch? And how about you, Mrs. Gjoerup? Yes or no?'

To find that honest statistician would make an eighth task for Hercules. Perhaps statistics as a profession shares one of the characteristic weaknesses of the acting fraternity. When your personality is used as a vehicle for the mounting of make-believes, there can be some fallout on the true person: what emerges at any moment not devoted to the art may never hold out to us any assurance that it is authentic. In practice, this is more a problem for others than for the actor, especially for those who forget that they are continually playing their own roles, that the word we use to define ourselves as individual entities, 'person,' means 'mask.'

The statistician, who honest and well-trained, knows that his knowledge is only of probabilities, has a difficult terrain to cross let alone abide in. He may have a tendency to move from the position that, given the accepted parameters of the method and the accuracy of the data, it is reasonable to consider the conclusion probably true; to the position that, either, because certainty is such an elusive little beast, there is no truth; or that, on the other hand, what may be so, given the parameters and the data, is so. Often, curiously enough, both positions alternate in the same minds in extreme cases.

Both the actor and the statistician occupy professions that model truth. Each is involved in manipulations that hide as much as they reveal. Their greatest dissimilarity resides in the fact that statistics has very bad dialogue, it has yet to produce its Shakespeare: 'All the world's a probability matrix' seems to lack something. But in neither case is the model any substitute for the real thing, for the pain in a man's bones or the guilt in his heart.

What can be described as doubtful in scientific parlance could better be called 'probable' in the popular tongue, because it is all too easy to conflate hard, accurate evidence and solid accepted statistical analyses with a conclusion that contains the word 'probable.' It is the fate of the word 'probable' that it can be caused to cast its shadow back over the method and the data to infect them in the weak or the untrained mind with 'doubt.' A probable conclusion, implying room for error, gets unfairly twisted back onto its premises and poisons them with ill-warranted unreliability. It is a sleight of hand performed with graphs and p-values.

One swallow does not a meal make. But, enough cancers make a heavy weight of probability, a tide that sweeps away the delicate fences of doubt.

It is the resident of these places of doubt, this honest broker, that the Professor despaired of ever finding. The system was designed to lose him in the paperwork.

Unfortunately, back in 1968, Koch had managed to get his way with Kofoed Hansen. Why Koch had gone to such lengths to intimidate and coerce him was a question that began to haunt him with increasing urgency during the next nineteen years of silence. In that time, the image of the ghostly activity on the blackened ice returned to him again and again, a silent film on a loop behind his eyes. Sometimes he imagined that, even from the distance of eight miles, in the preternatural clarity of the arctic air, he saw various figures turn his way and pause in their soundless activity as if contemplating him as he contemplated them. Occasionally, one would raise an arm in a slow, ambiguous gesture—was it a greeting, or a summons?

In 1986, the ghosts started appearing in the newspapers and on the TV screen, given flesh and voice. The men who had worked down on the ice that day so long ago stared out at him as definite persons all of a sudden: men with names, men with families and histories, men with stories to tell, men whose lives had been changed into lingering nightmares on that day on the ice. Kofoed Hansen would shudder and raise his shoulders against the chill of recognition. Eventually, he decided to speak before it was too late, before his own voice was silenced for good.

So, in 1987, in an attempt to redeem himself, and to see a grain of justice done, he submitted a report to Risoe reiterating the conclusions he had reached from his Thule investigations. He did so because he believed he could supply an independent and trustworthy account of some of the circumstances of the crash that might have been helpful in determining the outcome of the Thule Association members' claims. It was his testament, flung against the fortress of official silence.

But, a long story is cut short when it is told that Risoe, in its prurient variety of wisdom, sat on the report. It was not tabled at the meeting convened in April 1987 to consider the Thule Association's claims and has since disappeared into the bowels of the Agency's archives, swallowed by the same darkness that had taken everything else. Consequently, when finally Kofoed Hansen was moved to an act of heroism, it was, in the event, an act of the highest altruism, performed with no audience, no observer, and no hope of reward. A message in a bottle, thrown into a filing cabinet.

To cut a long story even shorter, Professor Otto Kofoed Hansen died in 1990. The cancers and the silence finally took him.

Requiescat in Pace. May he, at last, find a peace that was denied him in life.

* * * * * *

WHAT AMAZES ME is that the suggestion was never made, not once, that the personnel, whether US military or Danish civilian, who assisted in Operation Crested Ice, should be given any long-term medical follow-up. In the literature that exists, there is plenty of anxious attention given to whether there might be long-term effects in the area where HOBO 28 went down, whether the food chain had been infected, whether the local radiation levels were higher than average background after the accident than before. These are clean, academic questions, removed from the messy reality of men.

On the possible health effects on the very men who searched for and brought back aircraft and weapons fragments on dog-sledges, who handled the hot, twisted metal with their hands, who ploughed carbonated snow and ice and filled tanks with the melted products—on this, the silence is profound and eloquent. It is the sound of turning away.

This silence is scarcely disturbed in a very short article called 'Danish Health Physicists' Activities' written by Ole Walmod-Larsen in conjunction with Asker Aarkrog, Henry Gjoerup et al. There appears the plain, breathtaking assertion that 'All the measurements [nasal swabs, urine samples, geiger-counter readings etc.] proved that during the whole operation no Dane had been exposed to any radiation hazards.' To enjoy that degree of certainty must be a happy, unburdened state. And that degree of certainty is expressed in the same article that makes the following tremendous set of statements side by side, without a hint of irony:

'Some days after his [Henry Gjoerup's] departure, the "Operation Frying Pan" team concluded that the environmental hazards from Pu 239 outside the crash area were in fact comparable to the accumulated fallout from weapons testing. The team cabled this conclusion to Copenhagen.

'On the basis of the team's favorable report it was decided to scale-down the Danish scientific efforts in Thule.'

Ah, if we could only harness human stupidity for good, we could provide energy enough to make the donkey engine obsolete. The mind reels.

The article continues in an inoffensive, almost pastoral manner:

"One of the problems facing the Danish health physicist left on his own at the scene after the departure of the Frying Pan Team, was the layman's fear of the unknown: the fear of radiation, of contamination, of atomic weapons, and fear of all the new, unusual phenomena suddenly disturbing the quiet Arctic area at Thule."

Poor, put-upon Danish health physicist! Nasty, irrational laymen! I wonder how it is possible to make such a neat list of the 'unknowns' as is given here. I would like the recipe. I could then cook up some unknowns of my own, perhaps serve them with a sauce of condescension.

The article contains yet more gems of objective, indeed scientific, reporting. During a briefing of Danish workers on a bus (!) on the possible dangers, it seems the nasty laymen were at it again, their impertinent questions causing the briefing to last well over an hour. The author describes the American reaction to this 'undesirable delay' most amusingly:

"When the delay became known the smell of brimstone emanating from the SAC headquarters was detectable several miles off ..."

Unfortunately, what sort of detecting apparatus was used in detecting the devilish pyrophorus substance is left unexplained. A later briefing of Danish mechanics, laymen in the fields of nuclear physics and health, lasted an hour and a half. The unreasoning brutes were worried about sterility and impotence, the very real erosion of their futures. But:

"When it was explained that these fears were groundless, no further questions were asked!"

(The author's exclamation mark, not mine, a stamp of finality on their docility.)

In the silent, empty, cavern of care and attention to health and wellbeing given these civilian 'laymen' workers, the conclusion that, "during the whole operation no Dane had been exposed to any radiation hazards" echoes hollowly for a brief moment and quickly sinks, undetectably, into the baffles of muffling obdrivion.

(Obdrivion: n. Line of piffling argumentation causing instant forgetfulness. Webster's).

Pink socks pale in comparison with this foolishness.

* * * * * *

LARS MELGAARD IS well into his thirties, and yet has retained the almost eternal youthfulness which accompanies those whose idealism has not flagged or been diverted into lesser channels over the years. He is at odds with his surroundings—the sober, dull appurtenances of a typical lobbyist's office, lined mainly with nondescript green-bound volumes of Acts and Regulations, Journals of Jurisprudence, Environmental Impact Studies and goodness knows what else—in his scarcely contained sense of the import of what he is contending with. He is a David marvelling at his personal Goliath: and, like the original, that marvelling is exercised in the full, clear-eyed awareness of the possibility of being crushed.

One of the great mercies of life is that no matter how much one empathises, sympathises, imagines, projects and intuits, it is not possible to fully experience another's physical suffering. Dostoyevsky was right when he wrote, "Every man is responsible for everybody else: only people don't know it. If they knew it, it would be paradise at once." But the great Russian never imagined that we could actually directly experience another's pain as our own. Had he, had he imagined a mushroom cloud of a single child's pain billowing out across creation, infecting with that same pain every sentient being in its path, his vision would have been of shudders of Hell rather than of Paradise.

When Lars applies his considerable zest and purpose to the problem of nuclear waste, he is able to take advantage of that great mercy: he is protected from the direct somatic experience of the pain of those who have already suffered and died. A fortunate state of things, because, had he to contend with the weight of deep-mouthed groans screeching into the void, it may have blurred his vision. He might have lost his clear, legalistic sense of the injustice of what happened to the workers at Thule. Justice requires purpose; purpose requires meaning; and meaning dissolves in the solvent of chronic pain and all-absorbing death. Silence overtakes all in the end.

Lars, however, has no appetite for silence. Which is fortunate for his visitor. For Leonard Pinn, a finance journalist of some standing in his native Australia and boasting in addition considerable accomplishment in the rarified atmosphere of Shakespearean criticism, has come to Denmark, having taken an interest in the claims of the Thule Association after interviewing its International Representative, Jeffrey Carswell, (yours truly), to interview Lars.

Running his fingers through luxurious brown hair, parted in the middle, Lars purses his lips and warms to the task of expounding the truth of the matter to the largely silent and receptive Pinn. Pinn notes sardonically to himself that, despite being Lars' junior by two years, where Lars' hair is neatly parted, his own has simply departed.

When Lars begins, he is in a thoughtful, almost pedagogical mood.

"Reasonable risk is partly a scientific and partly an ethical measure. But the victim's point of view is never considered. The whole risk discussion is very strange, both in the nuclear industry and the chemical industry. The common definition of risk says that it is the potential qualitative amount of consequences multiplied by the statistical probability of the event occurring. That's funny, really."

"Why's that?" asks Pinn, leaning forward.

Lars grimaces slightly to indicate that any levity should in no way undermine the seriousness of his point. Sipping on his coffee, he burnishes his pursuit of the intangible with palpable logic. "Well, you end up multiplying together a quality and a quantity. That is bad mathematics. You just can't do it. The result is always going to be meaningless. The other point is that, with any population anywhere, including the Thule workers, the statistical probability of an accident occurring is beside the point. The point is the qualitative consequences of an accident once you have it on your hands. Once it's happened, probability is irrelevant. You're left with the consequence."

"I see." Pinn himself becomes very thoughtful, turning the idea over. "I suppose few military commanders throughout history have ever changed their strategy because it was pointed out to them that they might have made a category mistake. Had Aristotle appeared before Napoleon at Waterloo with sound advice on the correct way to systematise the different ways soldiers meet their death, the response would probably have been to put him in the front line to hasten his demise. A similar sort of realpolitik operates within the business world, and within the military-industrial complex."

"There is some cold comfort in knowing that things should make sense and don't." Lars sits back a moment to sip on his coffee and ponder the way things ought to be thought about. In that moment he is the epitome of the authentic modern idealist, surrounded by the grey tools of a grey system.

"All over the West, this is the definition of risk in use. None other ever gets a look in. It poses enormous problems to the scientific community in their own self understanding because they actually do know that it is a lie. The moment they return to the basics of their own specialist areas in mathematics and physics, they see you can't use statistics in this way. It's a shell game."

"So, why do they go along with it?" asks Pinn, though he knows the answer.

"The lie, this definition of risk, helps lubricate the wheels of a society that is stubbornly determined to use dangerous technologies no matter what. It provides a numerical alibi.

"But, the other definition is available. Risk is the same as the potential qualitative consequences of an accident. That is risk, and no other. But then, you see, an awful lot of activities all over the world would have to stop, because, under that definition, the risk becomes simply unacceptable. The worst possible consequences of a lot of these activities are too fearful to think about. So we don't. We multiply instead."

An uncharacteristic silence ensues. This silence is more like a fracture in the structure of the conversation than a bridge between its elements. Pinn's thoughts race out onto the Greenland ice with the Inuit and their *angagoks*, their shamans of meaning who focus the dispersed, still points of life into a sharp, incisive pathway between the glaciers of quietude. For Lars, the pathway through the polar darkness is intellectual control, a map of logic. He doesn't realise that the very tool which can offer the solutions to the worst of our fears—rational analysis—also creates for us the greatest of terrors when it is misapplied, even down to the technology that contrived his rapidly dwindling cup of coffee.

"What we need is a new paradigm: complex systems. Traditional science needs the knowledge of the philosophers and the social disciplines. I think that this current definition of risk will have run its course within a generation."

Pinn lets his minicassette do the work of listening for him for a few seconds and takes another look around Lars' office. There is no pretension: the rows of green-bound volumes are punctuated by several coffee cups put down in moments of revery and never retrieved. A couple of dusty computers occupy two corners and, in the centre of the room, are a number of large tables designed for the laying out of papers and maps, a battlefield of documents. An urn completes the furniture and the description. The effect is somewhere between that of a library and a bunker.

Everything smells of idealism, of sleepless nights and dogged determination. Or is it the smell of the gnawing sense of powerlessness to which idealism finds itself fatally bound that crinkles Pinn's olfactory sense? Pinn knows that you need no complex systems or improved cross-disciplinary knowledge to appreciate the raw folly and evil of the nuclear venture. A little basic accounting does the job quite nicely. The most common calculation in net present value—NPV to its friends—whereby dry little bean counters poring over their calculators work out the present value of something ten years in the future, after having properly considered the effects of inflation, fluctuating interest rates, the possible opportunity costs of alternative investments in emu farms, or short term cash in Brazil—and risk. This last being one of those corrosive little niceties that can spoil even the shiniest of calculators.

You very quickly run out of beans. If the half-life of nuclear waste is 125,000 years, then a standard net present value calculation spanning ten years leaves approximately 124,990 years without account, a yawning chasm of un-costed consequence. It is doubtful whether even the hardiest broad beans will last that long. Almost certainly there will not be any accountants around to see the end of the investment period, let alone a financial system to review the investment;

perhaps nothing resembling what we now call civilisation, nor even descendents of ourselves. The spreadsheet ends; the poison does not.

Pinn runs these thoughts past Lars' incredulous visage. "Perhaps an example might make it clear."

"It might, it might not. But, go on. I'm listening." Lars' tone suggests he is humouring his guest.

Pinn feels that Lars is listening more for the pauses between his words than the gaps in his thoughts, that he is waiting just for Pinn to take a breath to launch once more into his own well-rehearsed version of the state of things. "Oh, well," Pinn reflects to himself, "I can hardly blame him. After all, I'm here to interview him, not lecture him on monetary philosophy." But Pinn is wound up at this point, and a day-old baby would be interlocutor enough at this stage.

"Lets just look at how this sort of thing works within the financial system. In 1933, Frank Vanderlip made a vivid calculation in a story in the *Saturday Evening Post*. He pointed out that if the Medicis of Renaissance Florence had set aside $100,000, represented by a globe of gold nine inches in diameter, at 5% compound interest, by 1933, its value would have been in the region of $517,100,000,000,000,000. Five hundred and seventeen quadrillion dollars and some change. The 1933 figure would have been equal to forty-six million times the total then existing gold stock of the world."

Pinn risks a pause here to allow the monstrous figures to have their effect. They do so, as he can see by the new, arrested look of concentration on Lars' face. Pinn proceeds to his finale.

"With nuclear waste, the globes represent not capital and interest but an ever-accelerating cost of containment, monitoring, disaster. Long before the waste has lived out its semi-existence, the little globes each deposit represents will have well outgrown the earth's own shiny globe. The numbers become astronomical in the most literal sense—they leave our world behind.

"There's always shoelace insurance against risk: but while you're pulling yourself up by the shoelaces, the barque, itself held together by similar shoelaces, is sinking.

"The US Nuclear Regulatory Commission has estimated that a major nuclear accident would cost fifteen billion dollars at least. Keeping in mind that such a body is bound to be erring, as erring it certainly is, on the conservative side of the estimation. Even so, actuaries are refusing to insure against the real costs, whatever they may be, and will only cover for damages limited to around $500 million. One thirtieth of the Commission's estimate. EURATOM countries created a similar insurance scheme to protect the fledgling European nuclear industry. Nowhere for the buck to stop, but shoelaces looping bows over everything, pretending to hold it together."

"It really is unbelievable." Lars is quite taken with Pinn's examples, their sheer scale.

"And therein lies its greatest weakness," adds Pinn, closing the trap of his logic. "Your average John Doe puts his savings into a bank account and into a mortgage and sees it whittled away to nothing by inflation in no time. How is he to come to a true appreciation of the staggering, world-swallowing effects of compound interest on the scales we're dealing with here? You're only too right, Lars. The thing is simply, literally, outrageously unbelievable. You know, the thing I find it most like is the experience of looking at Van Gogh's 'Crows over a Wheat Field' as compared to the experience of remembering having seen it. You look at the picture and you go, 'Wow!' The colours seem to sink into your skin and you glow with them, you feel the turmoil.

"Later, you know full well what happened. But you know just as well that it has now stopped happening. If you want it to happen again, you're going to have to go and look at that painting again. True comprehension of any truth worth knowing is always like that. If you really desire comprehension, you have to live with the thing. It's not enough to know *about* it. You have to meet it like a friend or an enemy. The general doesn't look at his map once, note a marsh, a steep defile and a number of sand dunes upon the territory ahead, then put it away with the comment, "Well, I know they're there now." I would very reluctantly campaign with such a one. I, as his aide, would insist he look again and again at the map, even if it were a map of his own childhood district. To do otherwise is contempt of the thing you're dealing with."

"That's the right word alright when you start thinking about the military and civilian protagonists of the nuclear industry," Lars agrees, his voice low. "Contempt. Contempt for the earth and its future. Contempt for the men who clean up their mess."

"Pretty much so. The NPVs and insurance costs do not trouble the thoughts of your average garden-variety US military strategist. Only the annual budget figures for defence spending interest him. And the only relevant time period is maybe from now to ten years hence: in the case we're looking at, the crucial decade between 1960 and 1970. If Western democracy could survive that time, they argued, that would be long enough for the US to catch up with the Soviets in terms of nuclear missile technology. One hundred and twenty-five thousand years means nothing if the enemy can attack *now* and obliterate us all." Pinn finishes, and the silence returns, filled now with the ghost of that calculation, where millennia of future risk are discounted for the sake of a present advantage. It is the same calculation, he realizes, that buried Professor Kofoed Hansen's report, and with it, the truth.

* * * * * *

FINANCIAL LAWS ARE in the end, only a matter of opinion: shared values, not objective truths. The laws of motion are more satisfying in this respect: the same for all observers, undeniable. A rock dropped in Greenland falls as surely as one dropped in Washington, regardless of the political weather.

Is the universe just a play on words, or is it just that: a UNI-verse? Can there exist such things as different universes in which there is a spreading, bifurcating, diverging, sometimes converging, skein of times that embrace all possibilities and in which most of the people exist some of the time, all of the people exist some of the time, but no one exists all of the time? In the aftermath of Thule, it seemed less a theory of physics than a description of bureaucratic reality.

In Greenland in 1968, there was no doubt that parallel universes existed. Lars treads surely and unskeptically through the gritty, inconvenient truths of Universe One, where a great and lingering injustice was done to Danish workers at Thule.

"When it comes to the clean up, it is a very strange affair. There are just a host of contradictions," Lars begins, his fingers tracing the edge of a green-bound volume as if reading a tactile map of the folly. "All the radiation experts up there, American and Danish, agreed that any intake of plutonium is not risky at all if you take it up through the digestive system. You have to have open wounds somewhere in the system for the plutonium to get in. If you are healthy, it will pass all the way through you in a day and be expelled. This enabled them to say that it was not toxic in chemical terms. A tidy, comforting piece of logic.

"But it's another matter if you inhale it. Then it lodges. Then it stays.

"The funny thing is that they decided on a rather rough clean up involving the removal of snow from an area of about 500-800 yards square. From this area, snow was to be scraped up to the depth of about one foot, and taken away. This snow was very powdery, light and crispy and quite easy to kick around. It was dust waiting to become airborne."

"I was under the impression that the snow and ice had fused from the impact of the crash and the heat of the explosion," puts in Pinn.

"Oh, yeah, that's so, but there was a cap of lighter snow over the top of the hard crust. A fragile crust on a crust. But anyway, about the stupidest thing you could do was handle this powdery stuff. The Americans first thought that they would just retrieve the major parts of the wrecked bomber and the bombs, of course, and let the rest melt away into the ocean with the spring thaw. They actually considered this option a low-risk one. Sure, some contamination would spread through the food chain, but that would be through digestion: and, remember, it had already been agreed that, speaking of plutonium, that posed no danger. The amount of tritium was only a few grams per bomb. Uranium could be a problem but, apparently, they didn't discover traces of any."

Lars pauses as if lost in a silent, profound agnosticism at the idea that no traces of uranium could be found at the sight of the explosive demolition of a B-52 Stratofortress whose cargo was admitted by all parties to have been at least four nuclear bombs. His gaze returns from the middle distance and he shrugs off the doubting mood, a physical shedding of cognitive dissonance, to continue his narrative.

"Most of the waste was still in heavy particles that would quickly fall to the seabed and be overlaid by sediment in a year or two. The plutonium that did fall to the bottom at the point of impact is by now overlaid with a good foot of sediment, so it's more or less isolated from the biosphere."

Pinn nods and smiles wryly as Lars repeats the words, 'more or less' with a heavy, ironic emphasis that hangs in the air between them.

Meanwhile, in a quiet office far from the ice, Universe Two was being carefully prepared by SAC. According to documents from the United States Atomic Energy Commission, a paper prepared by Wright Langham, 'Some Plutonium Contamination Aspects of the Bomber Crash at Thule, Greenland,' which contained damning quantitative information concerning the amounts of plutonium on the ice after the crash, had been quietly doctored in preparation for its reception into this cleaner, safer Universe Two. The Americans and Danes had been alarmed at Langham's use of actual numbers, and suggested that 'it might be possible for him to present a paper which omitted quantitative data and which discussed the accident from the health physics point of view in general terms. Dr. Langham agreed—who can say with what degree of reluctance?—to rewrite his paper and to omit quantitative data to which the Danes were taking exception.'

So far so good. But perhaps we have only arrived at Universe 1.5 so far. Still a way to go to the pristine, contradiction-free Universe Two.

'The Thule Affair,' an article by Colonel O. J. Sundstrom, swings wide for us the door to that universe. Its sunny, congratulatory tone makes up for the sun's perpetual absence in the far northern regions it describes.

Colonel Sundstrom coos like a dove over the invincible competence of the US Military in Universe Two and over how the scientists discussed that the removal of the contaminated snow would be carried out merely as a 'housekeeping measure' even in 'the absence of hazards to the biosphere.' He hails the 'countless unsung participants' who contributed to the clean up and airily refers to the 'meticulous effort that severely tested the Air Force's ability to cope with a complex and costly situation.' All this despite, somewhat contradictorily, our Dear Colonel's own admission that 'the B-52 accident measurably raised the plutonium level in the marine environment.' A minor detail in the grand, heroic narrative.

In Universe Two, there is no threat to human life. The Honourable Colonel assures us that the village where the sled-drivers lived was monitored for radiation on January 25 and periodically thereafter and that no radiation was found 'except for small amounts on clothing.' No stone was left unturned to protect the workers. In addition to routine cleansing, nasal swabs were taken on all personnel and urine tests were made 'if it was considered desirable.' The discretion of the authorities was, of course, absolute.

In all, a masterpiece of logistics. The radiation represented merely an 'inconvenience' to on-site personnel because it was not possible to eat in the contaminated area. They were kept there for eight hour shifts and could only drink soup, hot chocolate and coffee. The Inuit nuclear tea was no longer available. Not that any of this was a problem: we remember that plutonium is absolutely harmless if consumed, provided you do not have any open wounds to let it into the bloodstream. Colonel Sundstrom was gleefully certain of that.

Colonel Sundstrom is the *Miles Triumphans* and can scarcely contain his pride: 'The cheerful patience of this group of dedicated workmen, their hours of productive effort, and their willingness to serve, were major factors in solving the many problems we faced.'

Back in Universe One with Lars, the Danish light becomes dark as the sun loses its daily battle with the horizon. The journals' dull green spines turn black in the gloom and, depending on which parallel of space-time you are occupying, heads become tails, cups of coffee become cockroaches and mushroom clouds become mere slabs of dirty ice.

Lars fortifies himself with another cup of coffee, the bitter liquid a tangible anchor, and continues his Universe One soliloquy.

"Apparently, there was Danish pressure on the Americans to make a more thorough clean up. Between them they agreed on a medium level clean up. That meant well over two hundred people out on the ice. Close to 250 Danes were working in some capacity out on the ice: Firefighters, carpenters, people providing electricity and so on. A small army of the expendable.

"Add this to the grand stupidity of taking all this scraped-off ice onto the base itself for preliminary storage. So, it was inevitable that some of this ice was being tramped daily into the dining hall. It came in on boots and overalls and even in pockets. A slow, invisible contamination of the very place of refuge."

Lars rubs his chin vigorously where his five-o-clock shadow reminds him of the real world and real time. How far they seem from the sterile realpolitik of the reports.

"They had a lot of problems with the alpha monitoring systems up there. Plutonium is a significant alpha emitter. Alpha particles have a very limited reach even in the air. Only a half to one inch. So, if you had to scan each man coming in from beyond the zero line, you'd have to scan every square inch of his clothes from up close and real slow. An impossible task.

"One of the monitors they used had been successful in the Palomares accident, but it was useless in the arctic conditions. The wiring inside became quickly fragile due to the cold and the thin little viewing windows kept cracking. After two weeks of this, they had to send for a repair team and have the machines redesigned to make them effective in arctic conditions."

Lars shakes his head and rubs his chin more forcefully, as if trying to stimulate a thought that could make sense of it. "All this makes any claim of a successful radiation monitoring program pretty damn dubious. It was theater.

"While overalls can give some protection from the large and slow alpha particles, they are little use against beta or gamma particles, which are a whole lot smaller and more penetrating. Tritium is an intense beta emitter and plutonium and uranium, as well as tritium, are all emitters of low levels of gamma radiation. Consequently, the workers were all exposed to long periods of low level radiation. But the US authorities concentrated only on alpha measurement. They ignored tritium altogether. They knew it was there, but decided—not concluded but decided—that it was probably a lesser threat because of a lower level than the alpha radiation." He spits the word 'decided' like a pit.

The pleasure of arguing his case, of laying out the damning sequence, outweighs the mere detail that the official verdict has long been decided. Lars warms visibly as he rubs his hands together, the energy of outrage fighting the encroaching evening chill.

"Any number of contaminated men could have passed through undetected quite easily. One screening method was to take nasal swabs. But, how do you breathe under arctic conditions? If you breathe through the nose at temperatures below minus fifteen, the hairs in your nose freeze when you inhale and fall out when you exhale. So, you have a tendency to open your mouth to breathe. And, there's another problem; when you inhale through your mouth, you breathe in cold air, whereas through the nose it is warmed. They did no mouth swabs at all." He leans forward. "None."

None of this was a problem in Universe Two, of course. There, Colonel G. S. Dressler, US commander at Thule, trumpets that on Friday 13 September, 1968—to most people a day of ill omen—he and those at Thule airbase experienced a 'day of elation.' For it was on that date that the last of the 600 containers of low-level radioactive residue from Project Crested Ice were loaded on board a US Navy cargo ship for transport to the United States. A victory parade without spectators.

The American physicist Joseph Gerver once commented, in a pyrotechnic display of historical revisionism eked out with the laws of physics, that, if we accept parallel-universe theory, then 'we no longer need to worry about what really happened in the past, because every possible past is equally real.' To avoid insanity, he adds (rather belatedly), we can, 'with clear consciences define reality as that branch of the past that agrees with our memories.'

By Gerver's standard, Colonel Dressler is a man of integrity and sanity. He has chosen the correct, heroic branch of the past and blithely recounts that, in the storage area, Danish crane operators lifted the boxes of contaminated snow in slings and tripped the hinge on the bottom to allow the snow to tumble through a specially constructed metal chute. There was no danger to those doing the disposing, which, of course, was precisely the reason why the waste was being loaded into containers to be hermetically sealed and shipped off to be buried in concrete bunkers in some isolated place in the US. The logic was circular, and perfect.

But, some universes admit of logical inconsistencies. Once you have dispensed with the finicky distinction between the possible and the actual, why should logic be a barrier to your creativity?

Another of the bizarre inhabitants of Universe Two is Risoe's own Jorgen Koch, friend and confidante of Otto Kofoed Hansen. He could confidently show that, although the contaminated waste was considered dangerous enough to ship across an ocean and bury in a mountain, this did not apply to those who cleaned it up. The proof was provided, for Koch, by an instrument volunteered by the Livermore laboratory in California, called FIDLER: Field Instrument for the Detection of Low Energy Radiation, or FIDLER on the roof of the world, as the USAF journal wittily commented. Koch, grinning broadly with the glories of scientific certitude at his back, notes that the survey team consisted of four men: an instrument operator, a recorder, a transit man and an operator's assistant. A personnel decontamination station was established in a vacant barracks building fitted out with hot running water and shower facilities. Everything was orderly, documented, clean.

Everything, he says, was monitored. He reminds us of the famous nasal swabs which came up with no detectable contamination. He admits to some minor problems with FIDLER, such as the fact that everything had to be dry, otherwise the readings could not be considered reliable. The measurements had to be taken not more than one-eighth of an inch from the surface to be monitored, yet direct contact had to be avoided to prevent the face of the instrument becoming damaged or punctured. Some of the readings were even 'false,' probably because of a static discharge from the wool and rayon clothing. But, in all, everything ran smoothly. Alpha contamination limits on US personnel were considered acceptable, and there was 'none detectable' on foreign nationals.

A curious racial preference on the subatomic level. Danish particles were apparently more obedient.

Of even greater satisfaction was the handling of the seventy-two newsmen from North America and Europe who deplaned at Thule. Given large quantities of alcohol, sanitised press releases, and sensing the soul-crushing depth of the cold in their bones, they found Universe Two the more congenial place. The arctic darkness and severe weather created some problems in accommodating the newsmen. Transport to the crash site was 'difficult and time-consuming.' Darkness, bulky clothing and extreme cold made identification difficult. All excellent reasons not to go.

Major General Richard O. Hunziger, DCT commander, ever the faithful servant of truth and defender of all things free, came up with the perfect solution: press conferences. Bring seventy-two media people thousands of miles, hide them in a warm room and lecture them. It suggests a new appreciation of the term 'covering the news.' There, he told the reporters that 'some radiation was present, but there had been no nuclear yield.' A masterpiece of understatement.

He had a captive audience. Hunziger remarked that 'credibility in the conferences was strengthened by the openness with which everyone answered questions and the maximum Danish and American scientific participation was achieved.' Many-worlds theory helped here. 'Public relations personnel had learned from the Palomares episode. The policy for release of information was determined before the newsmen arrived.' The story was written before the questions were asked.

Leakages from Universe One were as carefully prevented as they were from the containers of radioactive waste. A slightly paternalistic, stern note enters Dressler's manner to reassure us that this would not happen: 'because of the extreme sensitivity of all public affairs actions concerning the crash and recovery proceedings, the release of all information was triple-checked to make certain it did not mislead or distort, and that it was in the best interests of the nations concerned. Such a challenge was never-ending.' The challenge, it seems, was to maintain the fiction.

Many-Worlds theory does not allow for some commonalities of perception. The physicist David Z. Albert observes that there are many bizarre forms of overlap, such as 'cats, measuring instruments, my friend's brain, my own brain.' Lars, with his librarian's sensibility and fierce capacity for critical observation, knew some others: the madness of crowds, the depths of the potentiality for evil, the folly driven deep into human nature. As sternly spartan as his surroundings, he resumes his disquisition, pulling them both back to the cold, hard reality of Universe One.

"Whenever you have a Broken Arrow, you ring headquarters in Europe. The man receiving the call takes down the binder for Broken Arrow and follows the manual's steps. It is a totally strict set of commands to be followed very carefully. You don't take time to analyse the local conditions of the accident. You believe or trust that the commands in the set contain at least what is necessary to do the job. Somewhere in the manual is the need stipulated for twenty motorised lawnmowers. These were duly sent to Thule because it was in the book. Not much grass to mow seventy-eight degrees north, I fear.

"Most of the procedures were designed for temperate or subtropical climates and simply did not meet arctic conditions. It was a pantomime.

"They flew in people from all over. Some American soldiers went from the tropics to the arctic in a matter of hours, some even deplaning in tropical clothes. Most of the Americans that were flown in had never experienced cold like that in their lives.

"But, importantly, they had 1700 skilled Danes already working on the base, who knew the place, the machinery and the working conditions well. It was much easier to use these Danish workers and train them quickly for the special jobs to be done. All they had to do was offer them hard cash, and they became sedulous students. 'Will you join this? It isn't dangerous. And, oh, yeah, here's some money.' If it was not dangerous, why the hell were they doing the clean up at all? Why the containers, the shipping, the bunkers?

"It should never have been allowed that Danish and civilian workers were used in this clean up: it was an exclusively military action, with military consequences.

"When you look at the whole chain of command, which was set up by the chiefs in SAC, there remains no doubt of the essentially military nature of the action. Add to that that everybody knew at the time that plutonium was positively dangerous if inhaled. One inhaled molecule of plutonium could be enough to set off lung cancer in twenty-year's time. The security limit is zero—and the plutonium in the bombs totally disintegrated.

"We are talking about everything from small lumps of the stuff to powder to even isolated molecules. And who knows, maybe plutonium oxide, once inside the body, could change its chemical form on account of the explosion and fire. We just don't know. Like all nuclear accidents, it's brim-full of our lack of knowledge." His voice drops, weighted by the admission. "And our willingness to gamble with that ignorance."

No such lack of knowledge was suffered in Universe Two, though. For one thing, there was no such drearily binding thing as logical consistency, so no need to be troubled with the occasional contradiction. So, SAC Historical Study #113 on the accident can happily observe that, after taking readings of alpha and gamma radiation, 'no evidence of nuclear contamination was found.'

A mere two paragraphs later, the same document states that it was probable that the high explosives in all four nuclear weapons had detonated, which would have spread abroad 'significant amounts of contaminated weapons and aircraft.'

These inconsistencies are only apparent, because, as the SAC report observes, displaying an intimate understanding of Many-Worlds theory and the role of perception in arriving at the truth, 'exact levels of contamination would, of course, have to await the outcome of government-to-government negotiations.' Under this logic, Congress could legislate the law of gravity away; which once gone, might lead to a state of levity in the citizens, turning its legislative folly into a laughing-stock.

The report goes on to dispel all doubt. It notes with satisfaction that the Danish scientists were reassured by the fact that the searchers did not wear respirators, proof positive that the plutonium was fixed in the ice and consequently represented no inhalation hazard. Very comforting indeed. Nor did 'the Danes seem to be worried about contamination of the food supply of the local inhabitants; but they were interested in a joint ecological study.' A study, one assumes, to be conducted in Universe Two.

The laws of nature in Universe Two were different depending on who was observing. Although the Danes were already won over by the obvious lack of need for respirators, there might still be a problem for those subject to different laws of nature. The SAC report says, 'Because plutonium oxide can be dangerous when inhaled, the grader operators wore respirators. Air samplers inside and outside the cab recorded no contamination, however.' A few pages later, the report notes that after the graders had completed their first pass over the entire burn area, 'six areas still showed significant readings of contamination.' The graders made more cuts to remove the snow and reduce the contamination to 'acceptable levels.'

In all, a most satisfactory exercise in showing how deeply reality is dependent on how it is perceived, and by whom. The SAC report, always candid and professional, records that despite the public interest in the accident, much of it was partially diverted by the capture by the Koreans of the US intelligence ship *Pueblo* three days later. A fortunate distraction.

There was no need to worry about beans. The report notes that, in claims alone, the USAF paid over half a million dollars to Spanish citizens after the nuclear crash over Palomares, and the total cost was about $25 million. At Thule, in the 'icy twilight,' costs were kept to a minimum. 'No claims had been filed by Greenlanders to the date of the preparation of this history. The total cost of the operation is estimated at around $2 million.'

Ya larfin'!

* * * * * *

IN SHORT, A triumph of military professionalism, of the protection of human life, of political management, of the invention of new forms of logical consistency, and of the marriage of parallel-universe theory and techniques of post-modernist history. 'The Danes held all the cards, yet they chose not to be difficult. The decontamination effort then must be considered largely as fulfilling a political responsibility and completed in the interests of what has been called 'good housekeeping.''

There was the occasional loose end. Footnote 20 of the SAC report shows that, despite the fact that the monitoring of alpha and gamma radiation showed there was no risk of contamination, several Greenlanders had picked up contamination on their clothes during their activity. 'Some articles could not be cleaned and had to be replaced by polar bear skins purchased from Denmark.' A quaint, almost charming anecdote of native inconvenience.

There was also the occasional troublesome Dane. The report notes that our good Professor, Otto Kofoed Hansen, was 'unfriendly and difficult,' and, although a 'brilliant scientist,' was 'erratic and intellectual' to such an extent that he dared leave Greenland with a report damaging to the US government's interests. 'He was said to have concluded that the problem of contamination was very serious and that a large portion of Western Greenland and its adjacent waters were endangered.' Well, we know by what means Professor Kofoed Hansen was lured, at least for a time, into the quieter waters of Universe Two.

But, these were merely ripples in the space-time of Universe Two. Most of the Danes, even the workers, were much happier to repose there. Lars knows that, and the knowledge is a kind of torture.

"The US bases are pretty extraordinary in that the US does not pay any rent for base rights. Except for the base at Guantánamo in Cuba, it is probably the only foreign base the Americans get for free. The American attitude towards Denmark in military terms is again contradictory. We are a skillful and sophisticated nation. But, we are a ridiculously small country and consequently, are only a tiny part of the world-wide game of American foreign policy. The Americans look at Greenland as American territory. What they did is none of our business. I think that is their attitude. They think that the only problems in their foreign affairs dealings are the foreigners."

What a happy ending, thinks Pinn. But, there are some troubling questions thrown up by many-worlds theory. What does it mean if a person in World One knows what is happening in World Two, but the person in World Two does not know what is happening in World One? Sir Fred Hoyle, of 'The Black Cloud' fame, in another of his novels, 'October the First is Too Late,' talks of the possibility of waking each morning beside a different spouse in a parallel universe. The catch is that this would come with parallel perceptions:

"Our memory each morning will always be consistent with the spouse of the day, and we will therefore be entirely unaware of the other possibilities."

But, what if you can cross to the other world, see into its differences and absorb them into your own universe? Does this make you a bigamist of truth? Or, perhaps, morally superior: it might be said, in possession of a greater grasp of reality, even if that reality is agonizing and unwelcome?

Lars, who is quite capable of peering into Universe Two, sees it as no more than a flawed, self-serving fabrication. Even the coffee in his cup seems to boil over with his frustration. He parts his hair with both hands in a frenetic movement. He has just had a sudden, violent access of anger at an enemy that renders human emotion redundant, that operates on a scale where individual suffering is statistical noise.

"I have been working with the nuclear industry a long time and I am sick and tired of it. It's overloaded with nasty stories of this type. They are all different and they are all the same. The ineptness of the administration, slow political response and crazy attitudes towards the people affected. Whether it is Russia or the US makes no matter. Qualitatively, they are the same.

"You know, in the state of Washington they deliberately sent out nuclear material in gas form over an agricultural area of several hundreds of square miles as a full-scale test, to later on go out and make health examinations to assess what had happened. You see it all over, and they just don't give a damn."

Too young to sense his own mortality deeply, Lars barely ponders the bitter irony that the victims, too, are often complicit in the cover up. No one likes to die. No one likes to be sick, or to be seen as a victim. Even those most afflicted would rather have belonged to Universe Two, where the military is in flawless control, proper care and concern is shown to all, and radiation is never a problem provided everyone follows the manual and keeps quiet.

"A lot of Thule workers have been closed out by the doctors. And they have closed themselves out because they are macho boys, tough boys who don't need to go to doctors. Often it was only after their wives had told them to go, after ten years of silent suffering. Only a small number of them went into hospital under the national health system. Which is why so few of them appear in the Danish national health statistics. You need to spend at least two days straight in hospital before the statistics will pick you up. But, if the men themselves only rarely go and then, too late, and if the doctors try to exclude them at the lower preliminary levels, they will never be sent to the specialist parts of the hospital. They'll be checked and sent home with a prescription. And that is usually the last the system sees of them till they die inexplicably of cancer a little while later."

Superior vision never substitutes for effective action, although action is rarely effective without it. The laws of physics may allow more than one universe, but the laws of politics are simpler: 'Those with might write the history.' A hairline fracture appears in the frozen varnish of Lars's hope as his brown eyes deepen in a profound, weary sadness. Nothing seems left to him at this moment but to repeat himself, to circle the unspeakable truth. He reminds Pinn of the dog in the saying who cannot resist revisiting the undigested, poisonous refuse of his revulsion.

"I am sick of the doubts always being to the advantage of those responsible and not of the victims. The benefit of the doubt is a currency only the powerful mint.

"In the Arctic, you simply cannot use masks or protection. Any time you exhale, it freezes to ice immediately, which closes the mask off in half a minute. So they didn't. They breathed.

"All this polluted snow was taken up by bulldozers and loaded into open containers. Powdered snow was dropping on workers standing around the dozers. These open containers were driven into base areas and their contents reloaded into closed containers. So, it's being reloaded in an open area at least twice for every container with people all around, all day, inhaling the powdery stuff. The jet fuel containers were leaking, and Danes did the repairs. The containers often broke off at the taps, so they also started leaking. At one time, seventeen of them were leaking. A slow, toxic melt.

"Then, spring comes and the thaw begins. Water dripping everywhere from the containers. So, what happened to the plutonium? Why the heck do the clean up at all if the dangers were minimal? Why involve Danish civilians? To make it quicker? SAC could easily get their own people from the US. So, why involve foreign nationals, who are, by definition, a security risk? Why conclude so quickly that the clean up operations would not cause any damage, so there was very little follow-up medical analysis? In Spain, they made medical follow-up programs for 500 people, who were taken regularly to hospital in Madrid for US doctors to examine them. With the Thule workers, they did nothing. They did not even count them. Why should they count those who just don't count?" His voice rises, finally cracking with a raw, impotent fury. "They did nothing!"

The silence that follows is thick, filled with the ghost of that shouted word. It is the sound of Universe One colliding, futilely, with the immovable walls of Universe Two.

* * * * * *

PINN, LEAVING LARS' office, stepped out into the Copenhagen air, which felt no clearer than the moral atmosphere he had just departed. Lars' last words seemed to chase him down the street, rebounding on Lars himself, calling to him from the hollow heart of his own true, unacknowledged belief: the belief that, despite all the fist-shaking and letter-writing and earnest lobbying in rooms lined with green-bound volumes, what could be done was effectively, in the end, nothing. Which thought led directly to the cold, familiar fear that assailed Pinn too in his quieter moments: that, for all the grandstanding over issues of public importance and the finely crafted articles on what-have-you that earned his daily bread, he, Leonard Pinn, could do exactly what Lars Melgaard could and to the same definitive degree: nothing at all. They were both scribes in the archive of a disaster, cataloguing the fire while the building smouldered on.

"A good antidote to this feeling of hopelessness," Pinn ended the thought to himself, his breath a small cloud in the Nordic chill, "Is to keep in mind the reason you came here to talk to Lars in the first place. Carswell. Jeffrey Carswell." The name was a talisman. "If anyone is going to get around this fatal, polished barrier to success that confronts all these slot-machine revolutionaries—put in your coin of outrage, pull the lever, receive a printed statement of principle—he'll be the one. And he'll do it by simply refusing to bang his head against it. He'll find the crack, or make one."

With that sane remembrance of the new friend whose stubborn, almost anarchic persistence under duress had so impressed him that he had crossed hemispheres to get the background to the story, Pinn gladdened a little. The cynical fog lifted a fraction. He hailed a taxi, its yellow a splash of artificial sun in the grey afternoon, and gave the driver the address of his down town Copenhagen hotel, a temporary sanctuary from the pervasive taste of futility.

* * * * * *

SOME TIME IN about April 1995, I received a rather curious unsolicited package by mail. It lay on my Australian doorstep, an anomaly among the bills and circulars, its Danish postage stamps like bright, foreign eyes. I do not remember my hands shaking as I turned it over to see an Odense postmark on it, but my fingers did tingle momentarily, a physicist's tremor at the detection of an unseen field, as I broke the seal.

"Don't get paranoid!" I rebuked myself mildly, standing in my own quiet hallway. "No one is going to send you a bomb." I added the statement defiantly, aloud, to the empty house. As it turned out, the package did contain a subtle, sophisticated time-delay device: not of explosives, but of psychology. It was an extensive, daunting questionnaire from one Professor Joergen Halberg Bechmann, chief psychologist at the University of Odense. The pages felt heavy with implication.

I immediately got on the phone to Marius Schmidt in Denmark, the only time I ever took a cue from him and blithely ignored the brutal time difference between a waking Australia and a sleeping Denmark. The ringtone echoed into the Scandinavian night.

"Yes, who is it?" Marius's voice finally came, thick with sleep, a sniff and a yawn swallowed by the apparatus.

"It's the mother of all mothers-in-law," I replied, the old joke a weak vehicle for my alarm. I quickly went on, not giving him time to parse it. "I've just received an invitation to cut my own throat. Professionally speaking."

"What?" Marius spat out the word as if it had a bad taste, sleep receding.

"The illustrious Professor of Psychology at Odense ..." I began, holding the covering letter up as if he could see it.

"Oh, that. Yeah, I was about to give you a call on that." His voice shifted, assuming a tone of managerial calm. "Seems like an OK idea to me. Finally, someone is taking us seriously scientifically. All the guys are getting the questionnaire, you know."

"I don't think so, Marius." My own voice was tight. "It smells a bit fishy to me. Look, he says here that he wants to compare the health statistics of our members with those of a group of bank tellers exposed to armed robbery. What sort of a comparison is that, for God's sake? It smacks of an attempt to brand us as psychosomatic sufferers, a bunch of nervous wrecks who just *think* we're sick. Besides, what possible genuine interest does an Odense psychologist have in us? He couldn't give two shits about us or Thule. It's just an opportunity to write a 'learned' paper, to mine our misery for academic capital. I've seen this sort of thing too often before to trust it."

"Well, he might find that the differences between us and the bank tellers are greater than ..." Marius began, ever the optimist, trying to spin gold from lead.

"No, Marius, you miss my point." I cut him off, frustration sharpening my tone. "He could just as easily find—and phrase his findings to suggest—that we're just a disaffected, stressed-out bunch of nobodies, our illnesses born of anxiety, not alpha particles. I can see no point in submitting the guys to a psychological interrogation of this sort. These things can be skewed in a thousand subtle ways to get the results you want, or the results that cause the least trouble. And that seems to me to be a risk we ought not to take. If we were being compared with a control group of soldiers from Maralinga or the Marshall Islands nuclear tests, maybe it would seem fair, relevant. But, bank tellers? It's an insult disguised as science. And what if the results are presented in a way adverse to our cause? Then we'll have a prominent, respectable scientific voice raised against us, not just one of those known Risoe hacks. This whole thing makes me very uneasy. It's a trap baited with legitimacy."

"Well, there's not much to be done." Marius's sigh travelled twelve thousand miles, weighted with resignation. "It's really just up to each of the guys to fill out the questionnaire or not, now that they've got it."

"I just hope for the best, then, Marius." My hope felt thin. "But I feel strongly the guys should be advised against returning this thing. We should put out a warning."

"Maybe I could send out a special bulletin with the newsletter," he offered, the practical administrator rising to the surface.

"Well, just do what you can," I snapped rather abruptly, the distance and the dread shortening my patience. I rang off, the click final. I left Marius, I knew, with two of the biggest headaches he had ever had: one thudding behind his own temples from the rude awakening, and the other, larger one, walking the difficult line between welcoming scrutiny and fearing a setup. I stared at the questionnaire on my table. It was, I thought, a very clean, very polite way of asking a man to testify against himself.

Chapter 10: ...Then We Take Copenhagen

THE SNOW FELL and just kept on falling, a silent, white siege against the city. The streets of Washington were icy and treacherous underfoot, the gutters choked with grey, frozen sludge, the air so cold it felt like a personal rebuke. For Jeff Carswell, Proustian snapshots of Thule and its ghostly array of victims seemed at moments to block the very perspectives of the Capital of the Free World. The gleaming monuments and broad avenues were superimposed by images of dark ice, silent flames, and men whose faces were now etched in his memory. The past was not past; it was here, in this chill.

For the next three days, they followed much the same relentless routine as on their first twenty-four hours: days crammed with back-to-back meetings, evenings sacrificed to earnest journalists in noisy bars.

They met with such a bewildering number and variety of different interest and lobby groups, ranging from the sober Physicians for Social Responsibility to the spirited campaigners of Greenpeace, from Ralph Nader's meticulous subsidiary organisations to the quietly determined Council of Churches Environmental Watchdog, that specific individuals, promises of support, and fragments of encouragement remained in the memory only as a general, buzzing impression. Were it not for his meticulous written record of these few frenetic days, Carswell was sure he would quickly conclude that he had merely treated himself to a very pleasant though hectic dream, a fantasy of influence.

However, the general impression that did remain, firmly fixed in his mind, was of an almost overwhelming tide of sympathy and concrete support. It was a humbling, energizing force. As such, it had pushed their first, sharp disappointment with Mr. Christian of the American Legion quite out of consideration. He could see it now for the minor hiccough it was, a stumble on a long march. Although, he still wished some more tangible, constructive support could have been forthcoming from that quarter: he meant in kind, in political muscle, not just in well-wishes or token donations.

Among other results, the effect on him personally was to act as a powerful antidote to any sneaking, generalized anti-American sentiment that may have been seeping into his consciousness via the subterranean ways of frustration and bureaucratic encounters. Here were Americans—dedicated, informed, outraged on their behalf.

He came away from Washington with a revitalised, if nuanced, faith in the basic honorableness of the American people and quite refocused on the true object of their struggle: not a foreign nation, but their own Danish government in its quiet collusion with the American military machine. Their only lingering disquiet rested on Christel's unpleasant encounter at the hotel. Though the incident had no recurrence, Christel did think she saw her assailant from across the vast hotel foyer the morning of the day before they left—a flash of the same sullen face. By the time she had wended her way across the expanse through the knots of visitors and luggage, the beat-hippy on her beat had, appropriately, beat it.

But, the Americans are an honorable people, Carswell reaffirmed to himself, however dishonorable and wretched some of their institutions, and some of their agents, might occasionally prove to be.

They also came away from Washington with one of their most potent weapons yet secured: a televised interview that felt like a turning-point in the propaganda war they were waging against the stone wall of Danish government indifference.

Carswell had been fairly resistant to exposing himself to too much publicity to that time. He held the strong belief that one public face for the Association was enough, and that was Marius, the authentic everyman, the president. But, on the Thursday, their last day, as they prepared for departure to New York and thence for Copenhagen, Marius came up to him in the hotel lobby, smiling sheepishly and looking uncharacteristically spick and span, his hair combed, his tie straight.

"Who is it this time, Marius?" Carswell asked, bracing for another meeting.

"I've organised an encounter with the local representatives of Danish TV2." (One of Denmark's major TV stations). "Just a quick one. I shan't be long."

Carswell lay his hand on Marius' arm, his own gaze abstracted beyond the view of the Pentagon through the hotel window, that grim symbol of the power they were tangling with. Despite his habitual and much-expressed dislike of such media performances, he felt a sudden, decisive shift.

"The time is ripe, Marius, for some apocalyptic revelations over the airwaves," he said, his voice low and firm. "On this occasion, I think I'll join you."

So, off they went to the station's studios, across a town glittering coldly under a leaden sky. Once there, Carswell had to fight his natural inclination to flee as he sat and watched the usual, absurdly solemn rounds of disputes over lighting and shots and angles and what not. It felt like preparing for a stage play about a tragedy.

His mood was not enhanced when, before he could quite comprehend what was being required of him, he found himself, with a bemused Marius, in a repeat of their encounter with Chicago TV. They were out again on the ice-laden sidewalk of the Washington street in front of the studios, slipping and sliding comically up and down until the crew got the right video shots of the two of them 'arriving.' The farce of authenticity.

Back inside, under the hot lights, the producer, a large, wheezing man whose voice seemed to emanate from the next room bar one even when he spoke directly into your face from three inches away, which is precisely what he did now, addressed them.

"Mr. Schmidt. Mr. Carswell." He smiled a brisk, professional smile from Marius to Carswell. "We've scheduled to run the interview local time tonight in Denmark on our prime-time news program, so we'll have to put it all together in as short a time as possible to catch the satellite. OK?" He beamed with abrupt condescension and was gone, leaving a vacuum filled with tension.

In his absence, the interviewer, who had been there all along, occupying a swivel chair opposite, came into focus. He also smiled at them, looked at a camera, spoke a few words of introduction to the lens, and suddenly they were on. The red light glowed.

"No one in Denmark can be ignorant of the attention that a twenty-seven-year-old miscarriage of justice has been gaining over the last several months. We all know something of the story of HOBO 28 and the results of that disaster on the lives of hundreds of Danish citizens. However, it seems there has just been an exciting development in this matter issuing from Washington D.C. I have with me in our Washington studio Mr. Marius Schmidt, the president of the ex-Thulers' Association, and their international campaigner and board member, Mr. Jeff Carswell."

"Mr. Carswell," he addressed me, his tone suggesting a shared secret. "I understand that you have managed to locate evidence in the Pentagon archives of Danish and American connivance and malfeasance."

"Yes, Bjoern. We have." I leaned forward slightly, the documents a palpable weight in my briefcase by my feet. "However, first, let me just correct you on one point: it's not a miscarriage of justice we're talking about here; it's a total absence of justice. I want to make it clear that, to date, the Danish government has come nowhere near this matter either to address the issue of justice or to mismanage it. They have consistently denied any responsibility or any wrong-doing of any sort and, in short, are not admitting to there being any issue at all of either justice or injustice. They have pursued to this moment, and have done so for over twenty-five years, a policy of official indifference and crude obstructiveness. They have fobbed us off as cranks and malingerers, which was just adding cruel insult to very real and tangible injury. Not to mention our many friends who have already actually died."

I could feel myself warming to the task, the cold studio light burning away my reticence.

"Now, however, for the first time, we have located documents, previously kept secret, relating to the American airforce base at Thule, regarding in particular its alleged and true uses, as well as evidence that the Danish government was cognisant of those uses. In a few days, we will be in Denmark, to address the members of our association; at which time we will make documents selectively available to the media."

"Could we see any of those documents now?" The interviewer's question was predictable, eager.

The hair on my scalp thrilled as I thought of the effect my words would be having on any government types who might be watching at that very moment in cozy Copenhagen living rooms.

"I'm afraid not. I feel that our members deserve, having suffered the indifference and obtuseness of government officials and ministers for so long, to have the first viewing of these most important documents; documents that vindicate us completely and put the finger squarely on those who have made themselves their enemies. None of us went out to seek an enemy, you know, Bjoern: we just went out as citizens of a democratic nation to seek recognition and reparation. That's all!

"It is they themselves who have created in us some sort of enemy.

"Well, having created us, they will now have to deal with us!"

"You're being rather enigmatic, Mr. Carswell." A slight, challenging smile.

"Yes, I am." I answered curtly and deliberately, turning my gaze fully to the camera, speaking past the interviewer to the power behind him. "And I will declare my hand when I and my colleagues in the association are good and ready to do so; and not a moment before."

I added under my breath, a quiet aside to myself, "That should make 'em squirm."

"It sounds like you're calling the government's bluff, Mr. Carswell."

"Does it sound that way?" I asked, feigning curiosity.

The interviewer brightened and straightened in his chair, sensing a headline. "It certainly does."

"Good." I declared, the word a hammer tap. "Because that's precisely what I'm doing. Let them now call mine!"

I stared hard, unblinking, into the camera's unfeeling eye, hoping my gaze would carry across the ocean.

Afterwards, as the lights dimmed and the crew bustled, the interviewer came over to us as we were pulling on our coats and gloves against the remembered cold outside.

"That was just great!" he said, genuine admiration in his voice. "You said next to nothing of substance; but you'll have them scurrying for cover like frightened rats. I wish I could be back home to get some comments from the PM and the Minister for Defence; just for the joy of seeing them writhe. Congratulations." And he shook my glove-clad hand vigorously.

He could not resist leaning in once more, his voice dropping. "But really. What have you actually got?"

I smiled warmly, the enigmatic mask back in place, and said, "You must be kidding!"

At this he touched his forelock in a gesture of humorous surrender, laughed, and made off into the gloom of the studio.

* * * * * *

MAKE 'EM SQUIRM it did.

The Prime Minister, Poul Nyrup Rasmussen, had just settled into his favorite armchair with a generous tumbler of bourbon, hoping to enjoy the evening news bulletin as a neutral spectator for once. Then my face stared hard out at him from the Washington studio, my words cutting through the comfortable haze. The tumbler paused mid-air. The Prime Minister's eyes, usually so controlled, widened just a visible fraction. At the conclusion of the interview, the TV station played some dramatic file tape of B-52s taxiing and divers purported to be searching for dangerous materials following the Palomares accident—images meant to evoke danger and secrecy. There was also a long, desolate shot of Thule intercut with a shot of another B-52 idling ominously on a runway somewhere.

These ominous shots were then replaced by the florid, outraged features of Tommy Dinesen, a member of one of the parties in opposition. Tommy was expostulating excitedly behind the calm exterior of his well-tailored blue suit. Rasmussen did not pause to listen to the details of Tommy's argument; he simply blinked him blank with a jab of his remote, silencing the upstart.

Mrs. Rasmussen, who had been quietly watching her husband's reaction during the foregoing, now spoke from her own chair, her needlework forgotten in her lap. "This could be serious, dear."

The Prime Minister merely raised his eyebrows again, a master of understatement, and replied, "Indeed!" The single word was heavy with unspoken calculations.

The phone rang, a shrill intrusion. The Prime Minister said to his wife, "I've got it," his voice already shifting into its public, authoritative register.

He rose, still lightly grasping the tumbler of bourbon in his right hand, a symbol of the interrupted peace, and took up the handset.

"Yes, yes, Yvonne, I rather thought it would be you." A pause, listening. "Uhuh. Uhuh. Yes, I see. I understand—I agree. Yes, it would be useful to meet. Have the Chief Whip get the Cabinet together at Christiansborg. Yes, this evening—It is important—Yes. I think you're right. The Chief Minister for Greenland. Imperatively! And, Yvonne," his voice dropped a conspiratorial notch, "I rather think we should invite Tommy Dinesen to sit in, too—Yes, Yvonne, it touches both our portfolios very closely. That's right, not just Health, but Defence and my own office— Yes, of course. Please, Yvonne just calm down. Look, you'd better come on over here first and we'll work out a few lines—No, no, we can handle these fellows. They're just desperate hicks. Schmidt, I know; but I've heard nothing of this Carswell fellow before. He could be dangerous. He seems pretty bloody determined. But, we just have to play it as the cards fall. The real danger is to the Coalition. If Dinesen, God bless his pure-white little heart, if Dinesen can be stimmied before he gets to any of our allies, we should be safe—Of course this is all about our safety, Yvonne. Our political futures, yes, ours, not just mine, could be riding on the political fallout of this farce. That's the issue to be addressed here, not whether some bunch of smart-assed country bumpkins is carking it from the big C—Right. I'll see you in ten. And, just calm it, OK! We can ride this one out. Bye."

Rasmussen turned to his wife, who had stood quietly behind him, overhearing the local half of his conversation. He put his arm about her shoulders, a gesture of reassurance that felt automatic, and led her back to the couch. He turned the TV on again, the screen now showing a benign gardening program, and settled with her, sipping on his tumbler, to await the arrival of his flustered Health Minister. His demeanour was a masterclass in control, muffling completely the ringing alarms in his head.

* * * * * *

MY LUCK WITH the airlines continued as it had begun, which is to say it was non-existent. I was snowed-in at Washington's Dulles Airport, a prisoner of weather, and not to mention that a plane actually crashed while coming in to land there, a tragedy that delayed all flights for a numbing number of hours. I only made it to New York the next morning after an atrocious, bumpy flight, my stomach churning in sympathy with the turbid skies. Meanwhile, back in Washington on the evening of the interview, I got a curious, exhilarating call from my sister Hanne in Copenhagen.

"Everyone's up in arms," she laughed, the sound tinged with amazement. "The whole family's just called me. They just saw you on the news. What a story! You know, it was the major item on the 6.30 bulletin here! You were brilliant, by the way. But, getting back to the family. They were all complaining that I didn't let them know that you had arrived earlier than anticipated in Copenhagen. I had to explain to them all about modern satellite technology. What luddites they are sometimes! Phew! But all is well again, now."

"So, it went over well?" I was elated, the fatigue momentarily burned away.

"I'll say. You must have some incredible documents. What have you got?"

"Well, nothing new in essence, really. Nothing we didn't know in our bones, so to speak. But, what we do have is confirmation. Written, undeniable confirmation of the dishonesty of the entire government apparatus, from top to toe, from ministers down to the most minor bureaucrats. We can now point and say, `We know you're lying to us, because this document says the contrary to what you're telling me now.' That changes everything.

"I'm planning an extensive campaign of severe embarrassment for them. A political striptease."

"So, you'll be here in Copenhagen as planned tomorrow evening?"

"Yep. I get in around ten o'clock, if this weather and the gods of travel permit. I'll see you at the airport, then."

"Righto. See you then. All my love to Marius and Christel. Bye."

"Bye," I finished. And then, on a whim, I added, "And bye bye to you too, whoever you are, listening in to private conversations. We may be in Washington, but this is not the Watergate." I spoke clearly to the empty room around me.

"What?" came Hanne's amazed voice down the line.

"Just saying nigh-night to the buggers here in D.C.," I laughed, a dry, humorless sound, and rang off, wondering if I was being paranoid or prescient.

* * * * * *

WONDERFUL, WONDERFUL, COPENHAGEN. The city of slate skies, leaden waterways, and eyes that could turn as grey and cold as the winter sea. I have never spent much time there; and each time I return, my desire to do so diminishes. Were it not for Hanne's warm presence there, and the scattered remnants of my remaining family, I doubt the place would hold any charm at all for me. It felt like the administrative heart of the very machine we were fighting.

But, my presence there was now critically required for the upcoming General Meeting of the Association, at which I planned to finally prime and distribute the bombs we had so carefully manufactured in the archives of Washington.

Marius and Christel had flown in on an earlier, smoother flight than mine. On their way out of the customs clearance area, they were set upon by a school of feeding journalists, hungry for the next chapter.

Cameras, videos and cassette machines whirred and thrust forward as Marius, self-effacing yet firm, commented, at the end of yet another improvised spiel, that perhaps the ladies and gentlemen of the press would like to wait around for a couple of hours for the arrival of Mr. Carswell's flight; that gentleman being in a better position to answer any detailed queries that he himself was unable to address.

Thus was the dead winter lull of Copenhagen Airport quickened (I might have foreseen it!) on my own arrival by a rushing scrum of television and newspaper journalists, who had been awaiting my arrival for some two cold hours and were now in a veritable frenzy of anticipation.

"Look, off the record," I began, sighing heavily with barely suppressed irritation, my whole body aching from the journey. "I have just had an exhausting flight made even more uncomfortable by having been ill for a good part of the trip; and I am less than ecstatic to have electronic equipment shoved up my nose the moment I step from my plane."

I gently illustrated my point by pushing a persistent tape recorder away from under my nose with my right index finger. I had indeed spent the entire flight over the Atlantic going over the damning documents, making notes, preparing myself for the upcoming Association meeting. At that moment, I could feel the curious eyes of my fellow travellers upon me as they passed, wondering briefly who this harried man might be, besieged by media.

Maybe someone important?

Then I spotted Hanne over the bobbing heads of the journalists and waved, a lifeline to sanity.

"Will you be releasing any new documents, Mr. Carswell?" asked one tenacious cub reporter, his notebook poised.

I looked curiously at him, the glare of the airport lights harsh in my tired eyes, and answered, "As I have yet to release any documents at all, I can hardly release any *new* ones."

"Will you be bringing the government to the parley table, Mr. Carswell? Or is its fall what you have in mind?" asked a lady with a large microphone, an innocent smile, and an idiosyncratic idea of grammar.

"For the time being, I will say only this," I began, my voice weary but deliberate. "Since this fight is, at its core, about justice for the members of the ex-Thulers' Association, I think it only right and proper that they be the very first to hear the news I have to relate and view the documents I have to show. They have waited twenty-seven years; they can wait two more days."

I barely raised my voice above my usual conversing volume, forcing them to lean in, and deliberately ensured that I betrayed no emotion in it, no triumphalism, only steel.

"I will limit my comments for the present to merely asking the question of the government officials and ministers, lackeys, all of them, who have ignored our pleas for assistance and justice: just what professionalism has there been in their irresponsible and indecent behavior toward us, and how can they continue to hold public office when their moral standards would shame a donkey and a cuckoo at once?"

I stared directly down the barrel of the video camera nearest me, the lens a dark, unblinking eye. "These people have hidden behind a wall of bureaucratic paper-shuffling and incompetence for long enough; their time has come! Thank you. That is all." I ended dramatically, cutting off any further questions with a sharp, final hand gesture; and then pushed through the throng to greet Hanne and to escape to the sanctuary of her home, and a good, long rest before the storm.

* * * * * *

IN THE CABINET office at Christiansborg at that same moment, there was a considerable amount of braying and cawing and other unstatesmanlike noises as Poul Nyrup Rasmussen tried, with dwindling patience, to prevent his coalition government from dismantling itself before his eyes. Panic, not principle, was in the air. A number of old favours were called in that evening, a number of recalcitrants quietly reminded of past, buried misdemeanours, and no small number of shaky reaffirmations of faith and trust were demanded and, with reluctance, received.

After the initial uproar had died down into a tense murmur, the Prime Minister expressed his grim satisfaction with all present—members of his own ruling party and its coalition allies— all, that is, bar one. His eyes fell but for a brief, contemptuous instant on the still-reddened yet defiantly unassailed features of Tommy Dinesen, sitting like a thorn at the far end of the table.

"Contemptable sardine," he felt the thought come and go, and resolved to forget him as well as it is possible for a hardened public figure to forget the needle in his side.

His sure hand was back on the rudder, his voice regaining its accustomed dominance. His summary comments bore the unmistakable stamps of his authority and his focus: political survival.

"So, it is clear that we must convince the members of this… irritating group that everyone's interests—the nation's interests—will be best served if they agree to sharing their knowledge with us, the government. In a controlled manner. After all," he allowed a thin, dismissive smile, "it's not as if they can have unearthed anything that isn't already known to us, in broad strokes. It is merely a public relations challenge, a measure to ensure that the facts are not distorted by amateurs to create the false impression that the Danish government has been culpable of shilly-shallying or obstructionism. For, we are guilty of none such. We must insist that this information, which has ever been in the public domain in any case, be released in such a manner as to allow the truth of the matter to be appreciated and assimilated by the public in a leisurely and mature manner."

The PM paused and sipped at the glass of water on the polished table before him. Not as fortifying as bourbon, but more acceptable in this company. When he continued, he was like a general deploying his troops.

"The Minister for Health will speak with Mr. Schmidt personally and place him under an obligation, via persuasion and good sense, to hand over the documents to her department for 'proper evaluation.' The Chief Minister for Greenland, Torben Cordtz, will organise for, say, five or six, members of the Greenland State Government to make themselves available to come to Denmark should a hearing in this matter be viewed as the most efficacious way of deflecting this development. Emphasis on the Native Inuits," he said, tapping a finger on the table for emphasis, "will safely sidetrack the issue, I think, in the current climate of public opinion where anything regarding righting wrongs done to indigenous peoples can drown out just about anything else. Even," he added dryly, "the concerns of a few hundred Danish labourers.

"The Minister for Energy will be in touch with the scientific community at Risoe to secure their continuing, and silent, support in this matter. None of them is in any position to do anything but to keep his nose very clean. In this regard, I would also suggest we discreetly encourage a campaign in the press undermining any scientific credibility this association may claim to have, which I'm sure is very little. They are cranks; and we must ensure that the people of Denmark are let in on that secret of theirs. Have I missed anyone or anything?"

A low rumble of 'nos' and shaken heads around the room attested to the Prime Minister's efficient, if cynical, coverage of every possible angle. The ship of state would be steadied.

"Fine. Well, to borrow a favorite, melodramatic term of these agitators," he concluded, allowing himself a small, cold smile, "let's see that the only fallout from this incident is of the harmless type: nuclear and not political. Good night."

The relieved smiles and quiet, complicit laughs that greeted this essay in fine, political wit were the objective observer's greatest evidence of the single-minded, self-preserving spirit of the gathering. Following which, it dispersed into the Copenhagen night, its members tasked not with seeking justice, but with managing a nuisance.

* * * * * *

ABOUT SEVEN NEXT morning, I sat at breakfast in Hanne's cozy kitchen, the smell of coffee and fresh bread in the air. I was staring at a picture of myself in *Ekstra Bladet*, my own tired, determined face looking back from the newsprint, when Hanne came bustling in in her bathrobe, waving a video cassette about in her hand like a trophy.

"This is from last night's news, Jeff. I think you'll enjoy this with your coffee more than that unflattering photo."

She put the tape in the machine and we sat together on the worn couch, ready to enjoy the spectacle of my own media performance.

" ...a donkey and a cuckoo at once?"

My own televised voice filled the quiet room. "Did I really say that?" I was barely able to resist open laughter at my own frankness, a flush of elation mixing with the absurdity. They had actually run it to air, uncensored.

"A donkey and a cuckoo? Ha!" The laugh burst out of me. "Stubborn stupidity and parasitic imposture all at once! I love it. It has a certain ring."

"Well, it should serve to assure us of a certain amount of continued attention, anyway," Hanne said, smiling but pragmatic.

"You're not out to make friends in the government, are you Jeff?" Flemming walked in grinning from ear to ear, gave Hanne a kiss, and sat down on the couch to rewind the tape and view the segment himself, his engineer's mind appreciating the mechanics of the broadcast.

"I prefer to choose my friends from the vertebrates and above," I quipped, the morning's levity a brief respite from the weight.

"Donkeys are vertebrates, Jeff."

"So are cuckoos," added Hanne, playing along.

"In which case, I withdraw my calumnies against both those noble creatures," I said, raising my coffee cup in mock solemnity. "I had no intention of lowering their public reputations in any way by associating their names with flatworms and political mould."

"Ah, remember my namesake and penicillin," Flemming put in, ever the scientist. "Even mould is useful."

"Too true, too true," I sighed, the smile fading. "It seems there really is no adequate parallel between politicians and bureaucrats and any respectable member of any of the living kingdoms. They occupy a phylum of their own."

Hanne was quite in hysterics by now, so in the interests of her health—and the promise of a good dinner that afternoon—we desisted from any further ribaldry. But the shared moment of laughter was a buoy in the churning waters ahead.

That afternoon, I took a taxi through the grey Copenhagen streets to the venue set for a special meeting of the association, at which Marius and I were to report on the results of our tour of the States. The familiar knot of tension tightened in my stomach.

The first thing to negotiate, as I had feared it might be, was a pre-meeting conference with the national press, a scrum of expectant faces and poised recorders in the foyer. I had nothing genuinely new to report and said so in the darkest and most enigmatic manner I could muster, a performance of concealed power. I knew that this would ensure they all then stayed for the main show; which was precisely what I wanted. Mystery was our currency.

As little as I actively sought the glare of publicity, I nevertheless appreciated with cold clarity that publicity was now one of our most powerful tools. So, I quietly congratulated Marius on his inexhaustible capabilities in arranging it all and, with a few more vague pronouncements, took my leave of the press corps for the time being. Let them wait.

We had borrowed a hall in the Falck Office Complex near the main drag. As I looked out from a side room over the rapidly filling seating area, I could see that we would soon have a capacity crowd. Our largest ever. The low buzz of excited conversation grew to a steady, bass rumble as the place filled and then overfilled, chairs scraping, voices layering upon one another.

Once again, as it had during my recent interviews, a sharp, almost electric thrill coursed through me—part anxiety, part adrenaline.

Never before in my life had I experienced this galvanic charge of public attention and approbation, this illicit thrill of nascent power. It had not ever even occurred to me to seek it before. Nor, in truth, had I consciously sought it at this time, though now, in a minor but palpable degree, I held it.

"Well," I mused silently, watching the sea of faces. "There are two ways to enjoy power, such as it is in this case. One is to live to the full the sensual fulfilment that comes with the potential to exercise influence over the lives of others; the other is to use that potential as a catalyst by merely drawing attention to its presence, without ever actually touching it yourself. I know what happens when you touch high-voltage power lines: for one brief, pathetic moment you become the conductor of immense energy; then you're smoked pork. My job today, as unlikely as it seems given that I'm ostensibly here to reveal our discoveries, is to resist the terrible pressure to become a regular member of the Board, to become the conductor they want to grasp."

That private resolve was badly shaken when, the meeting having been opened by Marius and his having noticed my presence to the capacity crowd with a warm introduction, they rose to their feet in a loud and unseemly wave of applause and welcome. The sound was a physical force. I hardly knew how to acknowledge this enthusiastic, desperate demonstration of support: I half rose from my chair, a clumsy gesture, and nodded my head, my face hot, my mind reeling.

"My God! What do these people expect from me?" I thought, a spike of alarm piercing the adrenaline. "Do they think I have any more answers about this labyrinthine issue than they have? Do they really expect me to be able to help them any more than they can help themselves? If only they realized that the closer you look at this thing, as I have been forced to do, the less clear and simple it seems. The enemy is not a person, but a system; the truth is not a fact, but a pattern of concealment."

I became intensely, almost unbearably aware of their utter collective desperation, of their profound need to be injected with a serum of hope, of their craving for somebody on whom to rely so they could simply go on. To my shock and dismay, that somebody was clearly, in that moment, me.

Marius, much to my relief, spoke at animated length about the logistics of the trip, the meetings, the snow; enough, I hoped, to dampen their fervor a little and ground the proceedings. I retreated into the sanctuary of my own whirling thoughts.

"Well, I suppose I at least owe it to these people not to dash their hopes altogether. Nor should I let them see how deeply doubtful I am myself of a clean, positive outcome. No, I think my part here should be to stress the advances we've made, to give shape to their anger, and help them to keep up the necessary enthusiasm. What a narrow, treacherous course I have to tread; I have to put my own corrosive doubts aside and guide them, while at the same time avoid allowing them to make of me some sort of untouchable savior. A role I could never fulfil, and which would consume me."

I was jerked out of my reverie by the sound of renewed, thunderous applause. Marius was looking directly at me, clapping, as was every other person of the several hundred crammed into the hall. The expectation was a tangible pressure in the air. I supposed that I was to rise and speak now. So, I rose, my legs feeling less than steady, and began to speak.

"Ladies and gentlemen, I am flattered by your enthusiastic reception this afternoon. Flattered and frankly, stunned." My voice sounded calmer than I felt. "I have done nothing to deserve it, I can assure you; and I hope you can bear with me if I fail to live up to the expectations I see in your faces."

This humble disclaimer only provoked a fresh, warm round of applause, a wave of goodwill that threatened to sweep me off my feet. Luckily, some deep-seated stubbornness prevented panic; and, as the sound died out, I applied myself to the task at hand, my mind clicking into the gear of presentation.

"For nearly eight years now—need I tell you?—the major activity of this association has been to await patiently the good will of a government while suffering its persistent ill will. We have been little more than a punching bag for the bureaucrats, a helpless body of victims of whom they would take notice only to beat us down and humiliate us." I paused, the memory of my own futile expedition to Aarhus flashing before me, a personal emblem of that humiliation.

I stopped dramatically, letting a murmur of hard-won agreement ripple and disperse through the hall. I realized then, with a fresh jolt, the huge, unasked-for responsibility I had toward these people: not to deflate their small, fragile balloons of hope. It was a terrible duty.

The fatigue, the lingering jetlag, and my generally weakened condition on account of the cancer stirring within me—a secret I held close—all joined their leaden weight to the burden of responsibility in that moment. It made the task of communicating hope an ironically, cruelly difficult one; I felt little enough of it myself. Then, as there was nothing for it but to speak or collapse under the weight, I continued. Without alteration in my voice or delivery—I wanted the stark change in content to signal its own presence—I shifted gears.

"But, things have changed." The room seemed to hold its breath. "As Marius has just outlined to you, for the first time since we began this struggle, we have in our possession conclusive evidence. Written, undeniable proof of the underhanded policies, the contemptible practices, and the out-and-out lying of government and bureaucrats throughout this whole, sorry affair.

"We have contended with snow storms and plane crashes—literal ones—to promote the cause which is that of you all. In the few days we had in Washington, Marius and I attended more meetings on your behalf than any of you will have attended in your whole lives, I'd wager.

"At times," I paused and managed a genuine smile toward Marius. "At times, I actually forced our poor president here into a slow, undignified gallop across West Potomac Park, from one meeting to another, just so we'd be able to keep to our impossibly tight schedule. Which we did, but only with great difficulty. Not the least of which was the snow which, coming directly from an Australian summer, posed for me, in any case, quite a novel and formidable obstacle. And, I am pleased to report a considerable measure of success, both in relation to the information and documentation located, as well as in the broad and sincere support we gained from a wide range of interested and sympathetic groups across America."

I paused to let the applause, now tinged with relief, die down, and then leaned into the heart of the matter. I delivered the gist of, and quoted select, damning extracts from, the juiciest documentation we had prised from the archives of Washington. Names, dates, policy contraventions. The air in the room changed; it became charged with a new kind of energy—not just hope, but the sharp, clean fury of vindication.

I ended my presentation by returning to gestures of strength and defiance, channeling their renewed anger.

"I firmly believe, my friends, that with your continued, unwavering efforts and support, we can win this case. We're going to knock their socks off and chase them, barefoot and bare-arsed, beating them with birch sprays, out of their cosy offices and all the way to the Big Belt; where they'll have to either turn and confess their sins; or we'll make them swim all the way to Greenland to see for themselves the legacy of their neglect!"

I sat down, physically spent, into a roar of furious, cathartic applause that seemed to shake the very foundations of the Falck building.

And then, suddenly, I rose again as if I had forgotten a crucial piece of business. The applause subsided into a curious hush.

"Ladies and gentlemen, I cannot allow this meeting to proceed to any other item without publicly acknowledging the important—no, the indispensible—part played in the success of our American enterprise by Marius Schmidt and his wife, Christel." I turned to them. "Their energy seemed limitless, and Marius' adaptability in a country whose language he speaks only haltingly left me dumbfounded; his rare, innate ability to sniff out every single opportunity for positive publicity is a gift of immeasurable value. It contributed in a major degree to the high profile we gained both in the States and, as you've seen, back here in Denmark. And without profile, we are nothing. We are silent. So, please, your thanks—Marius and Christel Schmidt."

I gestured for the room's applause to find its rightful target. The ovation only revived, louder and more affectionate, when the secretary of the association himself got up to propose, as the next order of business, that the remainder of the meeting be devoted to voting in a new board. Marius, I noted, seemed not at all disturbed or overwhelmed by the attention I had redirected; he bore it with a quiet, steadfast grace, the figurehead steady on the prow of our ship.

* * * * * *

I HAD, EVEN at that moment of high drama, no intention of changing the long-distance strategy that had been till then our quiet strength. I continued, once more returned to the relative calm of my home in Melbourne, to script and stage-manage the whole affair from afar. Marius, on the ground in Denmark, remained the indispensable figure who drew to himself the heat and light of the media, keeping the story simmering on the front pages. And he succeeded admirably, a native son fighting for his people.

Particularly in the wake of our trip, whenever any new fragment of information came my way from the sources we had uncovered in the States, I would quickly translate it into Danish, add strategic emphasis, and fax it through the night to Marius; who would then feed it, still warm, to the hungry press. Marius was the face every Dane saw on their evening news, while I was the ghostwriter, the voice every one heard in the carefully crafted statements and damning quotes.

Nor was my voice limited to the press. I also made it a central part of the campaign to arm the opposition in the Danish Parliament. I drafted precise, pointed questions, based on the documents, designed to cause maximum embarrassment. The leader of the key opposition party was not in the least averse to using my ammunition to snipe at the reigning Socialist government, reading my words verbatim from the podium.

It is a peculiarly satisfying, almost surreal experience to read in the Danish equivalent of *Hansard*, as well as in the press coverage of parliament, questions just as I had written them weeks earlier at my kitchen table in Melbourne, Australia, over ten thousand miles and several time zones away. It was a form of political telekinesis.

Nor were these questions plucked from the air. I was relying on a steady drip-feed of factual information coming to me via phone and fax from the network of organisations and individuals I had established contact with in the States—physicians, historians, declassified documents researchers. And Mr. Rasmussen, the PM, knew they were facts. He could squirm, but he could not deny their provenance.

It was more than hectic at times, a perpetual, global juggling act: taking calls from Washington as my evening ended, receiving faxes from Copenhagen as I began my morning, preparing my parliamentary interrogations and then firing them back across the world to yet another time zone. But, it was deeply satisfying too: to know that I really could *do* something tangible for all those members of the association who were relying on a faint voice from the other side of the planet; and to know, with cold certainty, that the Dirty Denizens of Danish Duplicity were writhing under these long-distance, righteous assaults.

But my own personal profile I continued to keep as low as possible from Melbourne. To have done otherwise would have been strategically foolish because of the sheer impossibility of making myself readily available for television interviews, press conferences, and the like. For all these on-the-ground necessities, Marius remained the tactical linchpin. He was the focus of press attention and the conduit for the public outrage against the government, which was growing palpably by the day. Hardly a day passed without Thule figuring in one or another of the Danish media. I contented myself with the occasional, calculated telephone interview, my voice a disembodied presence in the Danish debate.

From the moment of our pivotal TV interview in Washington, we had stolen the publicity march on the Danish government. It was an advantage we clung to with grim determination. And the nub of our power, such as it was, lay in the great, tantalizing unknown of just what we had discovered in the vaults of the States.

What *was* in those documents that could make us voice such unequivocal confidence? What could allow us to use such scalding terms about the government and its officials as 'lackeys,' 'cronies,' 'spineless,' 'liars,' 'Mandarins'? What had we found that might prove significant enough to turn popular opinion decisively and perhaps cost them their exalted positions?

We made them squirm all the more precisely by releasing less. That was the core strategy I enforced: the Danish government grew increasingly strident in its demands that we release the information; our reply was to assume an ever-greater mantle of indignation and to allow more and more mystery to enshroud the issue, like fog on the Øresund.

Through Marius, I would let it become a matter of public knowledge—a whispered allegation—that those now in power were desperate to get hold of and suppress any document that might point to bad decisions they had taken in the past as junior bureaucrats or ambitious backbenchers. The more they pressed us, the more we made public revelations of their very attempts to intimidate and suppress us. It was a feedback loop of their own making.

Even the inevitable, sinister death threats that began to come the way of both myself and Marius could only operate, in our narrative, to intensify our resolve and underline the seriousness of what we held.

"Mr. Carswell?" asked an unfamiliar male voice, flat and without trace of a foreign accent (by which I mean he spoke with the electric, nasal twang of an Aussie) one Sunday morning in March 1994. The sun was streaming into my Melbourne kitchen, making a lie of the call.

"Yes? Who's that? Toby?" I asked, thinking it was a mate.

"No dramatics, Jeff." The voice was calm, almost friendly. "Just letting you know that your life is in danger. Take care, eh? Ha, ha!" The false laugh was followed by the cold, final click of disconnection, the malice ringing in my ear like a tinnitus.

I slammed the phone down, the sound too loud in the peaceful room. "Frigging little shits!" The anger was instant, hot, and cleansing.

I turned to confront the three sets of raised eyebrows round the breakfast table—Sophia and our two young children.

"Sorry," I said, forcing a casual smile. "I hate it when those wrong numbers treat you like it's your fault they can't dial properly." I improvised smoothly, the lie sour in my mouth.

Later, when we were alone, I told Sophia what had been the true essence of the morning call.

"God, Jeff. Call the police. Now. This is serious. Who knows what sort of lunatic they might get hold of to do this sort of thing." Her face was pale, her fear immediate and personal.

I sat still for a long moment, looking out at my own backyard, the ordinary Australian gums, so far from the ice of Thule.

"Jeff?"

"I'm thinking."

"Well? I'm going to call the police!"

"No. Leave it, Sophia." My voice was firm. "What are you going to say? That I got a nasty, obscene phone call? And what can they possibly do? Put a tap on my phone because I'm leading a campaign against a foreign government and I need protection from their hypothetical agents? Look, I think it's best to treat this as an aberration, an indicator. It tells me we've really put the wind up the Mandarins in Copenhagen. It's a sign of weakness, not strength."

"Well, I don't like it, Jeff." Her voice trembled.

"Well, neither do I, you know." I took her hand. "But I'm not going to allow this to make me paranoid. Sure, I'm concerned, but there is nothing effective I can do about it except to ignore it. To not let it change a thing."

Which is what I tried to do, until, a week later, a note came in the mail, typed on a cheap sheet:

"Is your mail safe, Mr. Carswell?????"

The following week, I walked out early one frosty autumn morning to my car. As the automatic garage door raised itself, a yellow slip of paper, folded and wedged into the space between the door and the wall, fluttered to the concrete at my feet:

"Is this car roadworthy, Mr. Carswell?????"

After that, I actually, despite my bravado, took to varying my route to work each morning. Each time I turned the ignition key, I felt a distinct, unwelcome pucker of anxiety deep in my groin. Apart from that small concession to vigilance, though, I did nothing. I would not give them the satisfaction.

On several occasions, leaving for work at my usual pre-dawn hour, I noticed a pattern. Just as I backed out of my driveway, a set of headlights would suddenly flick on in a car parked further down the quiet, sleeping street. It would follow me, a silent shadow, for a few blocks before turning off down a side street. Even if I left a few minutes earlier or later, there it would be, the timing too perfect. It would crawl along, maintaining distance, and then, as if bored, it would suddenly vanish.

"I see it this way," I explained to Sophia about a month after this wave of harassment had begun, trying to sound more convinced than I felt. "If they really want to get me, if there really is a serious, professional risk to my life, then whoever is behind this is likely expert enough that there is genuinely nothing I could do to avoid it. If they have stooped to these childish threats to try to stop what I'm doing, then it just won't work. They'll scare me, yes. But they can't bluff me into giving up. I'm calling their bluff. This is the cost of doing business."

Shortly after that, we came back from a drive in the nearby Dandenong Ranges one afternoon to find another note, this one lodged in the jamb of the security door to the house itself:

"Is this house liable to subsidence, Jeff?????"

I ground my teeth as I angrily screwed the note into a tight ball and hurled it into the garden. My resolve hardened into something cold and flinty. I would keep on. I would get those bastards in Copenhagen.

Once, Marius whispered to me over the phone, the line crackling with more than static: "Who do you think is behind it?"

I answered back very loudly, for the benefit of any listeners, "The Danish Secret Police, the CIA, ASIO, ASIS, the Boy Scouts of America. I don't know, Marius, and I don't care! But, if they're listening right now, it'll sure save me the postage on the letters I'd like to send them telling them to get stuffed! And that we're going to get them! Ha!" And I slammed the phone down, the violence of the gesture a release.

So, and not for the first time in my life, I was learning the lesson that you never truly get used to the presence of lunatics, whether they are state-sponsored or freelance. Whatever the motivation for such harassment, and whatever real or imagined anxiety it seeded, it has not, and I vowed it would not, ever stop me.

* * * * * *

SO, MY TACTIC of lying low and passing the ammunition to Marius had, I realized, a natural limit. When Marius' own concerns escalated—he called me, his voice tense, and said, "Jeff, I *know* they're tapping my phone and recording our conversations!"—I thought the time had come to step out from behind the curtain. The strategy of the hidden hand had been effective, but its utility was expiring.

The effectiveness of the low-profile approach was brought home to me with peculiar force in the middle of 1995 when *Ekstra Bladet* ran a major feature article on me, splashed with that photo from the airport. It was entitled, `The Unknown Hero of Thule.'

The article marveled at the fact that, though I was a key board member and the Director of International Affairs, I remained a ghost to the Danish political establishment—unknown personally to any minister, bureaucrat, or government official. I was a persistent, troubling voice from the ether. As information about me inevitably leaked out—my background, my location— they must have started piecing it together, eventually recognizing their long-time, tenacious correspondent from the Antipodes. The game was up; the ghost had acquired a face.

Around the time this article appeared, I consciously began adopting a more publicly visible persona. The cloak of anonymity had served its purpose; now it was time for the shield. And, so it came to pass, that when obscurity no longer served our cause, I stepped forward, reluctantly but deliberately, into the spotlight. I ceased to be the *éminence gris* and became, for better or worse, another target in the open field.

Chapter 11: Success Plus Failure Equals Experience

Hoc opus, hic labor est

Aenead vi 126   VIRGIL

WE ARE ALL familiar with the principles behind every ballistic weapon, strictly speaking, of whatever age. Whether it be a ballesta, a crossbow, a longbow, a blunderbuss, a revolver, a machinegun or an ICBM, the method is basically the same: a projectile is dismissed with great acceleration from the vicinity of the weapon when the accumulated energy built up behind the triggering device is all in an instant set free. What saves the trigger from following at close range its projectile is a damping device on the weapon, set there to insure not only that it will not fly off over the moon like an enigmatic cow, but also that it transfer the maximum possible amount of its kinetic energy to the projectile in question. The art is in the restraint within the release.

Sisyphus is perhaps, in this modern world of seemingly pointless enterprises and impossible tasks, the most immediately accessible of the many myths that have in some way informed Western Civilization over the past four thousand years. Engaged as he is in the task of pushing a rock up hill, we wonder whether he does not ask himself from time to time just what it is that he is pushing, and what might ensue should he unshoulder the burden. We might also ask why he persists in his task. But, has it ever been considered just what would happen if he succeeded in his task? Or, even in what would success consist? The myth assumes the eternal struggle, not the unimaginable moment of completion.

Imagine for a moment then, this figure; let it be man or woman, burdens take no account of gender; back and shoulders to the burden, legs bent for leverage, arms wrapped in an inverse embrace about it. Struggling, pushing with all disposable energy and force, uphill ever and again ever. Thus engaged, this figure is not in a position to see the approaching ridge lipping out at a stupendous height over a dizzying drop. It takes little imagination to understand that our modern Sisyphean figure is going to go right on over the edge, perhaps still clinging to its burden like a postmodern Wiley Coyote plunging into the depths of the Grand Canyon or the Painted Desert. Success, in such a scenario, is not victory but a sudden, terrifying absence of resistance.

On the morning of Tuesday July 4, 1995, at precisely 05.17am, I had just finished shaving and was taking a shower, the steam a cocoon against the Melbourne winter, getting ready for another early start to work. I heard the phone ring. My heart missed a beat, the memory of other recent early-morning calls—those cold, twanging voices—flooding back with a rush of unpleasant association.

But, this time it was Marius. He had not called to wish me a happy American Independence Day. Rather his news was the first glimpse, albeit only registered on a level of the motor-unconscious, of the margin of the prominence up which I had borne my burden, and as such was the herald of the most significant turn-around yet in the history of our many years of struggling. The summit, unseen, was near.

"What's new since last night, Marius?" I dripped into the phone, my body still beaded with water, the towel around my waist. "Has the Minister decided he can't fit you into his busy schedule? Do you know what time it is here?" I added testily, shifting my weight from one dripping foot to the other on the cold linoleum.

Late the previous evening, Marius had called to tell me that the Chief Minister of Greenland, who was on an official visit to Denmark, had requested a meeting with him. The position of Chief Minister of Greenland is probably most comparable to the Governor of a State in the US or to a state premier in Australia. This position had been created when Greenland was granted home rule in 1979. That Marius had been asked to meet him was admittedly a development of major significance, although Marius and I could only guess at what its true purpose might be. However, standing in my passageway on a freezing Melbourne July morning, I felt little enough inclined to make the admission of excitement. I was braced for another bureaucratic dance.

"Jeff, are you sitting down?" Marius was never one for grasping subtle hints that he might call at a more convenient hour; his excitement overrode all time zones.

"I'm not sitting down, Marius; nor am I about to just for news of the latest update since five hours ago!" My voice was sharp with cold and interrupted routine.

"Well, get ready. Because this is really news. The best news we've had since it all began! This is news you'll really want to hear. To be bearer of this news to you, Jeff, is one of the greatest pleasures I've yet had in life." His tone was buoyant, almost giddy.

I raised my eyebrows at the empty hallway and asked, scarcely mollified by all this verbiage, "Well? What's new? Out with it."

Marius went on to inform me on that July 4 morning that, owing directly to the continued pressure to give an adequate response to our enquiries and allow the truth to see the light, the Danish government had, much to its own consternation, suddenly and unexpectedly turned up a copy of a letter. A letter dated November 18, 1957. In it, the Danish Prime Minister of the day (who also held the portfolio of Minister for Foreign Affairs), H. C. Hansen, had communicated to the United States government his permission for them to enjoy, in the interests of world peace, unrestricted military access to Greenland.

Unrestricted. It is a difficult term to construe liberally, being a very liberal, even promiscuous, term in its own right. However that may be, the United States took it to mean, and quite rightly, that they were free to establish radar and electronic surveillance facilities, to overfly Greenland with their B-52 Strategic Bombers with nuclear payloads; that they could use Greenland as a launching pad for their nuclear missiles; that they could, presumably, if they felt like it, test nuclear weapons in Greenland. The word was a blank cheque, signed by the highest authority.

That they failed to do the last I can only put down to the fact that, all in all, the Americans are an honorable people. Or maybe that would have been taking unfair advantage. Or maybe it just did not occur to them. Whatever the explanation, it is truly one of the great unsolved mysteries of our time that they showed such restraint.

My first verbal response to Marius was to misquote, my mind scrambling for an anchor, some lines from a now long-forgotten Beatles song:

"Yesterday,

Deceit was such an easy game to play ...

Now I need a place to hide away ..."

"Looks like your bluff worked, Jeff, ol' boy." Marius was so excited I could hear the jingling of his keys or change down the line, a sound of restless energy.

"Worked?" I almost shouted, the word echoing in the tiled passage. "The shark didn't just take the bait, Marius. The shark swam up the river from the sea, waltzed out of the water up to us and gently, deliberately, placed the biggest hook in my tacklebox in its mouth and champed down hard on it. Have you seen this letter, Marius? 'Cos I certainly haven't. I'd like to know just what it says, verbatim."

"It's hot stuff, Jeff. It spells out a secret agreement that just happens to violate the Danish constitution and leave it bleeding in a ditch; and, what's more, the hand that signed the paper belonged to none other than H. C. Hansen himself."

The name H. C. Hansen is of as sacred memory in Denmark as is FDR or JFK in the United States. Since Hansen's death in 1960, he has become something of a national icon, a pillar of social democratic virtue, held to have been as close to the perfect Prime Minister as a country could wish to have. A most honorable man! And, more significantly for the present predicament, he was of the same political lineage as the current Danish government. This was not some distant, politically convenient villain; this was their own founding saint.

I am not one to disturb the bones of popular esteem lightly. I derive no pleasure from the vindictive demolishing of a man's reputation; especially when he is in no position to reach out of the grave and defend himself. No. But, the rights of the living take precedence over those of the dead, as sacred as is their memory. And while the deathless, unremembering nuclear waste still reaches out of its grave in South Carolina to touch and shrivel the flesh of the living, let justice not keep her peace. Let the record be set straight.

Where there is advantage in terms of justice for the living, let the monuments of the dead be shaken. Here there is indeed a crushing advantage to the living; so let the legend disintegrate!

Let it be known that the great and esteemed H. C. Hansen, Prime Minister of Denmark, acting in collusion with H. C. Hansen, Danish Minister for Foreign Affairs, contravened in secrecy the very constitution whose every term he had solemnly sworn to uphold and defend as a minister of the Crown. A dual violation, by a single hand.

If that were not enough, even if I could be accused of pedantry over a technical detail, then the further, staggering charge must stand: that a responsible servant of the Crown and people gave over—on his own personal initiative, without parliamentary consent—an entire province of Danish sovereign territory to the political and military use of a foreign power. He gave away a piece of the kingdom.

While attempts are afoot to disprove that the permission granted was ever fully exercised by the US, those attempts I can confidently say will be in vain. The evidence is mounting, my own personal observations and suspicions aside, that indeed nuclear bombs were stored in and around Thule Airbase as a part of the United States' defence policy of the time. The letter was the enabling fiction; the bombers were the fact.

Only two copies of the letter are believed to exist: one held in the archival basement at the Department of Foreign Affairs in Copenhagen, buried by shame or strategy; and the other in Washington, D.C., filed under agreements kept. The fact that the Danish government decided to unearth it and release it—as if these were two distinct acts of courage—was due entirely to our continued, unrelenting pressure on them, especially my policy of theatrical mysteriousness about what we had unearthed in Washington. We had forced their hand. And by releasing it themselves, the government was clearly hoping to seize the initiative from us by ostentatiously appearing to be open and helpful in the matter where we had been painted as obstructive. They also hoped to forestall the possibility of the association's releasing it, had we had it (which we had not); with all the predictable political damage that is the inevitable result of this type of revelation. It was a pre-emptive confession.

I said as much to Marius, and added, my mind racing ahead, "We're not letting the government off the hook at this stage of proceedings. They've found themselves in a no-win situation and are just trying to ingratiate themselves with us and with the Danish public by a display of forced openness and honesty. But it's an honesty motivated by sheer desperation and fear. We've got them on the hop, and now we're going to make them hop until they pay the piper."

I rang off filled with a profound feeling of having been vindicated in my persistence, and with a regained, fierce vigour to face the final leg of the struggle. Nor can I overstate the cold, sweet satisfaction I felt at having caused the Danish government to admit, publicly and irrevocably, to having been, at the very least, significantly mendacious for some forty years. They had lied, and now they had to say so.

People the world over know the date July 4, whether they have cause to celebrate it or not. Marius' news enabled me to join the American people, in spirit at least, in celebrating the happy denouement of a protracted and, seemingly from the outset, hopeless struggle. So, the date was not without its own fierce meaning even to me here in the antipodean winter.

At the feast of death, many decline to eat. At my dinner table, however, we eat our fill even in the presence of the ghosts of the ex-Thulers. On the evening of Friday, July 7, we had a close and dear friend, the Very Reverend Brian Bainbridge, over for dinner. The conversation was lively, the wine flowing, a momentary respite. Then, there was Marius on the phone again, the third time in three days; this time with news that made me blink with sheer disbelief. He surely had only the barest inkling that he was acting as the BMEWS of my nervous system, telling it that the burden's weight of eleven years pressure had just been dissolved away and exchanged for the dead weight of gravity, for the plunge.

Marius was ringing to tell me that we had won our case.

* * * * * *

THE BURDEN I had pushed up that slope for so long, for eleven restless years, had suddenly disappeared and I felt I was momently in danger of following it into the deeps into which it now plunged. The Sisyphean burden had gone, but yet I continued to push uphill, my muscles straining against nothing, struggling to contain the suddenly freed energies lately spent in shouldering the rock. The absence of resistance was itself a form of violence.

So many thoughts raced into my mind in rapid succession that they pushed each other over in their haste. Had I misunderstood Marius? Was he misinformed? Was it a tactical trick to hamstring our activities, to lull us? Was it a sick joke played by our enemies? Will they fob us off with paltry compensation, a sop to make us go away? I had to work hard to steady myself, to direct all my mental energies to the mere task of resisting my by now habitual, ingrained disbelief. Trust was the hardest muscle to flex.

After all, had we not been fobbed off for year after grinding year with delaying tactics, bureaucratic obfuscation and red tape? What had become of all those lies and deceits, the morally

271

vacuous continual handing-on of the buck down the line? Had we not been *proved* wrong, officially, legally, morally and scientifically? Had we not made it all up? Were we not the dupes of powerful, shadowy lobby groups? Were we not simply malingerers or stressed-out ex-hippies chasing a phantom?

Yet, here, out of the blue, we were being told that the Danish government had reviewed the situation and it appeared that we were not wrong at all: neither legally, morally nor scientifically; nor had we made it all up; nor, it seemed, were we the dupes of a powerful lobby. Nor were we all of a sudden right: we had been right *all along*, for all of the nine years that had passed since we started the struggle! The buck had finally come to a stop; and it sat queerly yet squarely on the Prime Minister of Denmark's desk, a paperweight of his own making.

I said as much to Marius, my voice thick with a skepticism born of too many defeats, but he merely insisted, his own voice cracking with emotion, that the good news really was as good as it seemed. That the battle was over.

When Marius had rung off, I put the handset of the phone back in its cradle, but still held it tight in my hand, as if it were the only solid thing in a shifting world. I found Sophia by my side who, with considerable difficulty, was wresting the cold plastic from my white-knuckled grip.

"Jeff," she spoke softly, her face etched with concern. "What's wrong? What did he say?"

"We've won." I said evenly, the words feeling alien on my tongue.

"Will you let go of the phone, dear?"

"We've won," I repeated, the meaning beginning to seep in. "But I can't let go. I just can't just let go just like that." I was now struggling to keep my voice from cracking, a dam threatening to break. Then I looked straight into Sophia's eyes and years of memories—of late-night faxes, of angry letters, of phone threats, of haunted faces from Denmark, of my own creeping illness— welled up and muffled out the sounds of the pleasant evening and blocked out its sights completely.

An anticipated pleasant evening of dinner and company dissolved as I plummeted with my familiar burden into very unfamiliar territory: a place where the struggle was over. All the intensity of feeling of injustice and humiliation I had experienced and had had to keep under tight control so as to be in a state to conduct our protracted campaign was in a moment set free, and I had no choice but to allow it to run its course. It was a torrent. And I knew, with a terrifying clarity, that I had to learn to let go my grip. To unclench.

Anyone who has similarly been freed of a Sisyphean burden will understand me in this: if not, no words can convey more than the most superficial impression of what Marius' news meant to me that evening. It was the sound of the rock, not hitting the bottom, but vanishing into silence.

It was not till that moment that the full impact of my earlier conversation with Marius on July 4 began to have its true, emotional effect. As I remembered it, Marius had advised me then that he was at that very moment rushing to get to his meeting in Copenhagen with the Chief Minister of Greenland. I had been barely able to do more than just congratulate him and to register to myself, in a detached way, that this meeting might possibly mean a measure of success in our enterprise. I had not dared feel it.

Then, all of a sudden, things were moving with the speed and fury of a hurtling B-52 where moments before they had seemed to be in their customary, frustrating stasis. The laws of political physics had changed.

The fuller substance of Marius' message that night was that, following his most revelatory encounter with the Chief Minister of Greenland, they had held a joint press conference with a large pack of journalists, both Danish and foreign. The story was now international. In a quiet moment between these two events, Marius had been asked to attend a private, one-on-one meeting with the Prime Minister himself, Poul Nyrup Rasmussen. The lion's den.

A meeting of this type, at this level, could only mean one thing: the buck was about to come to rest; and where it ought. And, sure enough, in that meeting, the Prime Minister advised the President of the Association that, given the present state of knowledge concerning the effects of exposure to radiation from plutonium, uranium, tritium and other radioactive substances such as are used in the manufacture and composition of nuclear bombs on the health of persons, and the fact that the problems experienced by our members correspond to the sort of problems that might be traceable to such exposure, on the balance it seemed favourable to both parties that the government no longer pursue its policy of comprehensive health examinations—which would have been just yet another one in a long line of such stalling examinations—and take the rap. They would fold.

The government was accepting responsibility and was already moving onto the next phase; which was to set about determining a suitable level of compensation to be paid to each member of the association. The words 'accepting responsibility' hung in the air, monumental.

Subsequent to that meeting, on the following Tuesday, July 11, Marius had a meeting with Yvonne Herloev Andersen, the Minister for Health. Also present on that occasion was the association's solicitor, Anders Boelskifte. It was there agreed to hold a formal parliamentary inquiry, a *hörning*, at Odense, the birth place of Hans Christian Andersen. The irony was almost too perfect.

This was no poetical gesture on behalf of the government, in the belief that they were making a fairytale come true: the mundane reason for the choice was that that was the only available location with a congress centre large enough to accommodate the expected large assembly. For, such a level of interest had been generated in the case that, in addition to the significant number of bureaucrats and members of the Association expected to attend, a large contingent of media was also expected to descend. There was then even a suggestion, quickly quashed, that the hearing be televised live. The government wanted a record, but not *that* kind of record.

About this time, simultaneously, the government went into full damage-control mode and the media into a feeding frenzy over the government's delicious discomfiture. Stories willy-nilly were being reported on these events while the stories the government would dearly have loved to be given the same prominence—stories of their cooperation and openness—were relegated to Page 7. The narrative had slipped from their grasp.

In the midst of this media feeding frenzy, strangely it occurred to no journalist or editor that the events they were turning into daily news stories were without precedent in the history of Denmark; that never before had such a public parliamentary hearing been proposed in the wake of a thirty-year governmental cover-up. They reported the spectacle, but missed the historical earthquake.

I, practical as ever, booked myself into a cheap tourist hotel in Copenhagen for the hearing, as I fully expected to be paying my own way. Then came one of the government's little, telling damage-control tactics: they offered to pay my fare to Denmark and to put me up in the Five-Star Radisson SAS Royal Hotel smack in the centre of Copenhagen, where the other delegates would also stay. The reason suggested to me was that it would be more convenient and make it easier to coordinate, if we all stayed in the same hotel. I saw it more clearly for what it was: a face-saving exercise, an attempt at co-option, given the government's till-then consistent policy of rejecting me out of hand. They were now offering me a luxury cage.

I was shortly to discover that my cynical feeling was accurate, that, far from repentant, the government had simply found a publicly useful way of fobbing us off with courtesy. And, that in the very hearing they had acquiesced to, they were about to deploy their strongest weapon yet: the full, draining, bureaucratic machinery of the state, arrayed in a circus tent.

I was given a forewarning of this returning hardness of heart when, within days, a disruptive quarrel over the venue broke out. The hearing was to go for one and a half days, over the weekend of the seventh and eighth of October, 1995. The first venue that had been suggested to us, at Odense, on the island of Funen, turned out not to be acceptable to the Greenlandic delegates. They argued, with perfect reason, that after the five-hour flight to Copenhagen, they ought not to have to do any further significant travelling once in Denmark. This was regrettable, as Odense was in a convenient central location for a large number of our members who live on the western side of the Great Belt, the waterway that separates Funen from Zealand to the east. The change of venue meant that many of our own people could not attend. The first fracture.

The next venue mooted was in suburban Copenhagen; but, among other things, this time it was just not big enough to accommodate the numbers expected to attend. Nor did the government see it as desirable to be at a location not right in the centre of the city, the seat of power.

Finally, after much wrangling, the venue selected was the National Circus Building in Copenhagen. By that time it seemed ironically, painfully appropriate, given the clowning about that we had already been through just to find a place to have our day in court. The universe has a dark sense of humour.

Were it the government's or God's sense of humour we were up against, we were not to be deterred by a circumstantial conspiracy to make the hearing look like a sideshow. The government officials might have seen themselves as ringmasters, cracking the whip; but we were not trained animals. We were not going to jump when they said jump! We were going to speak, and we were going to be heard, even under the big top.

* * * * * *

BEFORE I LEFT Australia, I prepared some nineteen pages of questions that I felt needed to be aired at the hearing, a meticulous catalogue of doubts and demands honed over years of frustration. I faxed them to Marius so that he could incorporate them into a single document along with the questions of the other delegates, a collective arsenal for our day in court.

After a brief hiccough on my trip over, when my luggage went astray at Heathrow, courtesy of British Airways—a mundane irritation that felt like an omen—I arrived pretty much on schedule in Copenhagen on Wednesday October 4. The grey autumnal light was familiar, a colour of memory. Marius was to have met me in Copenhagen and driven me to his home, one and a half hours outside of the capital, at Korsoer, for a couple of days of planning conferences. The evening of my arrival, however, I was not overly surprised to get a call from Marius at my hotel. Some patterns never change.

"Hello, Jeff. Look, I hope you don't mind; but, you see, I've managed to arrange an interview with *Jyllands Posten* for tonight. Would it be too bad of me to ask if you could catch the train to Korsoer and I can meet you at the station tomorrow?"

I may have sighed lightly inwardly, a breath of weariness, but acquiesced readily. I have known Marius long enough now to realize that, between a planning meeting and an opportunity to air our grievances publicly once again, it is no contest. Catching the public eye and ear is his major strength and has been of incalculable use to the association over the long years of struggle. To ask Marius to forego such an opportunity would have been equivalent to asking a sailor to ignore the wind. It is his element.

"I'll be on the first train tomorrow morning, Marius. Just be there, OK! Don't make any more plans for interviews before then." My voice carried a mock-sternness I didn't quite feel.

"Don't worry, I'll be there. It's just that this opportunity to talk again with the largest daily in the country..."

"Yes, Marius, I know, I know." I cut him off gently.

"And especially as it's Per Kanstrup. And I think it would be great for people to read about your part in the victory, working from the other side of the world."

"Couldn't all this wait till after the hearing? I'm still going to be pretty jetlagged tomorrow, Marius." A pause. "Oh, by the way, did you get my fax of questions for the hearing?"

"Oh, yeah, I did."

"Great. Well I'd like a little time to look over what other questions people want asked. Could I have a look at them tomorrow?"

Marius paused a moment and drew his breath in, a sound that conveyed hesitation. "Well, actually, Jeff, yours were the only questions submitted."

"What?" I could not believe my ears. The word was sharp in the quiet hotel room. After all this, were they sleepwalking to the finish line?

"Oh, hang on. No. That's right, Jens put in one or two as well."

"God, what's wrong with these people? Don't they think the hearing's important enough to prepare any questions for it? What, do they think it's a *fait accompli*? Well, I'll tell you what. If they think this is all a mere formality, they'll find it is just that: a *fait accompli* where the government walks all over us and screws us thoroughly to the floor. Bloody hell, Marius! Do you want them to go on writing history the way they wanted it to happen?"

"I guess not," Marius mumbled haltingly, chastened. Then he brightened up, his resilience irrepressible, and added blithely. "But I've set up a number of other interviews for when we get back to Copenhagen. I'll fill you in on all that when I see you tomorrow. Bye."

I looked bleary-eyed at the now dead telephone a few moments, said, "Good night, the irrepressible Marius," returned the set to its place, and wandered meanderingly over to my bed, the weight of the campaign and the journey heavy in my bones. I pulled on my pyjamas and fell between the crisp, cold sheets of the government-paid hotel.

"Well, at least I'm learning to let go," I mumbled into the pillow as I drifted off into a fitful and tiring sleep, my mind still churning with unanswered questions.

So, Thursday morning, I took the one-hour train ride through the damp Danish countryside to Korsoer, where Marius met me at the station, the untiring, ever-functioning repository of news and energy, a force of nature in a winter coat.

While we may have won a victory in principle, the deep sadness and personal tragedy of it all remained, a shadow beneath the surface of our business. Marius's first words, after our greeting, were not of strategy, but of loss.

"Anker Sønnichsen is seriously ill and might not last beyond the weekend."

* * * * * *

ANKER, WHO HAD been scheduled to replace me in my position with the DCC after I decided to leave Thule and move to Australia, was suffering from the same cancer I am, a thing called Barrett's Oesophagus. The symmetry was cruel.

The first indication that something was awry came only in September 1994, when Anker started complaining of a persistent hoarseness. The throat specialist advised him it was nothing, a common irritation. A month and ten kilos in weight-loss later, a more gaunt Anker visited his specialist again, who now prescribed a simple spray for his throat. On his third visit, his specialist, still baffled or indifferent, referred Anker to a speech therapist. The system was treating a symptom, blind to the cause.

It was not until January 1995, upon Anker's own dogged insistence, that he was finally admitted to hospital and biopsies taken of his throat. Then the truth, ugly and undeniable, came to light.

Less lucky than I, it had not been possible to check the illness's progress because it had not been detected in time—the time wasted on sprays and speech exercises. Anker was by then not even able to swallow his own saliva and, by the time of the hearing, things having moved with a shocking, ravaging rapidity, he relied on oxygen and intravenous feeding in a hospital bed to stay alive. A strong man reduced to tubes and whispers.

I spoke to his wife, Jette, on the phone when we reached Christel and Marius' house at Korsoer. Her voice sounded steady, though weary with the awful patience of waiting. Waiting for the news she now knew would never come: that Anker would recover.

"Hello, Jeff, thanks so much for calling. Well, actually, Anker's condition has improved over the last couple of days. Hmm, yes. It is good news. Yes, well, they're discharging him from the hospital tomorrow. Yes, we're having a room in the house fitted out with oxygen and all the equipment necessary to keep Anker alive. No, Jeff, he hasn't yet been told how serious his condition is. He doesn't know how little time he has left to live." Her voice broke slightly on the last sentence, then firmed again. She was protecting him to the end.

Anker died two days after the hearing. He was fifty-eight.

R.I.P. Anker. Another name on the list the government did not keep.

* * * * * *

I JOINED MARIUS for the interview with Per, the journalist from *Jyllands Posten*. It was always a relaxed, professional affair talking with one of the country's leading feature writers, even though his paper had for years been one of our subtle enemies in the battle, having chosen largely to take the side of the Risoe establishment, preferring official certainty to messy doubt.

This time it was over a pleasant lunch provided by Christel. A typical Danish smorgasbord was laid out with generous abundance: a wide range of cold cuts, herring, cheeses, and warm dishes. My pleasure was confined mainly to the eye and the smell, as my own condition constrains me from eating more than a sparrow's share at any one time. I was also reticent in the interview itself, merely contenting myself with listening and, where possible, subtly modulating any of Marius' more extravagant or optimistic phrases, keeping the tone firm, factual, undeluded.

After lunch, as I bid farewell to Christel, she smiled a tired, knowing smile and, jerking her thumb toward Marius, who was still engaged deeply with Per, joked, "The only thing that will outlast Marius' appetite for the media is this contaminated waste stuff itself."

"If that!" I laughed, gave her a hug, and dragged Marius away. He had to bring Per with us in the car, however, who we dropped off at the ferry to return to Funen, his notebook full.

We then drove straight on to Copenhagen where Marius had us booked up for a second round of press interviews. As it turned out, I was of more interest to the newsmen at that point, as

Marius had had about all the exposure the public could take; they needed a new face, a new quarry from the Antipodes. The interviews, though taking all the afternoon and sapping all my residual energy, went well enough: I was careful, measured, and pointed. I looked forward to reading the evening editions to see what I had actually said, and what had been made of it.

By that time, the jet lag was hitting in severely, a leaden fatigue behind the eyes, so Marius left me in Copenhagen at my 5-Star retreat and rushed back to Korsoer. He somehow managed to conduct several more interviews with radio and television stations in I-do-not-know-precicely-what towns on the way home. Sometimes I just have to take a step backwards and shake my head in wonder at that whirlwind of a man, a phenomenon of pure, driven persistence.

I had scarcely arrived in my room, I had not even set down my jacket, which still draped over my arm, when a slim, professionally bound volume on the desk caught my eye. Not big enough to be Gideon's Bible, I wondered what courtesy the government had left for me. I gave the hastily prepared volume a quick perusal and I could hardly believe that my eyes were reading the words I saw there. It was a cold plunge into bad faith.

The book contained Professor Halberg Bechmann's much-anticipated "assessment" of the questionnaires he had sent to our members some months previous. The result was as bad, as insultingly contrived, as I had initially feared. True to his word, Bechmann had used, as a control group against which to compare our members, a small sample of bank tellers, twelve to be precise, who had been exposed to armed robbery! The comparison was so absurd, so transparent in its intent to psychologize our physical suffering, that it took my breath away. My immediate reaction was to wonder if I might not from that moment serve as a comparison group of one—one sensible but tenacious ex-Dane who had been exposed to unarmed flummery and state-sponsored bullying. From where I stood, without moving, I pressed the volume solidly, urgently, and ungently against the opposite wall of my hotel room. It hit with a satisfying thud and slid to the floor. A petty, necessary gesture.

Friday morning: Marius picked me up and we drove to Anders Boelskifte's downtown legal suite. At last, I thought, down to some of the real business! Most members of the association's board were present, as was Anders himself. Anders had arranged a repast of coffee and *wienerbrød* (a variety of rich, sweet pastries), which I normally love but which I could not look at; having been ill already after my light breakfast at the hotel. I could barely even glance at the food without feeling a wave of nausea, my body rebelling against the stress and the latent sickness within me.

All that meeting lacked, to my growing dismay, to complete the resemblance to a distracted five-year-old's birthday party were paper hats and a clown. I looked on at what was more a series of minor squabbles over trivialities than a serious discussion of tactics for an association that had, against all odds, brought a howling and screaming Danish government to the parley table. The smell of potential money, of imminent closure, had turned even the soberest heads giddy; and, after nearly two hours of scratching the same itch, I intervened and suggested, with forced calm, that lunch be taken. I ate part of an open-faced sandwich for sustenance, but abstained from the beer everyone else was enjoying, realizing that I would need a crystal-clear head for the fray, especially after the others had dimmed their own with a drink or two.

The ghosts of the dead, however, again declined to partake of the repast: theirs is a different hunger, one that cannot be sated by smørrebrød.

Lunch was jolly and easy, and there was no shortage of casual, often black-humoured anecdote relating to the case flying around. In the afterglow of the bonhomie supplied by the beer and badinage, I felt in a position to suggest that the crucial job of preparing and refining the questions for the hearing was really a task for a smaller, focused task force of two or three persons. The larger meeting nodded in vague agreement to this and, my guess is with some relief, retired to continue the more popular tasks of comparing medical symptoms and relating grandiose, improbable plans for how they would spend the compensation money that hovered like a mirage on the horizon.

* * * * * *

"A PREJUDICE IS a self-fulfilling prophecy." Anders nodded gravely, the index fingers of each hand steepled together as if to support his lips and the weight of his statement. The three of us—Anders, Jens Zinglersen (now a farmer in Jutland and a prominent, steadfast board member of the Thule Association), and myself—had retired to Anders' quieter office at the nearby Organisation for Information on Nuclear Energy, to finally put together the questions and the basic framework of our attack for the following day. Anders caught me looking up at him somewhat askew from the Bechmann report I was flipping through with disgust, and broke into his customary muted, wheezing laugh.

"Struth, a hackneyed saw if ever there was one," I remarked and, sighing, dumped the offensive volume on his desk as if it were soiled.

"Maybe," he acknowledged, his eyes twinkling, "But it has a point; in fact several. In which case it would be a hacksaw. Ha ha ha!"

Anders is a tall, lithe, and still athletic man, having reached his mid-thirties without any of the disastrous physical incidents that usually attend the youthful years of those engaged in sports like pole vaulting and soccer—pursuits he had followed in addition to the unstinting pursuit of his high ideals. He could be mistaken for nothing if not a Dane on account of his shock of blond hair and striking Viking features: fierce steel-grey eyes, sensuous lips, and outrageously well-formed cheeks and chin. He looked the gentle brute he most assuredly was not, as he demonstrated in his totally unself-conscious sense of the absurd. He was the Thule Association's legal representative, our shield and our strategist.

I could hardly help but join in Anders' amusement at his pun. Jens, on the other hand, did manage that feat, his face a mask of preoccupation. Anders, in response to the abstracted intensity of Jens' visage, was tempted into a yet further foray into wordplay, a defence against despair.

"Our little gnome looks particularly gnomic this afternoon." His pen played a light tattoo on the papers in his hand and his eyebrows rose playfully. I screwed up my eyes in simulated pain, expecting more of the same verbal gymnastics. Jens recovered from his brown study and looked from Anders to me, not amused.

"I'll leave the maxim seeking to the expert," he said dryly.

"And I will seek to the maximum," laughed Anders, undeterred.

"Look, I'm really concerned about tomorrow's hearing." Jens's voice was low, urgent. He seemed a little irritated at Anders' light-heartedness. Jens's sense of humour was spent upon satire and irony, and he always turned authentically grave in the presence of serious, imminent matter.

"They're trying to write us off as a bunch of malingering troublemakers," he went on, leaning forward. "Or hypochondriacs, at best. Do you realize that the other members of the board are pretty well unanimous for throwing in the towel? Johanne and Gerda feel it's interfered enough in their lives, and would be happy to let it all go at this stage. Even Mogens has just about had it up to the eyebrows with this thankless task. And I swear, little believable as it is, that Marius himself looks like a man who could well do himself a favour and throw in the towel. Game, set and match. They feel completely out-manoeuvred, they reckon, and they just don't have the heart to go on with a struggle that brings no rewards and only slaps on the face and heartache. And I feel pretty much the same way." The confession hung in the air, heavy with the fatigue of years.

The smile did not fade from Anders' lips as he answered Jens, but it softened, became knowing. "Hey, we're concerned too, Jens. Deeply. But, the last thing we want to happen is they grind us down so we lose our sense of humour. Humour is the reverse of the coin of anger. It's what keeps the coin in the air."

Jens looked a moment blankly at Anders and then, out of nowhere, his inner Mr. Pecksniff—a persona of elaborate, theatrical sincerity—returned for our entertainment and edification. "No doubt, my dear chaps, our mistaken and ignorant opposition, may the good Lord forgive them, poor blind creatures, are this very moment celebrating our imminent downfall. Shall we surprise them?" His eyes glittered with a sudden, mischievous fire.

Suddenly he was on his feet in one of those electric moves that at times gave me the odd sensation that Jens was like one of those little cartoon sequences sometimes drawn in the top margins of a book and animated by flicking through the pages. He seemed to go from sitting to striding up and down the cramped office in just two or three flicks. As he moved around the room like a wound-up toy, he gave the impression of having overcome a considerable inertia: Jens was on the move, anger transmuting into energy.

"I'd like to think we could, Jens," said Anders, his tone now wholly serious. "The problem is that now the government has only to point to this piece of pseudo-scientific trash," he held aloft the volume I had thrust upon the desk, "which they can, in the absence of any counter-report that would hold similar authority in the eyes of the public, use to legitimize their position. Put that together with the pathetically limited medical examinations they conducted on the guys, and together they add up to pretty damning evidence *against* us. Bechmann's report faintly recognises that several ex-Thulers exhibit high levels of stress; and it's that very faintness, that lack of concrete physical diagnosis, that saves their bacon and cuts our throats. The Department of Health is going to have a field day with us. I don't know what it is, yet, Jens, but we have to find some other strategy to keep at them, or else come up with something extraordinary between now and tomorrow morning."

"Extraordinary? Like what?" Jens stopped pacing, his hands spread.

"You tell me! Jeez, I don't know. Maybe,... Maybe something that would undermine their cockiness a bit, like, say, a sex scandal or something distinctly illegal in their proceedings with us. I don't know, Jens, to be honest. They've really got me bluffed this time. Well, Jeff, what do you reckon?"

I had been listening and considering intently, turning the problem over in my mind, looking for the crack in their armour.

"Well," I said, slowly, "Wouldn't we all like to find a sex scandal in our stockings at Christmas! But, it's not going to happen, is it? We have to fight with the tools we have, not the ones we wish for."

I considered quietly another moment, the silence punctuated by the distant hum of Copenhagen traffic.

"We ignore this Bechmann rubbish. We dismiss it outright. It's as simple as that. We *know* this investigation is a worthless piece of baloney, a constructed narrative. It's as obvious as the nose on your face. But, whether the experts on the government panel could be made to see that physical protuberance, let alone be persuaded to blow it, is another matter. I just hope they can."

I paused for breath, gathering my thoughts. I had plenty more to say, the arguments forged in years of solitary study and correspondence.

"I think we have to insist, loudly and repeatedly, on this book being shoddy and inadmissible as serious evidence. We have to keep hammering at the pathetic, designed-to-fail way in which the medical examinations were conducted. We have to insist on our own doctors' reports, the ones that show real damage, being admissible as counter-evidence. We have to keep reminding the panel that not just now, but even back in 1968, the dangers of exposure to alpha-emitting particles like plutonium were recognised in the scientific literature. We've got to keep reminding them that, whatever soothing stories our allies over the pond may tell, hundreds of Danish civilians were exposed to contaminated waste, repeatedly and for extended periods of time. Danes collected the hot, twisted metal from the crash site with their hands, loaded it onto trucks for removal, worked around that toxic tank farm for days on end, walking around in the radioactive slush from the melting ice. And, in my own case, I can testify that I personally handled the very bombs themselves, the broken physics packages. We have to make them *see* that, not just hear about abstract 'exposures'."

Anders had by now sat back in his swivel-chair with one ankle resting on the opposite knee, and was spinning his pen into the air repeatedly; sometimes catching it, mostly dropping it in his lap. This action, I had learned, indicated his most intense listening attitude.

"Absolutely, Jeff," he said, the pen falling forgotten. "Our only course is to insist and insist and insist. Our greatest weapon remains, of course, the very fact of this hearing being called at all. It is a monumental admission. We have to make sure that they don't manage somehow to turn this very public event into yet another, more sophisticated effort at a cover-up. All these questions have to be asked, Jeff. We may never get another opportunity like this. And, at every step of the way, we have to be alert, ready to query every statement—*when it is made*—that contradicts our version or that is not of the highest scientific probity. We know we have justice and truth on our side. We have to show by our constant, informed intervention that we are convinced of that. After all, gents," he said, looking from Jens to me, a fierce grin returning, "it's *your* hearing, not theirs! They're just the reluctant hosts."

Three hours later, and the three of us had fairly well outlined our strategy and had determined on the necessary, piercing questions to be asked. The desk was a landscape of scribbled notes, underlined phrases, and coffee stains.

Anders looked up at me blearily from his block of note paper, by now covered in a dense thicket of scribbles and arrows. "I feel so fresh," he shook his head in tiny, exhausted oscillations, and the three of us burst into laughter, the release of tension. "Look, I'll spend the rest of the night getting these notes up into a more polished, formidable form. It should only take two or three hours. You guys may as well take off now, get what rest you can."

"School's out!" joked Jens and, with a wave, disappeared out the door to whatever appointment or solitary preparation he had for that evening.

"You don't have to tell him twice, do you?" I laughed, watching him go.

"Not even once!" assented Anders with the widest, most exhausted grin I've ever seen on the face of a lawman east of the Pecos or west of the Øresund.

As I left his office, I felt that, of these last-minute manoeuvres, the ghosts of the dead—Anker, the others—would have approved. We were still fighting.

* * * * * *

THE EARLIER PART of that evening I spent in the precious, normalizing company of my two sisters: Hanne, who had travelled in from Jutland with Flemming to visit me and to attend the hearing; and Paula, who lives in Copenhagen. I was able then to have a simple dinner with at least part of my family, not having time to get down to Jutland to visit them all. While it was, as always, an enjoyable and heartening reunion, my mind was continually reverting to the morrow's proceedings, darting back like a compass needle to magnetic north.

Having been largely responsible for things coming as far as they had, I could not rest at this moment just before the final climacteric. The weight of authorship was upon me. Besides which, I was constrained to attend a final, late meeting with the full board at the hotel at ten o'clock that same night. That meeting consisted primarily in my calming frayed nerves and reassuring other members that, however it might go tomorrow, whatever the immediate outcome, whatever clever trap the opposition might spring, whether we were going to be rhetorically shafted or not, the central, monumental issue had already been decided: the government had accepted liability. We were in the right and they had been in the wrong. That letter from 1957 had seen to that. No circus hearing could erase that fact. We had already pushed the rock over the crest; tomorrow was just about managing its descent.

* * * * * *

FINALLY, THE MAGICAL day arrived: the day of the hearing. The day the Danish government would, we dared hope, plead guilty, say it was sorry, and hand out adequate compensation. The day the rock would finally land, and we could stop pushing.

Or am I being prematurely ironic? A lifetime of bureaucratic disappointment had taught me to armor hope with skepticism.

Early Saturday morning was filled with even more preparatory meetings of the board; I was a largely mute attendant at these vain, circular meetings whose purpose seemed only to be for each board member to recount yet again how he or she would spend, invest, or give away his or her share of the booty that still existed only in theory. I put this all down to raw nerves, the giddiness before the plunge, and reserved my few comments to quietly assuring them of that charitable judgment. We then all proceeded through the crisp October air to the National Circus Building for the opening of the hearing at nine o'clock. The venue's name felt less like an irony and more like a diagnosis.

The tension was so high, so palpable in the lift lobbies and corridors of the hotel, that we were all perversely grateful to the government for at least one thing: that our luxury hotel was located within easy walking distance of the venue. No one's nerves could have handled a traffic jam.

To feel disoriented in an unfamiliar place is an uncomfortable and scary thing: to feel familiar scenes as though you had entered into the perceptions of a stranger whilst retaining your own memories is significantly eerie. That morning, Copenhagen itself felt unreal. It was as if everything was normal except that the sky was green or that everyone you passed in the street was wearing clothes one size too large for them. It is not something you can easily share or comment on to your neighbour except to say, perhaps, 'Boy, am I nervous!' And so we did, in muttered asides.

Lars Nordskov Nielsen, who was appointed to occupy the chair, was a powerful man: a doctor of jurisprudence and highly regarded in legal and parliamentary circles, he had been, till his retirement some years before, the Parliamentary Ombudsman (not the one I had famously harassed). His presence was meant to convey gravitas and impartiality. The Minister for Health was represented on the panel by Tommy Dinesen, a key parliamentarian who had been a long-time, vocal supporter of our cause. His familiar, earnest face helped to relax the tension a little, a lone ally in the fortress.

The government, however, had taken its careful, calculated measures to control the outcome of the proceedings. One measure was to have on the panel a selection of the very scientists from Risoe, of unhappy memory, who had for so many years made themselves our unofficial opposition. In addition, there was a sprinkling of the doctors from the supposedly independent medical inquiry of farcical memory—including the ridiculous Dr. Kay-Ole Larsen—several parliamentarians, a fairly large delegation representing the Greenlanders living in the affected areas, a few members of our association, and a few from Ole and Sally Markussen's original little splinter group. Dr. Hans Henrik Storm represented the Danish Anti-Cancer Council, while a small number of Norwegian and Swedish experts completed the picture. Twenty-three persons in all; of whom thirteen were already tainted with Risoe connections or state allegiance, and only two of whom directly represented the association that had forced the government's hand. The arithmetic was not encouraging.

Ole Markussen had already passed away by this time, so his group was represented principally by Sally, now in perpetual widow's weeds. Her attack strategy over the two days of the hearing—a tactic of utter secrecy veiled in impenetrable silence—led her to decline to ask a single question or to make any other contribution to the proceedings whatsoever. She was a monument to private grief and public inscrutability.

On Ole's death, Sally had had several of his internal organs removed for later examination. These she kept stored in a collection of glass jars in her lounge room, like grotesque preserves. It seems that she looks forward to the day when science will have discovered methods for testing the pickled parts for radiation. The overall impression she gave would leave Morticia Addams looking normal, well-adjusted, and not in the least funny. She was tragedy turned gothic.

A photo of Sally illustrates an interview she gave with a women's magazine since the hearing. It shows her propped up in her lounge-room like a dusty relic of the sixties, hair piled high on her head, and surrounded by her late de-facto's pickled innards. In it, she revealed that Ole had fathered an illegitimate child of whose existence she had known nothing, till the government informed her that she would have to share whatever compensation might come her way with this child. The absurdity of it all—the jars, the secret child, the bitter fight over future money—was almost Shakespearian.

It is generally felt that Ole may consequently find himself consigned to the attic, the broom-closet, or the garbage-bin, as a result. However that may be, he has joined the company of the silent presences at the table. For, I'm sure the ghosts, just as they have sat at the dinner tables of the yet-living members of the association, attended the hearing in as great a number as the living. Anker, and all the others, were there in the empty chairs.

I would only with great reluctance suggest that the government did all it could to influence the outcome of the hearing by loading the jury; reluctantly would I aver that such would be an act unworthy of a democratic regime; and reluctantly would I compare it to Uncle Joe's Show Trials of the thirties.

But I must. The parallels were too stark to ignore.

The setup of the hall was itself a masterclass in controlled discourse. The entire official group was ranged in a vast horseshoe, the experts facing the panel that was to ask them the questions, with the parliamentarians and the Greenlanders seated in between. A solitary podium sat at the open end of the horseshoe, a great distance from the audience seats. It was a layout designed for pronouncements, not conversations.

This setup was no accident; the government wanted to ensure that as little genuine debate as possible actually took place. Debate would involve spontaneous exchanges of opinions and data, perhaps truthful, damning interchanges between persons; and this had to be avoided at all costs!

The geography of the hall ensured that few from the floor would be encouraged, or even able, to ask questions of the panel. The message was clear: you will listen; we will speak.

Of course, I am wrong to suggest that the Royal Danish Government would be so distasteful as to rig the hearing so blatantly. Perish the thought.

That they flew in a large number of Greenlanders, most of whom had not personally been exposed to the plutonium or uranium or other toxic substances at the crash site, is of no consequence, I'm sure. It would be distasteful on my part, naturally, to suggest that the hearing was thus skewed in any way toward a politically convenient outcome, that the hearing was, in effect, hijacked to serve a different narrative. To suggest that a disproportionate representation of Greenlanders was a deliberate tactic used by the government to shift the focus of the hearing from justice for specific Danish workers to a broader, vaguer, and more manageable propaganda exercise on behalf of an ethnic minority would, well, I say again, be distasteful.

So, it is better to pass over the matter in silence and wonder, and let the truth speak for itself as the hearing gets under way. Let the proceedings reveal their own nature.

In the meantime, then, under the big top, let the circus begin.

* * * * * *

THE HEARING WAS divided into four main parts for as many issues, each of which was introduced by two persons. The inquiry was opened by the chairman, his voice dry and precise, who stated its purpose and the carefully delineated guidelines governing its powers and scope. The boundaries were set; the cage was closed.

Then, our own eloquent, steadfast Jens Zinglersen presented the first part. He sketched out the physical environment of the place where the crash occurred: the geography, the brutal climate, the condition of the ice and so on of Thule, setting the scene of the events so that the two days' discussions might have a context of concrete reality in which to rest. He spoke plainly, without flourish, and for a moment, the circus tent held the biting wind of North Star Bay.

Following Jens, Ole Walmod-Larsen from Risoe rose to take the stand, smoothing his jacket. His mandate was to give a rundown of the health precautions and checks in use at the time of the crash. As he adjusted the microphone, I caught sight of a flash of pink at his ankle and my eyes opened wide in sudden, vivid recollection. The pink socks. The man from the airport, all those years ago, with his ridiculous sartorial signal and his bland assurances. He was here, now, an official memory-keeper.

"At no time," finished Walmod-Larsen, his tone one of bureaucratic finality, "were Danish or Greenlander civilians allowed within the zero line. No Dane or Greenlander worked at the crash site or close to the radioactive wastes at the 'Tank Farm' that were being readied for transportation to the United States. All precautionary measures that were set in place were adhered to religiously. Moreover, the nasal swabs and urine samples that were continually being taken and tested for possible radioactive results yielded a comprehensive 'no' to the possibility of radiation poisoning among those workers."

The boos and mocking laughter from the auditorium, from the men who had *been* those workers, clearly expressed the raw incredulity with which these vague assertions and polished distortions were met. Following this expert's evidence there was to be a question time, but he spoke on and on in an expert filibuster, a river of reassuring jargon, till there only remained some three minutes of assigned time for questions to be put. The tactic was transparent.

This gambit quickly became the pattern of the day, as speaker after speaker spoke and spoke and spoke and, at the conclusion, looked at his watch with feigned surprise to exclaim, "I'm afraid there is only time for one or two brief questions."

Consequently, over the two days of the hearing, even I, positioned and persistent, managed only to get in about three or four questions. Dr. Troels Munckner alone of the specialists present, himself a specialist in nuclear medicine and a former employee of the Danish Anti-Cancer Council, showed a persistence equal to mine, a gadfly on the flank of the official beast.

Standing to deliver his queries in his immaculate sky-blue suit, his neat, Freudian whiskers framing a face of academic mildness, he seemed a ridiculous figure to some. Dr. Storm, head of the Anti-Cancer Council, was at the podium at the time and thrust a petulant jaw out when he saw Munckner rise, a bull seeing a matador.

"Dr. Munckner. You have a question?" enquired the chairman, his voice neutral.

"A number," Munckner answered unceremoniously, and launched straight in, his face still directed toward the papers his fingers lightly touched on the table before him, as if reading a shopping list of atrocities.

"Or rather," he began, "I have something more in the line of a demand."

Dr. Storm took a slug of water from the glass at the podium and his jaw stuck out even further as he swallowed, a gesture of theatrical irritation.

Neither looking up nor pausing to note the wrath that passed over Storm's face at his following words, Munckner remarked, "Don't do that, Doctor. It makes you look like a billy-goat. Now, it is a fact that the Anti-Cancer Council is refusing to release key information bearing on issues central to this hearing. I should like that information to be made available. Details of the relevant files are contained on this memo." He held high one of the sheets from the table and handed it to a page to pass to the chairman. "Let them be made available. Now, Dr. Storm."

By now, Storm was looking true to his name, a thundercloud of affronted authority. Munckner still did not pay him the courtesy of looking at him, intense on his remaining papers.

"Please confirm, if you will—for I know that you can—that doctors performing autopsies on deceased members of the Thule Association were directed by superiors to falsify their reports: that, if they found evidence of radiation—plutonium, for instance, in the corpses—they were to make no reference to it in their official findings."

Dr. Storm's jaw slackened, the theatrical anger replaced by something colder.

"Can you also confirm that at least two physicians who abided by this instruction were later found out, and that the authorities were embarrassed into sacking them?"

Dr. Storm put a hand to his jaw as if to manually stop it from falling any further. A vain attempt at control.

"Can you deny—I'm sure you will, but, really, you cannot—that any pathologist who refused the instruction was quickly moved into less attractive, dead-end positions as punishment? Difficult to prove in a court of law; easy to deny in a forum like this. I will not trouble the proceedings now with the evidence. But, I have it here, and it can be made available to any who wish it this afternoon."

Dr. Storm was visibly glad to see Dr. Munckner sit down, and was about to launch into his indignant reply, when Munckner popped up again like a Jack-in-the-Box and unceremoniously cut him off mid-breath.

"On a slightly different note, with regard to the composition of this very hearing." He paused and directed a conciliatory nod to the Greenlander delegation. "I have no desire to deny that a number of local Inuit were deeply affected by the incident which has brought us all here today so many years later. For which, naturally, it is right that they should seek equal justice to that sought by the Danes who were involved.

"However." Once more he paused and looked down at his notebook, which indicated clearly enough to all present, Dr. Storm included, that he was once more addressing the hapless speaker at the podium. "However, it is obvious that the panel is overloaded, in terms of raw numbers, with representatives of the affected Greenlanders. To do equal justice to the Danes affected, the panel would need at least another hundred and seventy members. That would make it unwieldy. However, I mention the number only in order to make the point that the panel—once more with my apologies to the Greenlanders present—has been stacked so as to yield a political rather than a social and just outcome."

With that, he sat down again; this time to an outbreak of applause and muffled 'hear hears' from the floor. A moment later, he rose yet again and added, as an aside, "I no longer work at the Council." And sat down a third and final time.

Dr. Storm denied everything short of having personally sunk the Titanic (which, now I come to think of it…!) and abruptly left the podium for what one presumed was a much heavier drink of water.

Notwithstanding such satisfying, explosive interludes, by the end of it all, I felt rather like the little terrier in the cartoon, teeth clamped tenaciously onto the tail of a huge, indifferent, and unfeeling adversary who barely notices the weight. One of my own questions, when I finally wrestled the moment, raised a visible grunt of discomfort from the blimpish opposition.

"Why," I asked, my voice carrying clearly in the sudden quiet, "has neither the Danish Government nor the Danish Atomic Energy Commission attempted to gain any of the easily available information regarding the legal action brought in the United States by a similar group to our own, representing the soldiers and civilians of that country involved in the clean up? Nor attempted to get hold of any of the documents relating to the Crested Ice disaster held by the US government. If they had wanted to find out any of this, they could have: after all, I did, and I was working alone, as a single private citizen with no budget, from the other side of the world."

My question was prompted by the clear, glaring indications in every report and statement issued by those two accused bodies that I had ever seen, that they professed to have no knowledge of the transatlantic developments with regard to this same affair; nor any idea of what Washington held in its vaults. I wondered out loud how it was that a large, well-funded government bureaucracy apparently lacked the resources or will to find out such obtainable information, when I, with a phone, a fax machine, and stubbornness, had had no trouble in tracking it down. The implication of willful ignorance hung in the air.

The response from the official side was very hostile, a bristling of shoulders and tightening of lips. Everyone understood the import of my question: I did, the panel did, the audience did, the pirate and his parrot could have. It was an accusation of bad faith.

But I got no joy where there was no shame. The answer was a muddle of procedural excuses and implied that my sources were likely unreliable. The stone wall remained, just better dressed.

Moving on from the circumstances of the crash and the fact of subsequent health problems, there came a long set of presentations of the scientific analyses of the possible causes of those problems. This was where the battle would be won or lost, in the realm of probability and causation.

The scientific community, despite its record of astounding discoveries of seismic consequence over the past couple of hundred years, is not given to making premature or sensational claims. It is known for its caution, its collective self-scrutiny, its reverence for the qualified 'maybe'. However, even given this natural and admirable professional carefulness, it was profoundly disappointing to watch some experts shy away from any shade of definitive statement that might help us, and deeply distressing to see others of that community toe a clearly party-political line with naked abandon.

Professor Hugh Zacharia, throughout the world an acknowledged expert in rare skin diseases, from whom I for one had expected great things, went to water in the event. Faced with the imposing horseshoe of officialdom, he was unwilling to make any strong statements about his own findings; despite them indicating that, from among the group of employees from Thule, an extremely high and statistically unexpected proportion had developed one or other of a number of very special, uncommon types of skin cancer.

Rather, he allowed himself to be grilled and intimidated by the Risoe contingent until eventually his tentative statements were submerged in a mire of quibbles about statistical significance, methodological purity, and 'precipitate inappropriateness'. 'Wait and see' became his muffled cry: a 'wait and see' that did not imply his own death from such and such a cancer, but that might imply a safe, breakthrough paper at some sunny medical conference in Bermuda early in the next century, when the last of the Ex-Thulers was safely dead and silent, and the political heat had dissipated.

* * * * * *

WHEN THE PROFESSOR of psychology at Odense University got up to deliver his specialist opinion based on the results of his questionnaire as outlined in his book, I gazed keenly upon his long, solemn, self-important visage and chewed my bottom lip. Halberg Bechmann lived to tell his grandchildren of that day, but whether he will ever want to is another matter entirely.

The Professor had just outlined his procedures, his voice droning with academic detachment, when the first question issued from the panel. One of the Swedish experts, a man with a sharp, intelligent face, had his hand in the air.

"Do you mean to say," the Swede asked, his tone one of pure, clinical disbelief, "that you pitted a control group of twelve bank tellers against a study group of many hundreds of ex-Thule workers and found the mental stress profiles *comparable*? You found in favour of the twelve?"

"Did he really say, 'bank tellers'?" inquired another voice from the expert panel, laden with incredulity. "Was there a radiation leak at the bank? Or perhaps an armed robbery with alpha particles?"

"Ha, ha, ha!" echoed a titter that spread shyly up and down the auditorium, growing in volume. The author's neck began to turn a mottled red.

"Did the witness say he carried out this research over a period of six years?" asked one of Risoe's lackeys, feigning confusion, playing to the crowd.

"Six, er, months," stuttered out the now beetroot-coloured professor, his authority deflating like a punctured balloon.

"Six months! My God. What happened to the careful, longitudinal assessment over thirty years of supposed radiation-induced illness? This was meant to be the definitive psychological study, was it not?"

"Farce! It's a farce!" shouted a voice from the auditorium, no longer muffled.

"Boo! Boo! Booo!" began at the back and rumbled to the front of the National Circus Building in a growing thunder of derision that forced the Professor out from his place of safety behind the podium and sent him scuttling for cover somewhere behind the heavy backdrop to the main stage, a clown chased by his own absurdity.

To some extent, even though the results of the study deserved nothing but studied derision, Halberg Bechmann suffered too from the built-up, explosive frustration of all the participants on both sides at the hearing, who happily used him as a collective whipping-boy. I felt we were lucky with this result, as the study could just as easily have been given a respectful, nodding hearing by our opposition, its flaws politely ignored. The crowd's visceral rejection was a small gift.

* * * * * *

THE EXPERTS IN general were very displeased at finding themselves so exposed in this manner; especially given the savaging of our chief psychologist from Odense. It turned into a situation where those giving evidence were made to feel as if they were being judged by a jury of their professional peers *and* the rabble: something like a scientific Star Chamber held in a public square.

Nor was it possible in this context to play their usual games of hide and seem: to hide behind their learned papers and technical jargon before an audience of their colleagues who would then ask polite, scientific, and safe questions, gently nudging them out into the open only so far. This was different.

This was a calling to account of the scientific community before the people they were supposed to serve, to answer for the social and human consequences of their search for knowledge, and for their silence. And many of them came out of it looking a pretty sorry lot, caught between truth and power.

And so it went for the experts on both sides. H. L. Gjoerup, one of the chief scientific whitewashers sent to Thule in January 1968, and a key opponent, must have had a premonition of the likely reception he would be given. He had been busily tiring the readers of our dailies with his disputatious letters for some months before the hearing, defending the indefensible. He refused to participate in it when the opportunity was given him. At one stage he had accused the association of ruining his peaceful retirement by our constant questioning of his professional views. I had indeed responded quite keenly in kind, my letter published in the same paper:

Dear sirs,

I refer to the letter printed in these columns yesterday from one H. L. Gjoerup, wherein he brands as malingerers the men of Thule who claim they are sick on account of their participation in the nuclear accident clean up operation there in 1968. Everyone is familiar with many of the details of that incident, so I will merely remark that, it seems that your correspondent believes that the only good malingerer is a dead one.

Well, he will be ecstatic then, when informed that a great number of those indigent troublemakers are indeed well and truly dead.

Some four hundred, average age 46, good malingerers, because dead, dead of malingering.

Thank you, Professor, for your insights into truth, justice and compassion.

J. Carswell
Melbourne, Australia

Although he did not participate in the hearing, I did see him there, sitting safely amongst the audience, protecting his anonymity, the anonymous coward I knew him to be, observing the damage control operation.

The basic, repeated position of the experts who opposed us was that plutonium was not dangerous unless inhaled. This is because it emits mainly the largish alpha particles which do not penetrate the skin as do X- and gamma-rays. If any adhered to your clothes, you only had to brush it off; and the dangers vanished with it. A theory neat, clean, and utterly divorced from the reality of men working in howling winds, melting ice, and clouds of vaporized debris.

Laughter, bitter and knowing, was heard throughout the auditorium when Mogens Boesen stood up and with a grave, deadpan demeanour asked whether it could be confirmed for him that an instruction had been issued on the base to the effect that 'thou shalt not breathe while on the ice or anywhere else on the base.' In any case, he added, when brushing invisible particles off the clothing in an Arctic gale, inhaling some can scarcely be entirely avoided. The laughter was a release of pent-up fury at the absurdity of the official fairy tale.

And the show went on. Lengthy, draining discussions into the circumstances of the crash, the level of contamination, the hypothetical dangers and so on and so on. The only new, chilling thing that emerged came, surprisingly enough, from the Greenlandic delegation. One of their representatives informed a suddenly silent auditorium that, of the healthy sled dogs that had been used to go into the crash site directly after the plane came down, the first to die died the next day. The rest died over the following few weeks; till not one remained alive. A whole pack, wiped out.

Well, dogs die. That's life. Even healthy dogs die; even dogs bred for that harsh environment die. But, *every single one* of them? ... The *day after*? ... No dangers? ... Open-mouthed disbelief settled even among those of us who knew and accepted the grim facts. Several questions that immediately irrupted in the hall are still left unanswered: such as, whether the dogs had been examined, and where might their bodies be today? The silence that followed was louder than any applause.

The Saturday sitting of the hearing went well beyond its six o'clock closing time, stretching into the evening. We finished up at seven-thirty, minds numb, and immediately convened for a provided dinner in an adjoining hall, a surreal transition from conflict to cutlery.

I found myself at dinner opposite the aging and very sick Henning Thorup, his face drawn with pain. He leaned carefully over the table to me and spoke, his voice a thin rasp.

"I find it incredible," he said, "that you could travel to the US and come up with a whole bunch of 'top secret' documents when the entire Danish authorities couldn't find their own fly-buttons with both hands."

He shook his head carefully and slowly so as not to aggravate the pain the tumours in his neck caused him. He paused a moment longer as if considering the sheer, monumental mendacity of the Danish officials in its full, darkness. He went on.

"I also suffered the ministrations of Doctor Kay-Ole Larsen at Aarhus. Just like you, they tapped my knee and asked for a specimen. I almost handed over my rabbit's foot. It would have been as useful."

I smiled at Henning's grim joke, but had few words for him. I could only reflect to myself on the bitter, circular irony that, what life he had left to him at that point, was being prolonged by the very thing that likely sickened him: radiation therapy to fight his tumours. Radiation to fight radiation. What a perfect, hellish state of affairs!

After my meagre meal, I took the time to seek out Dr. Storm, as I had a specific, pointed query to put to him. I found him over his dessert, a large slice of flan. In my hand I held an excerpt from the official report tabled by the Health Minister, outlining the results of the medical examinations conducted on our members. My name was notably absent.

"Doctor Storm?" I stood directly behind his chair as I addressed him, forcing him to twist about uncomfortably, his spoon hovering.

"Hmm?" His mouth was full of flan.

"I am Jeff Carswell."

"Uh huh." He swallowed, not offering a chair.

"Can you explain to me," I said, keeping my voice level, "why it is that the results of the medical examination I underwent in Aarhus do not figure in the statistics here? I was examined. I have the paperwork."

"Mr. Carswell," he said, shaking his jowls at me with disapproval, as if I were a naughty student. "You do not live in Denmark. You are not a resident. So, of course you do not figure in the *Danish* statistics!" he concluded, as if explaining something simple to a child, and turned his broad back on me to refill his cavernous mouth with flan. Dismissed.

As I moved off, fuming at the blunt illogic of it—the accident happened on Danish soil, I was a Danish citizen working there—an unwelcome shape obtruded into my path. The still-youthful, unlined figure of Dr. Kay-Ole Larsen swam smilingly into view. I stopped and frowned at it.

"Mr. Carswell. You remember me, I suppose?" His smile was unctuous, a professional display of benevolence.

"You suppose," I answered noncommittally. "And what else do you suppose?"

"That you're wondering why I should seek you out, when everyone else seems to be avoiding you. You are getting quite a reputation, you know." His smiling was like a disease spread over his face, immune to hostility. I kept looking at it and then looking away with physical distaste.

"I just wanted to say, Mr. Carswell, about that examination back at Aarhus. Well, how can I put it? I guess I just want to say that, well, we all learn over time, don't we? Methods improve. Understanding deepens." Then he skittered off, leaving me open-mouthed and nonplussed. Was that an apology? A disclaimer? A mere platitude? It was nothing, and it was infuriating.

I had not recovered from this weird encounter when I spotted Halberg Bechmann sidling up to me—how can I put it?—sheepishly, almost tearfully, to discuss his public whipping.

He smiled like a nine-day-old cadaver and spoke, his voice conciliatory: "Today went quite well, don't you think, Mr. Carswell? A robust exchange."

I looked at him blankly, unable to fathom the depth of his self-delusion.

"I suppose my conclusions were a little unexpected to the layman." He repeated his rigor mortis grin, seeking some form of academic solidarity.

"It wasn't the laymen calling you a farcical fool out there today," I replied curtly. "It was your fellow scientists."

"Oh, that!" He waved a dismissive hand. "Just a little interdisciplinary leg-pulling. You know, academics have their little ways. It's all part of the peer review process, in a way."

I scratched my neck with the expression of a dog beset by a persistent, stupid flea, said, "Very little!" and walked away, leaving him to his ruined dignity.

What a sight: a trained psychologist, an expert in the human mind, struggling there in the corner of a banquet hall to come to terms with a profound public humiliation, and to emerge from it with some vestige of professional pride. A vain struggle against the obvious verdict of the crowd, and of common sense.

* * * * * *

AS I MADE my way out of the dining hall, the clatter of cutlery and murmur of voices a dull roar in my ears, I brushed past a lady of about forty years of age. She was in quietly intense conversation with Dr. Joergen Winther, a conservative parliamentarian and member of the Danish opposition. Her posture was taut, leaning forward as if against a wind.

I thought to merely throw the Doctor a humorless grin of recognition—a fellow player in this tedious farce—and be on my weary way, except I overheard the lady hiss out, "Well, aren't you a doctor? A man of science?" To my astonishment, she threw out her hand and detained me by the shoulder with the words, "Please, Mr. Carswell… It is Mr. Carswell, isn't it? Do you mind giving the Doctor and me a few moments of your time?"

I then recognised her from the association's meetings as the determined and outspoken daughter of Finn Pettersen, R.I.P. 1970, aet. 45, from cancer. Ms. Pettersen threw a seductive, challenging smile at Doctor Winther, who merely froze her out with a stare into the middle of the vacant dance floor, as if studying a fascinating void. I acquiesced, curiosity cutting through my fatigue, and the lady went on with her quiet, relentless talking.

"As a doctor, Dr. Winther," she began again, her voice low but precise, "can you not explain to me why there has been no mention made at the hearing—not a whisper—that the men we are all talking about were in their physical prime, between twenty and forty, mostly closer to twenty, and that, just to get on the base, each had to undergo a thorough and much expanded medical examination? They were certified fit. The fittest of the fit. And now they are dying, decades early. How does your medical training reconcile that?"

The doctor's reply, had he more than the usual smattering of medical bastard Latin, and an awareness of the basic logic of precedence and consequence, he would himself have recognised as a textbook *non sequitur*. It was a dodge, not an answer.

"I do not know, madam," he began, his tone one of patronizing weariness. "But undoubtedly they were all smoking and drinking on the base. The lifestyle was... robust."

"Well, who doesn't?" the lady replied contemptuously, not giving an inch. "Do you think they were unique in that?"

"And they would all have been lonely," he continued, grasping at another straw, "away from their wives and children and familiar things. Stress of that nature..."

"They flew back home every nine months and could write and receive letters. So, that doesn't really stick, does it?" she shot back, her logic a cleaver. "My father wrote to us every week."

"Well, Ms. Pettersen," the doctor was clearly unsettled by the directness of the interrogation, his political polish wearing thin. "You must know that, if you don't even have, for example, a cat for a pet, the problem of loneliness can be greatly exacerbated. Companionship is a complex psychological need."

Ms. Pettersen's jaw dropped in perfect, horrified unison with mine. "You must be kidding me!" she let out emphatically, the words a slap. "A *cat*? You're blaming the absence of a *pet* for cancers that are killing men in their forties?"

"Well, that's the way it is, madam," he finished curtly with a shrug of the shoulders that dismissed thirty years of suffering, and walked off into the crowd, his dignity a shield against truth. We looked after him, she with a look of utter disbelief and dismay etched on her features, me with the alarming, sickening thought in my head, `My God, he's on our own steering committee! This man is meant to be fighting for us.'

We observed a few moments' stunned silence together, the noise of the dinner crowd swelling around us. Finally, Ms. Pettersen sighed, a sound of profound exhaustion, and spoke.

"I'm having a particularly bad evening."

"So I see," I said, my own voice flat.

"That's only half of it."

"Oh? Who else has turned the instant freeze on you?"

"Dr. Pink Socks."

"Who?" I asked, though I was sure I knew who she meant.

"Walmod-Larsen. The great vain baboon from Risoe."

I broke into a short, sharp laugh, the absurdity a relief. Ms. Pettersen recounted the event, her eyes flashing with remembered anger.

"Remember how Pink Socks," (I guffawed again at the nickname) "said that every time a person went out to the crash site, their signature had to be obtained on some official list? Proof of procedure? Well, during dinner, I thought I'd take the liberty of asking a few practical questions about this. I went and sat next to him, his neighbour having gone up to the buffet, and introduced myself.

"'Dr. Walmod-Larsen, my father was among those men who went out to the crash site. His name was Finn Pettersen. Could I see the list you mentioned today, just to check that his name is on it? For my own peace of mind.'

"'That is just not possible,' he said, not even looking at me. He didn't have the list with him, anyway, he said. I asked him if he could send me the list, or a copy. Not possible! If I gave him my name and phone number, would he at least call me and tell me whether my father's name is on the list? Not possible!"

She shook her head slowly, a gesture of defeat in the face of sheer, blank obstruction. "Why all this secrecy? There are no military secrets anymore, are there? The Cold War is over. Why can't a daughter have access to a piece of paper that might have her dead father's name on it? This doesn't make any sense at all. It makes me think the list doesn't exist. Or that his name isn't on it."

She wandered off sadly into the throng, and I continued on my own way to my next destination, the weight of her frustration added to my own. The walls of the state, it seemed, were not just stone, but endlessly receding mirrors.

* * * * * *

FOLLOWING DINNER, THE steering committee assembled in a stale, airless meeting room to compile the official document to be tabled and handed to the Minister for the morrow's final sessions. What should have been a concise statement of our case degenerated into a microcosm of the whole struggle: exhausting, fractious, and mired in disagreement. The submission was only finished at five-thirty on the Sunday morning, after many hours of stormy, circular debate. We emerged into the pre-dawn gloom, bleary-eyed and brittle.

The document was presented later that Sunday morning and, after some more perfunctory debate, slightly modified. One comment therein, which was utterly unacceptable to us, was a clause to the effect that radiation and plutonium-related health problems have a gestation period of up to, and not exceeding, thirty years. A neat, arbitrary deadline for our suffering.

There was a patent, glaring contradiction in placing this arbitrary thirty-year limit on the exhibition of symptoms: after all, was not the constant position from which the opposition argued that we do *not* yet know enough about the long-term effects of radiation poisoning, that it is still too young a science to give definitive results? To claim both ignorance and a precise cutoff date was hypocrisy of a pure, distilled kind. We therefore had that absurdity struck from the document, a small victory of logic.

On the committee, as well as Dr. Winther of 'pet-cure' fame, was one of his parliamentary colleagues, Henriette Kjaer. These state-appointed allies were the sort your worst enemy wishes on you—distracted, disengaged, and devoted to their own political performance.

Joergen and Henriette had spent the whole of the Saturday of the hearing like two bored future high-school dropouts, passing notes to each other and whispering. More specifically, Joergen would scribble on a slip of paper and pass it to Henriette, and her hand would obediently shoot up and she would read out the question Joergen had dictated for her. The glistening, smug complicity I caught in their interchanged glances from time to time caused me to blink at the unveiled affront of their exhibitionism. They were playing a game, and we were the tiresome backdrop.

So, I was scarcely surprised when, their minds clearly on other things—or on each other—they found the proceedings of the committee meeting much to their disliking and high-handedly walked out to formulate their own independent response; which they independently tabled the following morning. This show of disunion, this public fracturing of our front, no doubt did our cause a power of good in the eyes of the government, though I fail to see it myself. I am sure we humble citizens and dying workers are most thankful for the delicate attentions thus paid to us by our political betters.

A third, insignificant blister on the Danish government's rump was one Arne Melchior. Arne turned up to the two days' proceedings dressed in the most exquisite, undoubtedly Italian suit, a crimson silk handkerchief flowering like an exotic bloom from his jacket pocket. That he spoke with the Danish equivalent of the plum-in-mouth upper class twit accent and was obviously trying to smile the pants off all present females colors in the outline of this travesty of nobility and honor. Add to this the fact that he expressed publicly to the panel, and smilingly to the cameras of the media, that he held us sick men to be common whingers and worth not a dime in payouts, and the painting of self-inflated meretriciousness is complete. He was decoration, not deliberation.

The Sunday sessions were a dull, draining affair, most of us reacting to the overwhelming feeling that the merest of formalities were being observed, that the verdict was already in. The government was performing an elaborate, expensive charade for us and for the cameras. Until, that is, the proceedings were suddenly enlivened—electrified—by an unknown woman who rose from the audience and addressed to the Risoe scientists such a series of quiet, devastating questions that left them speechless and the audience leaning forward, keen for explanations.

She introduced herself as the daughter of one of *their own* former colleagues, a Doctor Frede Hermann, an oceanographer with the Danish Fishing and Marine Investigation, who had been sent to Thule immediately after the crash to report on the environmental situation there for the Commission. He died seven years later, in 1975, of a cancer not dissimilar to those suffered by many members of our association. A scientist felled by the very thing he was sent to measure.

"Why," she asked, her voice clear and steady, carrying in the hushed big top, "were my father's reports on the very real dangers, present and future, from radiation poisoning consigned to forgetfulness by an indifferent bureaucracy in the Commission; who then went on to exclude him pointedly from key debates within the Commission; why had they found it expedient to cultivate ignorance when my father had to stop work on account of his declining health, and not a single one of them paid him a visit even once during his terminal illness, or took the least interest in him when he was dying; and why had they arrived at his home the very day of his death and removed, and probably destroyed, all his personal papers? And, most importantly, what has become of the final report he was preparing on his findings, which also disappeared along with his other papers?"

It was a long and involved question, laden with a daughter's grief and a citizen's fury; so the profound silence and stony coldness that greeted it from the ranks of the Danish Atomic Energy Commission must, I suppose, be put down to that ever-present professional caution that must weigh every element of every question to its very death. It made me wonder just how it must look in their kitchens of a morning when their wives ask them whether they want bacon and eggs or Corn Flakes for breakfast. Tension must run high until, all the possibilities weighed and subjected to long and extended considerations of expected outcomes and possible side-effects, the bacon finally, cautiously, sizzles on the family hotplate.

The meagreness of the answer given her: a collective shuffling of feet and papers, a discreet cough, a muttered 'What's all this?' and a reddening of a number of highly trained, impassive visages; only spurred this hitherto unknown ally to continue her attack, her composure magnificent.

"Is anyone on this panel aware," she continued, "that my father was literally forced to burn the clothes of the scientists who conducted the examination of the bottom of the fiord? The clothes they came back in. Can anyone give me an explanation of why such an action was required? What were they afraid of?"

A similar, intensified silence was forthcoming, only this time it was a vacuum that seemed to suck the air from the room. Again, she spoke, her words dropping like stones into a still pond:

"My father told me and my brother, in 1969, that two of the sled dogs used on the ice the day the bomber crashed died the following day. The remains were wrapped in plastic and removed to an undisclosed location, after having been checked with geiger counters. The geiger counters, he said, reacted violently. Does anyone here have any notice of that story, admittedly anecdotal?"

Clasped professional hands played with their thumbs as their owners looked intently at their notepads, suddenly fascinating documents.

"I put it to you," she said, her voice gaining a sharper edge, "that the locals, both Inuit and Greenlander, advised the authorities of the fact that a total of seven of the dogs died within a few weeks of their treks over the ice the day of the crash. Can anybody on this panel of experts confirm or deny that report?"

Nobody could. Or would. No bacon, I imagined, would sizzle in several professional, guilt-ridden households that evening!

Somewhere, I felt, Otto Kofoed-Hansen's bones rested a little easier that evening as it came to light that he had not been the only honest expert snubbed, silenced, and betrayed by the Risoe fraternity.

So, too, R.I.P. Professor Frede Hermann. Another ghost given a voice, too late.

* * * * * *

IT IS HARDLY possible to give these developments their complete due in mere words; they are of such major political and social significance, with continuing, rippling consequence. The Prime Minister is on record now, irrevocably, as having publicly accepted liability for the sufferings caused to Danish civilians on Danish soil in the discharge of duties they ought never have been required to carry out. That is a seismic fact, however they now try to qualify it.

The British have long been accused, with some justice, of treating the soldiers put at her disposal by her Dominions (the countries that, by and large, now make up the Commonwealth) as common cannon fodder, expendable in the imperial cause.

The controversial, catastrophic sacrifice of Australian and New Zealander soldiers at Gallipoli in World War I, for instance, has given rise to enduring, mixed feelings toward the United Kingdom in those soldiers' homelands.

The valuable—because brutally informative—Dieppe raid of 1942, which yielded important knowledge about the Nazi's strength along the northern French coast pre D-Day, was undertaken primarily by Canadian soldiers after both British and US commanders concluded that their respective publics back home would not stand the inevitable, horrific losses. Of a force of six thousand, only two thousand returned. The price of knowledge.

But, at the very least, in both those cases, these were soldiers. They were enlisted men, trained for war, fighting in the fiercest, most explicit wars the world has known. There was a contract, however brutal.

The Danes and Greenlanders who helped clean up the American mess in Greenland were at peace. Nor were they soldiers; nor were they even citizens of the country whose mess they cleaned up. Yet they were conscripted, by economic necessity and official duplicity, into action in one of the hottest, most secret zones the Cold War ever produced. They were civilians treated as disposable biodecontamination units.

It has now been officially admitted that a nuclear disaster occurred on Danish territory and that the people working there at the time were exposed to grave dangers without being advised what those dangers were; nor even that there *were* any dangers. The admission is there, in the parliamentary record.

It would hardly be the act of an honorable person, or government, to try to back away from those asseverations at this point. None of this has gone entirely unnoticed by the media, I might add: every day, every single newspaper and radio and television station covered the developments closely. News of the case reached throughout Europe and beyond, even as far as Japan. And even in the United States, that refuge of the parochial, there was reporting of this very engaging, very damning series of events.

And yet, the final, bitter twist. The outcome of the hearing, the weasel-worded form in which the Minister finally framed the acceptance of liability, was based upon the deliberately shaky foundation of allusions to psychosomatic problems. The official narrative, crafted from the Bechmann farce, became this: because we had been under the impression for so many years that we had been exposed to radiation, this belief had created in us considerable, debilitating stress. And it was for *this* stress, for the suffering caused by our own fear and awareness, that we now deserved compensation. A compensation, I might add, that would not cover the expenses of a terminally ill person in hospital under intensive care for a single month! Such are the hues and contours of the picture painted by the so-called experts. They compensated us for worrying, not for dying.

Psychosomatic illnesses that had, in my own case, for example, a silent gestation period of some fourteen years before a single symptom appeared. A psychosomatic condition that presented itself full-grown in the very first instance *before* I even suspected that I may have been exposed to radiation poisoning; in fact, I knew of the disease before I consciously connected it to the cause. My body knew before my mind did.

Psychosomatic illnesses that simulate to the last degree of medical accuracy, even to the specific, rare detail of cell mutation and eventual death, the sorts of illnesses—not just their vague symptoms—that the world over are now admittedly known to be caused by radiation poisoning. What a clever, inventive hysteria we must have possessed!

Psychosomatic illnesses that require no other aggravating circumstances in the lives of those afflicted in order to manifest, apart from the single, unifying circumstance of having worked on the irradiated ice of North Star Bay. A mass delusion with a single, geographic trigger.

Psychosomatic illnesses!

Psychosomatic illnesses, indeed! Bosh! Humbug!

Psychosomatic illnesses, was what they said with their grave, scientific faces: when what they meant, what they hoped the public would hear, was that we were all a bit soft in the head, a little strung out, overreacting to an itsy-bitsy, harmless little bit of radiation. Just nerves. Just our imaginations killing us.

* * * * * *

A RESULT THAT was designed to save political face? I believe so, utterly. After all, reputations beyond the merely political were also jeopardized by the government's concession to our cause. From inside the Danish Atomic Energy Commission and the medical establishment, energetic, defensive letters questioning the wisdom of the government's decision began appearing in the press in the period between the decision and the hearing.

I have already mentioned the source of some of these letters. Others were rather irrelevantly claiming that the consequences of smoking and drinking to excess were yet to be fully understood and investigated and that the life style we all led on Thule was more likely to be the root cause of the illnesses we now suffered. The old, reliable vices of the working man were trotted out as the true culprits, a classic tactic of blame-shifting.

Not for the first time will I mention here the fact that we were all required to submit ourselves to thorough, invasive medical examinations before we even set foot on the plane to Thule. Furthermore, I will mention that we were required to undergo further tests every time we were in Denmark on holidays: the reports from these tests being forwarded to the DCC's Copenhagen office and approved before we were permitted to return to the base at the conclusion of our leave. We were monitored fit men.

Talking of life styles: compared to the life style of the average Dane at home, we were hardly worse, and in many ways we were better. For instance, the ordinary Dane smokes a great deal and I find it quite uncomfortable at times when I am visiting the country as I am quite unused to navigating so much tobacco smoke during a social encounter. And, when it comes to drink, the Danes put the Australians to shame; and the latter are a race proud of their legendary drinking heritage. Beside the Dane at home or in his local, the Aussies are small beer, amateurs.

As for living at Thule, inside the Arctic Circle, it could be argued that, living in so pure and remote an environment, quite pollution free, we were exposed to fewer industrial and urban dangers than the rest of the Danish population breathing the air of Copenhagen or Århus.

But such opposition we treated, perhaps foolishly, as a minor irritant, the last thrashings of a discredited beast. Besides which, as soon as any letters of this type reached the press, supporters of our case wrote sharp, intelligent replies. These have included professors and acknowledged medical experts from abroad, as well as our own members and colleagues from those fateful days. With hindsight, I now see that we might have taken this coordinated professional opposition a little more seriously, it being a stark index of how powerful, entrenched, and united the establishment was against us. They were not just disagreeing; they were closing ranks.

* * * * * *

AN ARTICLE APPEARED recently in the Melbourne daily, *The Age*, dealing with secret, unethical tests undertaken by the British scientific community in the 1950s and 60s, where they removed bones from children who had died, without parental consent, for radiation analysis. They had also used the same radiation testing procedures as have been discovered to have been used in United States hospitals. The ghost of the past is global.

From the point of view of myself and my colleagues, the most interesting part of the article was not the scandal, but the science it confirmed. It reported that the most highly respected experts in nuclear medicine have now stated categorically that "for years the medical community has been divided over the effects of small doses of radiation on the body, but a report in 1992 by the Medical Research Council at Didcot in Oxfordshire found that even the lowest possible doses of lowest energy nuclear radiation can cause abnormalities in some cells."

There is no safe minimum level of radiation exposure. Which is precisely what my own surgeon has declared in a written statement wherein he refers to specific, observed changes that cells in my body have undergone, changes that have directly affected my health. Which is precisely what Dr. Rosalie Bertell has been saying for years. The same goes for Dr. Alice Stewart and Dr. George Kneale and Dr. Thomas Mancuso and a long and illustrious *et alii*. The truth was not lacking for champions; it was lacking for political will.

The article proceeded to report remarks of Dr. Stewart of Birmingham University Medical School, who has carried out extensive studies over the past twenty years relating to radiation poisoning. She says: "it is something that always has to be watched, but things are much stricter now. The real benchmark was Nuremberg, when physicians began asking themselves questions about what they were doing. There are ethical committees today that would not allow the use of radioactive tracers in such a manner." The article concludes by flatly stating that "there is no doubt that exposure to radiation, even low doses, increases the risk of cancer."

Further and authoritative voices that support the claim we have been reiterating over so many years now. Yet, clearly, according to the official findings of our hearing, we have merely been victims of our own overactive imaginations, our anxieties making real what science (their science) says is impossible. We are liars of the body, telling falsehoods with our own cells.

* * * * * *

AT THE CLOSE of the hearing on Sunday lunchtime, many of us were in a deeply despondent mood, the anticlimax a physical weight. I am not sure quite how to describe my own mood, except to say that I was prompted by it to act entirely out of character in my immediate response. I was born a Dane: my spontaneity, my fire, lies buried beneath deep cultural layers of patience, forebearance, and a deep-seated aversion to public scenes. It is not dead; merely appropriated to the future, to private moments.

However, that day, in that circus tent, I felt stripped bare of all those layers. I felt little sympathy for cultural norms or social niceties of any sort. Very calmly (I may no longer have been a Dane in residence, but I was still myself, only more so), I left my chair, asked the gathering clutter of journalists if they would mind excusing me from the usual post-hearing commentaries—which I felt confident I could leave in the capable, candid hands of Marius—and went in search of the three afore-mentioned conservative parliamentarians who had so distinguished themselves by their indifference.

I found Joergen Winther first, holding court with his female cohort, Henriette Kjaer, for a small group of journalists. I tapped him on the shoulder, interrupting their rehearsed platitudes. As the journalistic pens paused and tapes rolled and a select, gaping audience of onlookers reeled, I made my position clear to him, my voice calm, almost conversational.

"As you will be aware," I began, "I no longer live in this country. I want you to know that, when I did, I usually supported your party at election time. However, you will no doubt be relieved that I now live elsewhere and cannot vote here; because, if I could, I would not vote for a party that has a person of your questionable character, immoral behaviour, and profoundly flawed judgement as a member. You have been a disgrace to this process."

When he exhibited a mien of little comprehension mixed, though, with the politician's acute, skin-crawling sense of public ridicule, I added, leaning in slightly, that I believed his behaviour during the hearing to be down-gradient from the ordinary woodlouse; that his moral standards must be so totally, synthetically integrated with his ego that they left no detectable trace in his actual behaviour; and that, as a representative member of the human race, he made me seriously consider handing in my own resignation from the species. My preternatural calmness during this diatribe never faltered and was probably the key factor, rather than any feeling of shame, that caused my victim to pale a little beneath his tan. I was about to move off, feeling severely, cleanly unburdened, in the shocked silence that dinned in my ears, when I realized I had very rudely failed to address myself to the female parliamentarian present. So, I gently turned to Henriette Kjaer, who was staring at me as if I were a madman, and added, with a small, polite nod, "And all that goes for you, too; and with bells on, you little shit!"

My sister, Hanne, who had formed part of the little coterie around me, caught her breath sharply at this raw manifestation of an utterly unknown side to her brother, and did not let it go again till I had taken her elbow and hurried her off in search of the Danish Dorian Gray, our beloved dandy, Arne Melchior. He, lucky man, had already absconded with his bare-arsed dignity the minute the final papers had been handed to the Minister. A pity: I only wanted to ask him one question; where he kept his mirror. His vanity would have failed his discretion then and he would have asked my meaning, to which I would have replied that I assumed he carried a mirror about with him, to be able to kiss his own reflection at every opportunity. I would have added that he might leave a better impression on the world if he simply sat on that mirror.

* * * * * *

BEFORE LEAVING THE National Circus Building for the last time—to go for a stiff, much-needed drink with Hanne, Flemming, and Mogens, a fellow suffering ex-Thuler and vice-president of the association—I managed to exchange a few final, unpleasantries with the Minister for Health herself, The Honorable Yvonne Herloev Andersen. She was surrounded by minders, a queen bee with drones. She only condescended to look down at me from her slight height, trying, but not quite succeeding, to make me feel like a supernumerary at an awards night, a bit player cluttering her stage.

"Do you have any children?" I asked, my opening gambit seemingly innocuous.

She looked at me, her expression one of weary impatience, wondering when I would finally go away, cease to be a problem. But I went on rather than away.

"I'm one of the luckier ex-Thulers. I do have children. But, you know well—or you should—that many of our members couldn't father children on their return from Thule. Their sterility is part of their medical record. And, of those who did manage to conceive, a much too high number of their children have been born with disabilities directly attributable to their fathers' own radiation sickness. Genetic damage. The legacy continues."

Her simple, chilling response was to offer a tight, social smile and say, "So nice to finally meet you in person, Mr. Carswell. Do enjoy your flight back to Australia," and move quickly off under the protective cover of her minders, the conversation, and the human consequences, terminated.

Democracy is a wonderful thing: it allows the ordinary person to be ignored or to be battened upon at will by those other ordinary persons who happen to have won the political lottery and are drawing a Minister's salary for the time being. Equal opportunity to feel the cool, refined dirt being heaped upon your head by a gloved hand.

* * * * * *

That same afternoon there was a final, impromptu gathering of the association members at the Central Railway Station. Most were heading home by train to their towns and villages around the country. The mood was heavy, defeated, and though no one felt much like talking about the Thule topic, we spent a few shambling minutes considering our several reactions to the proceedings. The straw consensus, grasped at weakly, was that it had all been far too short, too controlled, and had answered nothing. At that stage, we had no concrete idea of the next move the government would make; though we were by no means sanguine about what the eventual offer might be. A dread hung in the sooty station air.

The following morning, Monday, October 9, I left Copenhagen for Chicago via Heathrow, my body moving on autopilot. I could not believe my continuing, farcical luck as British Airways again managed to lose my baggage. This time they were not to reappear at all. A lesser man, a more mystical man, might have suspected a celestial conspiracy, a cosmic punchline. I just felt profoundly, pettily annoyed and, in a fit of righteous pique, I went shopping in down-town Chicago for the basic necessities I lacked on BA's account—underwear, a shirt, a razor—and charged it all, with grim satisfaction, to their account.

While in Chicago, I had some remaining business commitments to fulfil for my Australian employer. I still had a few moments to spare, though, for Greg Maas, still the president and effectively the entire board of our American brother organization, and Larry Leck, their drawling, sharp-eyed attorney. I principally wanted to brief them on how things had gone for us in Denmark and to demonstrate our continuing solidarity with them; as they had so steadfastly supported us.

Larry, it turned out, was also an informal adviser to the White House on a number of cultural and historical issues. Through those channels he was able to tell me something crucial: that, as agreed under longstanding NATO arrangements, the US government would reimburse the Danish government to the tune of seventy-five percent of any amount they might pay out to us in compensation. I was glad to have this confirmed from an American source, already being vaguely aware of such agreements; moreover, it seemed to me that such a reimbursement agreement, if adhered to, would dispose the Danish government to deal with us a little more generously than they might otherwise. After all, it would only be a quarter of the cost to them.

That afternoon, I spoke by phone to Marius and said to him that it would be a potent piece of information to feed to the press. "Make sure they understand the Americans are footing seventy-five percent of the bill. This should make our government careful as to just how stingy they want to appear to the public," he commented, a flicker of his old tactical confidence returning.

Later that same afternoon, the blow fell. I took another call from Marius in my Chicago hotel room. He was in shock, his voice thin and wavering. He could barely speak to tell me that the Prime Minister's office had just communicated their offer: each of us was to receive 50,000 Kroner (about US$9,000) as a once-off, final settlement. It was about five percent of the sum we had minimally, reasonably expected. The shock Marius felt was a live wire, easily communicated across the Atlantic, and I actually felt the blood drain from my face as the meaning of the insinuated insult—for it was nothing less—sank into my body. It was not compensation; it was a dismissal price.

For once, Marius was brought to a stunned silence and my own voice faltered for a moment, the wind knocked out of me. But just for a moment.

"Well, naturally," I said, my voice regaining its steel, "this laughable—no, offensive—offer must be declined. Immediately. Get on the phone to them and tell them to stock their arsenal with it. And get on to the press about it, and don't forget to impress upon them the fact that, with the NATO deal, the government is only actually paying out twenty-five percent of even this measly amount. Make sure that the whole board is informed. See if you can't get them together and draft a definitive reply in the negative to the government. Prepare a statement for the press saying that the struggle for justice will not finish even as our members one by one lay down to death, or something equally dramatic. And make sure it's clear that, after nearly thirty years of suffering, what we are rejecting is the equivalent to about six months' wages of a Copenhagen street cleaner. Go to it, Marius. We have to act quickly while our issue is still a live one for the press."

Marius, to his credit, went into action, firing off letters and calls. But the following day he got back to me with the flint-hearted, final response from the government, relayed through Anders Boelskifte. The message was simple, brutal:

"'Take it or leave it!' That's Anders' summary. He spoke directly to the Prime Minister's office. They reckon that if we reject the offer, we'll get nothing. Ever. This is the end of the line."

I was speaking to Marius from the hushed, carpeted solitude of Chicago-O'Hare's American Airlines Admirals Club lounge. I was on my way home to Australia via Los Angeles, a ghost between worlds. I wondered whether the combination of sheer exhaustion from the enormous amount of travelling, the blur of meetings, the intensity of the hearing, and the profound disappointment now clotting in my heart, was written plainly on my features as I sat in that very public, very private place. Rubbing my right forefinger through the stubble on my cheek, I pondered Marius' latest, irksome, devastating news.

"Well, Marius," I said finally, the fight leaching out of me into the plush chair, "I can't right now appreciate the full, grim import of this news. I'm frankly, at this moment, just worn out. Empty. Look, I'll trust your and Anders' judgement in this: if it is a true take-it-or-leave-it offer, perhaps we can accept it… but under the strongest protest. In other words, they can't stop us from continuing to fight for justice, and we can take this stingy amount as merely a first, insulting instalment on what they will *have* to pay us in the future. It's not over yet, my boy. It can't be."

I left Marius with those thin, hopeful considerations and boarded my flight to LA, which I thankfully slept through, a dead sleep. Changing to Qantas in Los Angeles, I felt comfortably, finally, at home even before I hit Australian soil, after a thoroughly demanding, ultimately crushing trip. The rock, it seemed, had not vanished over the cliff after all. It had simply been replaced in my hands, lighter now, but just as hard, and just as much mine to push.

* * * * * *

AT LEAST THE Danish media, in its hunger for a story, did not entirely let us down. The Monday I left, there was a goodly number of articles in the Danish dailies, one of which described me, with typical flourish, as the 'Hero of Thule'; which, having accounted for the generic exaggeration of the media, is not altogether untrue. Especially as it reported accurately that I was the one manufacturing the bullets for the struggle over the past few years from my distant sanctuary in Australia. A form, I suppose, of the classic tactic of the secret services the world over; wherein the centre of real power is protected by feints of seeming power invested at different times in different places and in diverse individuals. Behind M is always N; behind MI5 operates MI6; behind the throne is always a grey eminence. Like Newton's gravity, a difficult and unpopular concept when first proposed, I had learned to exercise power at a distance. It was effective, and it was safe.

Which is, I guess, from my bruising experience at the hearing, the best and most effective place from which to exercise it. My physical presence at the hearing was, without a trace of doubt, one of the major irritants and focal points for the opposition; as the Prime Minister's own conspicuous absence (the Minister for Health, as it were, deputizing for him) was another telling weapon in their arsenal. Power manifests in presence; ultimate power manifests in the ability to be absent.

This became painfully, bureaucratically evident to me after my return to Australia, via a frustrating series of faxes to the Head of Administration in the Department of Health, one Peter Bak Mortensen. I was attempting, against my better judgement, to claim some minor expenses I had incurred while in Copenhagen—taxi fares, a meal—on which they had been delaying refund with exquisite pettiness. In one of my faxes, that of November 3, 1995, I also included, as a matter of record, a copy of the comprehensive, damning medical report provided by my own specialist.

I was informed by Mortensen in a terse reply that he had received the report, but that he could not act on it, as the hearing had "concluded that there could be no claim for compensation on the grounds of radiation poisoning." The circular logic was breathtaking: the hearing they stage-managed to avoid that conclusion was now cited as proof that the conclusion was definitive. I also mentioned in that same fax, perhaps naively, that I should still like to see the Prime Minister on my next visit to Denmark, to discuss the matter further. I was curtly informed that, as far as the Prime Minister, and the Minister for Health too, were concerned, the matter was finalized and the case closed. They would not see me. Big Brother would not be disturbed! The door, so briefly and conditionally opened, was now not just shut but bricked over.

They had dealt with the problem: which they had always perceived to be a problem of public relations and political nuisance; not a problem of justice, or health, or moral responsibility. The hearing had been masterfully stage-managed by the bureaucrats for their political masters to give the convincing appearance of an attempt to administer justice, a simulacrum of due process. But, the limited, begrudging time that was available to the victims to voice their concerns over specific issues, or to ask relevant questions, as compared to the extended, leisurely time packets awarded to those making the opening comments for each panel, was clearly felt by all present to be an indication of a travesty in the making. We were allotted minutes; they held the hours.

Another of the government's deft public relations coups was to play, with great fanfare, the card of attending to native rights. Now, I am the last person to dispute that the Inuit involved in the search for the bomber's crew and in the initial stages of the clean up suffered, and suffered severely. Their plight is real and their justice is also delayed. But, at the hearing, the amount of time and emotional focus devoted to their case was way out of proportion to the actual numbers of them involved. They became a moral backdrop, a politically correct diversion.

In all fairness, to do justice to all those affected by the disaster on the same scale as that offered the Inuit, the hearing should have run for several weeks, or even months, and included hundreds more Danish voices. If we had made a fuss about this glaring imbalance in treatment, the bureaucrats would have seen to it that the media was fully apprised of our opposition to justice for the Inuit on account of race; or some such crafted absurdity. It was a trap we could not spring.

However, our true position is and always has been that the Inuit deserve to be compensated in a way appropriate to them and in proportion to their needs for exactly the same reasons for which we deserve it: for exposure to radiation. Not as a separate, more sympathetic ethnic narrative, but as part of the same terrible, unifying fact.

Not to be so easily dismissed after some nine years of dealing with this particular species of formalised insensitivity, the following day, November 4, a Saturday, I fired off another long fax to the Ministry of Health, once more outlining in detail my claim that my health problems can demonstrably be traced directly to my exposure to radiation from plutonium and the effects of other dangerous substances. I was shouting into a filing cabinet, but I would be damned if I'd stop.

I also felt I had better point out to them, because it is a long and involved document and they might easily 'miss' the fact, that the final report presented to the Minister at the conclusion of the hearing, had not stated in any way or form that there *could not* be health problems as a result of exposure to radiation. To the contrary, the original form of the document itself made that admission when it affirmed that up to thirty years might pass before symptoms of radiation poisoning became evident—a clause meant to limit, but which inherently conceded the possibility.

I reminded the Minister that the thirty-year reference had been struck out in accord with the wishes of all concerned, *even of the so-called scientific experts in the opposition to our cause*. The report then simply affirmed the undeniable: that radiation exposure can result in cancers that may only manifest after many years of incubation. They had removed their own arbitrary deadline, leaving the danger open-ended, as it truly is.

I now await the pleasure of Her Majesty's government; whether that be to reply, or to apply the old and well-trusted policy of ignoring this annoying, tenacious mutt attached irremoveably to their collective behind. I am not holding my breath.

* * * * * *

SURPRISINGLY, WITH THE greater, public struggle for recognition now ostensibly behind me, I find that I do feel at this point a certain, slow-burning bitterness. It has been a response I have always consciously kept at bay, not least because it is corrosive and not productive in a fight; and, in addition, because it is not, on the whole, a *personal* bitterness. It is not a feeling that I sit well with, nor does it find its target with any ease. It is a diffuse acid in the soul.

Nevertheless, it is indeed bitter to reflect that, in the heat of the Cold War, all Denmark's powerful ally had to do was express its wishes in a private letter and the Danish government would comply with an unquestioning, secret, and humiliating alacrity. Sovereignty was traded for a whisper of inclusion, for a seat at the grown-up table, and the bill was sent to the working men of Thule.

However, my bitterness has been more directed toward the Danish rather than the United States' government. They were, after all, our own. Our guardians. But, in all my struggle over the past ten years, what has motivated me most has been, as we say in Denmark, to make sure that I kept my eyes open and asked the pertinent questions as to what the *Smirches* were up to. (The *Smirches*: a wonderfully Danish term for the shadowy, powerful figures who operate just out of sight, the permanent government behind the elected one.)

And, the upshot of my looking is now clear: the Smirches have been wearing GI Army boots and dealing with their own allies with subterfuge and a callous disregard. They outsourced our safety, and then our truth.

It is not a personal bitterness, because I number among my best friends many Americans; I find them, as individuals, a people of unending hospitality and expansive kindness that has not been equalled anywhere in my wide experience. This is the enduring paradox.

The Americans: that most honorable of peoples. I repeat it like a mantra, testing its truth against the evidence.

I have certainly not overlooked the circumstance in all the flurry of recent events that perhaps the American government has been left a little nonplussed, a little irritated, at the unprecedented and inconvenient developments in the land of its usually cooperative little ally. I might put a number of pertinent questions at this point, which that most honorable people, whether in government or business, in the civil service or education, on the land or in the factory, might like to mull over in their quieter moments. For they are questions of truth, justice and honor; and they are questions that, excuse the solecism, *beg* answers, not more evasive questions.

As further evidence comes to light on this issue, some of the questions now being asked relate to the very purpose of the bases constructed on Greenland's soil, about their actual operation, and about their morality. Especially in view of the growing public perception that Thule existed solely for the protection of the United States, a giant radar eye pointed away from Denmark, toward a threat that was never truly Denmark's own.

The whole enormous, elaborate spying device that was BMEWS was set in place to watch the Soviet Union in case that country should send unfriendly and dangerous missives toward the United States. Had the USSR decided instead to make a sudden, horrific example of Copenhagen, would BMEWS have been of the least service to Denmark, even as a concession that might have won for it the vague promise of later US retaliation? We were a forward outpost for *their* defence, not partners in our own.

While the United States ran the global public relations campaign of the Cold War, portraying themselves as the 'World's Policeman,' the reality on the frozen ground was that it was wholly directed to the defence of the US and only the US. If anyone else should benefit incidentally: well and good; if not, well, too bad! Realpolitik on ice.

So, I ask, is American science so superior to Danish that it knows how to contain radiation in such a way that, while myself and Marius and all the other Danes who were involved in the clean up were unremittingly dosed with lethal levels, the young American soldiers flown in from US air bases all over the world to assist with the same clean up, being US citizens, were magically protected from the same dangers? If this protective science existed, why did not the United States military officials in charge of the operation, who treated the Danish civilians in exactly the same way as the US GIs—even up to lining them up on the same parades—extend that protection as far as us Danes, perhaps as a simple diplomatic courtesy if from no other motive?

Is American medical science so advanced that it is able to show conclusively that any illness suffered by their soldiers subsequent to the clean up must have been caused by just about anything other than by radiation exposure: by watching too much TV; by eating fast food; by the climate of Oregon? Is their epidemiology so precise it can exclude with certainty what ours, humbly, cannot prove?

Is American technology so perfected and its products so keenly devised that they cannot do harm to American citizens, only to enemies, or to inconvenient allies?

Is the United States government so immune to scientific results that are not its own, to moral questions that play themselves out on other soil, so immune to the honor of another people who equally say, just as the honorable American people say, `we too belong on this planet and have our part to play,' that it can turn away, shrug its collective shoulder and legitimise culpable ignorance as a weapon of diplomacy?

While the Danish government has belatedly, and squirming with discomfort at every turn, accepted a limited, parsing culpability, it is sobering to reflect that, in a profound manner, they are taking the rap for the United States government: a US bomber crashes, explodes and vomits radiation all over the Danish Arctic, on a mission in defence of the US, within spitting distance of a major US military installation; and the Danish government says, 'oops, sorry, our bad!' The absurdity would be comic if it were not so tragic.

Is the payment by the United States government of seventy-five percent of the eventual, paltry offer of compensation made by the Danish government a surreptitious, back-door way of admitting liability without ever having to say so in court, or to its own veterans? A financial wink in a confidential ledger?

Where does this leave the many hundreds of US GIs who assisted in the clean up? Does the fact of their having been subject to rigid military law and discipline at the time continue to mean that the US government need accept zero percent liability in their case? Is it a case of the voice silenced prematurely by oath and statute, consent assumed by the uniform?

A lot of attention has been paid, rightly, to that moving, polished memorial in Washington D.C. to the American victims of the Vietnam War: the black granite wall that speaks the unwritten lives of thousands upon thousands of American men and women who never came back to speak for themselves. It is a sacred space.

There is another, invisible wall in Washington D.C. A wall of silence, of classified documents, of denied claims, that effectively muffles the lives of hundreds of men who continue today to suffer on account of a job they did for their country twenty-eight years ago. A good job, well done, by all official accounts of the time. Yet, to us today, it is as if the escaping tribes of Israel had attempted to write their names on the raised waters of the Red Sea as they passed through: the waters, like as they are to a wall of stone, will not hold those names. They vanish. Only in the mind of the one who raised that wall—the state, the Pentagon—will those names live on, filed and forgotten.

Only in the voices of a few tenacious, stubborn men like Greg Maas in the US, and Marius here, will the lives of these hundreds of ignored men be ever told and, perhaps, one day, will the damage done to them be redressed by damages awarded them; or at least in recognition given them before they are all gone.

And, leaving aside all protective irony, I must ask once more, and plainly: are the American people an honorable people?

Irony is a powerful device whose efficacy depends on the cooperation of understanding with humility. Well, if I am to be shown by history to be wrong, let it be so. I will wear the fool's cap. However, I do think, from my own personal observations and friendships, that the Americans, as a people, are indeed an honorable people. It is the great, the tragic, disconnect: that the honor of a people can be so divorced from the actions of their institutions, that the decency of the citizen can exist in a parallel universe to the cynicism of the state. That is the bitterest lesson of all.

* * * * * *

EPILOGUE

'Mervayle nat, for I was

somtyme an erthely man'

The Miracle Of Galahad   MALORY

AND THAT, AS they say, is basically that.

While it has been my belief that the amount of compensation should have been the price of a B-52G, something of a symbolic gesture linking the cause to the effect, it is also a fact that much more than that will have to be paid out by the Danish government before it will have extinguished the debt of suffering, neglect and victimization it has burdened us with for so many years now.

If they imagine that a once-for-all take-it-or-leave-it payment the equivalent of US$9,000 is adequate compensation for the immense distress and death borne in their name, then their imaginations are clearly defective and do not reach as far into the future as mine does.

The problem of compensation is only going to grow, especially since the Danish government has just commissioned a comprehensive report to be prepared covering all activities at Thule air base over the entire period of its existence from the German capitulation in early May 1945 to date, with specific reference to nuclear issues such as the storage of nuclear warheads and missiles, nuclear bombs and the constant patrols over Greenland of nuclear-armed B-52s. Doubtless HOBO 28 will be exhumed in that report.

The fact that the government had, at that time conceded the need for such a report must be put down directly to the actions of the Thule Association in its discovery to the world of the secret life of Thule air base in the 1950s and 1960s.

They know they have been found out.

They know they have nowhere to hide.

They know they have been found wanting as human beings and as responsible politicians.

They know the world knows of their shameful and deceitful behaviour.

They know their time is running out.

They know that we are not giving up.

They know that we are going to win.

* * * * * *

IN THE FUTURE, I shall return to Thule;

and I will walk out onto the midnight icepack over the waters of Wolstenholme Fiord;

and I will drag my feet upon the upper crunching surface of the snow litter;

and I will play at arsarnerit with the Aurora;

and I will wander up and down in the company of those souls of Inuit and Danes

and Americans alike whose bodies' strengths were forever sapped and undermined irreparably at the micro-molecular level on that sunless day more than a generation ago when the devil dragged his finger nail over the pure white arctic ice and scarred it forever black.

JOURNALIST STATEMENT

As a journalist he has worked on the Thule case for a considerable number of years and is most likely the person in Denmark with the deepest knowledge of the different perspectives of the case.

A representative of the OHCHR (United Nations Office of the High Commissioner for Human Rights), Mr. Raphael Pangalangan requested him to highlight key mechanisms and practices from the Thule context that could be applied or are relevant to the situation in the Marshall Islands.

In an e-mail on 23rd February 2024, Mr. Pangalangan specified the following 5 issues:

1. **Truth Mechanisms:** This includes official investigations, radiological assessments, transparency, and the participation of affected communities.

2. **Accountability Mechanisms:** Procedures that establish state responsibility or individual liability for the nuclear exposure.

3. **Reparations:** Compensation programs and other reparative measures, such as recognition and apology to affected communities.

4. **Guarantees of Non-Repetition:** Institutional changes made to ensure that the initial nuclear exposure and its impacts are avoided and mitigated moving forward.

5. **Memorialization:** Measures adopted to preserve the memory and honour victims, which can include physical structures (memorials) or through education and memorial holidays.

These 5 areas were as requested commented on as follows:

1. Truth Mechanism:

- Since 1968, there have been a series of Danish so-called statistical register studies of the 1,200 Danish workers who helped the US Air Force in the clean-up "Project Crested Ice" after the nuclear accident, which ended on 17th September 1968.
- The 1,200 Danish Thule workers were never told that they were cleaning up after a nuclear accident.
- Individual measurements of radiation have never been made on the workers when most of them returned to Denmark after their stay at Thule Air Base. Only statistical register studies have been performed.
- During the clean-up, the Danes' exposure to ionizing radioactive radiation was measured by US military personnel when they had worked on the crash site on the B-52 – otherwise without protection unlike the American personnel – at the so-called Tank Farm. The contents of these lists have been kept secret.
- When drivers had been out at the crash site, they were given new clothes at every return to the base due to radiation, provided by the US Air Force. But this happened without recording the individual worker's radiation level.
- After the stay at Thule Air Base, no Danish worker has received individual measurement of their respective exposure by doctors specialized in ionizing radiation or other specialized health personnel.
- There has been no indication of openness from the Danish authorities regarding the individual worker's health information, which has been repeatedly pointed out by the Thule workers.
- The EU Parliament has also demanded that Denmark start monitoring the Thule workers, according to the EURATOM directive. This involved by an almost unanimous decision in the EU Parliament on 10th May 2007.
- Denmark has since refused to comply with the decision.
- Along the way there has been absolutely no involvement whatsoever of the Inuit population around Thule Air Base.

2. Accountability Mechanisms:

- No-one, neither of the authorities nor the then employer, Danish Construction Corporation (DCC), has taken any responsibility for the Thule workers.

- Denmark has never assumed responsibility for any radiation damage that the 1,200 Thule workers may have sustained.
- In 1968, the Danish workers were employed by the Danish-American company, DCC, of which E. Pihl & Son was a co-owner.
- As recently as 2023, lawyer Ian Anderson, raised claims for the Thule workers against E. Pihl & Son via the US Courts, which subsequently dismissed the case.

3. Reparations:

- The Danish Government paid out – after the so-called "Thule Hearing" in Copenhagen in October 1995, to everyone who had passed through the area of Thule Air Base from 21st January 1968 to 17th September 1968, a culance-wise compensation of DKK 50,000 – the Thule workers called the allowance a "team candy" to make them shut up.
- Danish authorities and the then employer DCC have never given an apology to the Thule Workers. It was therefore a very conscious thoughtfully accurate choice that the amount of DKK 50,000 was paid out as a "reimbursement in terms of compensation".
- In this way, Denmark and the then Danish Government avoided taking on legal responsibility.
The Thule case has been closed since 1995 both politically in the Danish Parliament, Folketinget, among all political parties and among all relevant authorities.
- The Thule workers have only been met with closed doors in their countless attempts to obtain information about their state of health.

4. Guarantees of Non-Repetition:

- Denmark has done nothing at all to prevent a possible repetition of the nuclear accident on 21st January 1968.
- The US Air Force has basically unlimited powers at Thule Air Base, and Denmark has never admitted that there have been nuclear weapons at the base, even though all Danish territory including Greenland is, and always have been, declared nuclear-weapon free.

5. Memorialization:

- There has never been and is not today any memorials or days of remembrance for the nuclear accident on 21st January 1968, nor for the efforts of the Thule workers.
- The Thule workers have never been given an excuse for working for half a year without protective equipment against ionizing radiation from plutonium PU239 and many other radioactive substances.
- A former Foreign Minister, Niels Helveg Pedersen, admitted to me (Journalist Torsten Raagaard) some years ago that "we have not treated Thule workers well enough." This is probably the closest the Thule workers will ever get to an apology from Denmark.

STATEMENT ON UN NUCLEAR LEGACY

"From my experience in cases I have argued on behalf of the victims of nuclear bomb accidents and deliberate detonations including against the United Kingdom (South Pacific indigenous populations and UK and Commonwealth military veterans), Denmark (Danish emergency workers in Greenland), and the United States Federal Labour Department, for the same Danish workers under the US Defence Base Act, and against the US under ILO Convention 150), all of these states have blatantly lied, fabricated false evidence, falsified case decisions, including US Supreme Court judgements, ignored peer-reviewed scientific studies and used strong-arm tactics against third parties (in the Danes' case, Bankruptcy Trustees in Copenhagen) to avoid any accountability or admission that radiation emitted by nuclear bombs, not used in war, is a health hazard.

That is not surprising since there is an unwritten understanding amongst all nuclear states never to expose each other's nuclear accidents for fear that their own accidents will in turn be exposed.

In some cases, involving military/civilian use of nuclear plants, such "exposure" is unavoidable, as in the case of Windscale in England (now erased from the map), and Chernobyl. In these instances, scientific government hacks move to minimize public health hazards and remediation issues. In Chernobyl, for example, by "airbrushing" out of existence the fact that thousands of children in Belarus subsequently developed thyroid cancers.

Since nuclear weapons are the "Holy Grail" of state power and international influence, states in possession of such weapons take ongoing measures to keep their respective populations isolated from knowledge of the real dangers they are exposed to. This includes minimizing remedial measures for accidentally exposed populations.

The state advantage in this regard is that few members of their respective populations have any specialized knowledge or understanding of ionizing radiation's serious long-term dangers, including decades prolonged internal irradiation of organs and tissues from inhalation or ingestion.

This is not a nuclear "legacy" but an ongoing international disinformation programme by major nuclear states, which if left unchecked, will inevitably lead to the destruction of all life on our planet."

~ Ian

Statement by the Author's lawyer, Ian

IN HONOUR OF THEIR MEMORY

"More than 400 men are known to have suffered devastating health consequences or to have lost their lives as a result of exposure to radiation and other hazardous substances. Many were never informed of the dangers they faced. Others remain unnamed, their suffering unrecorded, their exposure unacknowledged, and their voices unheard.

This memorial stands not only for the 400 whose names are known, but also for all those whose names were never written down, whose illnesses were never recognised, and whose deaths were never officially linked to what they endured. They worked in silence, without protection, without warning, and without justice.

Their lives, their suffering, and their courage demand remembrance. Their story demands truth. Their memory demands accountability."

Crested Ic9 - A Tribute to Heroes - History will not forget them!